Psychodiagnosis: Selected Papers

PSYCHODIAGNOSIS

****

SELECTED PAPERS

by PAUL E. MEEHL

UNIVERSITY OF MINNESOTA PRESS Minneapolis

© Copyright 1973 by the University of Minnesota.
All rights reserved. Printed in the
United States of America at Kingsport
Press, Kingsport, Tennessee.
Published in the United Kingdom and India
by the Oxford University Press, London
and Delhi, and in Canada by the Copp Clark
Publishing Co. Limited, Toronto.

Library of Congress Catalog Card Number: 72-95440

ISBN 0-8166-0685-4

To the memory of my wife

Alyce Roworth Meehl

October 8, 1920–September 4, 1972

Lux perpetua luceat ei

Preface

WHEN JOHN ERVIN, JR., director of the University of Minnesota Press, first proposed publishing a selection of my papers, I dragged my feet a little because I believe that such a gathering in one volume ought to have a strong thematic unity; and our initial tentative list (concocted over lunch in 1967) seemed to me lacking such a unity. Over the ensuing five years the list of candidate titles underwent considerable revision, and some of my most widely cited (and, I am led to suppose, "influential") publications do not appear in this volume. Despite these changes, which resulted in concentration on psychodiagnosis, it might still be asked what common core of aims, concepts, or methods justifies gathering these thirteen essays into a book.

I suppose it could suffice to say that they are all about psychodiagnosis, assessment of the human person, and let it go at that. I should like to think, however, that they possess a conceptual or methodological unity beyond mere specification of the psychodiagnostician's task. Despite their wide range of manifest content (from a speculative theory of schizophrenia to a polemic on the mediocrity of clinical case conferences) each of these papers involves some aspect of what might be called "The Great Struggle of the Psychoclinician" as mirrored in the experience of myself as scientist-practitioner. "How do I help my clients or patients, practicing an art that applies a primitive science?" Or, on the other side of the coin, "How do I preserve my scientific mental habits and values from attrition by the continual necessity, as a helper, to think, act, and decide on the basis of 'scientifically' inadequate evidence—relying willy-nilly on clinical experience, hunches, colleagues' anecdotes, intuition, common sense, far-out extrapolations from the laboratory, folklore, introspection, and sheer 'guesswork'?"

Doubtless every applied science (or would-be science) presents aspects of this problem to those working at the interface between science and technics, as is apparent when one listens to practicing attorneys talking about law professors, practitioners of medicine complaining about medical school teaching, "real engineers" in industry poking ambivalent fun at academic physicists, and the like. So I do not suggest that the existential predicament of the clinical psychologist is unique in this respect, which it certainly is not. But I strongly suspect that there are few if any fields of applied semiscientific knowledge in which the practitioner with scientific interests and training is presented *daily* with this problem in one guise or another, or in which its poignancy, urgency, and cognitive tensions are so acute. I am aware that there are *some* clinical psychologists who do not experience this conflict, but I have met, read, or listened to very few such during the thirty years since I first began working with patients as a clinical psychology trainee. Further, these rare exceptions have seemed to me in every case to be either lacking in perceptiveness and imagination or, more often, deficient in scientific training and critical habits of mind. When I encounter a hardnosed behaviorist clinician who "knows" (for sure) that Freud's theory of dreams is 100 percent hogwash and is not worth five hours of his serious attention; or, toward the other end of the continuum, when I converse with a devoted Rorschacher who "knows" (for sure) that the magic inkblots are highly valid no matter what the published research data indicate—I find both of these attitudes hard to understand or sympathize with.

One would, of course, like to believe the methodological dictum, enunciated by the Wittgenstein of the *Tractatus,* that "Everything that can be thought at all can be thought clearly. Everything that can be said can be said clearly" (4.116). One would also, unless one has obscurantist motives, like to be able to subscribe to the methodological dogmas of strict behaviorism and strict operationism. Unfortunately, no historically or philosophically informed mind can subscribe today to these dogmas. (I hasten to say that an *investigatory strategy* for certain domains of psychology may be deliberately confined to the ascertainment of first-order factual generalizations plus a cautiously limited use of dispositional concepts tied closely to them; such a strategy has been adopted by Professor Skinner and his disciples, with indisputable success *at the tasks they set themselves.*) The spirit of the essays in this volume intends to be that recommended by Aristotle in the first part of the *Nicomachean Ethics,* where we read, ". . . for it is the mark of an educated man to look for precision in each class of things just so far as the nature of the subject admits." The extent to which this ideal of openness-cum-criticality has been approximated in these essays is obviously not for me to judge.

The story is told of Bertrand Russell and Alfred North Whitehead (whose collaboration on the monumental *Principia Mathematica* seemed odd to some because of the marked dissimilarity of their minds) that many years later, having not seen much of one another in the interim, they happened to be at the same academic banquet. The toastmaster asked Whitehead if he would care to comment on his old co-author's subsequent philosophical development, and Whitehead (allegedly) said, after praising Russell's knowledge, humanity, intellect, and work habits, ". . . but he is, I fear, somewhat simpleminded." Russell's rejoinder was to admit cheerfully his own inclination to "simplemindedness" (*not,* of course, to be conflated with low intelligence), then went on to say that his friend and colleague Whitehead, surely not simpleminded, tended unfortunately to be somewhat "muddleheaded." With the possible exception of philosophy, I can think of no domain of technical knowledge where this simpleminded/muddleheaded dimension is so potent and pervasive a factor in professional disagreement. For a psychological reader, I need not define it; any knowledgeable person apprehends immediately what these polar opposites refer to. An explication of this dimension's meaning in clinical psychology could proceed ontologically ("How complicated is the mind?") or epistemologically ("How do we find out about somebody's mind?") while admitting the philosophical thesis that questions of ontology and epistemology cannot be sharply separated. In the perennial methodological controversies over personality assessment, epistemological simplemindedness could (almost) be articulated by the thesis: "Everything that can be said about a person is reducible to [translatable into, "definable in terms of"] statements about behavior or behavior dispositions." Epistemological muddleheadedness in personality assessment, rightly perceiving this thesis to be a simpleminded mistake, reacts with the muddleheaded thesis: "Since clinical psychology deals with the human person—that person being an inner entity not equatable with his overt behavior—the usual questions about behavioral implications of personological statements, and the usual 'academic, scientific' demands for behavioral evidence, are inappropriate in this field." The two errors could be formulated in a nutshell by saying that the simpleminded psychoclinician mistakenly supposes it to be a consequence of scientific empiricism that all legitimate statements in psychology must be *behavior-equivalent*; whereas the muddleheaded psychoclinician mistakenly supposes that, since psychological assertions are not required to be behavior-equivalent, he is free of the obligation—as theorist or practitioner—to try to make them *behavior-relevant*. The therapy I prescribe for these opposite methodological ailments is the (philosophically trite) meta-principle that statements in clinical psychology should be behavior-relevant but need not be behavior-equivalent.

While I do not generally urge my doctoral candidates to take formal courses in philosophy of science (a psychologist can spend his time much more profitably studying laboratory electronics, computer programming, genetics, biochemistry, neurophysiology, nonstatistical mathematics, and the like) I consider it indicative of the low level of philosophic sophistication in our profession that these two bloopers are so widely and dogmatically committed. I especially call the reader's attention to the temptation, widely succumbed to, to bolster up one of these methodological mistakes by criticizing the other. Point: They are contraries, not contradictories. So we cannot prove either by refuting the other. *Both* are unacceptable.

Linked to these core misconceptions at the simpleminded and muddlehead ends of the methodological-bias continuum are several interconnected but distinguishable kinds of mistakes. Some of these are decision-theoretical mistakes; some are quasi-ethical, economic, or even "political" mistakes; some are psychometric or statistical mistakes; and some are plain blunders in the ordinary principles of probabilistic inference. I have attempted to gather together into one rather unattractive mélange what I believe to be the commoner and more malignant of these mistakes in the thirteenth paper of this volume, "Why I Do Not Attend Case Conferences," published here for the first time. I am glad of the opportunity to include it in this selection, for I suspect I would have had considerable difficulty persuading the editor of any psychiatric or psychological journal to accept it for publication!

While I am hardly the person to evaluate my own success in steering between simplemindedness on the one side and muddleheadedness on the other, I permit myself a clarifying remark in this connection, which may save the reader some needless cognitive stomachaches. There is a tendency among intellectuals whose professional area is in the humanities, or "documentary" social science, which—surprisingly?—is also found among psychologists and psychiatrists with considerable frequency, to incompatibilize two things: (1) recognition of how rich, complex, subtle, and elusive are the entities and events of the human mind, and (2) the aim to attain maximum quantitative explicitness in the decision making forced upon us in practical situations where human behavior is the subject matter. That is, it seems to be widely believed, *by persons on opposite sides of the "argument,"* that one would not be justified in utilizing explicit actuarial methods, mathematical formulas, the tools of the statistician or computer programmer or life insurance actuary, unless one premised that "the mind is simple, and its workings are easily grasped." Consequently those who lean in their research, teaching, and clinical practice to "objective" modes of decision making tend, by and large, to link these technological preferences to a view of the human mind that is positivistic, operationistic, behavioristic, and the like; whereas those personologists and clinical practitioners whose world picture is relatively more open—one might say, quoting Professor Walter's famous remark about the field of animal behavior, those who refuse to accept the "postulate of impoverished reality"—have a characteristic tendency to be offended by automated, computerized, "mechanical" decision-making procedures, such as I have urged consistently for some twenty years in print, and thirty in class. Now this is an easy mistake to make, arising as it does from deep-seated temperamental differences among psychologists, and then reinforced by the dominant ideology in the particular psychologist's subculture; but it is a mistake nonetheless. There is no clear contradiction between (1) a substantive thesis that the human person is extraordinarily complex, quite possibly (as I believe) too complex ever to be captured by a set of causal laws and constructs in any stage, however utopian, of science; and (2) reliance upon actuarial decision procedures in those pragmatic contexts where decisions are forced upon the professional willy-nilly. From "The mind is terribly complicated" we cannot infer "Avoid mathematics in decision making."

In fact, respectable argument can be made in a direction opposite from the usual. Although this counterargument is found in a couple of my essays, it will do no harm to summarize it briefly here. Misunderstanding about it is one of the commonest reasons for fruitless disputes between clinicians of different "schools," and it is close to the core theme of the essays in this book. The counterargument runs thus: In order to apply a scientific causal theory powerfully in a technological context (e.g., in order to use theoretical physics for purposes of engineering) it is undergraduate methodology of the exact sciences that two epistemic conditions must be fulfilled. First, the theory relied upon for purposes of practical problem solving must be a theory of high verisimilitude (Bunge, 1964; Lakatos, 1968; Lakatos and Musgrave, 1970; references in Meehl, 1970c; Popper, 1959; Schilpp, in press). Second, the theory must have provided us with a powerful technology of measurement, by means of which we can ascertain the initial and boundary conditions of the system under study. *Both* of these conditions must be met, since the way in which a scientific theory is utilized for practical purposes of manipulation or forecasting is, of course, that we "plug in" particular empirical values (ascertained by our accurate measurement procedures) to the equations that describe how the system works (the formalism which, together with the necessary embedding text of words or diagrams, constitutes our causal theory of the subject-matter domain). If you don't have any well-corroborated general laws, you can't play this sort of game with high technological efficiency; and if you don't have accurate instruments by means of which the present values of the relevant causal variables can be ascertained, then you can't play this game either. You need the general laws, and you need the particular conditions. This is undergraduate chemistry and physics, not to say freshman philosophy of science.

Now no clinical psychologist with the slightest exposure to an advanced physical or biological science could possibly have any delusions that personology and psychopathology are fields in which *either* of these two conditions is remotely approximated in the present state of the science and art. (If there is any potential reader who disagrees with the previous sentence, I will save him a lot of trouble by suggesting that perusal of this book would be a waste of his time.) Life insurance companies rely upon actuarial methods *not* because they have a detailed theory of "mortality"; and even if they had such, decision making about individuals (insurable? special premium rating?) could not be made upon that basis, since the second condition is not fulfilled. Point: There are circumstances in physical and biological science (meteorology is an example in the physical sciences) where reliance upon statistical methods, such as a regression equation or an actuarial table, is rational *precisely because* neither a sufficiently powerful causal theory nor a sufficiently powerful measurement technology tied to that theory is available to us. I happen to believe with Hamlet that there are more things in heaven and earth than are dreamed of in any psychologist's philosophy. But I cannot see that this Jamesian "over-belief" of mine speaks against the rationality of seeking the most "objective, non-inferential, automated" prediction methods that can be had in the present state of the art. On the contrary, it speaks for it.

A second general theme which recurs with varying explicitness (and in different substantive guises) in these papers is my view that while many concepts in psychology are unfortunately quite vague or fuzzy, so that to set forth a purported "operational definition" of the concept would really amount to pseudoscientific pretentiousness (in violation of Aristotle's dictum), this does not excuse us from trying to be as precise, explicit, and clearheaded as we can *about that very conceptual fuzziness.* I have little patience with psychologists who deceive themselves about the degree of precision our science and art have presently achieved; but I also disapprove of an attitude (at the other end of the simpleminded/ muddleheaded dimension) where one has become so accustomed to the unavoidable fuzziness of "open concepts" that he does not accept the obligation to be *meta*-theoretically clear (or again, "as clear as the nature of the subject matter permits") about his open concepts. There is in psychology a deplorable tendency to push one's position, or to beat up on the opposition's position, by arguments that are not about facts, or about verbal and mathematical derivations, but are essentially "philosophical" arguments, *although they are usually not stated in the philosopher's language or conceived with the philosopher's technical competence.* One finds psychologists who loftily disclaim any interest or competence in "philosophy of science," but then proceed to deal with difficult substantive issues within psychology by dogmatic appeal to some outmoded, misconceived, and misstated philosophical principle. Example: It is absurd for a clinical psychologist to rule out of court a concept like, say, "subclinical manic depression" on the methodological ground that it is not (to use the favorite catchword again) "operationally defined." Any competent logician or historian of science will tell us that the meta-concept of something's being "operationally defined" is in at least as bad shape conceptually as that of "subclinical manic depression." The proper stance to take in respect to open concepts in personology and clinical practice is to *realize* that they are "open," and in the light of that realization, to exercise a mixture of imagination and rigor, conjecture and criticality that will help us better to deal with such "open concepts" in the daily decision process, meanwhile maintaining a healthy linkage of clinical practice with the research task that aims to "close" some of our open concepts a bit more.

This last consideration leads me to another comment. I am a one-worlder, ontologically speaking. I do not understand what it would mean to say that I "believe in" Freud's theory as a practitioner but do not "believe in" Freud's theory as a teacher or researcher. I understand the meaning of saying that an individual scientist or practitioner has different social roles, and confronts different tasks at different times and places; but I do not understand what it would mean for me to hold a view expressed in proposition p "as a psychotherapist," while holding $\sim p$ in a seminar on psychopathology. I suppose this convicts me of being somewhat old-fashioned, since it amounts to saying that a person should try to make his convictions intellectually *coherent*.

It might be thought, for example, that I contradict myself in the final paper, "Why I Do Not Attend Case Conferences," inasmuch as I criticize the pointless verbalizing of speculative psychodynamics that typically goes on in such conferences and yet I defend (against the super-operationist critic) the use of my own favorite open concepts, such as "compensated schizotypy." (I hope the reader would give me the benefit of the doubt and assume that when Meehl contradicts himself, he does it a *little* more interestingly than that!) But there is no contradiction here. The bootless, feckless psychodynamic speculation of case conferences is usually presented in the guise of something "clinically useful," meaning that it bears somehow upon the steps we might take to help this particular patient; but typically no such concrete therapeutic implications are drawn. And when they are, there is usually no consensus among the informed persons present—let alone quantitative research in the literature—to indicate that any such probability linkage *exists* between the particular bit of psychodynamic inference made and the proposed treatment technique. Nor, in my experience at case conferences, is there any serious attempt to hook up the particular piece of psychodynamic speculation with any larger theory, or with a proposed research project, or even with an ongoing research program in which the concepts mentioned would find their place. Whereas if I suggest that a patient, despite his having presented with primarily anxiety neurosis complaints, and despite his appearing totally free of the accessory symptoms of disintegrated schizotypy, is nevertheless *perhaps* a semicompensated (or decompensated but nondisintegrated) schizotype, that "open concept" is embedded in a rich network of connections, some corroborated and others as yet untested, ranging from behavior genetics to clinical neurology to speculative neurochemistry. Further, in conjecturing that somebody is "perhaps a pseudoneurotic schizophrenia" I am implicitly saying several things that are empirically falsifiable in the result, e.g., he should (probably) react rather well to one of the phenothiazines; he should probably not be treated psychoanalytically, and certainly not be put on the couch; he probably would do better with a therapist who scores high on the Whitehorn Betz A-B scale than with one who does not; the psychotherapeutic commitment one makes ought to be for a long period, possibly even "for life"; modest therapeutic goals should be set; the patient may have to learn to live with what Rado calls a "scarcity economy of pleasure"; remissions and exacerbations are to be expected; the long-term prognosis is rather poor; and if psychotherapists are in short supply (as they usually are) we lack adequate data to indicate that psychotherapeutic intervention makes enough difference with this type of patient to justify taking that many hours away from a nonschizoid patient with neurotic or situational problems.

I cannot understand the position of those who say that a given concept is "all right" in a seminar, or in designing an experiment or file study, but it is not "all right" in the clinical setting. How can that be? I repeat, I do not live in different worlds. If an open concept doesn't have anything going for it, I don't see why I would discuss it in a seminar any more than I would in a pool hall or at a cocktail party. If it *does* have something going for it—and the "something" may be merely that it is a fresh, interesting, and potentially refutable conjecture—then I don't see what kind of ground rules would exclude it from my thinking qua clinician. Of course the problem of what weight may properly be given to an open concept (and to conjectured lawlike relationships involving it) when it comes to decision making about patients is an ethical and economic question, examinable on the merits. It may well be that a certain concept has *at the moment* so little "empirical cash value" that it would be unethical to utilize it in prescribing a kind of therapy, and uneconomic to discuss it in a conference aimed at practical decisions. But this we conclude on the basis of the utilities and the aims of the case conference, not by dividing the world into different kinds or orders of reality.

Except for the paper on "The Cognitive Activity of the Clinician," the contributions reprinted in this volume are theoretical, methodological, or psychometric rather than empirical. While my empirical research in the area of psychodiagnosis exemplifies, more often than not, the pragmatic and epistemological viewpoints set forth in the essays here reprinted, it seemed more useful to round off the volume conceptually than to reprint empirical studies on specific diagnostic problems, e.g., brain damage. This is the more so since the diagnostic instrument with which I happen, for geographical reasons, to have been most concerned, the Minnesota Multiphasic Personality Inventory (MMPI), is not an instrument employed by all clinicians or researchers; the methodological themes of the book recur apart from a preference, whether biased or informed, for or against a particular diagnostic tool. Some of my earlier work on the MMPI has been either extended or refuted in subsequent research and is therefore of at most historical interest. A list of all publications by me in the broad area of psychodiagnosis, empirical and theoretical, is appended at the end of this volume.

Given the opportunity afforded by this preface, I cannot resist the impulse to make one more effort at clarifying a widespread misconception of my views about the clinical interview and the clinician's diagnostic skills and sensitivities. Despite repeated disclaimers, *including over half the total pages of my 1954 book on actuarial prediction,* I find to my continued amazement that most clinical psychologists attribute to me the view that the clinician has no special powers, that there are no skills which a bright, sensitive, empathic, and *seasoned* diagnostic or therapeutic interviewer possesses that cannot be found (or substituted for) in a beginning psychiatry resident or first-year clinical trainee or, for that matter, a computer or a clerk. I am at a loss to understand such selective reading of words as is represented in that misconception, and have long since abandoned efforts to understand it or counteract it. It seems to be a characteristic of the human mind that it cannot readily assimilate anything subtle or complicated, and the slovenly intellectual tradition in clinical psychology and psychiatry (discussed in the thirteenth essay) renders many professionals in these fields so habituated to superficiality of thought and stereotypes of "viewpoints" that trying to explain anything that involves the making of complex or subtle distinctions, whether of substance or method, is usually a waste of time. Despite my resignation to being stereotyped because of my 1954 book, I record here once again my belief that the skilled clinician possesses a set of cognitive and instrumental dispositions that are *not* to be found in just any clerk that we commandeer from the outer office. I have noted that clinical psychology trainees, who had formed an impression of my views as undergraduates elsewhere than Minnesota, are surprised at how much time I spend in class on "clinical lore" concerning the Mental Status Examination, including large amounts of unpublishable material about subtle aspects of posture, expressive movement, voice, and the like—in support of which I present so little quantitative data. In my day as a Ph.D. candidate, all Minnesota's clinical psychologists took a minor in neuropsychiatry which meant spending hundreds of hours in classes with medical students or residents and going on hospital rounds (neurology and psychiatry). A strong emphasis on the medical tradition has, until recent years, been characteristic of Minnesota's clinical psychologists. Coming out of that sort of background, and adding to it my own experience as analysand and at least 10,000 hours (the last time I computed it some years ago) of flying time as a practitioner, I have an interest in clinical assessment through interview and history which, I suspect, exceeds that of the average member of my profession. Further— as the thirteenth paper also indicates—my respect for the physician's diagnostic rubrics, and his general taxonomic model and mode of thought, is much greater than what is typical for American clinical psychologists at the present time. I therefore find it strange to be so consistently put into the role of superactuarial, hardnosed "anti-clinician" largely on the basis of a book devoted to a highly specific technological dilemma in decision making, to wit, *given* certain historical facts, test scores, and *clinical judgments* as the ("not-so-raw") data available for purposes of forecasting future behavior (or inferring concurrent behavior unobserved), how well does the typical clinical judge do at this information-combining job when put in competition with regression equations, actuarial tables, or, as I would emphasize today, the big computer? That was a sensible question to put in 1954, and (despite obscurantist efforts to pretend that the "dichotomy" is a misleading one) it remains a significant question to put today. Anybody who doesn't see that there is an important difference, both to patient and taxpayer, between a 60 percent hit rate achieved by fifteen high-paid clinicians sitting around a table in a smoke-filled room engaged in what is called a "case conference" and an 80 percent hit rate achieved by an actuarial table seems to me to have something wrong with his cerebration.

One final word. I am quite aware that the questions examined in these papers are not of the sort that "turn on" the majority of our current crop of clinical psychology trainees. This is not the place to discuss the deep social forces that underlie those frequent changes in problem definition (and what would count as an acceptable problem solution) regrettably so characteristic of the inexact sciences. What fledgling clinicians want to talk and hear about today, and why, deserves a whole book in its own right. I shall content myself with saying that the concerns of most of our young clinicians seem to me to reflect their understandable and valid protest against a dominant cultural ethos which is neither rational nor humane, together with personal preoccupations which, so far as I can discern, are not fundamentally different from those which "bugged" us who were in doctoral training programs thirty years ago. We, like them, were as young people intensely concerned with what Hesse (*The Glass Bead Game*) succinctly conjoins as "the struggle for position and the search for love." I am unable to see any really important differences, of either quality or quantity, between our generation and theirs in this respect. These two regnant motives appeared to me, whether openly expressed or thinly disguised, in the graduate students of 1940–45; and they appear to me the same way in the present crop. Nor can I discern a major qualitative or quantitative difference in the matter of "social awareness" or "rejection of the establishment." It puzzles me when I hear a twenty-three-year-old Ph.D. candidate complain that he doesn't find neuroanatomy "relevant" and can't make himself study it conscientiously because of the mess the world is in. I am willing to defend the proposition that those of us who, in our teens and young adulthood, were confronted with the Great Depression (my father killed himself as a result of it), the rise of world fascism, and the degeneration of the socialist ideal under Stalin's bloody tyranny lived in a world that was in pretty much of a mess; and those of us with any brains and social awareness were, as I retrospect, fully aware of this social fact. I have not as yet seen a psychological or sociological analysis of the "commitment problems" of the present generation that strikes me as persuasive. But graduate students, as a class, are of course "committed" to some minimal degree or they would not be graduate students. The biggest difference I see between my generation of fledgling clinicians and the current group is *not* a difference in personal motivations, or ambition, or altruism, or awareness of the world outside academia. Rather it is a difference in *what kind of subject matter mobilizes their intellectual passions*. In this respect I permit myself what may sound like a reactionary comment, but I want to lay my cards on the table. It seems to me that one characteristic of a first-rate intellect is that it demands a complex, difficult, abstract subject matter to grapple with in order to be fully alive. Natural-born mesomorphic athletes seem to "need" vigorous exercise. Creators in the arts report that they "need" to write music or paint pictures or write sonnets, and would do so even if they knew beforehand that their productions would never be appreciated or never even be seen or heard by anybody else. Analogously, I believe that first-class abstract ideator types "need" something complicated to think about, some conceptual food for thought. And I confess that the subjects which seem to interest many clinical students of the present generation are, whatever their ethical or political importance, just not subjects *capable* of commanding the prolonged and intense focus of an able mind. I shall no doubt be told that I am wrong about this, but I can't help it. It is hard for me to understand how persons with a Ph.D. in psychology can find it intellectually exhilarating to repeat "The patient seems to be relating well to the patients in our therapeutic community" 250 times a year, despite variation in terminology. The conceptual matter with which many of our students (and, unfortunately, some of our faculty) occupy themselves is, I submit, a rather dismal intellectual repast of stale bread and flat beer. You may say, "Well, what of it? What social relevance does it have whether or not the dominant themes of clinical psychology are exciting to the first-rate intellects among our students?" My response to this query is somewhat conjectural, but not without historical analogies that are disturbing. As I read the record, it is possible for the cognitive character of a field to degenerate (or merely stagnate) to such an extent that the field no longer attracts able persons. I suppose the most dramatic example of this in Western culture is theology. For many centuries, the ablest minds in our culture were theologians. And this was true, for England at least, even up into the early nineteenth century, witness Sir Francis Galton's finding that a remarkably high proportion of English eminent scholars and scientists were the sons of clergymen. It is a matter of common knowledge that this is no longer true, at least so far as Protestantism is concerned (I do not happen to have any data or impressions with regard to the Roman or Eastern churches). The Protestant ministry today attracts almost no first-rate brains, and this is so overwhelming a tendency that when a large doctoral training program in psychology—to which a fair number of clergy or ex-clergy are attracted these days—finds a clergyman of high intellectual ability and cognitive zeal, it is a subject for amazed comment among the faculty ("Why, believe it or not, I actually have a preacher in my course who isn't dumb!"). The differences in average intellectual level in various graduate study fields are too well known to require documentation, and I shall avoid making those invidious comparisons which all informed readers know about as well as I. It is also commonly believed, by students and faculty alike, that a pronounced circular influence operates here, in that the presence of numerous mediocrities tends to render even a potentially interesting subject matter dull to the brights and super-brights. This in turn means that the intellectual level of the rejected field is likely to remain low, or even to sink lower. I am reliably informed that it is a matter of grave concern to socially conscious business executives that the intellectually ablest college majors in economics and business administration are today showing a pronounced disinclination to enter the business world upon graduation; and it goes without saying that in a society like ours, a dearth of incisive and creative minds among the power elite of the business community could have very bad social consequences. Point: Whether the subject matter of clinical psychology includes substantive and methodological content capable of engaging the passionate attention of high-caliber intelligences is not merely a matter of academic interest or personal snobbery. In the long run, it is likely to have a profound effect upon the statistical composition of the discipline's teachers, investigators, and practitioners. If, as I suppose, clinical psychology is (as Einstein once said about physics) "too hard for us," and if, as I think at least plausible, some of the problems considered in this collection of essays will resist solution unless the field experiences some powerful conceptual "breakthroughs," then it is of supreme importance that we present to advanced undergraduate students and beginning graduate students who are making career decisions a subject matter capable of attracting and holding the interest of at least a few persons sufficiently bright, creative, clearheaded, and intellectually passionate to make such conceptual breakthroughs. Furthermore, given the shortage of mental health personnel and the squeeze on the taxpayer's dollar, it is hardly justifiable to put would-be psychological helpers through eight years (and more) of higher education in order to render them capable of propounding such earthshaking truths as "The patient is a person" or "Successful psychotherapy is a growth process." If one really believes that there *is* no appreciable validity in the existing corpus of psychological knowledge that bears upon mental health problems, as to either substance or method, then the obvious conclusion is that we should liquidate our training programs and turn to making an honest living selling shoes. I record my prediction that this "thin-beer phase" of clinical psychology is a passing fad, and that the kinds of topics to which these collected papers address themselves will again become the focus of serious attention.

I want here to record an intellectual debt to my teacher, colleague, and friend Professor Emeritus Starke R. Hathaway, which the papers make obvious to anyone familiar with the Minnesota tradition of clinical psychology. There are few persons on this campus with whom I have at times disagreed so profoundly and debated so vehemently (on topics ranging from epistemology and the limitations of science to the merits of factor analysis and the truth content of Freud's system) since I first became Dr. Hathaway's assistant in 1943. But there are also few men from whom I have learned so much. Scientific content and habits, clinical skills, and professional values are all among the learnings involved in that three-decade association.

Gratitude is due to the staff of the University of Minnesota Press for its encouragement and support; and to my excellent secretary, Mrs. Cheryl Yano, whose high competence, conscientiousness, and nurturant acceptance of my oral impatience have been most helpful.

Paul E. Meehl

Minneapolis, Minnesota
August 17, 1972

Table of Contents

Psychodiagnosis: Selected Papers

1

Construct Validity
in Psychological Tests

VALIDATION of psychological tests has not yet been adequately concep-
tualized, as the APA Committee on Test Standards learned when it
undertook (1950–54) to specify what qualities should be investigated
before a test is published. In order to make coherent recommendations
the committee found it necessary to distinguish four types of validity,
established by different types of research and requiring different interpretation. The chief innovation in the committee's report was the
term *construct validity*.[1] This idea was first formulated by a subcom-
mittee (Meehl and R. C. Challman) studying how proposed recommendations would apply to projective techniques, and later modified
and clarified by the entire committee (Bordin, Challman, Conrad, Cronbach, Humphreys, Meehl, and Super). The statements agreed upon by
the committee (and by committees of two other associations) were
published in the "Technical Recommendations" (APA Committee on

AUTHOR'S NOTE: This paper was written in collaboration with Lee J. Cronbach,
then of the University of Illinois. It first appeared in *Psychological Bulletin*, vol.
52, 1955; copyright 1955 by the American Psychological Association, Inc.
  I worked on this problem in connection with my appointment to the Minnesota
Center for Philosophy of Science. Both Professor Cronbach and I are indebted
to the other members of the Center (Herbert Feigl, Michael Scriven, Wilfrid
Sellars), and to D. L. Thistlethwaite of the University of Illinois, for their major
contributions to our thinking and their suggestions for improving this paper.
  [1] Referred to in a preliminary report (APA Committee on Test Standards, 1952)
as *congruent validity*.

Test Standards, 1954). The present interpretation of construct validity is not "official" and deals with some areas where the committee would probably not be unanimous. The present writers are solely responsible for this attempt to explain the concept and elaborate its implications.

Identification of construct validity was not an isolated development. Writers on validity during the preceding decade had shown a great deal of dissatisfaction with conventional notions of validity, and introduced new terms and ideas, but the resulting aggregation of types of validity seems only to have stirred the muddy waters. Portions of the distinctions we shall discuss are implicit in Jenkins' paper, "Validity for What?" (1946), Gulliksen's "Intrinsic Validity" (1950), Goodenough's distinction between tests as "signs" and "samples" (1949), Cronbach's separation of "logical" and "empirical" validity (1949), Guilford's "factorial validity" (1946), and Mosier's papers on "face validity" and "validity generalization" (1947, 1951). Helen Peak (1953) comes close to an explicit statement of construct validity as we shall present it.

Four Types of Validation

The categories into which the "Recommendations" divide validity studies are predictive validity, concurrent validity, content validity, and construct validity. The first two of these may be considered together as *criterion-oriented* validation procedures.

The pattern of a criterion-oriented study is familiar. The investigator is primarily interested in some criterion which he wishes to predict. He administers the test, obtains an independent criterion measure on the same subjects, and computes a correlation. If the criterion is obtained some time after the test is given, he is studying *predictive validity*. If the test score and criterion score are determined at essentially the same time, he is studying *concurrent validity*. Concurrent validity is studied when one test is proposed as a substitute for another (for example, when a multiple-choice form of spelling test is substituted for taking dictation), or a test is shown to correlate with some contemporary criterion (e.g., psychiatric diagnosis).

Content validity is established by showing that the test items are a sample of a universe in which the investigator is interested. Content validity is ordinarily to be established deductively, by defining a universe

4

of items and sampling systematically within this universe to establish the test.

Construct validation is involved whenever a test is to be interpreted as a measure of some attribute or quality which is not "operationally defined." The problem faced by the investigator is "What constructs account for variance in test performance?" Construct validity calls for no new scientific approach. Much current research on tests of personality (Child, 1954) is construct validation, usually without the benefit of a clear formulation of this process.

Construct validity is not to be identified solely by particular investigative procedures, but by the orientation of the investigator. Criterion-oriented validity, as Bechtoldt emphasizes (1951, p. 1245), "involves the *acceptance* of a set of operations as an adequate definition of whatever is to be measured." When an investigator believes that no criterion available to him is fully valid, he perforce becomes interested in construct validity because this is the only way to avoid the "infinite frustration" of relating every criterion to some more ultimate standard (Gaylord, unpublished). In content validation, *acceptance* of the universe of content as defining the variable to be measured is essential. Construct validity must be investigated whenever no criterion or universe of content is accepted as entirely adequate to define the quality to be measured. Determining what psychological constructs account for test performance is desirable for almost any test. Thus, although the MMPI was originally established on the basis of empirical discrimination between patient groups and so-called normals (concurrent validity), continuing research has tried to provide a basis for describing the personality associated with each score pattern. Such interpretations permit the clinician to predict performance with respect to criteria which have not yet been employed in empirical validation studies (cf. Meehl, 1954a, pp. 49–50, 110–111).

We can distinguish among the four types of validity by noting that each involves a different emphasis on the criterion. In predictive or concurrent validity, the criterion behavior is of concern to the tester, and he may have no concern whatsoever with the type of behavior exhibited in the test. (An employer does not care if a worker can manipulate blocks, but the score on the block test may predict something he cares about.) Content validity is studied when the tester *is* concerned with the type of behavior involved in the test performance. Indeed, if the test is a work sample, the behavior represented in the test may be an end in itself. Construct validity is ordinarily studied when the tester has no definite criterion measure of the quality with which he is concerned, and must use indirect measures. Here the trait or quality underlying the test is of central importance, rather than either the test behavior or the scores on the criteria. [APA Committee on Test Standards, 1954, p. 14.]

Construct validation is important at times for every sort of psychological test: aptitude, achievement, interests, and so on. Thurstone's statement is interesting in this connection:

In the field of intelligence tests, it used to be common to define validity as the correlation between a test score and some outside criterion. We have reached a stage of sophistication where the test-criterion correlation is too coarse. It is obsolete. If we attempted to ascertain the validity of a test for the second space-factor, for example, we would have to get judges [to] make reliable judgments about people as to this factor. Ordinarily their [the available judges'] ratings would be of no value as a criterion. Consequently, validity studies in the cognitive functions now depend on criteria of internal consistency . . . [Thurstone, 1952, p. 3.]

Construct validity would be involved in answering such questions as To what extent is this test of intelligence culture-free? Does this test of "interpretation of data" measure reading ability, quantitative reasoning, or response sets? How does a person with A in Strong Accountant, and B in Strong CPA, differ from a person who has these scores reversed?

Example of construct validation procedure. Suppose measure X correlates .50 with $Y,$ the amount of palmar sweating induced when we tell a student that he has failed a Psychology I exam. Predictive validity of X for Y is adequately described by the coefficient, and a statement of the experimental and sampling conditions. If someone were to ask, "Isn't there perhaps another way to interpret this correlation?" or "What other kinds of evidence can you bring to support your interpretation?" we would hardly understand what he was asking because no interpretation has been made. These questions become relevant when the correlation is advanced as evidence that "test X measures anxiety proneness." Alternative interpretations are possible; e.g., perhaps the test measures "academic aspiration," in which case we will expect different results if we induce palmar sweating by economic threat. It is then reasonable to inquire about other *kinds* of evidence.

Add these facts from further studies: Text X correlates .45 with fraternity brothers' ratings on "tenseness." Test X correlates .55 with amount of intellectual inefficiency induced by painful electric shock,

6

and .68 with the Taylor Anxiety Scale. Mean X score decreases among four diagnosed groups in this order: anxiety state, reactive depression, "normal," and psychopathic personality. And palmar sweat under threat of failure in Psychology I correlates .60 with threat of failure in mathematics. Negative results eliminate competing explanations of the X score; thus, findings of negligible correlations between X and social class, vocational aim, and value orientation make it fairly safe to reject the suggestion that X measures "academic aspiration." We can have substantial confidence that X does measure anxiety proneness if the current theory of anxiety can embrace the variates which yield positive correlations, and does not predict correlations where we found none.

Kinds of Constructs

At this point we should indicate summarily what we mean by a construct, recognizing that much of the remainder of the paper deals with this question. A construct is some postulated attribute of people, assumed to be reflected in test performance. In test validation the attribute about which we make statements in interpreting a test is a construct. We expect a person at any time to possess or not possess a qualitative attribute (amnesia) or structure, or to possess some degree of a quantitative attribute (cheerfulness). A construct has certain associated meanings carried in statements of this general character: Persons who possess this attribute will, in situation X, act in manner Y (with a stated probability). The logic of construct validation is invoked whether the construct is highly systematized or loose, used in ramified theory or a few simple propositions, used in absolute propositions or probability statements. We seek to specify how one is to defend a proposed interpretation of a test; *we are not recommending any one type of interpretation.*

The constructs in which tests are to be interpreted are certainly not likely to be physiological. Most often they will be traits such as "latent hostility" or "variable in mood," or descriptions in terms of an educational objective, as "ability to plan experiments." For the benefit of readers who may have been influenced by certain eisegeses of Mac-Corquodale and Meehl (1948), let us here emphasize: Whether or not an interpretation of a test's properties or relations involves questions of construct validity is to be decided by examining the entire body of evidence offered, together with what is asserted about the test in the context

7

of this evidence. Proposed identifications of constructs allegedly measured by the test with constructs of other sciences (e.g., genetics, neuro-anatomy, biochemistry) make up only *one* class of construct-validity claims, and a rather minor one at present. Space does not permit full analysis of the relation of the present paper to the MacCorquodale-Meehl distinction between hypothetical constructs and intervening variables. The philosophy of science pertinent to the present paper is set forth later in the section entitled "The Nomological Net."

The Relation of Constructs to "Criteria"

Critical View of the Criterion Implied

An unquestionable criterion may be found in a practical operation, or may be established as a consequence of an operational definition. Typically, however, the psychologist is unwilling to use the directly operational approach because he is interested in building theory about a generalized construct. A theorist trying to relate behavior to "hunger" almost certainly invests that term with meanings other than the operation "elapsed-time-since-feeding." If he is concerned with hunger as a tissue need, he will not accept time lapse as *equivalent* to his construct because it fails to consider, among other things, energy expenditure of the animal.

In some situations the criterion is no more valid than the test. Suppose, for example, that we want to know if counting the dots on Bender-Gestalt figure five indicates "compulsive rigidity," and take psychiatric ratings on this trait as a criterion. Even a conventional report on the resulting correlation will say something about the extent and intensity of the psychiatrist's contacts and should describe his qualifications (e.g., diplomate status? analyzed?).

Why report these facts? Because data are needed to indicate whether the criterion is any good. "Compulsive rigidity" is not really intended to mean "social stimulus value to psychiatrists." The implied trait involves a range of behavior dispositions which may be very imperfectly sampled by the psychiatrist. Suppose dot counting does not occur in a particular patient and yet we find that the psychiatrist has rated him as "rigid." When questioned the psychiatrist tells us that the patient was a rather easy, freewheeling sort; however, the patient *did* lean over to straighten out a skewed desk blotter, and this, viewed against certain other facts,

8

tipped the scale in favor of a "rigid" rating. On the face of it, counting Bender dots may be just as good (or poor) a sample of the compulsive-rigidity domain as straightening desk blotters is.

Suppose, to extend our example, we have four tests on the "predictor" side, over against the psychiatrist's "criterion," and find generally positive correlations among the five variables. Surely it is artificial and arbitrary to impose the "test-should-predict-criterion" pattern on such data. The psychiatrist samples verbal content, expressive pattern, voice, posture, etc. The psychologist samples verbal content, perception, expressive pattern, etc. Our proper conclusion is that, from this evidence, the four tests and the psychiatrist all assess some common factor.

The asymmetry between the "test" and the so-designated "criterion" arises only because the terminology of predictive validity has become a commonplace in test analysis. In this study where a construct is the central concern, any distinction between the merit of the test and criterion variables would be justified only if it had already been shown that the psychiatrist's theory and operations were excellent measures of the attribute.

Inadequacy of Validation in Terms of Specific Criteria

The proposal to validate constructual interpretations of tests runs counter to suggestions of some others. Spiker and McCandless (1954) favor an operational approach. Validation is replaced by compiling statements on how strongly the test predicts other observed variables of interest. To avoid requiring that each new variable be investigated completely by itself, they allow two variables to collapse into one whenever the properties of the operationally defined measures are the same: "If a new test is demonstrated to predict the scores on an older, well-established test, then an evaluation of the predictive power of the older test may be used for the new one." But accurate inferences are possible only if the two tests correlate so highly that there is negligible reliable variance in either test, independent of the other. Where the correspondence is less close, one must either retain all the separate variables operationally defined or embark on construct validation.

The practical user of tests must rely on constructs of some generality to make predictions about new situations. Test X could be used to predict palmar sweating in the face of failure without invoking any construct, but a counselor is more likely to be asked to forecast behavior in diverse or even unique situations for which the correlation of test X is unknown. Significant predictions rely on knowledge accumulated around the generalized construct of anxiety. The "Technical Recommendations" state:

It is ordinarily necessary to evaluate construct validity by integrating evidence from many different sources. The problem of construct validation becomes especially acute in the clinical field since for many of the constructs dealt with it is not a question of finding an imperfect criterion but of finding any criterion at all. The psychologist interested in construct validity for clinical devices is concerned with making an estimate of a hypothetical internal process, factor, system, structure, or state and cannot expect to find a clear unitary behavioral criterion. An attempt to identify any one criterion measure or any composite as *the* criterion aimed at is, however, usually unwarranted. [APA Committee on Test Standards, 1954, pp. 14–15.]

This appears to conflict with arguments for specific criteria prominent at places in the testing literature. Thus Anastasi (1950) makes many statements of the latter character: "It is only as a measure of a specifically defined criterion that a test can be objectively validated at all . . . To claim that a test measures anything over and above its criterion is pure speculation" (p. 67). Yet elsewhere this article supports construct validation. Tests can be profitably interpreted if we "know the relationships between the tested behavior . . . and other behavior samples, none of these behavior samples necessarily occupying the preeminent position of a criterion" (p. 75). Factor analysis with several partial criteria might be used to study whether a test measures a postulated "general learning ability." If the data demonstrate specificity of ability instead, such specificity is "useful in its own right in advancing our knowledge of behavior; it should not be construed as a weakness of the tests" (p. 75).

We depart from Anastasi at two points. She writes, "The validity of a psychological test should not be confused with an analysis of the factors which determine the behavior under consideration." We, however, regard such analysis as a most important type of validation. Second, she refers to "the will-o'-the-wisp of psychological processes which are distinct from performance" (p. 77). While we agree that psychological processes are elusive, we are sympathetic to attempts to formulate and clarify constructs which are evidenced by performance but distinct from

10

it. Surely an inductive inference based on a pattern of correlations cannot be dismissed as "pure speculation."

Specific Criteria Used Temporarily: The "Bootstraps" Effect

Even when a test is constructed on the basis of a specific criterion, it may ultimately be judged to have greater construct validity than the criterion. We start with a vague concept which we associate with certain observations. We then discover empirically that these observations covary with some other observation which possesses greater reliability or is more intimately correlated with relevant experimental changes than is the original measure, or both. For example, the notion of temperature arises because some objects feel hotter to the touch than others. The expansion of a mercury column does not have face validity as an index of hotness. But it turns out that (a) there is a statistical relation between expansion and sensed temperature; (b) observers employ the mercury method with good interobserver agreement; (c) the regularity of observed relations is increased by using the thermometer (e.g., melting points of samples of the same material vary little on the thermometer; we obtain nearly linear relations between mercury measures and pressure of a gas). Finally (d) a theoretical structure involving unobservable microevents—the kinetic theory—is worked out which explains the relation of mercury expansion to heat. This whole process of conceptual enrichment begins with what in retrospect we see as an extremely fallible "criterion"—the human temperature sense. That original criterion has now been relegated to a peripheral position. We have lifted ourselves by our bootstraps, but in a legitimate and fruitful way.

Similarly, the Binet scale was first valued because children's scores tended to agree with judgments by schoolteachers. If it had not shown this agreement, it would have been discarded along with reaction time and the other measures of ability previously tried. Teacher judgments once constituted the criterion against which the individual intelligence test was validated. But if today a child's IQ is 135 and three of his teachers complain about how stupid he is, we do not conclude that the test has failed. Quite to the contrary, if no error in test procedure can be argued, we treat the test score as a valid statement about an important quality, and define our task as that of finding out what other variables—personality, study skills, etc.—modify achievement or distort teacher judgment.

11

Experimentation to Investigate Construct Validity

Validation Procedures

We can use many methods in construct validation. Attention should particularly be drawn to Macfarlane's survey of these methods as they apply to projective devices (1942).

Group differences. If our understanding of a construct leads us to expect two groups to differ on the test, this expectation may be tested directly. Thus Thurstone and Chave validated the Scale for Measuring Attitude toward the Church by showing score differences between church members and nonchurchgoers. Churchgoing is not *the* criterion of attitude, for the purpose of the test is to measure something other than the crude sociological fact of church attendance; on the other hand, failure to find a difference would have seriously challenged the test.

Only coarse correspondence between test and group designation is expected. Too great a correspondence between the two would indicate that the test is to some degree invalid, because members of the groups are expected to overlap on the test. Intelligence-test items are selected initially on the basis of a correspondence to age, but an item that correlates .95 with age in an elementary school sample would surely be suspect.

Correlation matrices and factor analysis. If two tests are presumed to measure the same construct, a correlation between them is predicted. (An exception is noted where some second attribute has positive loading in the first test and negative loading in the second test; then a low correlation is expected. This is a testable interpretation provided an external measure of either the first or the second variable exists.) If the obtained correlation departs from the expectation, however, there is no way to know whether the fault lies in test *A,* test *B,* or the formulation of the construct. A matrix of intercorrelations often points out profitable ways of dividing the construct into more meaningful parts, factor analysis being a useful computational method in such studies.

Guilford (1948) has discussed the place of factor analysis in construct validation. His statements may be extracted as follows: "The personnel psychologist wishes to know 'why his tests are valid.' He can place tests and practical criteria in a matrix and factor it to identify 'real dimensions of human personality.' A factorial description is exact and stable; it is economical in explanation; it leads to the creation of pure

12

tests which can be combined to predict complex behaviors." It is clear that factors here function as constructs. Eysenck, in his "criterion analysis" (1950), goes farther than Guilford, and shows that factoring can be used explicitly to test hypotheses about constructs.

Factors may or may not be weighted with surplus meaning. Certainly when they are regarded as "real dimensions" a great deal of surplus meaning is implied, and the interpreter must shoulder a substantial burden of proof. The alternative view is to regard factors as defining a working reference frame, located in a convenient manner in the "space" defined by all behaviors of a given type. Which set of factors from a given matrix is "most useful" will depend partly on predilections, but in essence the best construct is the one around which we can build the greatest number of inferences, in the most direct fashion.

Studies of internal structure. For many constructs, evidence of homogeneity within the test is relevant in judging validity. If a trait such as *dominance* is hypothesized, and the items inquire about behaviors subsumed under this label, then the hypothesis appears to require that these items be generally intercorrelated. Even low correlations, if consistent, would support the argument that people may be fruitfully described in terms of a generalized tendency to dominate or not dominate. The general quality would have power to predict behavior in a variety of situations represented by the specific items. Item-test correlations and certain reliability formulas describe internal consistency.

It is unwise to list uninterpreted data of this sort under the heading "validity" in test manuals, as some authors have done. High internal consistency may *lower* validity. Only if the underlying theory of the trait being measured calls for high item intercorrelations do the correlations support construct validity. Negative item-test correlations may support construct validity, provided that the items with negative correlations are believed irrelevant to the postulated construct and serve as suppressor variables (Horst, 1941, p. 431–436; Meehl, 1945c).

Study of distinctive subgroups of items within a test may set an upper limit to construct validity by showing that irrelevant elements influence scores. Thus a study of the PMA space tests shows that variance can be partially accounted for by a response set, a tendency to mark many figures as similar (Cronbach, 1950). An internal factor analysis of the PEA Interpretation of Data Test shows that in addition to measuring reasoning skills, the test score is strongly influenced by a tendency to

13

say "probably true" rather than "certainly true," regardless of item content (Damrin, 1952). On the other hand, a study of item groupings in the DAT Mechanical Comprehension Test permitted rejection of the hypothesis that knowledge about specific topics such as gears made a substantial contribution to scores (Cronbach, 1951).

Studies of change over occasions. The stability of test scores ("retest reliability," Cattell's "N-technique") may be relevant to construct validation. Whether a high degree of stability is encouraging or discouraging for the proposed interpretation depends upon the theory defining the construct.

More powerful than the retest after uncontrolled intervening experiences is the retest with experimental intervention. If a transient influence swings test scores over a wide range, there are definite limits on the extent to which a test result can be interpreted as reflecting the typical behavior of the individual. These are examples of experiments which have indicated upper limits to test validity: studies of differences associated with the examiner in projective testing, of change of score under alternative directions ("tell the truth" vs. "make yourself look good to an employer"), and of coachability of mental tests. We may recall Gulliksen's distinction (1950): When the coaching is of a sort that improves the pupil's intellectual functioning in school, the test which is affected by the coaching has validity as a measure of intellectual functioning; if the coaching improves test taking but not school performance, the test which responds to the coaching has poor validity as a measure of this construct.

Sometimes, where differences between individuals are difficult to assess by any means other than the test, the experimenter validates by determining whether the test can detect induced intra-individual differences. One might hypothesize that the Zeigarnik effect is a measure of ego involvement, i.e., that with ego involvement there is more recall of incomplete tasks. To support such an interpretation, the investigator will try to induce ego involvement on some task by appropriate directions and compare subjects' recall with their recall for tasks where there was a contrary induction. Sometimes the intervention is drastic. Porteus (1950) found that brain-operated patients showed disruption of performance on his maze, but did not show impaired performance on conventional verbal tests, and argued therefrom that his test is a better measure of planfulness.

14

Studies of process. One of the best ways of determining informally what accounts for variability on a test is observation of the person's process of performance. If it is supposed, for example, that a test measures mathematical competence, and yet observation of students' errors shows that erroneous reading of the question is common, the implications of a low score are altered. Lucas (1953) in this way showed that the Navy Relative Movement Test, an aptitude test, actually involved two different abilities: spatial visualization and mathematical reasoning.

Mathematical analysis of scoring procedures may provide important negative evidence on construct validity. A recent analysis of "empathy" tests is perhaps worth citing (Cronbach, 1955b). "Empathy" has been operationally defined in many studies by the ability of a judge to predict what responses will be given on some questionnaire by a subject he has observed briefly. A mathematical argument has shown, however, that the scores depend on several attributes of the judge which enter into his perception of *any* individual, and that they therefore cannot be interpreted as evidence of his ability to interpret cues offered by particular others, or his intuition.

The Numerical Estimate of Construct Validity

There is an understandable tendency to seek a "construct-validity coefficient." A numerical statement of the degree of construct validity would be a statement of the proportion of the test score variance that is attributable to the construct variable. This numerical estimate can sometimes be arrived at by a factor analysis, but since present methods of factor analysis are based on linear relations, more general methods will ultimately be needed to deal with many quantitative problems of construct validation.

Rarely will it be possible to estimate definite "construct saturations," because no factor corresponding closely to the construct will be available. One can only hope to set upper and lower bounds to the "loading." If "creativity" is defined as something independent of knowledge, then a correlation of .40 between a presumed test of creativity and a test of arithmetic knowledge would indicate that at least 16 percent of the reliable test variance is irrelevant to creativity as defined. Laboratory performance on problems such as Maier's "hatrack" would scarcely be an ideal measure of creativity, but it would be somewhat relevant. If its correlation with the test is .60, this permits a tentative estimate of 36 percent as a lower bound. (The estimate is tentative because the test might overlap with the irrelevant portion of the laboratory measure.) The saturation seems to lie between 36 and 84 percent; a cumulation of studies would provide better limits.

It should be particularly noted that rejecting the null hypothesis does not finish the job of construct validation (Kelly, 1954, p. 284). The problem is not to conclude that the test "is valid" for measuring the construct variable. The task is to state as definitely as possible the degree of validity the test is presumed to have.

The Logic of Construct Validation

Construct validation takes place when an investigator believes that his instrument reflects a particular construct, to which are attached certain meanings. The proposed interpretation generates specific testable hypotheses, which are a means of confirming or disconfirming the claim. The philosophy of science which we believe does most justice to actual scientific practice will now be briefly and dogmatically set forth. Readers interested in further study of the philosophical underpinning are referred to the works by Braithwaite (1953, especially Chapter III), Carnap (1939, pp. 56–69; 1950), Pap (1953), Sellars (1948, 1954), Feigl (1950, 1951), Beck (1950), Kneale (1949, pp. 92–110), Hempel (1950; 1952, sec. 7).

The Nomological Net

The fundamental principles are these:

1. Scientifically speaking, to "make clear what something *is*" means to set forth the laws in which it occurs. We shall refer to the interlocking system of laws which constitute a theory as a *nomological network*.

2. The laws in a nomological network may relate (a) observable properties or quantities to each other; or (b) theoretical constructs to observables; or (c) different theoretical constructs to one another. These "laws" may be statistical or deterministic.

3. A necessary condition for a construct to be scientifically admissible is that it occur in a nomological net, at least *some* of whose laws involve observables. Admissible constructs may be remote from observation, i.e., a long derivation may intervene between the nomologicals which implicitly define the construct, and the (derived) nomologicals of

16

type a. These latter propositions permit predictions about events. The construct is not "reduced" to the observations, but only combined with other constructs in the net to make predictions about observables.

4. "Learning more about" a theoretical construct is a matter of elaborating the nomological network in which it occurs, or of increasing the definiteness of the components. At least in the early history of a construct the network will be limited, and the construct will as yet have few connections.

5. An enrichment of the net such as adding a construct or a relation to theory is justified if it generates nomologicals that are confirmed by observation or if it reduces the number of nomologicals required to predict the same observations. When observations will not fit into the network as it stands, the scientist has a certain freedom in selecting where to modify the network. That is, there may be alternative constructs or ways of organizing the net which for the time being are equally defensible.

6. We can say that "operations" which are qualitatively very different "overlap" or "measure the same thing" if their positions in the nomological net tie them to the same construct variable. Our confidence in this identification depends upon the amount of inductive support we have for the regions of the net involved. It is not necessary that a direct observational comparison of the two operations be made—we may be content with an intranetwork proof indicating that the two operations yield estimates of the same network-defined quantity. Thus, physicists are content to speak of the "temperature" of the sun and the "temperature" of a gas at room temperature even though the test operations are nonoverlapping because this identification makes theoretical sense.

With these statements of scientific methodology in mind, we return to the specific problem of construct validity as applied to psychological tests. The preceding guide rules should reassure the "toughminded," who fear that allowing construct validation opens the door to nonconfirmable test claims. *The answer is that unless the network makes contact with observations, and exhibits explicit, public steps of inference, construct validation cannot be claimed.* An admissible psychological construct must be behavior-relevant (APA Committee on Test Standards, 1954, p. 15). For most tests intended to measure constructs, adequate criteria do not exist. This being the case, many such tests have been left unvalidated, or a finespun network of rationalizations has been offered as if it were validation. Rationalization is not construct validation. One who claims that his test reflects a construct cannot maintain his claim in the face of recurrent negative results because these results show that his construct is too loosely defined to yield verifiable inferences.

A rigorous (though perhaps probabilistic) chain of inference is required to establish a test as a measure of a construct. To validate a claim that a test measures a construct, a nomological net surrounding the concept must exist. When a construct is fairly new, there may be few specifiable associations by which to pin down the concept. As research proceeds, the construct sends out roots in many directions, which attach it to more and more facts or other constructs. Thus the electron has more accepted properties than the neutrino: *numerical ability* has more than *the second space factor*.

"Acceptance," which was critical in criterion-oriented and content validities, has now appeared in construct validity. Unless substantially the same nomological net is accepted by the several users of the construct, public validation is impossible. If *A* uses *aggressiveness* to mean overt assault on others, and *B*'s usage includes repressed hostile reactions, evidence which convinces *B* that a test measures *aggressiveness* convinces *A* that the test does not. Hence, the investigator who proposes to establish a test as a measure of a construct must specify his network or theory sufficiently clearly that others can accept or reject it (cf. Macfarlane, 1942, p. 406). A consumer of the test who rejects the author's theory cannot accept the author's validation. He must validate the test for himself, if he wishes to show that it represents the construct as *he* defines it.

Two general qualifications are in order with reference to the methodological principles 1–6 set forth at the beginning of this section. Both of them concern the amount of "theory," in any high-level sense of that word, which enters into a construct-defining network of laws or lawlike statements. We do not wish to convey the impression that one always has a very elaborate theoretical network, rich in hypothetical processes or entities.

Constructs as inductive summaries. In the early stages of development of a construct or even at more advanced stages when our orientation is thoroughly practical, little or no theory in the usual sense of the word need be involved. In the extreme case the hypothesized laws are formu-

18

lated entirely in terms of descriptive (observational) dimensions although not all of the relevant observations have actually been made.

The hypothesized network "goes beyond the data" only in the limited sense that it purports to *characterize* the behavior facets which belong to an observable but as yet only partially sampled cluster; hence, it generates predictions about hitherto unsampled regions of the phenotypic space. Even though no unobservables or high-order theoretical constructs are introduced, an element of inductive extrapolation appears in the claim that a cluster including some elements not yet observed has been identified. Since, as in any sorting or abstracting task involving a finite set of complex elements, several nonequivalent bases of categorization are available, the investigator may choose a hypothesis which generates erroneous predictions. The failure of a supposed, hitherto untried, member of the cluster to behave in the manner said to be characteristic of the group, or the finding that a nonmember of the postulated cluster does behave in this manner, may modify greatly our tentative construct.

For example, one might build an intelligence test on the basis of his background notions of "intellect," including vocabulary, arithmetic calculation, general information, similarities, two-point threshold, reaction time, and line bisection as subtests. The first four of these correlate, and he extracts a huge first factor. This becomes a second approximation of the intelligence construct, described by its pattern of loadings on the four tests. The other three tests have negligible loading on any common factor. On this evidence the investigator reinterprets intelligence as "manipulation of words." Subsequently it is discovered that test-stupid people are rated as unable to express their ideas, are easily taken in by fallacious arguments, and misread complex directions. These data support the "linguistic" definition of intelligence and the test's claim of validity *for* that construct. But then a block design test with pantomime instructions is found to be strongly saturated with the first factor. Immediately the purely "linguistic" interpretation of Factor I becomes suspect. This finding, taken together with our initial acceptance of the others as relevant to the background concept of intelligence, forces us to reinterpret the concept once again.

If we simply *list* the tests or traits which have been shown to be saturated with the "factor" or which belong to the cluster, no construct is employed. As soon as we even *summarize the properties* of this group

19

of indicators we are already making some guesses. Intensional characterization of a domain is hazardous since it selects (abstracts) properties and implies that new tests sharing those properties will behave as do the known tests in the cluster, and that tests not sharing them will not.

The difficulties in merely "characterizing the surface cluster" are strikingly exhibited by the use of certain special and extreme groups for purposes of construct validation. The Pd scale of the MMPI was originally derived and cross-validated upon hospitalized patients diagnosed "Psychopathic personality, asocial and amoral type" (McKinley and Hathaway, 1944). Further research shows the scale to have a limited degree of predictive and concurrent validity for "delinquency" more broadly defined (Blair, 1950; Hathaway and Monachesi, 1953). Several studies show associations between Pd and very special "criterion" groups which it would be ludicrous to identify as *the* criterion" in the traditional sense. If one lists these heterogeneous groups and tries to characterize them intensionally, he faces enormous conceptual difficulties. For example, a recent survey of hunting accidents in Minnesota showed that hunters who had "carelessly" shot someone were significantly elevated on Pd when compared with other hunters (*Minnesota Hunter Casualty Study,* 1954). This is in line with one's theoretical expectations; when you ask MMPI "experts" to predict for such a group they invariably predict Pd or Ma or both. The finding seems therefore to lend some slight support to the construct validity of the Pd scale. But of course it would be nonsense to *define* the Pd component "operationally" in terms of, say, accident proneness. We might try to subsume the original phenotype and the hunting-accident proneness under some broader category, such as "Disposition to violate society's rules, whether legal, moral, or just *sensible.*" But now we have ceased to have a neat operational criterion, and are using instead a rather vague and wide-range class. Besides, there is worse to come. We want the class specification to cover a group trend that (nondelinquent) high school students judged by their peer group as least "responsible" score over a full sigma higher on Pd than those judged most "responsible" (Gough, McClosky, and Meehl, 1952, p. 75). Most of the behaviors contributing to such sociometric choices fall well within the range of socially permissible action; the proffered criterion specification is still too restrictive. Again, any clinician familiar with MMPI lore would predict an elevated Pd on a sample of (nondelinquent) professional actors. Chyatte's confirmation

20

of this prediction (1949) tends to support *both* (a) the theory sketch of "what the Pd factor is, psychologically," and (b) the claim of the Pd scale to construct validity for this hypothetical factor. Let the reader try his hand at writing a brief phenotypic criterion specification that will cover both trigger-happy hunters and Broadway actors! And if he should be ingenious enough to achieve this, does his definition also encompass Hovey's report that high Pd predicts the judgments "not shy" and "unafraid of mental patients" made upon nurses by their supervisors (1953, p. 143)? And then we have Gough's report that *low* Pd is associated with ratings as "good-natured" (Gough, McKee, and Yandell, 1953, p. 40), and Roessel's data showing that high Pd is predictive of "dropping out of high school" (1954). The point is that all seven of these "criterion" dispositions would be readily guessed by any clinician having even superficial familiarity with MMPI interpretation; but to mediate these inferences explicitly requires quite a few hypotheses about dynamics, constituting an admittedly sketchy (but far from vacuous) network defining the genotype *psychopathic deviate*.

Vagueness of present psychological laws. This line of thought leads directly to our second important qualification upon the network schema. The idealized picture is one of a tidy set of postulates which jointly entail the desired theorems; since some of the theorems are coordinated to the observation base, the system constitutes an implicit definition of the theoretical primitives and gives them an indirect empirical meaning. In practice, of course, even the most advanced physical sciences only approximate this ideal. Questions of "categoricalness" and the like, such as logicians raise about pure calculi, are hardly even statable for empirical networks. (What, for example, would be the desiderata of a "well-formed formula" in molar-behavior theory?) Psychology works with crude, half-explicit formulations. We do not worry about such advanced formal questions as "whether all molar-behavior statements are decidable by appeal to the postulates" because we know that no existing theoretical network suffices to predict even the *known* descriptive laws. Nevertheless, the sketch of a network is there; if it were not, we would not be saying *anything* intelligible about our constructs. We do not have the rigorous implicit definitions of formal calculi (which still, be it noted, usually permit of a multiplicity of interpretations). Yet the vague, avowedly incomplete network still gives the constructs whatever meaning they do have. When the network is very incomplete, having many strands missing entirely and some constructs tied in only by tenuous threads, then the "implicit definition" of these constructs is disturbingly loose; one might say that the meaning of the constructs is underdetermined. *Since the meaning of theoretical constructs is set forth by stating the laws in which they occur, our incomplete knowledge of the laws of nature produces a vagueness in our constructs* (see Hempel, 1952; Kaplan, 1946; Pap, 1953). We will be able to say "what anxiety is" when we know all of the laws involving it; meanwhile, since we are in the process of discovering these laws, we do not yet know precisely what anxiety is.

Conclusions Regarding the Network after Experimentation

The proposition that x percent of test variance is accounted for by the construct is inserted into the accepted network. The network then generates a testable prediction about the relation of the test scores to certain other variables, and the investigator gathers data. If prediction and result are in harmony, he can retain his belief that the test measures the construct. The construct is at best adopted, never demonstrated to be "correct."

We do not first "prove" the theory, and then validate the test, nor conversely. In any probable inductive type of inference from a pattern of observations, we examine the relation between the total network of theory and observations. The system involves propositions relating test to construct, construct to other constructs, and finally some of these constructs to observables. In ongoing research the chain of inference is very complicated. Kelly and Fiske (1951, p. 124) give a complex diagram showing the numerous inferences required in validating a prediction from assessment techniques, where theories about the criterion situation are as integral a part of the prediction as are the test data. A predicted empirical relationship permits us to test all the propositions leading to that prediction. Traditionally the proposition claiming to interpret the test has been set apart as the hypothesis being tested, but actually the evidence is significant for all parts of the chain. If the prediction is not confirmed, any link in the chain may be wrong.

A theoretical network can be divided into subtheories used in making particular predictions. All the events successfully predicted through a subtheory are of course evidence in favor of that theory. Such a subtheory may be so well confirmed by voluminous and diverse evidence that we can reasonably view a particular experiment as relevant only to the test's validity. If the theory, combined with a proposed test interpretation, mispredicts in this case, it is the latter which must be abandoned. On the other hand, the accumulated evidence for a test's construct validity may be so strong that an instance of misprediction will force us to modify the subtheory employing the construct rather than deny the claim that the test measures the construct.

Most cases in psychology today lie somewhere between these extremes. Thus, suppose we fail to find a greater incidence of "homosexual signs" in the Rorschach records of paranoid patients. Which is more strongly disconfirmed—the Rorschach signs or the orthodox theory of paranoia? The negative finding shows the bridge between the two to be undependable, but this is all we can say. The bridge cannot be used unless one end is placed on solider ground. The investigator must decide which end it is best to relocate.

Numerous successful predictions dealing with phenotypically diverse "criteria" give greater weight to the claim of construct validity than do fewer predictions, or predictions involving very similar behaviors. In arriving at diverse predictions, the hypothesis of test validity is connected each time to a subnetwork largely independent of the portion previously used. Success of these derivations testifies to the inductive power of the test-validity statement, and renders it unlikely that an equally effective alternative can be offered.

Implications of Negative Evidence

The investigator whose prediction and data are discordant must make strategic decisions. His result can be interpreted in three ways:

1. The test does not measure the construct variable.

2. The theoretical network which generated the hypothesis is incorrect.

3. The experimental design failed to test the hypothesis properly. (Strictly speaking this may be analyzed as a special case of 2, but in practice the distinction is worth making.)

For further research. If a specific fault of procedure makes the third a reasonable possibility, his proper response is to perform an adequate study, meanwhile making no report. When faced with the other two alternatives, he may decide that his test does not measure the construct adequately. Following that decision, he will perhaps prepare and validate a new test. Any rescoring or new interpretative procedure for the original instrument, like a new test, requires validation *by means of a fresh body of data.*

The investigator may regard interpretation 2 as more likely to lead to eventual advances. It is legitimate for the investigator to call the network defining the construct into question, if he has confidence in the test. Should the investigator decide that some strand in the network is unsound, he may be able to invent an alternative network. Perhaps he modifies the network by splitting a concept into two or more portions, e.g., by designating types of *anxiety,* or perhaps he specifies added conditions under which a generalization holds. When an investigator modifies the theory in such a manner, he is now required to *gather a fresh body of data* to test the altered hypotheses. This step should normally precede publication of the modified theory. If the new data are consistent with the modified network, he is free from the fear that his nomologicals were gerrymandered to fit the peculiarities of his first sample of observations. He can now trust his test to some extent, because his test results behave as predicted.

The choice among alternatives, like any strategic decision, is a gamble as to which course of action is the best investment of effort. Is it wise to modify the theory? That depends on how well the system is confirmed by prior data, and how well the modifications fit available observations. Is it worthwhile to modify the test in the hope that it will fit the construct? That depends on how much evidence there is—apart from this abortive experiment—to support the hope, and also on how much it is worth to the investigator's ego to salvage the test. The choice among alternatives is a matter of research planning.

For practical use of the test. The consumer can accept a test as a measure of a construct only when there is a strong positive fit between predictions and subsequent data. When the evidence from a proper investigation of a published test is essentially negative, it should be reported as a stop sign to discourage use of the test pending a reconciliation of test and construct, or final abandonment of the test. If the test has not been published, it should be restricted to research use until some degree of validity is established (American Psychological Association, 1953). The consumer can await the results of the investigator's gamble with confidence that proper application of the scientific method will ultimately tell whether the test has value. Until the evidence is in, he has no justification for employing the test as a basis for terminal decisions. The test may serve, at best, only as a source of suggestions about individuals to be confirmed by other evidence (Cronbach, 1955a; Meehl and Rosen, 1955—reprinted here as Chapter 2).

There are two perspectives in test validation. From the viewpoint of the psychological practitioner, the burden of proof is on the test. A test should not be used to measure a trait until its proponent establishes that predictions made from such measures are consistent with the best available theory of the trait. In the view of the test developer, however, both the test and the theory are under scrutiny. He is free to say *to himself privately,* "If my test disagrees with the theory, so much the worse for the theory." This way lies delusion, unless he continues his research using a better theory.

Reporting of Positive Results

The test developer who finds positive correspondence between his proposed interpretation and data is expected to report the basis for his validity claim. Defending a claim of construct validity is a major task, not to be satisfied by a discourse without data. The "Technical Recommendations" have little to say on reporting of construct validity. Indeed, the only detailed suggestions under that heading refer to correlations of the test with other measures, together with a cross-reference to some other sections of the report. The two key principles, however, call for the most comprehensive type of reporting. The manual for any test "should report all available information which will assist the user in determining what psychological attributes account for variance in test scores" (APA Committee on Test Standards, 1954, p. 27). And "The manual for a test which is used primarily to assess postulated attributes of the individual should outline the theory on which the test is based and organize whatever partial validity data there are to show in what way they support the theory" (p. 28). It is recognized, by a classification as "very desirable" rather than "essential," that the latter recommendation goes beyond the present practice of test authors.

The proper goals in reporting construct validation are to make clear (a) what interpretation is proposed, (b) how adequately the writer believes this interpretation is substantiated, and (c) what evidence and

25

reasoning lead him to this belief. Without a the construct validity of the test is of no use to the consumer. Without b the consumer must carry the entire burden of evaluating the test research. Without c the consumer or reviewer is being asked to take a and b on faith. The test manual cannot always present an exhaustive statement on these points, but it should summarize and indicate where complete statements may be found.

To specify the interpretation, the writer must state what construct he has in mind, and what meaning he gives to that construct. For a construct which has a short history and has built up few connotations, it will be fairly easy to indicate the presumed properties of the construct, i.e., the nomologicals in which it appears. For a construct with a longer history, a summary of properties and references to previous theoretical discussions may be appropriate. It is especially critical to distinguish proposed interpretations from other meanings previously given the same construct. The validator faces no small task; he must somehow communicate a theory to his reader.

To evaluate his evidence calls for a statement like the conclusions from a program of research, noting what is well substantiated and what alternative interpretations have been considered and rejected. The writer must note what portions of his proposed interpretation are speculations, extrapolations, or conclusions from insufficient data. The author has an ethical responsibility to prevent unsubstantiated interpretations from appearing as truths. A claim is unsubstantiated unless the evidence for the claim is public, so that other scientists may review the evidence, criticize the conclusions, and offer alternative interpretations.

The report of evidence in a test manual must be as complete as any research report, except where adequate public reports can be cited. Reference to something "observed by the writer in many clinical cases" is worthless as evidence. Full case reports, on the other hand, may be a valuable source of evidence so long as these cases are representative and negative instances receive due attention. The report of evidence must be interpreted with reference to the theoretical network in such a manner that the reader sees why the author regards a particular correlation or experiment as confirming (or throwing doubt upon) the proposed interpretation. Evidence collected by others must be taken fairly into account.

Validation of a Complex Test "as a Whole"

Special questions must be considered when we are investigating the validity of a test which is aimed to provide information about several constructs. In one sense, it is naive to inquire "Is this test valid?" One does not validate a test, but only a principle for making inferences. If a test yields many different types of inferences, some of them can be valid and others invalid (cf. Technical Recommendation C2: "The manual should report the validity of each type of inference for which a test is recommended"). From this point of view, every topic sentence in the typical book on Rorschach interpretation presents a hypothesis requiring validation, and one should validate inferences about each aspect of the personality separately and in turn, just as he would want information on the validity (concurrent or predictive) for each scale of the MMPI.

There is, however, another defensible point of view. If a test is purely empirical, based strictly on observed connections between response to an item and some criterion, then of course the validity of one scoring key for the test does not make validation for its other scoring keys any less necessary. But a test may be developed on the basis of a theory which in itself provides a linkage between the various keys and the various criteria. Thus, while Strong's Vocational Interest Blank is developed empirically, it also rests on a "theory" that a youth can be expected to be satisfied in an occupation if he has interests common to men now happy in the occupation. When Strong finds that those with high engineering interest scores in college are preponderantly in engineering careers nineteen years later, he has partly validated the proposed use of the engineer score (predictive validity). Since the evidence is consistent with the theory on which all the test keys were built, this evidence alone increases the presumption that the *other* keys have predictive validity. How strong is this presumption? Not very, from the viewpoint of the traditional skepticism of science. Engineering interests may stabilize early, while interests in art or management or social work are still unstable. A claim cannot be made that the whole Strong approach is valid just because one score shows predictive validity. But if thirty interest scores were investigated longitudinally and all of them showed the type of validity predicted by Strong's theory, we would

27

indeed be caviling to say that this evidence gives no confidence in the long-range validity of the thirty-first score.

Confidence in a theory is increased as more relevant evidence confirms it, but it is always possible that tomorrow's investigation will render the theory obsolete. The "Technical Recommendations" suggest a rule of reason, and ask for evidence for each *type* of inference for which a test is recommended. It is stated that no test developer can present predictive validities for all possible criteria; similarly, no developer can run all possible experimental tests of his proposed interpretation. But the recommendation is more subtle than advice that a lot of validation is better than a little.

Consider the Rorschach test. It is used for many inferences, made by means of nomological networks at several levels. At a low level are the simple unrationalized correspondences presumed to exist between certain signs and psychiatric diagnoses. Validating such a sign does nothing to substantiate Rorschach theory. For other Rorschach formulas an explicit a priori rationale exists (for instance, high F percent interpreted as implying rigid control of impulses). Each time such a sign shows correspondence with criteria, its rationale is supported just a little. At a still higher level of abstraction, a considerable body of theory surrounds the general area of *outer control,* interlacing many different constructs. As evidence cumulates, one should be able to decide what specific inference-making chains within this system can be depended upon. One should also be able to conclude—or deny—that so much of the system has stood up under test that one has some confidence in even the untested lines in the network.

In addition to relatively delimited nomological networks surrounding *control* or *aspiration,* the Rorschach interpreter usually has an overriding theory of the test as a whole. This may be a psychoanalytic theory, a theory of perception and set, or a theory stated in terms of learned habit patterns. Whatever the theory of the interpreter, whenever he validates an inference from the system, he obtains some reason for added confidence in his overriding system. His total theory is not tested, however, by experiments dealing with only one limited set of constructs. The test developer must investigate far-separated, independent sections of the network. The more diversified the predictions the system is required to make, the greater confidence we can have that only minor parts of the system will later prove faulty. Here we begin to

28

glimpse a logic to defend the judgment that the test and its whole interpretative system is valid at some level of confidence.

There are enthusiasts who would conclude from the foregoing paragraphs that since there is some evidence of correct, diverse predictions made from the Rorschach, the test as a whole can now be accepted as validated. This conclusion overlooks the negative evidence. Just one finding contrary to expectation, based on sound research, is sufficient to wash a whole theoretical structure away. Perhaps the remains can be salvaged to form a new structure. But this structure now must be exposed to fresh risks, and sound negative evidence will destroy it in turn. There is sufficient negative evidence to prevent acceptance of the Rorschach and its accompanying interpretative structures as a whole. So long as any aspects of the overriding theory stated for the test have been disconfirmed, this structure must be rebuilt.

Talk of areas and structures may seem not to recognize those who would interpret the personality "globally." They may argue that a test is best validated in matching studies. Without going into detailed questions of matching methodology, we can ask whether such a study validates the nomological network "as a whole." The judge does employ some network in arriving at his conception of his subject, integrating specific inferences from specific data. Matching studies, if successful, demonstrate only that each judge's interpretative theory has some validity, that it is not completely a fantasy. Very high consistency between judges is required to show that they are using the same network, and very high success in matching is required to show that the network is dependable.

If inference is less than perfectly dependable, we must know which aspects of the interpretative network are least dependable and which are most dependable. Thus, even if one has considerable confidence in a test "as a whole" because of frequent successful inferences, one still returns as an ultimate aim to the request of the "Technical Recommendations" for separate evidence on the validity of each type of inference to be made.

Recapitulation

Construct validation was introduced in order to specify types of research required in developing tests for which the conventional views on validation are inappropriate. Personality tests, and some tests of ability, are interpreted in terms of attributes for which there is no adequate criterion. This paper indicates what sorts of evidence can substantiate such an interpretation, and how such evidence is to be interpreted. The following points made in the discussion are particularly significant.

1. A construct is defined implicitly by a network of associations or propositions in which it occurs. Constructs employed at different stages of research vary in definiteness.

2. Construct validation is possible only when some of the statements in the network lead to predicted relations among observables. While some observables may be regarded as "criteria," the construct validity of the criteria themselves is regarded as under investigation.

3. The network defining the construct, and the derivation leading to the predicted observation, must be reasonably explicit so that validating evidence may be properly interpreted.

4. Many types of evidence are relevant to construct validity, including content validity, interitem correlations, interest correlations, test-"criterion" correlations, studies of stability over time, and stability under experimental intervention. High correlations and high stability may constitute either favorable or unfavorable evidence for the proposed interpretation, depending on the theory surrounding the construct.

5. When a predicted relation fails to occur, the fault may lie in the proposed interpretation of the test or in the network. Altering the network so that it can cope with the new observations is, in effect, redefining the construct. Any such new interpretation of the test must be validated by a fresh body of data before being advanced publicly. Great care is required to avoid substituting a posteriori rationalizations for proper validation.

6. Construct validity cannot generally be expressed in the form of a single simple coefficient. The data often permit one to establish upper and lower bounds for the proportion of test variance which can be attributed to the construct. The integration of diverse data into a proper interpretation cannot be an entirely quantitative process.

7. Constructs may vary in nature from those very close to "pure description" (involving little more than extrapolation of relations among observation variables) to highly theoretical constructs involving hypothesized entities and processes, or making identifications with constructs of other sciences.

30

8. The investigation of a test's construct validity is not essentially different from the general scientific procedures for developing and confirming theories.

Without in the least *advocating* construct validity as preferable to the other three kinds (concurrent, predictive, content), we do believe it imperative that psychologists make a place for it in their methodological thinking, so that its rationale, its scientific legitimacy, and its dangers may become explicit and familiar. This would be preferable to the widespread current tendency to engage in what actually amounts to construct-validation research and use of constructs in practical testing, while talking an "operational" methodology which, if adopted, would force research into a mold it does not fit.

2

Antecedent Probability and the Efficiency of Psychometric Signs, Patterns, or Cutting Scores

IN CLINICAL PRACTICE, psychologists frequently participate in the making of vital decisions concerning the classification, treatment, prognosis, and disposition of individuals. In their attempts to increase the number of correct classifications and predictions, psychologists have developed and applied many psychometric devices, such as patterns of test responses as well as cutting scores for scales, indices, and sign lists. Since diagnostic and prognostic statements can often be made with a high degree of accuracy purely on the basis of actuarial or experience tables (referred to hereinafter as *base rates*), a psychometric device, to be efficient, must make possible a greater number of correct decisions than could be made in terms of the base rates alone.

The efficiency of the great majority of psychometric devices reported in the clinical psychology literature is difficult or impossible to evaluate for the following reasons:

1. Base rates are virtually never reported. It is, therefore, difficult to determine whether or not a given device results in a greater number of

AUTHOR'S NOTE: This paper was written in collaboration with Albert Rosen, then with the Neuropsychiatric Service, Veterans Administration Hospital, Minneapolis, Minnesota, and the Divisions of Psychiatry and Clinical Psychology of the University of Minnesota Medical School. It first appeared in the *Psychological Bulletin*, vol. 52, 1955; copyright 1955 by the American Psychological Association, Inc.

I carried on my part of this work in connection with my appointment to the Minnesota Center for Philosophy of Science.

correct decisions than would be possible solely on the basis of the rates from previous experience. When, however, the base rates can be estimated, the reported claims of efficiency of psychometric instruments are often seen to be without foundation.

2. In most reports, the distribution data provided are insufficient for the evaluation of the probable efficiency of the device in other settings where the base rates are markedly different. Moreover, the samples are almost always too small for the determination of optimal cutting lines for various decisions.

3. Most psychometric devices are reported without cross-validation data. If a psychometric instrument is applied solely to the criterion groups from which it was developed, its reported validity and efficiency are likely to be spuriously high, especially if the criterion groups are small.

4. There is often a lack of clarity concerning the type of population in which a psychometric device can be effectively applied.

5. Results are frequently reported only in terms of significance tests for differences between groups rather than in terms of the number of correct decisions for individuals within the groups.

The purposes of this paper are to examine current methodology in studies of predictive and concurrent validity (APA Committee on Test Standards, 1954) and to present some methods for the evaluation of the efficiency of psychometric devices as well as for the improvement in the interpretations made from such devices. Actual studies reported in the literature will be used for illustration wherever possible. It should be emphasized that these particular illustrative studies of common practices were chosen simply because they contained more complete data than are commonly reported, and were available in fairly recent publications.

Importance of Base Rates

Danielson and Clark (1954) have reported on the construction and application of a personality inventory which was devised for use in military induction stations as an aid in detecting those men who would not complete basic training because of psychiatric disability or AWOL recidivism. One serious defect in their article is that it reports cutting lines which have not been cross-validated. Danielson and Clark state that inductees were administered the Fort Ord Inventory within two days after induction into the army, and that all of these men were allowed to undergo basic training regardless of their test scores.

Two samples (among others) of these inductees were selected for the study of predictive validity: (a) A group of 415 men who had made a good adjustment (Good Adjustment Group), and (b) a group of 89 men who were unable to complete basic training and who were sufficiently disturbed to warrant a recommendation for discharge by a psychiatrist (Poor Adjustment Group). The authors state that "the most important task of a test designed to screen out misfits is the detection of the [latter] group" (p. 139). The authors found that their most effective scale for this differentiation picked up, at a given cutting point, 55 percent of the Poor Adjustment Group (valid positives) and 19 percent of the Good Adjustment Group (false positives). The overlap between these two groups would undoubtedly have been greater if the cutting line had been cross-validated on a random sample from the *entire population* of inductees, but for the purposes of the present discussion, let us assume that the results were obtained from cross-validation groups. There is no mention of the percentage of all inductees who fall into the Poor Adjustment Group, but a rough estimate will be adequate for the present discussion. Suppose that in their population of soldiers, as many as 5 percent make a poor adjustment and 95 percent make a good adjustment. The results for 10,000 cases would be as depicted in Table 1.

Table 1. Number of Inductees in the Poor Adjustment and Good Adjustment Groups Detected by a Screening Inventory (55 Percent Valid Positives; 10 Percent False Positives)

Predicted Adjustment	Actual Adjustment				Total Predicted
	Poor		Good		
	No.	%	No.	%	
Poor...........	275	55	1,805	19	2,080
Good.........	225	45	7,695	81	7,920
Total.......	500	100	9,500	100	10,000

Efficiency in detecting poor adjustment cases. The efficiency of the scale can be evaluated in several ways. From the data in Table 1 it can be seen that if the cutting line given by the authors were used at Fort Ord, the scale could not be used directly to "screen out misfits." If all those predicted by the scale to make a poor adjustment were screened out, the number of false positives would be extremely high. Among the 10,000 potential inductees, 2080 would be predicted to make a poor adjustment. Of these 2080, only 275, or 13 percent, would actually make a poor adjustment, whereas the decisions for 1805 men, or 87 percent of those screened out, would be incorrect.

Efficiency in prediction for all cases. If a prediction were made for every man on the basis of the cutting line given for the test, 275 + 7695, or 7970, out of 10,000 decisions would be correct. Without the test, however, every man would be predicted to make a good adjustment, and 9500 of the predictions would be correct. Thus, use of the test has yielded a drop from 95 percent to 79.7 percent in the total number of correct decisions.

Efficiency in detecting good adjustment cases. There is one kind of decision in which the Inventory can improve on the base rates, however. If only those men are accepted who are predicted by the Inventory to make a good adjustment, 7920 will be selected, and the outcome of 7695 of the 7920, or 97 percent, will be predicted correctly. This is a 2 percent increase in hits among predictions of "success." The decision whether or not the scale improves on the base rates sufficiently to warrant its use will depend on the cost of administering the testing program, the administrative feasibility of rejecting 21 percent of the men who passed the psychiatric screening, the cost to the army of training the 225 maladaptive recruits, and the intangible human costs involved in psychiatric breakdown.

Populations to which the scale is applied. In the evaluation of the efficiency of any psychometric instrument, careful consideration must be given to the types of populations to which the device is to be applied. Danielson and Clark have stated that "since the final decision as to disposition is made by the psychiatrist, the test should be classified as a screening adjunct" (1954, p. 138). This statement needs clarification, however, for the efficiency of the scale can vary markedly according to the different ways in which it might be used as an adjunct.

It will be noted that the test was administered to men who were already in the army, and not to men being examined for induction. The reported validation data apply, therefore, specifically to the population of *recent inductees.* The results might have been somewhat different if the population tested had consisted of *potential inductees.* For the sake of illustration, however, let us assume that there is no difference in the test results of the two populations.

An induction station psychiatrist can use the scale cutting score in one or more of the following ways, i.e., he can apply the scale results to a variety of populations. (a) The psychiatrist's final decision to accept or reject a potential inductee may be based on both the test score and his usual interview procedure. The population to which the test scores are applied is, therefore, *potential inductees interviewed by the usual procedures for whom no decision was made.* (b) He may evaluate the potential inductee according to his usual procedures, and then consult the test score *only if* the tentative decision is to reject. That is, a decision to accept is final. The population to which the test scores are applied is *potential inductees tentatively rejected by the usual interview procedures.* (c) An alternative procedure is for the psychiatrist to consult the test score only if the tentative decision is to accept, the population being *potential inductees tentatively accepted by the usual interview procedures.* The decision to reject is final. (d) Probably the commonest proposal for the use of tests as screening adjuncts is that the more skilled and costly psychiatric evaluation should be made only upon the test positives, i.e., inductees classified by the test as good risks are not interviewed, or are subjected only to a very short and superficial interview. Here the population is *all potential inductees,* the test being used to make either a *final* decision to "accept" or a decision to "examine."

Among these different procedures, how is the psychiatrist to achieve maximum effectiveness in using the test as an adjunct? There is no answer to this question from the available data, but it can be stated definitely that the data reported by Danielson and Clark apply only to the third procedure described above. The test results are based on a selected group of men *accepted* for induction and not on a random sample of potential inductees. If the scale is used in any other way than the third procedure mentioned above, the results may be considerably inferior to those reported, and, thus, to the use of the base rates without the test.[1]

The principles discussed thus far, although illustrated by a single study, can be generalized to any study of predictive or concurrent validity. It can be seen that many considerations are involved in determining the efficiency of a scale at a given cutting score, especially

---

[1] Goodman (1953) has discussed this same problem with reference to the supplementary use of an index for the prediction of parole violation.

the base rates of the subclasses within the population to which the psychometric device is to be applied. In a subsequent portion of this paper, methods will be presented for determining cutting points for maximizing the efficiency of the different types of decisions which are made with psychometric devices.

Another study will be utilized to illustrate the importance of an explicit statement of the base rates of population subgroups to be tested with a given device. Employing an interesting configural approach, Thiesen (1952) discovered five Rorschach patterns, each of which differentiated well between 60 schizophrenic adult patients and a sample of 157 gainfully employed adults. The best differentiator, considering individual patterns or number of patterns, was Pattern A, which was found in 20 percent of the patients' records and in only .6 percent of the records of normals. Thiesen concludes that if these patterns stand the test of cross-validation, they might have "clinical usefulness" in early detection of a schizophrenic process or as an aid to determining the gravity of an initial psychotic episode (p. 369). If by "clinical usefulness" is meant efficiency in a clinic or hospital for the diagnosis of schizophrenia, it is necessary to demonstrate that the patterns differentiate a higher percentage of schizophrenic patients from *other diagnostic groups* than could be correctly classified without any test at all, i.e., solely on the basis of the rates of various diagnoses in any given hospital. If a test is to be used in differential diagnosis among psychiatric patients, evidence of its efficiency for this function cannot be established solely on the basis of discrimination of diagnostic groups from normals. If by "clinical usefulness" Thiesen means that his data indicate that the patterns might be used to detect an early schizophrenic process among nonhospitalized gainfully employed adults, he would do better to discard his patterns and use the base rates, as can be seen from the following data.

Taulbee and Sisson (1954) cross-validated Thiesen's patterns on schizophrenic patient and normal samples, and found that Pattern A was the best discriminator. Among patients 8.1 percent demonstrated this pattern and among normals none had this pattern. There are approximately 60 million gainfully employed adults in this country, and it has been estimated that the rate of schizophrenia in the general population is approximately .85 percent (Anastasi and Foley, 1949, p. 558). The results for Pattern A among a population of 10,000 gainfully em-

ployed adults would be as shown in Table 2. In order to detect 7 schizophrenics, it would be necessary to test 10,000 individuals.

In the neurology service of a hospital a psychometric scale is used
which is designed to differentiate between patients with psychogenic and
organic low back pain (Hanvik, 1949). At a given cutting point, this
scale was found to classify each group with approximately 70 percent
effectiveness upon cross-validation, i.e., 70 percent of cases with no

Table 2. Number of Persons Classified as Schizophrenic and Normal by
a Test Pattern among a Population of Gainfully Employed Adults (8.1 Percent Valid Positives; 0.0 Percent False Positives)

| Classification by Test | Criterion Classification | | | | Total Classified by Test |
| | Schizophrenia | | Normal | | |
	No.	%	No.	%	
Schizophrenia......7		8.1	0	0	7
Normal............78		91.9	9,915	100	9,993
Total............81		100.0	9,915	100	10,000

organic findings scored above an optimal cutting score, and 70 percent
of surgically verified organic cases scored below this line. Assume that
90 percent of all patients in the neurology service with a primary complaint of low back pain are in fact "organic." Without any scale at all
the psychologist can say every case is organic, and be right 90 percent
of the time. With the scale the results would be as shown in Section A
of Table 3. Of 10 psychogenic cases, 7 score above the line; of 90 organic cases, 63 score below the cutting line. If every case above the line
is called psychogenic, only 7 of 34 will be classified correctly or about
21 percent. Nobody wants to be right only one out of five times in this
type of situation, so that it is obvious that it would be imprudent to call
a patient psychogenic on the basis of this scale. Radically different results occur in prediction for cases below the cutting line. Of 66 cases
63, or 95 percent, are correctly classified as organic. Now the psychologist has increased his diagnostic hits from 90 to 95 percent on the condition that he labels only cases falling below the line, and ignores the
34 percent scoring above the line.

In actual practice, the psychologist may not, and most likely will not,
test every low back pain case. Probably those referred for testing will
be a select group, i.e., those who the neurologist believes are psycho-

Table 3. Number of Patients Classified as Psychogenic and
Organic on a Low Back Pain Scale Which Classifies Correctly
70 Percent of Psychogenic and Organic Cases

Classification by Scale	Actual Diagnosis		Total Classified by Scale
	Psychogenic	Organic	
A. Base Rates in Population Tested: 90 Percent Organic; 10 Percent Psychogenic			
Psychogenic.................	7	27	34
Organic...................	3	63	66
Total...................	10	90	100
B. Base Rates in Population Tested: 90 Percent Psychogenic; 10 Percent Organic			
Psychogenic.................	63	3	66
Organic...................	27	7	34
Total...................	90	10	100

genic because neurological findings are minimal or absent. This fact
changes the population from "all patients in neurology with a primary
complaint of low back pain," to "all patients in neurology with a
primary complaint of low back pain *who are referred for testing.*" Suppose that a study of past diagnoses indicated that of patients with minimal or absent findings, 90 percent were diagnosed as psychogenic and
10 percent as organic. Section B of Table 3 gives an entirely different
picture of the effectiveness of the low back pain scale, and new limitations on interpretation are necessary. Now the scale correctly classifies
95 percent of all cases above the line as psychogenic (63 of 66), and
is correct in only 21 percent of all cases below the line (7 of 34). In
this practical situation the psychologist would be wise to refrain from
interpreting a low score.

From the illustrations above it can be seen that the psychologist in
interpreting a test and in evaluating its effectiveness must be very much
aware of the population and its subclasses and the base rates of the behavior or event with which he is dealing at any given time.

It may be objected that no clinician relies on just one scale but would
diagnose on the basis of a configuration of impressions from several
tests, clinical data, and history. We must, therefore, emphasize that the
preceding single-scale examples were presented for simplicity only, but
that the main point is not dependent upon this "atomism." *Any complex
configurational procedure in any number of variables, psychometric or*

39

otherwise, eventuates in a decision. Those decisions have a certain objective success rate in criterion case identification; and for present purposes we simply treat the decision function, whatever its components and complexity may be, as a single variable. It should be remembered that the literature does not present us with cross-validated methods having hit rates much above those we have chosen as examples, regardless of how complex or configural the methods used. So that even if the clinician approximates an extremely complex configural function "in his head" before classifying the patient, for purposes of the present problem this complex function is treated as the scale. In connection with the more general "philosophy" of clinical decision making see Bross (1953) and Meehl (1954a).

Applications of Bayes' Theorem

Many readers will recognize the preceding numerical examples as essentially involving a principle of elementary probability theory, the so-called Bayes' Theorem. While it has come in for some opprobrium on account of its connection with certain pre-Fisherian fallacies in statistical inference, as an algebraic statement the theorem has, of course, nothing intrinsically wrong with it and it does apply in the present case. One form of it may be stated as follows:

If there are k antecedent conditions under which an event of a given kind may occur, these conditions having the antecedent probabilities P_1, P_2, . . . , P_k of being realized, and the probability of the event upon each of them is p_1, p_2, p_3, . . . , p_k, then, given that the event is observed to occur, the probability that it arose on the basis of a specified one, say j, of the antecedent conditions is given by

$$P_{j(o)} = \frac{P_j p_j}{\sum_{i=1}^{k} P_i p_i}.$$

The usual illustration is the case of drawing marbles from an urn. Suppose we have two urns, and the urn-selection procedure is such that the probability of our choosing the first urn is 1/10 and the second is 9/10. Assume that 70 percent of the marbles in the first urn are black, and 40 percent of those in the second urn are black. I now (blindfolded)

40

"choose" an urn and then, from it, I choose a marble. The marble turns out to be black. What is the probability that I drew from the first urn?

$$P_1 = .10 \qquad P_2 = .90$$
$$p_1 = .70 \qquad p_2 = .40$$

Then

$$P_{1(b)} = \frac{(.10)(.70)}{(.10)(.70) + (.90)(.40)} = .163.$$

If I make a practice of inferring under such circumstances that an observed black marble arose from the first urn, I shall be correct in such judgments, in the long run, only 16.3 percent of the time. Note, however, that the "test item" or "sign" *black marble* is correctly "scored" in favor of Urn No. 1, since there is a 30 percent difference in black marble rate between it and Urn No. 2. But this considerable disparity in symptom rate is overcome by the very low base rate ("antecedent probability of choosing from the first urn"), so that inference to first-urn origin of black marbles will actually be wrong some 84 times in 100. In the clinical analogue, the urns are identified with the subpopulations of patients to be discriminated (their antecedent probabilities being equated to their base rates in the population to be examined), and the black marbles are test results of a certain ("positive") kind. The proportion of black marbles in one urn is the valid positive rate, and in the other is the false positive rate. Inspection and suitable manipulations of the formula for the common two-category case, viz.,

$$P_{(o)} = \frac{Pp_1}{Pp_1 + Qp_2}$$

$P_{d(o)}$ = Probability that an individual is diseased, given that his observed test score is positive
P = Base rate of actual positives in the population examined
$P + Q = 1$
p_1 = Proportion of diseased identified by test ("valid positive" rate)
$q_1 = 1 - p_1$
p_2 = Proportion of nondiseased misidentified by test as being diseased ("false positive" rate)
$q_2 = 1 - p_2$

yields several useful statements. Note that in what follows we are operating entirely with exact population parameter values; i.e., sampling

41

errors are not responsible for the dangers and restrictions set forth. See Table 4.

Table 4. Definition of Symbols*

Diagnosis from Test	Actual Diagnosis	
	Positive	Negative
Positive.....................	p_1	p_2
	Valid positive rate (proportion of positives called positive)	False positive rate (proportion of negatives called positive)
Negative....................	q_1	q_2
	False negative rate (proportion of positives called negative)	Valid negative rate (proportion of negatives called negative)
Total with actual diagnosis...	$p_1 + q_1 = 1.0$ (total positives)	$p_2 + q_2 = 1.0$ (total negatives)

* For simplicity, the term *diagnosis* is used to denote the classification of any kind of pathology, behavior, or event being studied, or to denote "outcome" if a test is used for prediction. Since horizontal addition (e.g., $p_1 + p_2$) is meaningless in ignorance of the base rates, there is no symbol or marginal total for these sums. *All values are parameter values.*

1. In order for a positive diagnostic assertion to be "more likely true than false," the ratio of the positive to the negative base rates in the examined population must exceed the ratio of the false positive rate to the valid positive rate. That is,

$$\frac{P}{Q} > \frac{p_2}{p_1}.$$

If this condition is not met, the attribution of pathology on the basis of the test is more probably in error than correct, *even though the sign being used is valid* (i.e., $p_1 \neq p_2$).

Example: If a certain cutting score identifies 80 percent of patients with organic brain damage (high scores being indicative of damage) but is also exceeded by 15 percent of the nondamaged sent for evaluation, in order for the psychometric decision "brain damage present" to be more often true than false, the ratio of actually brain-damaged to nondamaged cases among all seen for testing must be at least one to five (.19).

Piotrowski (1937) has recommended that the presence of five or more Rorschach signs among ten "organic" signs is an efficient indicator of brain damage. Dorken and Kral (1952), in cross-validating Piotrowski's index, found that 63 percent of organics and 30 percent of a mixed, nonorganic, psychiatric patient group had Rorschachs with five or more signs. Thus, our estimate of $p_2/p_1 = .30/.63 = .48$, and in order for the decision "brain damage present" to be correct more than one-half the time, the proportion of positives (P) in a given population must exceed .33 (i.e., $P/Q > .33/.67$). Since few clinical populations requiring this clinical decision would have such a high rate of brain damage, especially among psychiatric patients, the particular cutting score advocated by Piotrowski will produce an excessive number of false positives, and the positive diagnosis will be more often wrong than right. Inasmuch as the base rates for any given behavior or pathology differ from one clinical setting to another, *an inflexible cutting score should not be advocated for any psychometric device.* This statement applies generally—thus, to indices recommended for such diverse purposes as the classification or detection of deterioration, specific symptoms, "traits," neuroticism, sexual aberration, dissimulation, suicide risk, and the like. When P is small, it may be advisable to explore the possibility of dealing with a restricted population within which the base rate of the attribute being tested is higher. This approach is discussed in an article by Rosen (1954) on the detection of suicidal patients in which it is suggested that an attempt might be made to apply an index to subpopulations with higher suicide rates.

2. If the base rates are equal, the probability of a positive diagnosis being correct is the ratio of valid positive rate to the sum of valid and false positive rates. That is,

$$p_{d(o)} = \frac{p_1}{p_1 + p_2}$$

if $P = Q = \frac{1}{2}$.

Example: If our population is evenly divided between neurotic and psychotic patients the condition for being "probably right" in diagnosing psychosis by a certain method is simply that the psychotics exhibit the pattern in question more frequently than the neurotics. This is the intuitively obvious special case; it is often misgeneralized to justify use of the test in those cases where base-rate asymmetry $(P \neq Q)$ counteracts the $(p_1 - p_2)$ discrepancy, leading to the paradoxical consequence that *deciding on the basis of more information can actually worsen the chances of a correct decision.* The apparent absurdity of such an idea has often misled psychologists into behaving as though the establishment of "validity" or "discrimination," i.e., that $p_1 \neq p_2$, indicates that a procedure should be used in decision making.

Example: A certain test is used to select those who will continue in outpatient psychotherapy (positives). It correctly identifies 75 percent of these good cases but the same cutting score picks up 40 percent of the poor risks who subsequently terminate against advice. Suppose that in the past experience of the clinic 50 percent of the patients terminated therapy prematurely. Correct selection of patients can be made with the given cutting score on the test 65 percent of the time, since $p_1/(p_1 + p_2) = .75/(.75 + .40) = .65$. It can be seen that the efficiency of the test would be exaggerated if the base rate for continuation in therapy were actually .70, but the efficiency were evaluated solely on the basis of a research study containing equal groups of continuers and noncontinuers, i.e., if it were assumed that $P = .50$.

3. In order for the hits in the entire population which is under consideration to be increased by use of the test, the base rate of the more numerous class (called here positive) must be less than the ratio of the valid negative rate to the sum of valid negative and false negative rates. That is, unless

$$P < \frac{q_2}{q_1 + q_2},$$

the making of decisions on the basis of the test will have an adverse effect. An alternative expression is that $(P/Q) < (q_2/q_1)$ when $P > Q$, i.e., the ratio of the larger to the smaller class must be less than the ratio of the valid negative rate to the false negative rate. When $P < Q$, the conditions for the test to improve upon the base rates are

$$Q < \frac{p_1}{p_1 + p_2}$$

and

$$\frac{Q}{P} < \frac{p_1}{p_2}.$$

Rotter, Rafferty, and Lotsof (1954) have reported the scores on a sentence completion test for a group of thirty-three "maladjusted" and thirty-three "adjusted" girls. They report that the use of a specified cutting score (not cross-validated) will result in the correct classification of 85 percent of the maladjusted girls and the incorrect classification of only 15 percent of the adjusted girls. It is impossible to evaluate adequately the efficiency of the test unless one knows the base rates of maladjustment (P) and adjustment (Q) for the population of high school girls, although there would be general agreement that $Q > P$. Since $p_1/(p_1 + p_2) = .85/(.85 + .15) = .85$, the over-all hits in diagnosis with the test will not improve on classification based solely on the base rates unless the proportion of adjusted girls is less than .85. Because the reported effectiveness of the test is spuriously high, the proportion of adjusted girls would no doubt have to be considerably less than .85. Unless there is good reason to believe that the base rates are similar from one setting to another, it is impossible to determine the efficiency of a test such as Rotter's when the criterion is based on ratings unless one replicates his research, including the criterion ratings, with a representative sample of each new population.

4. In altering a sign, improving a scale, or shifting a cutting score, the increment in valid positives per increment in valid positive *rate* is proportional to the positive base rate; and analogously, the increment in valid negative *rate* is proportional to the negative base rate. That is, if we alter a sign the net improvement in over-all hit rate is

$$H'_T - H_T = \Delta p_1 P + \Delta q_2 Q,$$

where $H_T =$ original proportion of hits (over all) and $H'_T =$ new proportion of hits (over all).

5. A corollary of this is that altering a sign or shifting a cut will improve our decision making if, and only if, the ratio of *improvement* Δp_1 in valid positive rate to *worsening* Δp_2 in false negative rate exceeds the ratio of actual negatives to positives in the population.

$$\frac{\Delta p_1}{\Delta p_2} > \frac{Q}{P}$$

Example: Suppose we improve the intrinsic validity of a certain "schizophrenic index" so that it now detects 20 percent more schizophrenics than it formerly did, at the expense of only a 5 percent increase in the false positive rate. This surely looks encouraging. We are, however, working with an outpatient clientele only one-tenth of whom are actually schizophrenic. Then, since

$$\Delta p_1 = .20 \qquad P = .10$$
$$\Delta p_2 = .05 \qquad Q = .90$$

applying the formula we see that

$$\frac{.20}{.05} \leq \frac{.90}{.10}$$

i.e., the required inequality does not hold, and the routine use of this "improved" index will result in an increase in the proportion of erroneous diagnostic decisions.

In the case of any pair of unimodal distributions, this corresponds to the principle that the optimal cut lies at the intersection of the two distribution envelopes (Horst, 1941, pp. 271–272).

Manipulation of Cutting Lines
for Different Decisions

For any given psychometric device, no one cutting line is maximally efficient for clinical settings in which the base rates of the criterion groups in the population are different. Furthermore, different cutting lines may be necessary for various decisions within the same population. In this section, methods are presented for manipulating the cutting line of any instrument in order to maximize the efficiency of a device in the making of several kinds of decisions. Reference should be made to the scheme presented in Table 5 for understanding of the discussion which

Table 5. Symbols to Be Used in Evaluating the Efficiency of a Psychometric Device in Classification or Prediction*

Diagnosis from Test	Actual Diagnosis		Total Diagnosed from Test
	Positive	Negative	
Positive...	NPp_1 (number of valid positives)	NQp_2 (number of false positives)	$NPp_1 + NQp_2$ (number of test positives)
Negative..	NPq_1 (number of false negatives)	NQq_2 (number of valid negatives)	$NPq_1 + NQq_2$ (number of test negatives)
Total...	NP (number of actual positives)	NQ (number of actual negatives)	N (total number of cases)

* For simplicity, the term *diagnosis* is used to denote the classification of any kind of pathology, behavior, or event studied, or to denote "outcome" if a test is used for prediction. *Number* means "absolute frequency," not rate or probability.

follows. This scheme and the methods for manipulating cutting lines are derived from Duncan, Ohlin, Reiss, and Stanton (1953).

A study in the prediction of juvenile delinquency by Glueck and Glueck (1950) will be used for illustration. Scores on a prediction index for 451 delinquents and 439 nondelinquents (p. 261) are listed in Table 6. If the Gluecks' index is to be used in a population with a given juvenile delinquency rate, cutting lines can be established to maximize the efficiency of the index for several decisions. In the following illustration, a delinquency rate of .20 will be used. From the data in Table 6, optimal cutting lines will be determined for maximizing the proportion of correct predictions, or hits, for all cases (H_T), and for maximizing the proportion of hits (H_P) among those called delinquent (positives) by the index.

In the first three columns of Table 6, "f" denotes the number of delinquents scoring in each class interval, "cf" represents the cumulative frequency of delinquents scoring above each class interval (e.g., 265 score above 299), and p_1 represents the proportion of the total group of 451 delinquents scoring above each class interval. Columns 4, 5, and 6 present the same kind of data for the 439 nondelinquents.

Maximizing the number of correct predictions or classifications for all cases. The proportion of correct predictions or classifications (H_T) for any given cutting line is given by the formula $H_T = Pp_1 + Qq_2$. Thus, in column 11 of Table 6, labeled H_T, it can be seen that the best cutting line for this decision would be between 299 and 300, for 85.9 percent of all predictions would be correct if those above the line were predicted to become delinquent and all those below the line nondelinquent. Any other cutting line would result in a smaller proportion of correct predictions, and, in fact, any cutting line set lower than this point would make the index inferior to the use of the base rates, for if all cases were predicted to be nondelinquent, the total proportion of hits would be .80.

Maximizing the number of correct predictions or classifications for positives. The primary use of a prediction device may be for *selection* of (a) students who will succeed in a training program, (b) applicants who will succeed in a certain job, (c) patients who will benefit from a certain type of therapy, etc. In the present illustration, the index would most likely be used for detection of those who are likely to become delinquents. Thus, the aim might be to maximize the number of hits only

Table 6. Prediction Index Scores for Juvenile Delinquents ($N = 451$) and Nondelinquents ($N = 439$) and Other Statistics for Determining Optimal Cutting Lines for Certain Decisions in a Population with a Delinquency Rate of .20*

Prediction Index Score	Delinquents			Nondelinquents			q_2 $1-p_2$ (7)	Pp_1 $.2p_1$ (8)	Qp_2 $.8p_2$ (9)	Qq_2 $.8q_2$ (10)	H_T Pp_1+Qq_2 (11)	R_P Pp_1+Qp_2 (12)	H_P Pp_1/R_P (13)
	f (1)	cf (2)	p_1 (3)	f (4)	cf (5)	p_2 (6)							
400+	51	51	.1131	1	1	.0023	.9977	.0226	.0018	.7982	.821	.024	.926
350–399	73	124	.2749	8	9	.0205	.9795	.0550	.0164	.7836	.839	.071	.770
300–349	141	265	.5876	23	32	.0729	.9271	.1175	.0583	.7417	.859	.176	.668
250–299	122	387	.8581	70	102	.2323	.7677	.1716	.1858	.6142	.786	.357	.480
200–249	40	427	.9468	68	170	.3872	.6128	.1894	.3098	.4902	.680	.499	.379
150–199	19	446	.9889	102	272	.6196	.3804	.1978	.4957	.3043	.502	.694	.285
<150	5	451	1.0000	167	439	1.0000	.0000	.2000	.8000	.0000	.200	1.000	.200

* Frequencies in columns 1 and 4 are from Glueck and Glueck (1950, p. 261).

Table 7. Percentage of Delinquents and Nondelinquents in Each Prediction Index Score Interval in a Population in Which the Delinquency Rate Is .20.

Prediction Index Score Interval	Number			Percentage in Score Interval		
	Delinquents	Nondelinquents	Total	Delinquents	Nondelinquents	Total
400+	51	4	55	92.7	7.3	100
350–399	73	33	106	68.9	31.1	100
300–349	141	95	236	59.7	40.3	100
250–299	122	288	410	29.8	70.2	100
200–249	40	279	319	12.5	87.5	100
150–199	19	419	438	4.3	95.7	100
<150	5	686	691	.7	99.3	100
Total	451	1,804	2,255			

SOURCE: Modification of Table XX–2, p. 261, from Glueck and Glueck (1950).

within the group predicted by the index to become delinquents (predicted positives $= NPp_1 + NQp_2$). The proportion of correct predictions for this group by the use of different cutting lines is given in column 13, labeled H_P. Thus, if a cutting line is set between 399 and 400, one will be correct over 92 times in 100 if predictions are made *only* for persons scoring above the cutting line. The formula for determining the efficiency of the test when only positive predictions are made is $H_P = Pp_1/(Pp_1 + Qp_2)$.

One has to pay a price for achieving a very high level of accuracy with the index. Since the problem is to select potential delinquents so that some sort of therapy can be attempted, the proportion of this selected group in the total sample may be considered as a selection ratio. The selection ratio for positives is $R_P = Pp_1 + Qp_2$, that is, predictions are made only for those above the cutting line. The selection ratio for each possible cutting line is shown in column 12 of Table 6, labeled R_P. It can be seen that to obtain maximum accuracy in selection of delinquents (92.6 percent), predictions can be made for only 2.4 percent of the population. For other cutting lines, the accuracy of selection and the corresponding selection ratios are given in Table 6. The worker applying the index must use his own judgment in deciding upon the level of accuracy and the selection ratio desired.

Maximizing the number of correct predictions or classifications for negatives. In some selection problems, the goal is the selection of negatives rather than positives. Then, the proportion of hits among all predicted negatives for any given cutting line is $H_N = Qq_2/(Qq_2 + Pq_1)$, and the selection ratio for negatives is $R_N = Pq_1 + Qq_2$.

In all of the above manipulations of cutting lines, it is essential that there be a large number of cases. Otherwise, the percentages about any given cutting line would be so unstable that very dissimilar results would be obtained on new samples. For most studies in clinical psychology, therefore, it would be necessary to establish cutting lines according to the decisions and methods discussed above, and then to cross-validate a specific cutting line on new samples.

The amount of shrinkage to be expected in the cross-validation of cutting lines cannot be determined until a thorough mathematical and statistical study of the subject is made. It may be found that when criterion distributions are approximately normal and large, cutting lines should be established in terms of the normal probability table rather than on the basis of the observed p and q values found in the samples. In a later section dealing with the selection ratio we shall see that it is sometimes the best procedure to select all individuals falling above a certain cutting line and to select the others needed to reach the selection ratio by choosing at random below the line; or in other cases to establish several different cuts defining *ranges* within which one or the opposite decision should be made.

Decisions based on score intervals rather than cutting lines. The Gluecks' data can be used to illustrate another approach to psychometric classification and prediction when scores for large samples are available with a relatively large number of cases in each score interval. In Table 7 are listed frequencies of delinquents and nondelinquents for prediction index score intervals. The frequencies for delinquents are the same as those in Table 6, whereas those for nondelinquents have been corrected for a base rate of .20 by multiplying each frequency in column 4 of Table 6[2] by

$$4.11 = \frac{(.80)\,(459)}{(.20)\,(431)}.$$

Table 7 indicates the proportion of delinquents and nondelinquents among all juveniles who fall within a given score interval when the base rate of delinquency is .20. It can be predicted that of those scoring 400 or more, 92.7 percent will become delinquent, of those scoring between 350 and 399, 68.9 percent will be delinquent, etc. Likewise, of those scoring between 200 and 249, it can be predicted that 87.5 percent will not become delinquent. Since 80 percent of predictions will be correct without the index if all cases are called nondelinquent, one would not predict nondelinquency with the index in score intervals over 249. Likewise, it would be best not to predict delinquency for individuals in the intervals under 250 because 20 percent of predictions will be correct if the base rate is used.

It should be emphasized that there are different ways of quantifying one's clinical errors, and they will, of course, not all give the same

[2] The Gluecks' Tables XX-2, 3, 4, 5 (1950, pp. 261–262) and their interpretations therefrom are apt to be misleading because of their exclusive consideration of approximately equal base rates of delinquency and nondelinquency. Reiss (1951), in his review of the Gluecks' study, has also discussed their use of an unrepresentative rate of delinquency.

evaluation when applied in a given setting. "Percentage of valid positives" ($= p_1$) is rarely if ever meaningful without the correlated "percentage of false positives" ($= p_2$), and clinicians are accustomed to the idea that we pay for an increase in the first by an increase in the second, whenever the increase is achieved not by an improvement in the test's intrinsic validity but by a shifting of the cutting score. But the two quantities p_1 and p_2 do not define our over-all hit frequency, which depends also upon the base rates P and Q. The three quantities p_1, p_2, and P do, however, contain all the information needed to evaluate the test with respect to any given sign or cutting score that yields these values. Although p_1, p_2, and P contain the relevant information, other forms of it may be of greater importance. No two of these numbers, for example, answer the obvious question most commonly asked (or vaguely implied) by psychiatrists when an inference is made from a sign, viz., "How sure can you be on the basis of that sign?" The answer to this eminently practical query involves a probability different from any of the above, namely, the *inverse* probability given by Bayes' Formula:

$$H_P = \frac{Pp_1}{Pp_1 + Qp_2}.$$

Even a small improvement in the hit frequency to $H'_T = Pp_1 + Qq_2$ over the $H_T = P$ attainable without the test may be adjudged as worthwhile when the increment ΔH_T is multiplied by the N examined in the course of one year and is thus seen to involve a dozen lives or a dozen curable schizophrenics. On the other hand, the simple fact that an actual *shrinkage* in total hit rate may occur seems to be unappreciated or tacitly ignored by a good deal of clinical practice. One must keep constantly in mind that numerous diagnostic, prognostic, and dynamic statements can be made about almost all neurotic patients (e.g., "depressed," "inadequate ability to relate," "sexual difficulties") or about very few patients (e.g., "dangerous," "will act out in therapy," "suicidal," "will blow up into a schizophrenia"). A psychologist who uses a test sign that even cross-validates at $p_1 = q_2 = 80$ percent to determine whether "depression" is present or absent, working in a clinical population where practically everyone is fairly depressed except a few psychopaths and old-fashioned hysterics, is kidding himself, the psychiatrist, and whoever foots the bill.

51

"Successive-Hurdles" Approach

Tests having low efficiency, or having moderate efficiency but applied to populations having very unbalanced base rates $(P \ll Q)$ are sometimes defended by adopting a "crude initial screening" frame of reference, and arguing that certain other procedures (whether tests or not) can be applied to the subset identified by the screener ("successive hurdles"). There is no question that in some circumstances (e.g., military induction, or industrial selection with a large labor market) this is a thoroughly defensible position. However, as a general rule one should examine this type of justification critically, with the preceding considerations in mind. Suppose we have a test which distinguishes brain-tumor from non–brain-tumor patients with 75 percent accuracy and no differential bias $(p_1 = q_2 = .75)$. Under such circumstances the test hit rate H_T is .75 regardless of the base rate. If we use the test in making our judgments, we are correct in our diagnoses 75 times in 100. But suppose only one patient in 10 actually has a brain tumor; we will drop our over-all "success" from 90 percent (attainable by diagnosing "No tumor" in all cases) to 75 percent. We do, however, identify 3 out of 4 of the real brain tumors, and in such a case it seems worth the price. The "price" has two aspects to it: We take time to give the test, and, having given it, we call many "tumorous" who are not. Thus, suppose that in the course of a year we see 1000 patients. Of these, 900 are non-tumor, and we erroneously call 225 of these "tumor." To pick up $(100)(.75) = 75$ of the tumors, *all* 100 of whom would have been called tumor-free using the base rates alone, we are willing to mislabel three times this many as tumorous who are actually not. Putting it another way, whenever we say "tumor" on the basis of the test, the chances are 3 to 1 that we are mistaken. When we "rule out" tumor by the test, we are correct 96 percent of the time, an improvement of only 6 percent in the confidence attachable to a negative finding over the confidence yielded by the base rates.[3]

Now, picking up the successive-hurdles argument, suppose a major

---

[3] Improvements are expressed throughout this article as *absolute* increments in percentage of hits, because (a) this avoids the complete arbitrariness involved in choosing between original hit rate and miss rate as starting denominator; and (b) for the clinician, the person is the most meaningful unit of gain, rather than a proportion *of* a proportion (especially when the reference proportion is very small).

decision (e.g., exploratory surgery) is allowed to rest upon a second test which is infallible but for practically insuperable reasons of staff, time, etc., cannot be routinely given. We administer Test 2 only to "positives" on (screening) Test 1. By this tactic we eliminate all 225 false positives left by Test 1, and we verify the 75 valid positives screened in by Test 1. The 25 tumors that slipped through as false negatives on Test 1 are, of course, not picked up by Test 2 either, because it is not applied to them. Our total hit frequency is now 97.5 percent, since the only cases ultimately misclassified out of our 1000 seen are these 25 tumors which escaped through the initial sieve Test 1. We are still running only 7½ percent above the base rate. We have had to give our short-and-easy test to 1000 individuals and our cumbersome, expensive test to 300 individuals, 225 of whom turn out to be free of tumor. But we have located 75 patients with tumors who would not otherwise have been found.

Such examples suggest that, except in "life-or-death" matters, the successive-screenings argument merely tends to soften the blow of Bayes' Rule in cases where the base rates are very far from symmetry. Also, if Test 2 is not assumed to be infallible but only highly effective, say 90 percent accurate both ways, results start looking unimpressive again. Our net false positive rate rises from zero to 22 cases miscalled "tumor," and we operate on 67 of the actual tumors instead of 75. The total hit frequency drops to 94.5 percent, only 4½ percent above that yielded by a blind guessing of the modal class.

The Selection Ratio

Straightforward application of the preceding principles presupposes that the clinical decision maker is free to adopt a policy solely on the basis of maximizing hit frequency. Sometimes there are external constraints such as staff time, administrative policy, or social obligation which further complicate matters. It may then be impossible to make all decisions in accordance with the base rates, and the task given to the test is that of selecting a subset of cases which are decided in the direction opposite to the base rates but will still contain fewer erroneous decisions than would ever be yielded by opposing the base rates without the test. If 80 percent of patients referred to a mental hygiene clinic are recoverable with intensive psychotherapy, we would do better to treat everybody than to utilize a test yielding 75 percent correct predictions. But suppose that available staff time is limited so that we *can* treat only half the referrals. The Bayes-type injunction to "follow the base rates when they are better than the test" becomes pragmatically meaningless, for it directs us to make decisions which we cannot implement. The imposition of an *externally* imposed selection ratio, not determined on the basis of any maximizing or minimizing policy but by nonstatistical considerations, renders the test worthwhile.

Before imposition of any arbitrary selection ratio, the fourfold table for 100 referrals might be as shown in Table 8. If the aim were simply

Table 8. Actual and Test-Predicted
Therapeutic Outcome

| | Therapeutic Outcome | | |
Test Prediction	Good	Poor	Total
Good.............60	5	65
Poor..............20	15	35
Total............80	20	100

to minimize total errors, we would predict "good" for each case and be right 80 times in 100. Using the test, we would be right only 75 times in 100. But suppose a selection ratio of .5 is externally imposed. We are then forced to predict "poor" for half the cases, even though this "prediction" is, in any given case, likely to be wrong. (More precisely, we handle this subset *as if* we predicted "poor," by refusing to treat.) So we now select our 50 to-be-treated cases from among those 65 who fall in the "test-good" array, having a frequency of $60/65 = 92.3$ percent hits among those selected. This is better than the 80 percent we could expect (among those selected) by choosing half the total referrals at random. Of course we pay for this, by making many "false negative" decisions; but these are necessitated, whether we use the test or not, by the fact that the selection ratio was determined without regard for hit maximization but by external considerations. Without the test, our false negative rate q_1 is 50 percent (i.e., 40 of the 80 "good" cases will be called "poor"); the test reduces the false negative rate to 42.5 percent ($= 34/80$), since 15 cases from above the cutting line must be selected at random for inclusion in the not-to-be-treated group below the cutting line (i.e., $20 + (60/65)15 = 34$). Stated in terms of corrcct decisions, without the test 40 out of 50 selected for therapy will have a good therapeutic outcome; with the test, 46 in 50 will be successes.

Reports of studies in which formulas are developed from psychometrics for the prediction of patients' continuance in psychotherapy have neglected to consider the relationship of the selection ratio to the specific population to which the prediction formula is to be applied. In each study the population has consisted of individuals who were *accepted for therapy* by the usual methods employed at an outpatient clinic, and the prediction formula has been evaluated *only* for such patients. It is implied by these studies that the formula would have the same efficiency if it were used for the *selection* of "continuers" from all those *applying* for therapy. Unless the formula is tested on a random sample of applicants who are allowed to enter therapy without regard to their test scores, its efficiency for selection purposes is unknown. The reported efficiency of the prediction formula in the above studies pertains only to its use in a population of patients who have already been selected for therapy. There is little likelihood that the formula can be used in any practical way for further selection of patients unless the clinic's therapists are carrying a far greater load than they plan to carry in the future.

The use of the term "selection" (as contrasted with "prediction" or "placement") ought not to blind us to the important differences between industrial selection and its clinical analogue. The incidence of false negatives—of potential employees screened out by the test who would actually have made good on the job if hired—is of little concern to management except as it costs money to give tests. Hence the industrial psychologist may choose to express his aim in terms of minimizing the false positives, i.e., of seeing to it that the job success *among those hired* is as large a rate as possible. When we make a clinical decision to treat or not to treat, we are withholding something from people who have a claim upon us in a sense that is much stronger than the "right to work" gives a job applicant any claim upon a particular company. So, even though we speak of a "selection ratio" in clinical work, it must be remembered that those cases *not selected* are patients about whom a certain kind of important negative decision is being made.

For any *given* selection ratio, maximizing total hits is always equivalent to maximizing the hit rate for either type of decision (or minimizing the errors of either, or both, kinds), since cases shifted from one cell of the table have to be exactly compensated for. If m "good" cases that were correctly classified by one decision method are incorrectly classified by another, maintenance of the selection ratio entails that m cases correctly called "poor" are also miscalled "good" by the new method. Hence an externally imposed selection ratio eliminates the often troublesome value questions about the relative seriousness of the two kinds of errors, since they are unavoidably increased or decreased at exactly the same rate.

If the test yields a score or a continuously varying index of some kind, the values of p_1 and p_2 are not fixed, as they may be with "patterns" or "signs." Changes in the selection ratio, R, will then suggest shifting the cutting scores or regions on the basis of the relations obtaining among R, P, and the p_1, p_2 combinations yielded by various cuts. It is worth special comment that, in the case of continuous distributions, the optimum procedure is *not* always to move the cut until the total area truncated $= NR$, selecting all above that cut and rejecting all those below. Whether this "obvious" rule is wise or not depends upon the distribution characteristics. We have found it easy to construct pairs of distributions such that the test is "discriminating" throughout, in the sense that the associated cumulative frequencies q_1 and q_2 maintain the same direction of their inequality everywhere in the range, i.e.,

$$\frac{1}{N_2} \int_{-\infty}^{x_i} f_2(x)dx > \frac{1}{N_1} \int_{-\infty}^{x_i} f_1(x)dx \text{ for all } x_i;$$

yet in which the hit frequency given by a single cut at R is inferior to that given by first selecting with a cut which yields $N_c < NR$, and then picking up the remaining $(NR - N_c)$ cases at random below the cut. Other more complex situations may arise in which different types of decisions should be made in different regions, actually reversing the policy as we move along the test continuum. Such numerical examples as we have constructed utilize continuous, unimodal distributions, and involve differences in variability, skewness, and kurtosis not greater than those which arise fairly often in clinical practice. Of course the utilization of any very complicated pattern of regions requires more stable distribution frequencies than are obtainable from the sample sizes ordinarily available to clinicians.

It is instructive to contemplate some of the moral and administrative issues involved in the practical application of the preceding ideas. It is our impression that a good deal of clinical research is of the "So what?" variety, not because of defects in experimental design such as inadequate cross-validation but because it is hard to see just what are the useful changes in decision making which could reasonably be expected to follow. Suppose, for example, it is shown that "duration of psychotherapy" is 70 percent predictable from a certain test. Are we prepared to propose that those patients whose test scores fall in a certain range should not receive treatment? If not, then is it of any real advantage therapeutically to "keep in mind" that the patient has 7 out of 10 chances of staying longer than fifteen hours, and 3 out of 10 chances of staying less than that? We are not trying to poke fun at research, since presumably almost any lawful relationship stands a chance of being valuable to our total scientific comprehension some day. But many clinical papers are ostensibly inspired by practical aims, and can be given theoretical interpretation or fitted into any larger framework only with great difficulty if at all. It seems appropriate to urge that such "practical"-oriented investigations should be really *practical,* enabling us to see how our clinical decisions could rationally be modified in the light of the findings. It is doubtful how much of current work could be justified in these terms.

Regardless of whether the test validity is capable of improving on the base rates, there are some prediction problems which have practical import only because of limitations in personnel. What other justification is there for the great emphasis in clinical research on "prognosis," "treatability," or "stayability"? The very formulation of the predictive task as "maximizing the number of hits" already presupposes that we intend *not* to treat some cases; since if we treat all comers, the ascertainment of a bad prognosis score has no practical effect other than to discourage the therapist (and thus hinder therapy?). If intensive psychotherapy could be offered to all veterans who are willing to accept referral to a VA mental hygiene clinic, would it be licit to refuse those who had the poorest outlook? Presumably not. It is interesting to contrast the emphasis on prognosis in clinical psychology with that in, say, cancer surgery, where the treatment *of choice* may still have a very low probability of "success," but is nevertheless carried out on the basis of that low probability. Nor does this attitude seem unreasonable, since no patient would refuse the best available treatment on the ground that even it was only 10 percent effective. Suppose a therapist, in the course

57

of earning his living, spends 200 hours a year on nonimprovers by following a decision policy that also results in his unexpected success with one 30-year-old "poor bet." If this client thereby gains $16 \times 365 \times 40 = 233,600$ hours averaging 50 percent less anxiety during the rest of his natural life, it was presumably worth the price.

These considerations suggest that, with the expansion of professional facilities in the behavior field, the prediction problem will be less like that of industrial *selection* and more like that of *placement*. "To treat or not to treat" or "How treatable" or "How long to treat" would be replaced by "What *kind* of treatment?" But as soon as the problem is formulated in this way, the external selection ratio is usually no longer imposed. Only if we are deciding between such alternatives as classical analysis and, say, fifty-hour interpretative therapy would such personnel limitations as can be expected in future years impose an arbitrary R. But if the decision is between such alternatives as short-term interpretative therapy, Rogerian therapy, Thorne's directive therapy, hypnotic retraining, and the method of tasks (Herzberg, 1945; Salter, 1949; Wolpe, 1952), we could "follow the base rates" by treating every patient with the method known to have the highest success frequency among patients "similar" to him. The criteria of similarity (class membership) will presumably be multiple, both phenotypic and genotypic, and will have been chosen because of their empirically demonstrated prognostic relevance rather than by guesswork, as is current practice. Such an idealized situation also presupposes that the selection and training of psychotherapists will have become socially realistic so that therapeutic personnel skilled in the various methods will be available in some reasonable proportion to the incidence with which each method is the treatment of choice.

How close are we to the upper limit of the predictive validity of personality tests, such as was reached remarkably early in the development of academic aptitude tests? If the now-familiar two-thirds to three-fourths proportions of hits against even-split criterion dichotomies are already approaching that upper limit, we may well discover that for many decision problems the search for tests that will significantly better the base rates is a rather unrewarding enterprise. When the criterion is a more circumscribed trait or symptom ("depressed," "affiliative," "sadistic," and the like), the difficulty of improving upon the base rates is combined with the doubtfulness about how valuable it is to have such information with 75 percent confidence anyhow. But this involves larger issues beyond the scope of the present paper.

Availability of Information on Base Rates

The obvious difficulty we face in practical utilization of the preceding formulas arises from the fact that actual quantitative knowledge of the base rates is usually lacking. But this difficulty must not lead to a dismissal of our considerations as clinically irrelevant. In the case of many clinical decisions, chiefly those involving such phenotypic criteria as overt symptoms, formal diagnosis, subsequent hospitalization, persistence in therapy, vocational or marital adjustment, and the numerous "surface" personality traits which clinicians try to assess, *the chief reason for our ignorance of the base rates is nothing more subtle than our failure to compute them.* The file data available in most installations having a fairly stable source of clientele would yield values sufficiently accurate to permit minimum and maximum estimates which might be sufficient to decide for or against use of a proposed sign. It is our opinion that this rather mundane taxonomic task is of much greater importance than has been realized, and we hope that the present paper will impel workers to more systematic efforts along these lines.

Even in the case of more subtle, complex, and genotypic inferences, the situation is far from hopeless. Take the case of some such dynamic attribution as "strong latent dependency, which will be anxiety-arousing as therapy proceeds." If this is so difficult to discern *even during intensive therapy* that a therapist's rating on it has too little reliability for use as a criterion, it is hard to see just what is the value of guessing it from psychometrics. If a skilled therapist cannot discriminate the personality characteristic after considerable contact with the patient, it is at least debatable whether the characteristic makes any practical difference. On the other hand, if it can be reliably judged by therapists, the determination of approximate base rates again involves nothing more complex than systematic recording of these judgments and subsequent tabulation. Finally, "clinical experience" and "common sense" must be invoked when there is nothing better to be had. Surely if the q_1/q_2 ratio for a test sign claiming validity for "difficulty in accepting inner drives" shows from the formula that the base rate must not exceed .65 to justify use of the sign, we can be fairly confident in discarding it for use with

59

any psychiatric population! Such a "backward" use of the formula to obtain a maximum useful value of *P*, in conjunction with the most tolerant common-sense estimates of *P* from daily experience, will often suffice to answer the question. If one is really in complete ignorance of the limits within which *P* lies, then obviously no rational judgment on the probable efficiency of the sign can be made.

Estimation versus Significance

A further implication of the foregoing thinking is that the exactness of certain small sample statistics, or the relative freedom of certain non-parametric methods from distribution assumptions, has to be stated with care lest it mislead clinicians into an unjustified confidence. When an investigator concludes that a sign, item, cutting score, or pattern has "validity" on the basis of small-sample methods, he has rendered a certain very broad null hypothesis unplausible. To decide, however, whether this "validity" warrants clinicians in using the test is (as every statistician would insist) a further and more complex question. To answer this question, we require more than knowledge that $p_1 \neq p_2$. We need in addition to know, with respect to each decision for which the sign is being proposed, whether the appropriate inequality involving p_1, p_2, and P is fulfilled. More than this, since we will usually be extrapolating to a somewhat different clinical population, we need to know whether altered base rates P' and Q' will falsify these inequalities. To do this demands *estimates* of the test parameters p_1 and p_2, the setting up of confidence belts for their difference $p_1 - p_2$ rather than the mere proof of their nonidentity. Finally, if the sign is a cutting score, we will want to consider shifting it so as to *maintain* optimal hit frequency with new base rates. The effect upon p_1 and p_2 of a contemplated movement of a critical score or band requires a knowledge of distribution form such as only a large sample can give.

As is true in all practical applications of statistical inference, non-mathematical considerations enter into the use of the numerical patterns that exist among P, p_1, p_2 and R. But "pragmatic" judgments initially require a separation of the several probabilities involved, some of which may be much more important than others in terms of the human values associated with them. In some settings, over-all hit rate is all that we care about. In others, a redistribution of the hits and misses even without much total improvement may concern us. In still others, the proportions p_1 and q_2 are of primary interest; and, finally, in some instances the confrontation of a certain increment in the absolute frequency (NPp_1) of one group identified will outweigh all other considerations.

Lest our conclusions seem unduly pessimistic, what constructive suggestions can we offer? We have already mentioned the following: (a) searching for subpopulations with different base rates; (b) successive-hurdles testing; (c) the fact that even a very small *percentage* of improvement may be worth achieving in certain crucial decisions; (d) the need for systematic collection of base-rate data so that our several equations can be applied. To these we may add two further "constructive" comments. First, test research attention should be largely concentrated upon behaviors having base rates nearer a 50–50 split, since it is for these that it is easiest to improve on a base-rate decision policy by use of a test having moderate validity. There are, after all, a large number of clinically important traits which do not occur "almost always" or "very rarely." Test research might be slanted more toward them; the current popularity of Q-sort approaches should facilitate the growth of such an emphasis, by directing attention to items having a reasonable "spread" in the clinical population. Exceptions to such a research policy will arise, in those rare domains where the pragmatic consequences of the alternative decisions justify focusing attention almost wholly on maximizing Pp_1, with relative neglect of Qp_2. Secondly, we think the injunction "quit wasting time on noncontributory psychometrics" is really constructive. When the clinical psychologist sees the near futility of predicting rare or near-universal events and traits from test validities incapable of improving upon the base rates, his clinical time is freed for more economically defensible activities, such as research which will improve the parameters p_1 and p_2; and for *treating* patients rather than uttering low-confidence prophecies or truisms about them (in this connection see Meehl, 1954a, pp. vii, 7, 127–128). It has not been our intention to be dogmatic about "what is worth finding out, how often." We do suggest that the clinical use of patterns, cutting scores, and signs, or research efforts devoted to the discovery of such, should always be evaluated in the light of the simple algebraic fact discovered in 1763 by Mr. Bayes.

Summary

1. The practical value of a psychometric sign, pattern, or cutting score depends jointly upon its intrinsic validity (in the usual sense of its discriminating power) and the distribution of the criterion variable (base rates) in the clinical population. Almost all contemporary research reporting neglects the base-rate factor and hence makes evaluation of test usefulness difficult or impossible.

2. In some circumstances, notably when the base rates of the criterion classification deviate greatly from a 50 percent split, use of a test sign having slight or moderate validity will result in an *increase* of erroneous clinical decisions.

3. Even if the test's parameters are precisely known, so that ordinary cross-validation shrinkage is not a problem, application of a sign within a population having these same test parameters but a different base rate may result in a marked change in the proportion of correct decisions. For this reason validation studies should present trustworthy information respecting the criterion distribution in addition to such test parameters as false positive and false negative rates.

4. Establishment of "validity" by exact small-sample statistics, since it does not yield accurate information about the test parameters (a problem of estimation rather than significance), does not permit trustworthy judgments on test usefulness in a new population with different or unknown base rates.

5. Formulas are presented for determining limits upon relations among the (a) base rates, (b) false negative rate, and (c) false positive rate which must obtain if use of the test sign is to improve clinical decision making.

6. If, however, external constraints (e.g., available staff time) render it administratively unfeasible to decide all cases in accordance with the base rates, a test sign may be worth applying even if following the base rates *would* maximize the total correct decisions, were such a policy possible.

7. Trustworthy information on the base rates of various patient characteristics can readily be obtained by file research, and test development should (other things being equal) be concentrated on those characteristics having base rates nearer .50 rather than close to .00 or 1.00.

8. The basic rationale is that of Bayes' Theorem concerning the calculation of so-called inverse probability.

3

Wanted—A Good Cookbook

ONCE UPON A TIME there was a young fellow who, as we say, was "vocationally maladjusted." He wasn't sure just what the trouble was, but he knew that he wasn't happy in his work. So, being a denizen of an urban, sophisticated, psychologically oriented culture, he concluded that what he needed was some professional guidance. He went to the counseling bureau of a large midwestern university (according to some versions of the tale, it was located on the banks of a great river), and there he was interviewed by a world-famous vocational psychologist. When the psychologist explained that it would first be necessary to take a fourteen-hour battery of tests, the young man hesitated a little; after all, he was still employed at his job and fourteen hours seemed like quite a lot of time. "Oh, well," said the great psychologist reassuringly, "don't worry about *that*. If you're too busy, you can arrange to have my assistant take these tests *for* you. I don't care who takes them, just so long as they come out in quantitative form."

Lest I, a Minnesotan, do too great violence to your expectations by telling this story on the dust-bowl empiricism with which we Minnesotans are traditionally associated, let me now tell you a true story having the opposite animus. Back in the days when we were teaching as-

AUTHOR'S NOTE: This paper was delivered as the Presidential Address, Midwestern Psychological Association, Chicago, April 29, 1955. It first appeared in the *American Psychologist*, vol. 11, 1956. Copyright 1956 by the American Psychological Association, Inc.

sistants, my colleague MacCorquodale was grading a young lady's elementary laboratory report on an experiment which involved a correlation problem. At the end of an otherwise flawless report, this particular bobbysoxer had written, "The correlation was seventy-five, with a standard error of ten, which is significant. However, I do not think these variables are related." MacCorquodale wrote a large red "FAIL" and added a note: "Dear Miss Fisbee: The correlation coefficient was devised expressly to relieve you of all responsibility for deciding whether these two variables are related."

If you find one of these anecdotes quite funny, and the other one rather stupid (I don't care which), you are probably suffering from a slight case of bias. Although I have not done a factor analysis with these two stories in the matrix, my clinical judgment tells me that a person's spontaneous reactions to them reflect his position in the perennial conflict between the toughminded and the tenderminded, between those for whom the proper prefix to the word "analysis" is "factor" and those for whom it is "psycho," between the groups that Lord Russell once characterized as the "simpleminded" and the "muddleheaded." In a recent book (Meehl, 1954a) I have explored one major facet of this conflict, namely the controversy over the relative merits of clinical and statistical methods of *prediction*. Theoretical considerations, together with introspections concerning my own mental activities as a psychotherapist, led me to conclude that the clinician has certain unique, practically unduplicable powers by virtue of being himself an organism like his client; but that the domain of straight *prediction* would not be a favorable locus for displaying these powers. Survey of a score of empirical investigations in which the actual predictive efficiency of the two methods could be compared gave strong confirmation to this latter theoretical expectation. After reading these studies, it almost looks as if the first rule to follow in trying to predict the subsequent course of a student's or patient's behavior is carefully to avoid talking to him, and that the second rule is to avoid thinking about him!

Statisticians (and rat men) with castrative intent toward clinicians should beware of any temptation to overextend these findings to a generalization that "clinicians don't actually add anything." Apart from the clinician's therapeutic efforts—the power of which is a separate issue and also a matter of current dispute—a glance at a sample of clinical diagnostic documents, such as routine psychological reports submitted in a VA installation, shows that a kind of mixed predictive-descriptive statement predominates which is different from the type of gross prediction considered in the aforementioned survey. (I hesitate to propose a basic distinction here, having learned that proposing a distinction between two classes of concepts is a sure road to infamy.) Nevertheless, I suggest that we distinguish between (a) the clinician's predictions of such gross, outcome-type, "administrative" dimensions as recovery from psychosis, survival in a training program, persistence in therapy, and the like; and (b) a rather more detailed and ambitious enterprise roughly characterizable as "describing the person." It might be thought that a always presupposes b, but a moment's reflection shows this to be false; since there are empirical prediction systems in which the sole property ascribed to the person *is* the disposition to a predicted gross outcome. A very considerable fraction of the typical clinical psychologist's time seems to be spent in giving tests or semitests, the intention being to come out with some kind of characterization of the individual. In part this characterization is "phenotypic," attributing such behavior dispositions as "hostile," "relates poorly," "loss in efficiency," "manifest anxiety," or "depression"; in part it is "genotypic," inferring as the causes of the phenotype certain inner events, states, or structures, e.g., "latent n aggression," "oral-dependent attitudes," or "severe castration anxiety." While the phenotypic-genotypic question is itself deserving of careful methodological analysis, in what follows I shall use the term "personality description" to cover both phenotypic and genotypic inferences, i.e., statements of all degrees of internality or theoreticalness. I shall also assume, while recognizing that at least one group of psychologists has made an impressive case to the contrary, that the description of a person is a worthwhile stage in the total clinical process. Granted, then, that we wish to use tests as a means to securing a description of the person, how shall we go about it? Here we sit, with our Rorschach and Multiphasic results spread out before us. From this mess of data we have to emerge with a characterization of the person from whose behavior these profiles are a highly abstracted, much-reduced distillation. How to proceed?

Some of you are no doubt wondering, "What is the fellow talking about? You look at the profiles, you call to mind what the various test dimensions mean for dynamics, you reflect on other patients you have seen with similar patterns, you think of the research literature; then you combine these considerations to make inferences. Where's the problem?" The problem is *whether or not this is the most efficient way to do it.* We ordinarily do it this way; in fact, the practice is so universal that most clinicians find it shocking, if not somehow sinful, to imagine any other. We feed in the test data and let that rusty digital computer in our heads go to work until a paragraph of personality description emerges. It requires no systematic study, although some quantitative data have begun to appear in the literature (Dailey, 1953; Davenport, 1952; Holsopple and Phelan, 1954; Kostlan, 1954; Little and Shneidman, 1954, 1955), to realize that there is a considerable element of vagueness, hit-or-miss, and personal judgment involved in this approach. Because explicit rules are largely lacking, and hence the clinician's personal experience, skill, and creative artistry play so great a role, I shall refer to this time-honored procedure for generating personality descriptions from tests as the *rule-of-thumb method.*

I wish now to contrast this rule-of-thumb method with what I shall call the *cookbook method.* In the cookbook method, any given configuration (holists please note—I said "configuration," not "sum"!) of psychometric data is associated with each facet (or configuration) of a personality description, and the closeness of this association is explicitly indicated by a number. This number need not be a correlation coefficient—its form will depend upon what is most appropriate to the circumstances. It may be a correlation, or merely an ordinary probability of attribution, or (as in the empirical study I shall report upon later) an average Q-sort placement. Whatever its form, the essential point is that the transition from psychometric pattern to personality description is an automatic, mechanical, "clerical" kind of task, proceeding by the use of explicit rules set forth in the cookbook. I am quite aware that the mere prospect of such a method will horrify some of you; in my weaker moments it horrifies me. All I can say is that many clinicians are also horrified by the cookbook method as applied in the crude prediction situation, whereas the studies reported to date indicate this horror to be quite groundless (Meehl, 1954a, Chapter 8). As Fred Skinner once said, some men are less curious about nature than about the accuracy of their guesses (1938, p. 44). Our responsibility to our patients and to the taxpayer obliges us to decide between the rule-of-thumb and the cookbook methods on the basis of their empirically demonstrated efficiency, rather than upon which one is more exciting, more "dynamic," more like what psychiatrists do, or more harmonious with the clinical psychologist's self-concept.

Let us sneak up the clinician's avoidance gradient gradually to prevent the negative therapeutic reaction. Consider a particular complex attribute, say, "strong dependency with reaction formation." Under what conditions should we take time to give a test of moderate validity as a basis for inferring the presence or absence of this complex attribute? Putting it negatively, it appears to me pretty obvious that there are two circumstances under which we should *not* spend much skilled time on testing even with a moderately valid test, because we stand to lose if we let the test finding influence our judgments. First, when the attribute is found in almost all our patients; and second, when it is found in almost none of our patients. (A third situation, which I shall not consider here, is one in which the attribute makes no practical difference anyhow.) A disturbingly large fraction of the assertions made in routine psychometric reports or uttered by psychologists in staff conferences fall in one of these classes.

It is not difficult to show that when a given personality attribute is almost always or almost never present in a specified clinical population, rather severe demands are made upon the test's validity if it is to contribute in a practical way to our clinical decision making. A few simple manipulations of Bayes' Rule for calculating inverse probability lead to rather surprising, and depressing, results. Let me run through some of these briefly. In what follows,

P = Incidence of a certain personality characteristic in a specified clinical population. ($Q = 1 - P, P > Q$)

p_1 = Proportion of "valid positives," i.e., incidence of positive test finding among cases who actually have the characteristic. ($q_1 = 1 - p_1$)

p_2 = Proportion of "false positives," i.e., incidence of positive test findings among cases who actually lack the characteristic. ($q_2 = 1 - p_2$)

1. When is a positive assertion (attribution of the characteristic) on the basis of a positive test finding more likely to be correct than incorrect?

$$\frac{P}{Q} > \frac{p_2}{p_1}.$$

Example: A test correctly identifies 80 percent of brain-damaged patients at the expense of only 15 percent false positives, in a neuropsychiatric population where one-tenth of all patients are damaged. The decision "brain damage present" on the basis of a positive test finding is more likely to be false than true, since the inequality is unsatisfied.

2. When does the use of a test improve over-all decision making?

$$P < \frac{q_2}{q_1 + q_2}.$$

If $P < Q$ this has the form

$$Q < \frac{p_1}{p_1 + p_2}.$$

Example: A test sign identifies 85 percent of "psychotics" at the expense of only 15 percent of false positives among the "nonpsychotic." It is desired to make a decision on each case, and both kinds of errors are serious.[1] Only 10 percent of the population seen in the given setting are psychotic. Hence, the use of the test yields more erroneous classifications than would proceeding without the test.

3. When does improving a sign, strengthening a scale, or shifting a cut improve decision making?

$$\frac{\Delta p_1}{\Delta p_2} > \frac{Q}{P}.$$

Example: We improve the intrinsic validity of a "schizophrenic index" so that it now detects 20 percent more schizophrenics than it formerly did, at the expense of only a 5 percent rise in the false positive rate. This surely looks encouraging. However, we work with an outpatient clientele only one-tenth of whom are actually schizophrenic. Since these values violate the inequality, "improvement" of the index will result in an increase in the proportion of erroneous diagnoses. N.B.—*Sampling errors are not involved in the above.* The values are assumed to be parameter values, and the test sign is valid (i.e., $p_1 > p_2$ in the population).

Further inequalities and a more detailed drawing out of their pragmatic implications can be found in a recent paper by Albert Rosen and myself (1955—reprinted here as Chapter 2). The moral to be drawn

---

[1] Inequalities 2 and 3 are conditions for improvement if there is no reason to see one kind of error as worse than the other. In trait attribution this is usually true; in prognostic and diagnostic decisions it may or may not be. If one is willing to say how many errors of one kind he is prepared to tolerate in order to avoid one of the other kind, these inequalities can be readily corrected by inserting this ratio. A more general development can be found in a paper by Ward Edwards (1954), which came to my attention only after I had written this essay.

from these considerations, which even we clinicians can follow because they involve only high school algebra, is that a great deal of skilled psychological effort is probably being wasted in going through complex, skill-demanding, time-consuming test procedures of moderate or low validity, in order to arrive at conclusions about the patient which could often be made with high confidence without the test, and which in other cases ought not to be made (because they still tend to be wrong) even with the test indications positive. Probably most surprising is the finding that there are certain quantitative relations between the base rates and test-validity parameters such that the use of a "valid" test will produce a net rise in the frequency of clinical mistakes. The first task of a good clinical cookbook would be to make explicit quantitative use of the inverse probability formulas in constructing efficient "rules of attribution" when test data are to be used in describing the personalities of patients found in various clinical populations. For example, I know of an outpatient clinic which has treated, by a variety of psychotherapies, in the course of the past eight years, approximately 5000 patients, not one of whom has committed suicide. If the clinical psychologists in this clinic have been spending much of their time scoring suicide keys on the Multiphasic or counting suicide indicators in Rorschach content, either these test indicators are close to infallible (which is absurd), or else the base rate is so close to zero that the expenditure of skilled time is of doubtful value. Suicide is an extreme case, of course (Rosen, 1954); but the point so dramatically reflected there is valid, with suitable quantitative modifications, over a wider range of base rates. To take some examples from the high end of the base-rate continuum, it is not very illuminating to say of a known psychiatric patient that he has difficulty in accepting his drives, experiences some trouble in relating emotionally to others, and may have problems with his sexuality! Many psychometric reports bear a disconcerting resemblance to what my colleague Donald G. Paterson calls "personality description after the manner of P. T. Barnum" (in Blum and Balinsky, 1951, p. 47; Dunnette, 1957, p. 223). I suggest—and I am quite serious—that we adopt the phrase *Barnum effect* to stigmatize those pseudo-successful clinical procedures in which personality descriptions from tests are made to fit the patient largely or wholly by virtue of their triviality; and in which any nontrivial, but perhaps erroneous, inferences are hidden in a context of assertions or denials which carry high confidence simply because of the population base rates, regardless of the test's validity. I think this fallacy is at least as important and frequent as others for which we have familiar labels (halo effect, leniency error, contamination, etc.). One of the best ways to increase the general sensitivity to such fallacies is to give them a name. We ought to make our clinical students as acutely aware of the Barnum effect as they are of the dangers of countertransference or the standard error of r.

The preceding mathematical considerations, while they should serve as a check upon some widespread contemporary forms of tea-leaf reading, are unfortunately not very "positive" by way of writing a good cookbook. "Almost anything needs a little salt for flavor" or "It is rarely appropriate to put ketchup on the dessert" would be sound advice but largely negative and not very helpful to an average cook. I wish now to describe briefly a piece of empirical research, reported in a thesis just completed at Minnesota by Charles C. Halbower (1955), which takes the cookbook method 100 percent seriously; and which seems to show, at least in one clinical context, what can be done in a more constructive way by means of a cookbook of even moderate trustworthiness.[2] By some geographical coincidence, the psychometric device used in this research was a structured test consisting of a set of 550 items, commonly known as the MMPI. Let me emphasize that the MMPI is not here being compared with anything else, and that the research does not aim to investigate Multiphasic validity (although the general order of magnitude of the obtained correlations does give some incidental information in that respect). What Dr. Halbower asked was this: given a Multiphasic profile, how does one arrive at a personality description from it? Using the rule-of-thumb method, a clinician familiar with MMPI interpretation looks at the profile, thinks awhile, and proceeds to describe the patient he imagines would have produced such a pattern. Using the cookbook method, we don't need a clinician; instead, a $230-per-month clerk-typist in the outer office simply reads the numbers on the profile, enters the cookbook, locates the page on which is found some kind of "modal description" for patients with such a profile, and this description is then taken as the best available approximation to the patient. We know, of course, that every patient is unique—absolutely, unqualifiedly unique.

[2] I am indebted to Dr. Halbower for permission to present this summary of his thesis data in advance of his own more complete publication [1973 addendum: he did not subsequently publish his data].

Therefore, the application of a cookbook description will inevitably make errors, some of them perhaps serious ones. If we knew *which* facets of the cookbook sketch needed modification as applied to the present unique patient, we would, of course, depart from the cookbook at these points; but we don't know this. It we start monkeying with the cookbook recipe in the hope of avoiding or reducing these errors, we will in all likelihood improve on the cookbook in some respects but, unfortunately, will worsen our approximation in others. Given a finite body of information, such as the thirteen two-digit numbers of a Multiphasic profile, there is obviously *in fact* (whether we have yet succeeded in *finding* it or not) a "most probable" value for any personality facet, and also for any configuration of facets, however complex or "patterned" (Meehl, 1954a, pp. 131–134). It is easy to prove that a method of characterization which departs from consistent adherence to this "best guess" stands to lose. Keep in mind, then, that the raw data from which a personality description was to be inferred consisted of an MMPI profile. In other words, the Halbower study was essentially a comparison of the rule-of-thumb versus the cookbook method where each method was, however, functioning upon the same information—an MMPI. We are in effect contrasting the validity of two methods of "reading" Multiphasics.

In order to standardize the domain to be covered, and to yield a reasonably sensitive quantification of the goodness of description, Dr. Halbower utilized Q sorts. From a variety of sources he constructed a Q pool of 154 items, the majority being phenotypic or intermediate and a minority being genotypic. Since these items were intended for clinically expert sorters employing an "external" frame of reference, many of them were in technical language. Some sample items from his pool are "reacts against his dependency needs with hostility"; "manifests reality distortions"; "takes a dominant, ascendant role in interactions with others"; "is rebellious toward authority figures, rules, and other constraints"; "is counteractive in the face of frustration"; "gets appreciable secondary gain from his symptoms"; "is experiencing pain"; "is naive"; "is impunitive"; "utilizes intellectualization as a defense mechanism"; "shows evidence of latent hostility"; "manifests inappropriate affect." The first step was to construct a cookbook based upon these 154 items as the ingredients; the recipes were to be in the form of directions for the optimal Q-sort placement of each item.

How many distinguishable recipes will the cookbook contain? If we had infallible criterion Q sorts on millions of cases, there would be as many recipes as there are possible MMPI profiles. Since we don't have this ideal situation, and never will, we have to compromise by introducing coarser grouping. Fortunately, we know that the validity of our test is poor enough so that this coarseness will not result in the sacrifice of much, if any, information. How coarsely we group, i.e., how different two Multiphasic curves have to be before we refuse to call them "similar" enough to be coordinated with the same recipe, is a very complicated matter involving both theoretical and practical considerations. Operating within the limits of a doctoral dissertation, Halbower confined his study to four profile "types." These curve types were specified by the first two digits of the Hathaway code plus certain additional requirements based upon clinical experience. The four MMPI codes used were those beginning 123', 13', 27', and 87' (Hathaway, 1947). The first three of these codes are the most frequently occurring in the Minneapolis VA Mental Hygiene Clinic population, and the fourth code, which is actually fifth in frequency of occurrence, was chosen in order to have a quasi-psychotic type in the study. It is worth noting that these four codes constitute 58 percent of all MMPI curves seen in the given population; so that Halbower's gross recipe categories already cover the majority of such outpatients. The nature of the further stipulations, refining the curve criteria within each two-digit code class, is illustrated by the following specifications for code 13', the "hysteroid valley" or "conversion V" type:

1. H_s and $H_y \geqq 70$.
2. $D < (H_s$ and $H_y)$ by at least one sigma.
3. K or L $> $? and F.
4. $F \leqq 65$.
5. Scales 4, 5, 6, 7, 8, 9, 0 all $\leqq 70$.

For each of these MMPI curve types, the names of nine patients were then randomly chosen from the list of those meeting the curve specifications. If the patient was still in therapy, his therapist was asked to do a Q sort (eleven steps, normal distribution) on him. The MMPI had been withheld from these therapists. If the patient had been terminated, a clinician (other than Halbower) did a Q sort based upon study of the case folder, including therapist's notes and any available psychometrics (except, of course, the Multiphasic). This yields Q sorts for nine patients of a given curve type. These nine sorts were then pair-wise inter-correlated, and by inspection of the resulting 36 coefficients, a subset of five patients was chosen as most representative of the curve type. The Q sorts on these five "representative" patients were then averaged, and this average Q sort was taken as the cookbook recipe to be used in describing future cases having the given MMPI curve. Thus, this modal, crystallized, "distilled-essence" personality description was obtained by eliminating patients with atypical sortings and pooling sortings on the more typical, hoping to reduce errors both of patient sampling and of clinical judgment. This rather complicated sequence of procedures may be summarized thus:

Deriving cookbook recipe for a specified curve type, such as the "conversion V" above:

1. Sample of N = nine patients currently or recently in therapy and meeting the MMPI specifications for conversion V curve.

2. 154-item Q sort done on each patient by therapist or from therapist notes and case folder. (These sorts MMPI-uncontaminated.)

3. Pairwise Q correlations of these nine patients yields 36 intercorrelations.

4. Selection of subset N' = five "modal" patients from this matrix by inspectional cluster method.

5. Mean of Q sorts on these five "core" patients is the cookbook recipe for the MMPI curve type in question.

Having constructed one recipe, he started all over again with a random sample of nine patients whose Multiphasics met the second curve-type specifications, and carried out these cluster-and-pooling processes upon them. This was done for each of the four curve types which were to compose the cookbook. If you have reservations about any of the steps in constructing this miniature cookbook, let me remind you that this is all preliminary, i.e., *it is the means of arriving at the cookbook recipe*. The proof of the pudding will be in the eating, and any poor choices of tactics or patients up to this point should merely make the cookbook less trustworthy than it would otherwise be.

Having thus written a miniature cookbook consisting of only four recipes, Halbower then proceeded to cook some dishes to see how they would taste. For cross-validation he chose at random four new Mental Hygiene Clinic patients who met the four curve specifications and who had been seen in therapy for a minimum of ten hours. With an eye to validity generalization to a somewhat different clinical population, with different base rates, he also chose four patients who were being seen as inpatients at the Minneapolis VA Hospital. None of the therapists involved had knowledge of the patients' Multiphasics. For purposes of his study, Halbower took the therapist's Q sort, based upon all of the case folder data (minus the MMPI) plus his therapeutic contacts, as the best available criterion, although this "criterion" is acceptable only in the sense of construct validity (Cronbach and Meehl, 1955—reprinted here as Chapter 1). An estimate of its absolute level of trustworthiness is not important since it is being used as the common reference basis for a comparison of two methods of test reading.

Given the eight criterion therapist Q sorts (two patients for each MMPI curve type), the task of the cookbook is to predict these descriptions. Thus, for each of the two patients having MMPI code 123', we simply assign the Q-sort recipe found in the cookbook as the best available description. How accurate this description is can be estimated (in the sense of construct validity) by Q correlating it with the criterion therapist's description. These eight "validity" coefficients varied from .36 to .88 with a median of .69. As would be expected, the hospital inpatients yielded the lower correlations. The Mental Hygiene Clinic cases, for whom the cookbook was really intended, gave validities of .68, .69, .84, and .88 (see Table 1).

How does the rule-of-thumb method show up in competition with the cookbook? Here we run into the problem of differences in clinical skill, so Halbower had each MMPI profile read blind by more than one clinician. The task was to interpret the profile by doing a Q sort. From two to five clinicians thus "read" each of the eight individual profiles, and the resulting twenty-five sorts were Q correlated with the appropriate therapist criterion sorts. These validity coefficients run from .29 to .63 with a median of .46. The clinicians were all Minnesota trained and varied in their experience with the MMPI from less than a year (first-year VA trainees) through all training levels to Ph.D. staff psychologists with six years' experience. The more experienced clinicians had probably seen over two thousand MMPI profiles in relation to varying amounts of other clinical data, including intensive psychotherapy. Yet not one of the twenty-five rule-of-thumb readings was as valid as the cookbook reading. Of the twenty-five comparisons which can be made between the validity of a single clinician's rule-of-thumb reading and that of the

Table 1. Validation of the Four Cookbook Descriptions on New Cases
and Comparative Validities of the Cookbook Readings and Rule-
of-Thumb Readings by Clinicians*

	MMPI Curve Type				Mean of Curve Types (through z_r)
Validities	Code 123'	Code 27'	Code 13'	Code 87'	
	Outpatient Sample†				
Cookbook...........	.88	.69	.84	.68	.78
Rule-of-thumb (4–5 readers)					
Mean.............	.75	.50	.50	.58	.48‡
Range............55–.63		.29–.54	.37–.52	.34–.58	
	Inpatient Sample§				
Cookbook...........	.63	.64	.36	.70	.60
Rule-of-thumb					
First reader........	.37	.29	.30	.50	
Second reader......	.49	.42	.30	.50	
Both readers.......					.41

* (1) Four patients currently in therapy (the outpatient sample) were Q described by the therapist (ten hours or more of therapy plus case folder minus MMPI). This is taken as the best available criterion description of each patient. (2) The MMPI cookbook recipe was Q correlated with this criterion description. (3) For each patient, four or five clinicians "read" his MMPI in the usual rule-of thumb way, doing Q sorts. (4) These rule-of-thumb Q sorts were also Q correlated with the criterion description. (5) The validity generalization was extended to patients in a psychiatric hospital (inpatient sample) with different base rates; hence an "unfair" test of the cookbook.

† The cookbook's superiority in validly predicted variance for the outpatient sample = 38 percent.

‡ Total of seventeen rule-of-thumb validations.

§ The cookbook's superiority in validly predicted variance for the inpatient sample = 19 percent.

corresponding cookbook reading of the same patient's profile, eighteen are significant in favor of the cookbook at the .01 level of confidence and four at the .05 level. The remaining three are also in favor of the cookbook but not significantly so.

Confining our attention to the more appropriate outpatient population, for (and upon) which the cookbook was developed, the mean r (estimated through z transformation) is .78 for the cookbook method, as contrasted with a mean (for seventeen rule-of-thumb descriptions) of only .48, a difference of 30 points of correlation, which in this region amounts to a difference of 38 percent in the validly predicted variance! The cookbook seems to be superior to the rule-of-thumb not merely in the sense of statistical significance but by an amount which is of very practical importance. It is also remarkable that even when the cookbook recipes are applied to patients from a quite different kind of population, their validity still excels that of rule-of-thumb MMPI readers who are in daily clinical contact with that other population. The improvement in valid variance in the hospital sample averages 19 percent (see item 6 in Table 1).

A shrewd critic may be thinking, "Perhaps this is because all kinds of psychiatric patients are more or less alike, and the cookbook has simply taken advantage of this rather trivial fact." In answer to this objection, let me say first that to the extent the cookbook's superiority did arise from its actuarially determined tendency to "follow the base rates," that would be a perfectly sound application of the inverse probability considerations I at first advanced. For example, most psychiatric patients are in some degree depressed. Let us suppose the mean Q-sort placement given by therapists to the item "depressed" is seven. "Hysteroid" patients, who characteristically exhibit the so-called "conversion V" on their MMPI profiles (Halbower's cookbook code 13), are less depressed than most neurotics. The clinician, seeing such a conversion valley on the Multiphasic, takes this relation into account by attributing "lack of depression" to the patient. But maybe he overinterprets, giving undue weight to the psychometric finding and understressing the base rate. So his rule-of-thumb placement is far down at the nondepressed end, say at position three. The cookbook, on the other hand, "knows" (actuarially) that the mean Q placement for the item "depressed" is at five in patients with such profiles—lower than the over-all mean seven but not displaced as much in the conversion subgroup as the clinician thinks. If patients are so homogeneous with respect to a certain characteristic that the psychometrics ought not to influence greatly our attribution or placement in defiance of the over-all actuarial trend, then the clinician's tendency to be unduly influenced is a source of erroneous clinical decisions and a valid argument in favor of the cookbook.

However, if this were the chief explanation of Halbower's findings, the obvious conclusion would be merely that the MMPI was not differentiating, since any test-induced departure from a description of the "average patient" would tend to be more wrong than right. Our original question would then be rephrased, "What is the comparative efficiency of the cookbook and the rule-of-thumb method *when each is applied to psychometric information having some degree of intrinsic validity?*"

76

Time permits me only brief mention of the several lines of evidence in Halbower's study which eliminate the Barnum effect as an explanation. First of all, Halbower had selected his 154 items from a much larger initial Q pool by a preliminary study of therapist sortings on a heterogeneous sample of patients in which items were eliminated if they showed low interpatient dispersal. Second, study of the placements given an item over the four cookbook recipes reveals little similarity (e.g., only two items recur in the top quartile of all four recipes; 60 percent of the items occur in the top quartile of only one recipe). Third, several additional correlational findings combine to show that the cookbook was not succeeding merely by describing an "average patient" four times over. For example, the clinicians' Q description of their conception of the "average patient" gave very low validity for three of the four codes, and a "mean average patient" description constructed by pooling these clinicians' stereotypes was not much better (see Table 2). For Code

Table 2. Validities of Four Clinicians' Description of "Average Patient," of the Mean of These Stereotypes, and of the Cookbook Recipe (Outpatient Cases Only)

MMPI Curve Type	Validities of "Average Patient" Descriptions by Four Clinicians	Validity of Mean of These Four "Average Patient" Stereotypes	Validity of Cookbook Recipe
Code 123′.............	.63–.69	.74	.88
Code 27′..............	−.03–.20	.09	.69
Code 13′..............	.25–.37	.32	.84
Code 87′..............	.25–.35	.31	.68

123′ (interestingly enough, the commonest code among therapy cases in this clinic) the pooled stereotype was actually more valid than rule-of-thumb Multiphasic readings. (This is Bayes' Theorem with a vengeance!) Nevertheless, I am happy to report that this "average patient" description was still inferior to the Multiphasic cookbook (significant at the .001 level).

Let me ruminate about the implications of this study, supposing it should prove to be essentially generalizable to other populations and to other psychometric instruments. From a theoretical point of view, the trend is hardly surprising. It amounts to the obvious fact that the human brain is an inefficient recording and computing device. The cookbook method has an advantage over the rule-of-thumb method because it (a) samples more representatively, (b) records and stores information better, and (c) computes statistical weights which are closer to the optimal. We can perhaps learn more by putting the theoretical question negatively: when should we *expect* the cookbook to be inferior to the brain? The answer to this question presumably lies in the highly technical field of computing machine theory, which I am not competent to discuss. As I understand it, the use of these machines requires that certain rules of data combination be fed initially into the machine, followed by the insertion of suitably selected and coded information. Putting it crudely, the machine can "remember" and can "think routinely," but it cannot "spontaneously notice what is relevant" nor can it "think" in the more high-powered, creative sense (e.g., it cannot invent theories). To be sure, noticing what is relevant must involve the exemplification of some rule, perhaps of a very complex form. But it is a truism of behavior science that organisms can *exemplify* rules without *formulating* them. To take a noncontroversial example outside the clinical field, no one today knows how to state fully the rules of "similarity" or "stimulus equivalence" for patterned visual perception or verbal generalization; but of course we all exemplify daily these undiscovered rules. This suggests that as long as psychology cannot give a complete, explicit, quantitative account of the "dimensions of relevance" in behavior connections, the cookbook will not completely duplicate the clinician (Meehl, 1954b). The clinician *here* acts as an inefficient computer, but that is better than a computer with certain major rules completely left out (because we can't build them in until we have learned how to formulate them). The use of the therapist's own unconscious in perceiving verbal and imaginal relations during dream interpretation is, I think, the clearest example of this. But I believe the exemplification of currently unformulable rules is a widespread phenomenon in most clinical inference. However, you will note that these considerations apply chiefly (if not wholly) to matters of *content,* in which a rich, highly varied, hard-to-classify content (such as free associations) is the input information. The problem of "stimulus equivalence" or "noticing the relevant" does not arise when the input data are in the form of preclassified responses, such as a Multiphasic profile or a Rorschach psychogram. I have elsewhere (1954a, pp. 110–111) suggested that even in the case of such prequantified patterns there arises the possibility of causal-theory-mediated idiographic extrapolations into regions of the profile space in which we lack adequate statistical experience; but I am now inclined to view that suggestion as a mistake. The underlying theory must itself involve some hypothesized function, however crudely quantified; otherwise, how is the alleged "extrapolation" possible? I can think of no reason why the estimation of the parameters in this underlying theoretical function should constitute an exception to the cookbook's superiority. If I am right in this, my "extrapolation" argument applies strictly only when a clinician literally *invents new theoretical relations or variables* in thinking about the individual patient. In spite of some clinicians' claims along this line, I must say I think it very rarely happens in daily clinical practice. Furthermore, even when it does happen, Bayes' Rule still applies. The *joint* probability of the theory's correctness, and of the attribute's presence (granting the theory but remembering nuisance variables) must be high enough to satisfy the inequalities I have presented; otherwise use of the theory will not pay off.

What are the pragmatic implications of the preceding analysis? Putting it bluntly, it suggests that for a rather wide range of clinical problems involving personality description from tests, the clinical interpreter is a costly middleman who might better be eliminated. An initial layout of research time could result in a cookbook whose recipes would encompass the great majority of psychometric configurations seen in daily work. I am fully aware that the prospect of a "clinical clerk" simply looking up Rorschach pattern number 73 J 10-5 or Multiphasic curve "Halbower Verzeichnis 626" seems very odd and even dangerous. I reassure myself by recalling that the number of phenotypic and genotypic attributes is, after all, finite; and that the number which are ordinarily found attributed or denied even in an extensive sample of psychological reports on patients is actually very limited. A best estimate of a Q-sort placement is surely more informative than a crude "Yes-or-No" decision of low objective confidence. I honestly cannot see, in the case of a *determinate trait domain* and a *specified clinical population,* that there is a serious intellectual problem underlying one's uneasiness. I invite you to consider the possibility that the emotional block we all experience in connection with the cookbook approach could be dissolved simply by trying it out until our daily successes finally get us accustomed to the idea.

Admittedly this would take some of the "fun" out of psychodiagnostic activity. But I suspect that most of the clinicians who put a high value on this kind of fun would have even more fun doing intensive psychotherapy. The great personnel needs today, and for the next generation or more, are for psychotherapists and researchers. (If you don't believe much in the efficacy of therapy, this is the more reason for research.) If all the thousands of clinical hours currently being expended in concocting clever and flowery personality sketches from test data could be devoted instead to scientific investigation (assuming we are still selecting and training clinicians to be scientists), it would probably mean a marked improvement in our net social contribution. If a reasonably good cookbook could help bring about this result, the achievement would repay tenfold the expensive and tedious effort required in its construction.

4

When Shall We
Use Our Heads instead
of the Formula?

MY TITLE QUESTION, "When shall we use our heads instead of the formula?" is not rhetorical. I am sincerely asking what I see as an important question. I find the two extreme answers to this question, namely, "Always" and "Never," equally unacceptable. But to formulate a satisfactory answer upon the present evidence seems extraordinarily difficult.

I put the question in the practical clinical context. This is where Sarbin (1942) put it in his pioneering study fourteen years ago, and this is where it belongs. Some critics of my book (1954a) have repudiated the whole question by saying that, always and necessarily, we use *both* our heads and the formula. No, we do not. In research, we use both; the best clinical research involves a shuttling back and forth between clever, creative speculation and subsequent statistical testing of empirical derivations therefrom. So far as I am aware, nobody has ever denied this. Even the arch-actuary George Lundberg approved of the clinician as hypothesis maker. In research one cannot design experiments or con-

AUTHOR'S NOTE: This paper was presented at the 1956 convention of the American Psychological Association, Chicago. It first appeared in *Journal of Counseling Psychology*, vol. 4, 1957; copyright 1957 by the American Psychological Association, Inc.

coct theories without using his head, and he cannot test them rigorously without using a formula. This is so obvious that I am surprised to find that people will waste time in discussing it. The clinical-statistical issue can hardly be stated so as to make sense in the research context, and I should have thought it clear that a meaningful issue can be raised only in the context of daily clinical activity.

In the clinical context, on the other hand, the question is sensible and of great practical importance. Here we have the working clinician or administrator, faced with the necessity to make a decision at *this* moment in time, regarding *this* particular patient. He knows that his evidence is inadequate. He can think of several research projects which, *had* they been done already, would be helpful to him in deciding the present case. If he is research-oriented he may even make a note of these research ideas and later carry them out or persuade someone else to do so. But none of that helps him *now*. He is in a sort of Kierkegaardian existential predicament, because he has to act. As Joe Zubin kept repeating when I last tangled with him on this subject, "Every clinical decision is a *Willensakt*." And so it is; but the question remains, how do we make our *Willensakts* as rational as possible upon limited information? *What clinician X knows today* and *what he could find out by research in ten years* are two very different things.

The question "When shall we use our heads instead of the formula?" presupposes that we are about to make a clinical decision at a given point in time, and must base it upon what is known to us at that moment. In that context, the question makes perfectly good sense. It is silly to answer it by saying amicably, "We use both methods, they go hand in hand." If the formula and your head invariably yield the same predictions about individuals, you should quit using the more costly one because it is not adding anything. If they don't always yield the same prediction—and they clearly don't, as a matter of empirical fact—then you obviously can't "use both," because you cannot predict in opposite ways for the same case. If one says then, "Well, by 'using both,' I mean that we follow the formula except on special occasions," the problem becomes how to identify the proper subset of occasions. And this of course amounts to the very question I am putting. For example, does the formula tell us "Here, use your heads," or do we rely on our heads to tell us this, thus countermanding the formula?

The Pragmatic Decision Problem Stated

Most decisions in current practice do not pose this problem because no formula exists. Sometimes there is no formula because the prediction problem is too open-ended, as in dream analysis; sometimes the very categorizing of the raw observations involves gestalted stimulus equivalences for which the laws are unknown, and hence cannot be mathematically formulated (although the clinician himself exemplifies these laws and can therefore "utilize" them); in still other cases there is no formula because nobody has bothered to make one. In any of these three circumstances, we use our heads because there isn't anything else to use. This presumably will be true of many special prediction situations for years to come. The logical analysis of the first two situations—open-endedness and unknown psychological laws—is a fascinating subject in its own right, especially in relation to psychotherapy. But since our original question implies that a formula does exist, we will say no more about that subject here.

Suppose then that we have a prediction equation (or an actuarial table) which has been satisfactorily cross-validated. Let us say that it predicts with some accuracy which patients will respond well to intensive outpatient therapy in our VA clinic. We are forced to make such predictions because our staff-patient ratio physically precludes offering intensive treatment to all cases; also we know that a minority, such as certain latent schizophrenias, react adversely and even dangerously. The equation uses both psychometric and nonpsychometric data. It may include what the Cornell workers called "Stop" items—items given such a huge weight that when present they override any combination of the remaining factors. It may be highly patterned, taking account of verified interaction effects.

So here is veteran Jones, whose case is under consideration at therapy staff. The equation takes such facts as his Rorschach F+, his Multiphasic code, his divorce, his age, his 40 percent service connection, and grinds out a probability of .75 of "good response to therapy." (The logicians and theoretical statisticians are still arguing over the precise meaning of this number as applied to Jones. But we are safe in saying, "If you accept patients from this population who have this score, you will be right three times in four.") Here is Jones. We want to do what is best for him. We don't *know for sure,* and we can't, by any method,

83

actuarial or otherwise. We act on the probabilities, as everyone does who chooses a career, takes a wife, bets on a horse, or brings a lawsuit. (If you object, as some of the more cloud-headed clinikers do, to acting on "mere probabilities," you will have to shut up shop, because probabilities are all you'll ever get.)

But now the social worker tells us that Jones, age forty, said at intake that his mother sent him in. The psychology trainee describes blocking and a bad F— on Rorschach VII; the psychiatrist adds his comments, and pretty soon we are concluding that Jones has a very severe problem with mother figures. Since our only available therapist is Frau Dr. Schleswig-Holstein, who would traumatize anybody even without a mother problem, we begin to vacillate. The formula gives us odds of 3 to 1 on Jones; these further facts, not in the equation, raise doubts in our minds. What shall we do?

Importance of "Special Cases"

In my little book on this subject, I gave an example which makes it too easy (1954a, p. 24). If a sociologist were predicting whether Professor X would go to the movies on a certain night, he might have an equation involving age, academic specialty, and introversion score. The equation might yield a probability of .90 that Professor X will go to the movie tonight. But if the family doctor announced that Professor X had just broken his leg, no sensible sociologist would stick with the equation. Why didn't the factor of "broken leg" appear in the formula? Because broken legs are very rare, and in the sociologist's entire sample of 500 criterion cases plus 250 cross-validating cases, he did not come upon a single instance of it. He uses the broken leg datum confidently, because "broken leg" is a subclass of a larger class we may crudely denote as "relatively immobilizing illness or injury," and movie attending is a subclass of a larger class of "actions requiring moderate mobility." There is a universally recognized "subjective experience table" which cuts across sociological and theatrical categories, and the probabilities are so close to zero that not even a sociologist feels an urge to tabulate them! (That this is the correct analysis of matters can be easily seen if we ask what our sociologist would do if he were in a strange culture and had seen *even a few* legs in casts at the movies?)

I suppose only the most anal of actuaries would be reluctant to aban-

don the equation in the broken leg case on the ground that we were unable to cite actual statistical support for the generalization "People with
broken legs don't attend movies." But clinicians should beware of over-
doing the broken leg analogy. There are at least four aspects of the
broken leg case which are very different from the usual "psychodynamic" reversal of an actuarial prediction. First, a broken leg is a
pretty objective fact, determinable with high accuracy, if you care to
take the trouble; second, its correlation with relative immobilization is
near perfect, based on a huge N, and attested by all sane men regardless of race, creed, color, or what school granted them the doctorate;
third, interaction effects are conspicuously lacking—the immobilization
phenomenon cuts neatly across the other categories under study; fourth,
the prediction is mediated without use of any doubtful theory, being
either purely taxonomic or based upon such low-level theory as can be
provided by skeletal mechanics and common sense. The same cannot be
said of such an inference as "Patient Jones has an unconscious problem
with mother figures, and male patients with such problems will not react
well in intensive therapy with Frau Dr. Schleswig-Holstein."

Theoretical Derivation of Novel Patterns

When the physicists exploded the first atomic bomb, they had predicted
a novel occurrence by theoretical methods. No actuarial table, based
upon thousands of combinations of chemicals, would have led to this
prediction. But these kinds of theoretical derivations in the developed
sciences involve combining rigorously formulated theories with exact
knowledge of the state of the particular system, neither of which we
have in clinical psychology. Yet we must do justice to the basic *logical*
claim of our clinician. I want to stress that he is not in the untenable
position of denying the actuarial data. He freely admits that 75 percent
of patients having Jones' formula score are good bets for therapy. But
he says that Jones belongs to the other 25 percent, and therefore thinks
we can avoid one of our formula's mispredictions by countermanding
the formula in this case. There is nothing intrinsically wrong with this
suggestion. Perhaps the clinician *can* identify a subclass of patients
within the class having Jones' actuarial attributes for which the success
rate is less than .5. This would be perfectly compatible with the over-all
actuarial data, provided the clinician doesn't claim it too often.

At this point the actuary, a straightforward fellow, proposes that we tabulate the new signs mentioned in staff conference as indicating this subclass before proceeding further. Here we again reduce our clinician to a hypothesis suggestor, and seem to put the current prediction problem back on an actuarial basis. But wait. Are we really prepared to detail someone to do such "case-oriented" research every time a clinical prediction is made? Actually it is impossible. It would require a super-file of punch cards of colossal N to be available in each clinic, and several major staff doing nothing but running case-oriented minor studies while clinical conferences went into recess pending the outcomes.

However, this is a "practical" objection. Suppose we circumvent it somehow, so that when a sign or pattern is used clinically to support a counteractuarial prediction, we can proceed immediately to subject the sign to actuarial test on our clinic files. There are serious difficulties even so. Unless the several staff who produced these records had in mind all of the signs that anybody subsequently brings up, we have no assurance that they were looked for or noted. Anyone who has done file research knows the frustration of having no basis for deciding when the lack of mention of a symptom indicates its absence. But even ignoring this factor, what if we find only three cases in the files who show the pattern? *Any split* among these three cases as to therapy outcome is statistically compatible with a wide range of parameter values. We can neither confirm nor refute, at any respectable confidence level, our clinician's claim that this pattern brings the success probability from .75 to some value under .5 (he doesn't say how far under).

Here the statistician throws up his hands in despair. What, he asks, can you do with a clinician who wants to countermand a known probability of .75 by claiming a subclass probability which we cannot estimate reliably? And, of course, one wonders how many thousands of patients the clinician has seen, to have accumulated a larger sample of the rare configuration. He also is subject to sampling errors, isn't he?

Nonfrequentist Probability and Rational Action

This brings us to the crux of the matter. Does the clinician need to have seen *any* cases of "mother-sent-me-in" and Card VII blockage who were treated by female therapists? Here we run into a philosophical issue about the nature of probability. Many logicians (including notably Car-

86

nap, Kneale, Sellars, and most of the British school) reject the view (widely held among applied statisticians) that *probability* is always *frequency*. Carnap speaks of "inductive probability," by which he means the logical support given to a hypothesis by evidence. We use this kind of probability constantly, both in science and in daily life. No one knows how to compute it exactly, except for very simple worlds described by artificial languages. Even so, we cannot get along without it. So our clinician believes that he has inductive evidence from many different sources, on different populations, partly actuarial, partly experimental, partly anecdotal, that there is such a psychological structure as a "mother-surrogate problem." He adduces indirect evidence for the construct validity (see Cronbach and Meehl, 1955—reprinted here as Chapter 1) of Rorschach Card VII reactions. I am not here considering the actual scientific merits of such claims in the clinical field, on which dispute still continues. But I think it important for us to understand the methodological character of the clinician's rebuttal. If Carnap and some of his fellow-logicians are right, the idea that *relative frequency* and *probability* are synonymous is a philosophical mistake.

Of course there is an implicit future reference to frequency even in this kind of inductive argument. Carnap identifies inductive probability with the betting odds which a reasonable man should accept. I take this to mean that if the clinician decided repeatedly on the basis of what he thought were high inductive probabilities, and we found him to be wrong most of the time, then he was presumably making erroneous estimates of his inductive probabilities. The claim of a high inductive probability implies an expectation of being right; in the long run, he who (correctly) bets odds of 7 to 3 will be able to point to a hit rate of 70 percent. But this *future* reference to success frequency is not the same as the *present evidence for* a hypothesis. This seems a difficult point for people to see. As a member of a jury, you might be willing to bet 9 to 1 odds on the prisoner's guilt, and this might be rational of you; yet no calculation of frequencies constituted your inductive support in the present instance. The class of hypotheses where you have assigned an inductive probability of .9 should "pan out" 90 percent of the time. But the assignment of that inductive probability to each hypothesis need not itself have been done by frequency methods. If we run a long series on Sherlock Holmes, and find that 95 percent of his "reconstructions" of crimes turn out to be valid, our confidence in his guesses is good *in part just because they are his.* Yet do we wish to maintain that a rational man, ignorant of these statistics, could form no "probable opinion" about a *particular* Holmesian hypothesis based on the evidence available? I cannot think anyone wants to maintain this.

The philosophical recognition of a nonfrequency inductive probability does not help much to solve our practical problem. No one has quantified this kind of probability (which is one reason why Fisher rejected it as useless for scientific purposes). Many logicians doubt that it can be quantified, even in principle. What then are we to say? The clinician thinks he has "high" (how high? who knows?) inductive support for his particular theory about Jones. He thinks it is so high that we are rationally justified in assigning Jones to the 25 percent class permitted by the formula. The actuary doubts this, and the data do not allow a sufficiently sensitive statistical test. Whom do we follow?

Monitoring the Clinician

Well, the actuary is not quite done yet. He has been surreptitiously spying upon the clinician for, lo, these many years. The mean old scoundrel has kept a record of the clinician's predictions. What does he find, when he treats the clinician as an empty decision maker, ignoring the inductive logic going on inside him? Let me bring you up to date on the empirical evidence. As of today, there are twenty-seven empirical studies in the literature which make some meaningful comparison between the predictive success of the clinician and that of the statistician. The predictive domains include success in academic or military training, recidivism and parole violation, recovery from psychosis, (concurrent) personality description, and outcome of psychotherapy. Of these twenty-seven studies, seventeen show a definite superiority for the statistical method; ten show the methods to be of about equal efficiency; none of them show the clinician predicting better. I have reservations about some of these studies; I do not believe they are optimally designed to exhibit the clinician at his best; but I submit that it is high time that those who are so sure that the "right kind of study" will exhibit the clinician's prowess, should *do* this right kind of study and back up their claim with evidence. Furthermore, *a good deal of routine clinical prediction is going on all over the country in which the data available, and the intensity of clinical contact, are not materially different from that in the published comparisons.* It is highly probable that current predictive methods are costly to taxpayers and harmful to the welfare of patients.

Lacking quantification of inductive probability, we have no choice but to examine the clinician's success rate. One would hope that the rule-of-thumb assessment of inductive probability is not utterly unreliable. The indicated research step is therefore obvious: We persuade the clinician to state the odds, or somehow rate his "confidence," in his day-by-day decisions. Even if he tends over all to be wrong when countermanding the actuary, he may still tend to be systematically right for a high-confidence subset of his predictions. Once having proved this, we could thereafter countermand the formula in cases where the clinician expresses high confidence in his head. It is likely that studies in a great diversity of domains will be required before useful generalizations can be made.

In the meantime, we are all continuing to make predictions. I think it is safe to say, on the present evidence, that we are not as good as we thought we were. The development of powerful actuarial methods could today proceed more rapidly than ever before. Both theoretical and empirical considerations suggest that we would be well advised to concentrate effort on improving our actuarial techniques rather than on the calibration of each clinician for each of a large number of different prediction problems. How should we meanwhile be making our decisions? Shall we use our heads, or shall we follow the formula? Mostly we will use our heads, because there just isn't any formula, but suppose we have a formula, and a case comes along in which it disagrees with our heads? Shall we then use our heads? I would say, yes—provided the psychological situation is as clear as a broken leg; otherwise, very, *very* seldom.

5

Some Ruminations on the Validation of Clinical Procedures

IT IS BECOMING ALMOST A CLICHÉ to say that "clinical psychology is in a state of ferment," a remark which is ambiguous as to whether the "ferment" is a healthy or pathological condition. Dr. E. Lowell Kelly finds upon follow-up that about 40 percent of the young clinicians who were studied in the early days of the Veterans Administration training program now state that they would not go into clinical psychology if they had it to do over again (personal communication). In recent textbooks, such as Garfield's, one can detect a note of apology or defensiveness which was not apparent even a decade ago (1957, pp. vi, 28, 88, 97, 101, 109, 116, 152, 166, 451, and *passim*). No doubt economic and sociological factors, having little to do with the substance of clinical psychology, contribute in some measure to this state of mind within the profession. But I believe that there are also deeper reasons, involving the perception by many clinicians of the sad state of the science and art which we are trying to practice (Hathaway, 1958). The main function of the clinical psychologist is psychodiagnosis; and the statistics indicate that, while the proportion of his time spent in this activity has tended to decrease in favor of therapy, it nevertheless continues to occupy the largest part of his working day. Psychodiagnosis was the original basis

AUTHOR'S NOTE: This paper was delivered as an invitational address to the Canadian Psychological Association's convention at Edmonton, Alberta, June 12, 1958. It first appeared in the *Canadian Journal of Psychology*, vol. 13, 1959; copyright 1959 by Paul E. Meehl.

upon which the profession became accepted as ancillary to psychiatry, and it is still thought of in most quarters as our distinctive contribution to the handling of a patient. One is therefore disturbed to note the alacrity with which many psychologists move out of psychodiagnosis when it becomes feasible for them to do so. I want to suggest that this is only partly because of the even higher valence of competing activities, and that it springs also from an awareness, often vague and warded off, that our diagnostic instruments are not very powerful. In this paper I want to devote myself entirely to this problem, and specifically to problems of validity in the area broadly labeled "personality assessment."

I have chosen the word "ruminations" in my title. It helps from time to time for us to go back to the beginning and to formulate just what we are trying to do. I shall have to make some points which are perhaps obvious, but in the interest of logical completeness I trust that the reader will bear with me. In speaking about validity and validation, I shall employ the terminology proposed by the APA Committee on Test Standards, making the fourfold distinction between predictive, concurrent, content, and construct validity (APA Committee on Test Standards, 1954; see also Cronbach and Meehl, 1955—reprinted here as Chapter 1).

The practical uses of tests can be conveniently divided into three broad functions: *formal diagnosis* (the attachment of a nosological label); *prognosis* (including "spontaneous" recoverability, therapy-stay-ability, recidivism, response to therapy, indications for one kind of treatment rather than another); and *personality assessment* other than diagnosis or prognosis. This last function may be divided, somewhat arbitrarily, into *phenotypic* and *genotypic* characterization, the former referring to what we would ordinarily call the descriptive or surface features of the patient's behavior, including his social impact; and the latter covering personality structure and dynamics, and basic parameters of a constitutional sort (for example, anxiety threshold). Taking this classification of test functions as our framework, let us look at each one, asking the two questions "Why do we want to know this?" and "How good are we at finding it out?"

Consider first the problem of formal psychiatric diagnosis. This is a matter upon which people often have strong feelings, and I should tell you at the outset that I have some prejudices. I consider that there are such things as disease entities in functional psychiatry, and I do not

91

think that Kraepelin was as mistaken as some of my psychological contemporaries seem to think. It is my belief, for example, that there is a *disease* schizophrenia, fundamentally of an organic nature, and probably of largely constitutional etiology. I would explain the viability of the Kraepelinian nomenclature by the hypothesis that there is a considerable amount of truth contained in the system; and that, therefore, the practical implications associated with these labels are still sufficiently great, especially when compared with the predictive power of competing concepts, that even the most antinosological clinician finds himself worrying about whether a patient whom he has been treating as an obsessional character "is really a schizophrenic."

The fundamental argument for the utility of formal diagnosis can be put either causally or statistically, but it amounts to the same kind of thing one would say in defending formal diagnosis in organic medicine. One holds that there is a sufficient amount of etiological and prognostic homogeneity among patients belonging to a given diagnostic group so that the assignment of a patient to this group has probability implications which it is clinically unsound to ignore.

There are three commonly advanced objections to a nosological orientation in assessment, each of which is based upon an important bit of truth but which, as it appears to me, have been used in a somewhat careless fashion. It is first pointed out that there are studies indicating a low agreement among psychiatrists in the attachment of formal diagnostic labels. I do not find these studies very illuminating (Ash, 1949; Masserman and Carmichael, 1939; Mehlman, 1952). If you are accustomed to asserting that "It is well known that formal psychiatric diagnoses are completely unreliable," I urge you to reread these studies with a critical set as to whether they establish that thesis. The only study of the reliability of formal psychiatric diagnosis which approximates an adequate design is that of Schmidt and Fonda (1956); and the results of this study are remarkably encouraging with regard to the reliability of psychiatric diagnosis. As these authors point out, some have inferred unreliability of formal diagnosis from unreliable assessment of other behavioral dimensions. Certainly our knowledge of this question is insufficient and much more research is needed.

I suppose that we are all likely to be more impressed by our personal experience than by what someone else reports when the published reports are not in good agreement and there is insufficient information to indicate precisely why they come to divergent results. For example, it is often said that the concept "psychopathic personality" is a wastebasket category that does not tell us anything about the patient. I know that many clinicians have used the category carelessly, and it is obvious that one who uses this term as an approximate equivalent to saying that the patient gets in trouble with the law is not doing anything very profound or useful by attaching a nosological label. I, on the other hand, consider the asocial psychopath (or, in the revised nomenclature, the sociopath) to be a very special breed of cat, readily recognized, and constituting only a small minority of all individuals who are in trouble because of what is socially defined as delinquent behavior (in this connection see Lykken, 1957; Simons and Diethelm, 1946). I consider it practically important to distinguish (a) a person who becomes legally delinquent because he is an "unlucky" sociopath, that is, got caught; (b) one who becomes delinquent because he is an acting-out neurotic; and (c) a psychiatrically normal person who learned the wrong cultural values from his family and neighborhood environment.

Being interested in the sociopath, I have attempted to develop diagnostic skills in identifying this type of patient, and some years ago I ran a series on myself to check whether I was actually as good at it as I had begun to believe. I attempted to identify cases "at sight," that is, by observing their behavior in walking down the hall or sitting in the hospital lounge, without conversing with the patient but snatching brief samples of verbal behavior and expressive movements, sometimes for a matter of a few seconds and never for more than five minutes. In the majority of cases I had no verbal behavior at all. In the course of a year, I spotted thirteen patients as "psychopathic personality, asocial amoral type"; accepting staff diagnosis *or* an MMPI profile of psychopathic configuration as a disjunctive criterion, I was "correct" in twelve of the thirteen. This does not, of course, tell us anything about my false negative rate; but it does indicate that if I think a patient is a psychopath, there is reason to think I am correct. Now if I were interested in examining the "reliability" of the *concept* of the psychopathic personality, I should want to have clinicians like myself making the judgments.

Imagine, if you will, a psychologist trained to disbelieve in nosological categories and never alerted to those fascinating minor signs (lack of normal social fear, or what I call "animal grace," a certain intense, restless look about the eyes, or a score of other cues); suppose a study shows that such a psychologist tends not to agree with me, or that we both show low agreement with some second-year psychiatric resident whose experience with the concept has been limited to an hour lecture stressing the legal delinquency and "immaturity" (whatever that means) of the psychopath. What importance does such a finding have?

This matter of diagnostic skill involves a question of methodological presuppositions that is of crucial importance in interpreting studies of diagnostic agreement. The psychologist, with his tendency to an operational (Hempel, 1954) or "pure intervening variable" type of analysis (MacCorquodale and Meehl, 1948; Rozeboom, 1956) and from his long tradition of psychometric thinking in which reliability constrains validity, is tempted to infer directly from a finding that people disagree on a diagnostic label that a nosological entity has no objective reality. This is a philosophical mistake, and furthermore, it is one which would not conceivably be made by one trained in medical habits of thinking. When we move from the question of whether a certain sign or symptom should be given a high weight to the quite different question whether a certain disease entity has reality and is worth working hard to identify, disagreement between observers is (quite properly) conceived by physicians as *diagnostic error*. Neurological diagnoses by local physicians in outstate Minnesota are confirmed only approximately 75 percent of the time by biopsy, exploratory surgery, or autopsy at the University of Minnesota Hospitals. The medical man does not infer from this result that the received system of neurological disease entities is unsound; rather he infers that physicians make diagnostic mistakes.

Furthermore, it is not even assumed that all of these mistakes could be eliminated by an improvement in diagnostic skill. One of the most highly skilled internists in Minneapolis (Peppard, 1949) published a statistical analysis of his own diagnoses over a period of twenty-eight years based on patients who had come to autopsy. Imposing very stringent conditions upon himself (such as classifying a diagnostic error as eliminable if evidence could have been elicited by sufficient reexamination), he nevertheless found that 29 percent of his diagnoses were errors which could not in principle have been eliminated because they fell in the category of "no evidence; symptoms or signs not obtained." How is this possible? Because not only are there diseases which are *difficult* to diagnose; there are individual cases which are for all practical purposes *impossible* to diagnose so long as our evidence is confined to the clinical and historical material.

Presumably anyone who takes psychiatric nosology seriously believes that schizophrenia (like paresis, or an early astrocytoma in a neurologically silent area) is an *inner state,* and that the correct attachment of a diagnostic label involves a probability transition from what we see on the outside to what is objectively present on the inside. The less that is known about the nature of a given disease, or the less emphasis a certain diagnostician gives to the identification of that disease, the more diagnostic errors we can expect will be made. That some psychiatrists are not very clever in spotting pseudoneurotic schizophrenia is no more evidence against the reality of this condition as a clinical entity than the fact that in 1850, long before the clinching demonstration of the luetic origin of paresis by Noguchi and Moore, even competent neurologists were commonly diagnosing other conditions, both functional and organic, as "general paralysis of the insane." By 1913 the luetic etiology was widely accepted, and hence such facts as a history of chancre, secondary-stage symptoms, positive spinal Wassermann, and the like were being given a high indicator weight in making the diagnosis (Kraepelin, 1913). Yet the entity could not properly be *defined* by this (probable) etiology; and those clinicians who remained still unconvinced were assigning no weight to the above-mentioned indicators. This must inevitably have led to diagnostic errors even by very able diagnosticians. It is impossible for diagnostic activity and research thinking to be suspended during the period—frequently long—that syndrome description constitutes our only direct knowledge of the disorder (Major, 1932).

A second argument advanced against nosology is that it puts people in a pigeonhole. I have never been able to understand this argument since whenever one uses *any* nomothetic language to characterize a human being one is, to that extent, putting him in a pigeonhole (or locating him at a point in conceptual space); and, of course, every case of carcinoma of the liver is "unique" too. That some old-fashioned diagnosticians, untrained in psychodynamics, use diagnostic labels as a substitute for understanding the patient is not an unknown occurrence, but what can one say in response to this except *abusus non tollit usum?* We cannot afford to decide about the merits of a conceptual scheme on the grounds that people use it wrongly.

A derivative of this argument is that diagnostic categories are not

95

dynamics, and do not really tell us anything about what is wrong with the patient. There is some truth in this complaint, but again the same complaint could be advanced with regard to an organic disease concept at any stage in the development of the conception of it before the elucidation of its pathology and etiology.

There is some confusion within our profession about the relation between content or dynamics and taxonomic categories. Many seem to think that when we elucidate the content, drives, and defenses with which a patient is deeply involved, we have thereby explained why he is ill. But in what sense is this true? When we learn something about the inner life of a psychiatric patient, we find that he is concerned with aggression, sex, pride, dependence, and the like, that is, the familiar collection of human needs and fears. Schizophrenics are people, and if you are clever enough to find out what is going on inside a schizophrenic's head, you should not be surprised that these goings-on involve his self-image and his human relationships rather than, say, the weather. The demonstration that patients have psychodynamics, that they suffer with them, and that they deal with them ineffectively, does *not* necessarily tell us what is the matter with them, that is, why they are patients.

One is reminded in this connection of what happened when, after several years of clinicians busily overinterpreting "pathological" material in the TAT stories of schizophrenic patients, Dr. Leonard Eron (1948) took the pains to make a normative investigation and discovered that most of the features which had been so construed occurred equally or more often in a population of healthy college students.

There is no contradiction between classifying a patient as belonging to a certain taxonomic group and attempting concurrently to understand his motivations and his defenses. Even if a certain major mental disease were found to be of organic or genetic origin, it would not be necessary to abandon any well-established psychodynamic interpretations. Let me give you an analogy. Suppose that there existed a color-oriented culture in which a large part of social, economic, and sexual behavior was dependent upon precise color discriminations. In such a culture, a child who makes errors in color behavior will be teased by his peer group, will be rejected by an overanxious parent who cannot tolerate the idea of having produced an inferior or deviant child, and so on. One who was unfortunate enough to inherit the gene for color blindness might develop a color neurosis. He might be found as an adult on the couch of a color therapist, where he would produce a great deal of material which would be historically relevant and which would give us a picture of the particular pattern of his current color dynamics. But none of this answers the question "What is fundamentally the matter with these people?"—that is, what do all such patients have in common? What they have in common, of course, is that defective gene on the X chromosome; and this, while it does not provide a *sufficient* condition for a color neurosis in such a culture, docs provide the *necessary* condition. It is in this sense that a nosologist in that culture could legitimately argue that "color neuroticism" is an inherited disease.

I think that none of these commonly heard objections is a scientifically valid reason for repudiating formal diagnosis, and that we must consider the value of the present diagnostic categories on their merits, on their relevance to the practical problems of clinical decision making. One difficulty is that we do not have available for the validation of our instruments an analogue of the pathologist's report. It makes sense in organic medicine to say that the patient was actually suffering from disease X even though there was no evidence for it at the time of the clinical examination, so that the best clinician in the world could not have made a correct diagnosis on the data presented before autopsy. We have nothing in clinical psychology which bears close resemblance to the clinicopathological conference in organic medicine. Our closest analogue to pathology is "structure" and psychodynamics, and our closest analogue to the internist's concept of etiology is a composite of constitution and learning history. If we had a satisfactory taxonomy of either constitution or learning history, we would be able to define what we meant by saying that a given patient is a schizophrenic. A well-established historical agent would suffice for this purpose, and Freud (1896 as reprinted 1948), for example, made an attempt at this in the early days (before he had realized how much of his patients' anamnesis was fantasy) by identifying the obsessional neurosis with a history of active and pleasurable erotic prepubescent activity, and hysteria with a history of passive and largely unpleasurable erotic experience.

Since anyone who takes formal diagnosis as a significant part of the psychologist's task must be thinking in terms of construct validity (APA Committee on Test Standards, 1954; Cronbach and Meehl, 1955), he should have at least a vague sketch of the structure and etiology of the disorders about which he speaks diagnostically. I do not think that it is appropriate to ask for an operational definition. My own view is that theoretical constructs are defined "implicitly" by the entire network of hypothesized laws concerning them; in the early stages of understanding a taxonomic concept, such as a disease, this network of laws is what we are trying to discover. Of course, when a clinician says, "I think this patient is really a latent schizophrenic," he should be able to give us *some* kind of picture of what he means by this statement. It could, however, be rather vague and still sufficient to justify itself at this stage of our knowledge. He might say:

I mean that the patient has inherited an organic structural anomaly of the proprioceptive integration system of his brain, and also a radical deficiency in the central reinforcement centers (or, to use Rado's language, a deficiency in his "hedonic capacity"). The combination of these proprioceptive and hedonic defects leads in turn to developmental disturbances in the body image and in social identification; the result at the psychological level being a pervasive disturbance in the cognitive functions of the ego. It is this defective ego organization that is responsible for the primary associative disturbance set forth as the fundamental symptom of schizophrenia by Bleuler. The other symptoms of this disease, which may or may not be present, I would conceive as Bleuler does, and therefore my conception of the disorder is perhaps wider than is modal for American clinicians. By "pseudoneurotic schizophrenia" I would mean a patient with schizophrenia whose failure to demonstrate the accessory symptoms (and whose lower quantitative amount of even the primary symptoms) leads to his being readily misdiagnosed. Pseudoneurotic schizophrenia is just schizophrenia that is likely to go unrecognized.

Such a sketch is, to my mind, sufficient to justify the use of the schizophrenia concept at the present state of our knowledge. It is not very tight, and it is not intellectually satisfying. On the other hand, when combined with the set of indicators provided by Bleuler (1911 as reprinted 1950), Hoch and Polatin (1949), and others, it is not much worse than the concept of general paresis as understood during most of the nineteenth century following Bayle's description in 1822. In this connection it is sometimes therapeutic for psychologists to familiarize themselves with the logicians' contributions to the methodological problems of so-called "open concepts," "open texture," and "vagueness" (Hempel, 1950, 1952; Kaplan, 1946; Pap, 1953; Scriven, 1958; Waismann, 1945; Wittgenstein, 1953). Even a slight acquaintance with the history of the more advanced sciences gives one a more realistic perspective on the relation of "operational" indicators to theoretical constructs during the early stages of a construct's evolution. (See, for example, Nash, 1950; Roller, 1950, 1954; Taylor, 1941.)

The formal nosological label makes a claim about an inner structure or state; therefore, the concurrent validity of a test against our psychiatrist as criterion is not an end in itself, but rather is one piece in the pattern of evidence which is relevant to establishing the *construct* validity of *both* the test and the psychiatrist. If I really accept the psychiatric diagnosis as *"the* criterion," what am I doing with my test anyway? If I want to know what the psychiatrist is going to call patient Jones when he has just finished interviewing, the obvious way to find out is to leave my own little cubicle with its Rorschach and Multiphasic materials and walk down the hall to ask the psychiatrist what he is going to call the patient. This is a ludicrous way of portraying the enterprise, but the only thing which saves it from really being this way is that implicitly we reject concurrent validity with the psychiatrist's diagnosis as criterion, having instead some kind of construct validity in the back of our minds. The phrase "the criterion" is misleading. Because of the whole network of association surrounding the term "criterion," I would myself prefer to abandon it in such contexts, substituting the term "indicator." The impact of a patient upon a psychiatrist (or upon anyone else, for that matter) is one of a *family of indicators of unknown relative weights*; when we carry out a "validation" study on a new test, we are asking whether or not the test belongs to this family.

Note that the uncertainty of the link between nosology and symptom (or test) is a two-way affair. Knowing the formal diagnosis we cannot infer with certainty the presence of a given symptom or the result of a given test; conversely, given the result on a test, or the presence of a certain symptom, we cannot infer with certainty the nosology. (There are rare exceptions to this, such as thought disorder occurring in the presence of an unclouded sensorium and without agitation, which I would myself consider pathognomonic of schizophrenia.) This uncertainty is found also in organic medicine, where there are very few pathognomonic symptoms and very few diseases which invariably show any given symptom. An extreme (but not unusual) example is the prevalence of those subclinical infections which are responsible for immunizing us as adults, but which were *so* subclinical that they were only manifested by a mild malaise and possibly a little fever, symptoms which, singly or jointly, do not enable us to identify one among literally hundreds of diagnostic possibilities.

One "statistical" advantage contributed by a taxonomy even when it is operating wholly at the descriptive or syndrome level is so obvious that it is easy to miss; I suspect that the viability of the traditional nosological rubrics, which could not be well defended upon etiological grounds at present, is largely due to this contribution. When the indicators of membership in the class constitute a long list, none of which is either necessary or sufficient for the class membership, the descriptive information which is conveyed by the taxonomic name has a "statistical-disjunctive" character. That is, when we say that a patient belongs to category X, we are at least claiming that he displays indicators a or b or c with probability p (and separate probabilities p_a, p_b, and p_c). This may not seem very valuable, but considering how long it would take to convey to a second clinician the entire list of behavior dispositions whose probability of being present is materially altered by placing a patient in category X, we see that from the standpoint of sheer economy even a moderately good taxonomic system does something for us. More important in the long run is the fact that only a huge clinical team, with a tremendous amount of money to spend on a large number of patients over a long period of time, could hope to discover and confirm all $N(N-1)/2$ of the pair-wise correlations among the family of N indicators that relate to the concept, to say nothing of the higher order configural effects (Horst, 1954) that will arise in any such material. The research literature can yield cumulative knowledge and improvement of clinical practice in different settings by virtue of the fact that in one hospital an investigator, working with limited means, is able to show that patients diagnosed as schizophrenic tend to perform in a special way on a proverbs test; while another investigator in another hospital is showing that male patients diagnosed as schizophrenic have a high probability of reacting adversely to sexually attractive female therapists. Imagine a set of one hundred indicator variables and one hundred output variables; we would have to deal with ten thousand pair-wise correlations if we were to study these in one grand research project. The advantages in communicative economy and in cumulating research knowledge cannot, of course, be provided by a descriptive taxonomy which lacks intrinsic merit (that is, the syndrome does not objectively exist with even a moderate degree of internal tightness), or which, while intrinsically meritorious, is applied in an unskillful manner.

Let us turn now to our second main use of tests—prognosis. Sometimes the forecasting of future behavior is valuable even if no special treatment is contemplated, because part of the responsibility of many clinical installations is to advise other agencies or persons, such as a court, on the probabilities. But the main purpose of predictive statements is the assistance they give us in making decisions about how to treat a patient. Predictive statements of the form "If you treat the patient so-and-so, the odds are 8 to 2 that such-and-such will happen" will be with us for a very long time. As more knowledge about behavioral disorders is accumulated, we can expect a progressive refinement and differentiation of techniques; their differential impact will thereupon become greater, so that the seriousness of a mistake will be correspondingly increased. Furthermore, even if—as I consider highly unlikely but as we know some therapists are betting—it is discovered that for all patients the same kind of treatment is optimal, it is easily demonstrated from the statistics of mental illness, together with the most sanguine predictions concerning the training of skilled professional personnel, that there will not be adequate staff to provide even moderately intensive treatment for any but a minority of patients during the professional lifetime of anybody at present alive. So we can say with confidence that the decision to treat or not to treat will be a decision which clinicians are still going to be making when all of us have retired from the scene. As I read the published evidence, our forecasting abilities with current tests are not what you could call distinguished (see, for example, Zubin and Windle, 1954).

In connection with this problem of prognosis, let me hark back a moment to our discussion of formal nosology. One repeatedly hears clinicians state that they make prognostic decisions, not on the basis of a formal diagnosis, but on their assessment of the individual's structure and dynamics. Where is the evidence that we can do this? So far as I am aware there is as much evidence indicating that one can predict the subsequent course of an illness from diagnostic categories (Hastings, 1958)—or from crude life-history statistics—as there is that one can predict the course of an illness or the response to therapy from any of the psychological tests available. I should like to offer a challenge to any

101

clinician who thinks that he can cite a consistent body of published evidence to the contrary.

In order to employ dynamic constructs to arrive at predictions, it would be necessary to meet two conditions. In the first place, we must have a sound theory about the determinative variables. Secondly, we must be in possession of an adequate technology for making measurements of those variables. As any undergraduate major in physics or chemistry knows, in order to predict the subsequent course of a physical system, it is necessary both to understand the laws which the system obeys and to have an accurate knowledge of the initial and boundary conditions of the system. Since clinical psychology is nowhere near meeting *either* of these two requirements, it must necessarily be poor at making predictions which are mediated by dynamic constructs. It is a dogma of our profession that we predict what people will do by understanding them individually, and this sounds so plausible and humanitarian that to be critical of it is like criticizing Mother's Day. I can only reiterate that neither theoretical considerations nor the data available in the literature lend strong support to this idea in practice.

Let us turn to the third clinical task which the psychologist attempts to solve by the use of his tests, that of "personality assessment." Phenotypic characterization of a person includes the attribution of the ordinary clinical terms involving a minimal amount of inference, such as "patient hallucinates" or "patient has obsessional trends"; trait names from common English, such as the adjectives found in the lists published by Cattell (1946, p. 219) or Gough, McKee, and Yandell (1953); and, increasingly important in current research, characterizations in the form of a single sentence or a short paragraph of the type employed by Stephenson (1950), the Chicago Counseling Center (Rogers and Dymond, 1954), Block and Bailey (1955), and others. (Example: "The patient characteristically tries to stretch limits and see how much he can get away with.") A logical analysis of the nature of these phenotypic trait attributions is a formidable task although a very fascinating one. I am not entirely satisfied with any account which I have seen, or have been able to devise for myself. Perhaps not too much violence is done to the truth if we say that these are all in the nature of dispositional statements, the evidence for which consists of some kind of sampling, usually not representative, of a large and vaguely specified domain of episodes from the narrative that constitutes a person's life. It is complicated by the fact that even if we attempt to stay away from theoretical inferences, almost any single episode is susceptible of multiple classification under different families of atomic dispositions constituting a descriptive trait. The fact that the evidence for a trait attribution represents only a sample of the concrete episodes that exemplify atomic dispositions introduces an inferential element into such trait attributions, even though the trait name is intended to perform a purely summarizing rather than a theoretical function (Cronbach and Meehl, 1955—see pp. 18–21 above).

Phenotypic characterization presents a special problem which differentiates it from the functions of diagnosis and prognosis in the establishment of validity. Since it involves concurrent validity, its pragmatic justification is rather more obscure. Suppose we have a descriptive trait, say, "uncooperative with hospital personnel," an item which is not uncommon in various rating scales and clinical Q pools in current use in the United States. Why administer an MMPI in order to guess, with imperfect confidence, whether or not the patient is being currently judged as uncooperative by the occupational therapist, the nursing supervisor, and the resident in charge of his case? This is even a more fruitless activity than our earlier example of using a test to guess the diagnosis given by the psychiatrist. From the theoretical point of view, the obvious reply is that the sampling of the domain of the patient's dispositions which is made by these staff members is likely to be deficient, both in regard to its *qualitative* diversity and representativeness as seen within the several contexts in which they interact with the patient, and *quantitatively* (simply from the statistical standpoint of size) during the initial portion of a patient's stay in the hospital. This reply leads to a suggestion concerning the design of studies which are concerned with phenotypic assessment from tests. Such designs should provide a "criterion" which is considerably superior in reliability to that which would routinely be available in the clinic on the basis of the ordinary contacts. If it is concurrent validity in which we are really interested (upon closer examination this often turns out not to be the case), there is little point in administering a time-consuming test and applying the brains of a trained psychologist in order to predict the verbal behavior of the psychiatric aid or the nurse. If it is our intention to develop and validate an instrument which will order or classify patients according to phenotypic features which are *not* reliably assessed by these persons in their ordinary contacts with the patient, then we need a design which will enable us to show that we have actually achieved this result.

As to the power of our tests in the phenotypic characterization of an individual, the available evidence is not very impressive when we put the practical question in terms of the *increment in valid and semantically clear information transmitted*. (See, for example, the studies by Kostlan, 1954; Dailey, 1953; Winch and More, 1956; Kelly and Fiske, 1951; Davenport, 1952; Sines, 1957; and Soskin, 1954.)

The question of concurrent validity in the phenotypic domain can be put at any one of four levels, in order of increasing practical importance. It is surprising to find that research on concurrent validity has been confined almost wholly to the first of these four levels. The weakest form of the validation question is "How accurate are the semantically clear statements which can be reliably derived from the test?" It is a remarkable social phenomenon that we still do not know the answer to this question with respect to the most widely used clinical instruments. I do not see how anyone who examines his own clinical practice critically and who is acquainted with the research data could fail to make at least the admission that the power of our current techniques is seriously in doubt.

A somewhat more demanding question, which incorporates the preceding, would be "To what extent does the test enable us to make, reliably, accurate statements which we cannot *concurrently* and *readily* (that is, at low effort and cost) obtain from clinical personnel routinely observing the patient *who will normally be doing so anyway* (that is, whose observations and judgments we will not administratively eliminate by the introduction of the test)?" In the preceding discussion regarding diagnosis and concurrent validity I oversimplified so grossly as to be a bit misleading. "How the staff rates" cannot be equated with "What the staff sees," which cannot in turn be equated with "What the patient does in the clinic"; and that, in turn, is not the equivalent of "What the patient does." If a patient beats his wife and does not tell his therapist about it, and the wife does not tell the social worker, the behavior domain has been incompletely sampled by those making the ratings; they might *conclude* that he had beaten his wife, and this conclusion, while it is an inference, is still a conclusion regarding the phenotype. We cannot, of course, classify a certain concept as "theoretical" merely on the grounds that we have to make an inference in order to decide about a concrete instance of its application. This is a sampling problem, and therefore mainly (although not wholly) a matter of the time required to accumulate a sufficiently extensive sample. On the other hand, in our sampling of the patient's behavioral dispositions in the usual clinical context, it is not wholly a numerical deficiency in accumulation of episodes, because the sample which we obtain arises from a population of episodes that is in itself systematically biased. That is, the population of episodes which can be expected to come to our attention in the long run is itself a nonrepresentative subpopulation of all the behavioral events which constitute the complete narration of the patient's life.

A very stimulating paper is that of Kostlan (1954). There are elements of artificiality in his procedure (of which he is fully aware) and these elements will no doubt be stressed by those clinicians who are determined to resist the introduction of adverse evidence. Nevertheless, his procedure was an ingenious compromise between the necessity of maintaining a close semblance to the actual clinical process and a determination to quantify the incremental validity of tests. What he did, in a word, was to begin with a battery of data such as were routinely available in his own clinical setting and with which his clinicians were thoroughly familiar, consisting of a Rorschach, an MMPI, a sentence completion test, and a social case history. He then systematically varied the information available to his clinicians by eliminating one of these four sources at a time, arguing that the power of a device is probably studied better by showing the effect of its *subtraction* from the total mass of information than by studying it alone. The clinicians were required to make a judgment, from the sets of data presented to them, on each of 283 items which had been culled from a population of 1000 statements found in the psychological reports written by this staff. The most striking finding was that on the basis of all three of these widely used tests his clinicians could make no more accurate inferences than they could make utilizing the Barnum effect (Meehl, 1956c—reprinted here as Chapter 3; Dailey, 1952; Forer, 1949; Soskin, 1954; Sundberg, 1955; Tallent, 1958) when the all-important social history was deleted from their pool of data. A further fact, not stressed by Kostlan in his published report (but see Kostlan, 1954, 1955), is that the absolute magnitude of incremental information, even when the results are statistically significant, is not impressive. For example, clinicians knowing only the age, marital status, occupation, education, and source of referral of a patient (that is, relying essentially upon the Barnum effect for their ability to make correct statements) yield an average of about 63 percent correct statements about the patient. If they have the Rorschach, Multiphasic, and sentence completion tests *but are deprived of the social case history,* this combined psychometric battery results in almost exactly the same percentage of correct judgments. On the other hand, if we consider their success in making inferences based on the social history together with the sentence completion test and the MMPI (that is, eliminating only the Rorschach, which made no contribution) we find them making 72 percent correct inferences (my calculations from his Table 3), that is, a mere 9 percent increment.

A thesis just completed at the University of Minnesota by Dr. Lloyd K. Sines is consistent with Kostlan's findings (1957). Taking a Q sort of the patient's therapist as his criterion, Sines investigated the contribution by a four-page biographical sheet, an MMPI profile, a Rorschach (administered by the clinician making the test-based judgments), and a diagnostic interview by this clinician. He determined the increment in Q correlation with the criterion (therapist sort) when each of these four sources of information was inserted at different places in the sequence of progressively added information. The contribution of either of the two psychological tests, or both jointly, was small (and, in fact, knowledge of the Rorschach tended to exert an adverse effect upon the clinician's accuracy). For some patients, the application of a stereotype personality description based upon actuarial experience in this particular clinic provided a more accurate description of the patient than the clinician's judgment based upon any, or all, of the available tests, history, and interview data!

A third level of validation demand, in which we become really tough on ourselves, takes the form "If there are kinds of clear nontrivial statements which can be reliably derived from the test, which are accurate, and which are not concurrently and readily obtainable by other means routinely available, *how much earlier in time* does the test enable us to make them?" It might be the case that we can make accurate statements from our tests at a time in the assessment sequence when equally trustworthy nonpsychometric data have not accumulated sufficiently to make such judgments, but from the practical point of view there is still a need to know just how "advanced" this advance information is. So

106

far as I know, there are no published investigations which deal with this question.

A final and most demanding way of putting the question, which is ultimately the practically significant one by which the contribution of our techniques must be judged, is the following: "If the test enables us to make reliably clear, differentiating statements which are accurate and which we cannot readily make from routinely available clinical bases of judgment, and if this additional information is not rapidly picked up from other sources during the course of continued clinical study of the patient, in what way, *and to what extent,* does this incremental advance information help us in treating the patient?" One might have a clear-cut positive answer to the first three questions and be seriously in error if he concluded therefrom that his tests were paying off in practice. On this fourth question, there is also no published empirical evidence.

In the absence of any data I would like to speculate briefly on this one. Suppose that a decision is made to undertake the intensive psychotherapy of a patient. A set of statements, either of a dichotomous variety or involving some kind of intensity dimension or probability-of-correctness, is available to the psychotherapist on the basis of psychological test results. How does the therapist make use of this knowledge? It is well known that competent therapists disagree markedly with regard to this matter, and plausible arguments on both sides have been presented. Presumably the value of such information will depend upon the kind of psychotherapy which is being practiced; therapists of the Rogerian persuasion are inclined to believe that this kind of advanced knowledge is of no use; in fact they prefer to avoid exposure to it. Even in a more cognitively oriented or interpretative type of treatment, it may be argued that by the time the therapeutic interaction has brought forth sufficient material for interpretation and working-through to be of benefit to the patient, the amount of evidential support for a construction will be vastly greater than the therapist could reasonably expect to get from a psychological test report. It does not help the patient that there is "truth" regarding him in the therapist's head; since there is going to be a lot of time spent before the patient comes around to seeing it himself, and since this time will have to be spent regardless of what the therapist knows, perhaps there is no advantage in his knowing something by the second interview rather than by the seventh. On the other side, it may be argued that any type of therapy which involves even a moderate amount of selective attention and probing by the therapist does present moment-to-moment decision problems (for example, how hard to press, when to conclude that something is a blind alley, what leads to pickup) so that advance information from psychometrics can set the therapist's switches and decrease the probability of making mistakes or wasting time. It seems to me that the armchair arguments pro and con in this respect are pretty evenly balanced, and we must await the outcome of empirical studies.

One rather disconcerting finding which I have recently come upon is the rapidity with which psychotherapists arrive at a stable perception of the patient which does not undergo much change as a result of subsequent contacts. I was interested in this matter of how early in the game the psychological test results enable us to say what the therapist *will be saying later on.* In our current research at Minnesota we are employing a Q pool of 183 essentially "phenotypic" items drawn from a variety of sources. We are also using a "genotypic" pool of 113 items which consists of such material as the Murray needs, the major defense mechanisms, and various other kinds of structural-dynamic content. I was hoping to show that as the therapist learns more and more about his patient, his Q correlation with the Q description of the patient based upon blind analysis of the MMPI profile would steadily rise; furthermore, it is of interest to know whether there are *sub*domains of this pool, such as mild and well-concealed paranoid trends, with respect to which the MMPI is highly sensitive early in the game. (From my own therapeutic work, I have the impression that a low Pa score has almost no value as an exclusion test, but that any patient, however nonpsychotic he may be, who has a marked *elevation* on this scale will, sooner or later, present me with dramatic corroborating evidence.) However, I can see already that I have presented the test with an extraordinarily difficult task, because the Q sorts of these therapists stabilize so rapidly. The therapists Q described their patients after the first therapeutic hour, again after the second, then after the fourth, eighth, sixteenth, and twenty-fourth contact. If one plots the Q correlation between each sorting and the sorting after twenty-four hours of treatment (or between each sorting and a pooled sorting; or between each sorting and the next successive sorting), one finds that by the end of the second or fourth hour, the coefficients with subsequent hours are pushing the sort-resort reliabilities. The convergence of the therapist's perception of his patient is somewhat

108

faster in the phenotypic than in the genotypic pool, but even in the latter his conception of the patient's underlying structure, defense mechanisms, need-variable pattern, and so on seems to crystallize very rapidly. Even before examining the MMPI side of my data, I can say with considerable assurance that it will be impossible for the test to "prove" itself by getting ahead, and staying ahead, of the therapist to a significant extent. Of course, we are here accepting the psychotherapist's assessment as one which does converge to the objective truth about the patient in the long run, and this may not be true for all subdomains of the Q pool. The extent to which this rapid convergence to a stable perception represents invalid premature "freezing" is unknown (but see Dailey, 1952).

Personality characterization at the genotypic level will undoubtedly prove to be the most difficult test function to evaluate. A genotypic formulation, even when it is relatively inexplicit, seems to provide a kind of background which sets the therapist's switches as he listens to the patient's discourse. What things he will be alert to notice, how he will construe them, what he will say and when, and even the manner in which he says it, are all presumably influenced by this complicated and partly unconscious set of perceptions and expectancies. Process research in psychotherapy is as yet in such a primitive state that one hardly knows even how to begin thinking about experiments which would inform us about the pragmatic payoff of having advanced information, at various degrees of confidence, regarding specific features of the genotype. Even if it can be demonstrated that the therapist's perception of the patient tends with time to converge to that provided in advance by the test findings, this will never be more than a statistical convergence; therefore, in exchange for correctly raising the probability that one subset of statements is true of the patient, we will always be paying the price of expecting confirmation of some other unspecified subset which is erroneous.

Let me illustrate the problem by a grossly oversimplified example. Suppose that before either testing or interviewing, a dichotomously treated attribute has a base-rate probability of .60 in our particular clinic population. Suppose further that it requires an average of five therapeutic interviews before the therapist can reach a confidence of .80 with regard to the presence of this attribute. Suppose finally that a test battery yields this same confidence at the conclusion of diagnostic study (that is, before the therapy begins). During the five intervening hours, the therapist is presumably fluctuating in his assessment of this attribute between these two probability values, and his interview behavior (as well as his inner cognitive processes) are being influenced by his knowledge of the test results. Perhaps because of this setting of his switches he is able to achieve a confidence around the .80 mark by the end of the fourth session, that is, two hours earlier than he would have been able to do without the test. Meanwhile, he has been concurrently proceeding in the same way with respect to a second attribute; but, unknown to him, in the present case the test is giving him misinformation about that attribute (which will happen in one patient out of five on our assumptions). It is impossible to say from our knowledge of the cognitive processes of interpretive psychotherapists, or from what we know of the impact of the therapeutic interaction upon the patient, whether a net gain in the efficacy of treatment will have been achieved thereby. The difficulties in unscrambling these intricate chains of cumulative, divergent (London, 1946), and interactive causation are enormous.

I suspect that the present status of process research in psychotherapy does not make this type of investigation feasible. Alternatively, we shift to "outcome" research. Abandoning an effort to understand the fine causal details of the interaction between patient and therapist, we confine ourselves to the crude question "Are the outcomes of psychotherapy influenced favorably, on the average, by making advance information from a psychometric assessment available to the therapist?" Granting the variability of patients and therapists, and the likely interaction between these two factors and the chosen therapeutic mode, it seems feasible to carry out factorial-design research in which this question might be answered with some degree of assurance. When so much of the clinical psychologist's time is expended in the effort to arrive at a psychodynamic formulation of the patient through the integration of psychological test data, to the point that in some outpatient settings the total number of hours spent on this activity is approximately equal to the median number of hours of subsequent therapeutic contact, I believe that we should undertake research of this kind without delay.

Whatever the future may bring with regard to the pragmatic utility of the genotypic information provided by psychometrics, I am inclined to agree with Jane Loevinger's view that tests should be constructed in a framework of a well-confirmed psychological theory and with attention devoted primarily to construct validity. In her monograph (1957), Dr.

110

Loevinger has suggested that it is inconsistent to lay stress on construct validity and meanwhile adopt the "blind, empirical, fact-to-fact" orientation I have expressed (Meehl, 1956c, 1957—reprinted here as Chapters 3 and 4). I do not feel that the cookbook approach is as incompatible with a dedication to long-term research aimed at construct validity as Dr. Loevinger believes. The future use of psychological tests, if they are to become more powerful than they are at present, demands, as Loevinger points out, cross-situational power. It would be economically wasteful to have clinicians in each of the hundreds of private and public clinical facilities deriving equations, actuarial tables, or descriptive cookbooks upon each of the various clinical populations. I would also agree with Loevinger that such cross-situational power is intimately tied to construct validity, and that the construction of a useful cookbook does not, in general, contribute appreciably to the development of a powerful theoretical science of chemistry.

On the other hand, there is room for legitimate disagreement, among those who share this basic construct-validity orientation, on an important interim question. If the development of construct-valid instruments which will perform with a high degree of invariance over different clinical populations hinges upon the elaboration of an adequate psychological theory concerning the domain of behavior to be measured, then the rate of development of such instruments has a limit set upon it by the rate of development of our psychodynamic understanding. I personally am not impressed with the state of psychological theory in the personality domain, and I do not expect the edifice of personality constructs to be a very imposing one for a long time yet. Meanwhile, clinical time is being expended in the attempt to characterize patients by methods which make an inefficient use of even that modest amount of valid information with which our present psychometric techniques provide us.

The number of distinct attributes commonly viewed by clinicians as worth assessing is actually rather limited. The total number of distinguishable decision problems with which the psychiatric team is routinely confronted is remarkably small (see, for example, Dailey, 1953). It is not possible to say, upon present evidence, what are the practical limits upon the validity generalization of configural mathematical functions set up on large samples with respect to these decision classes. It is possible that the general *form* of such configural functions, and even the parameters, can be generalized over rather wide families of clinical populations, with each clinical administrator making correction of cutting scores or reassigning probabilities in the light of his local base rates (Meehl and Rosen, 1955—reprinted here as Chapter 2). One could tolerate a considerable amount of shrinkage in validity upon moving to a similar but nonidentical clinical population without bringing the efficiency of an empirical cookbook down to the low level of efficiency manifested by clinicians who are attempting to arrive at such decisions on an impressionistic basis from the same body of psychometric and life-history evidence. Halbower (1955), for instance, showed that moving from an outpatient to an inpatient veteran population, while it resulted in considerable loss in the descriptive power of a cookbook based upon MMPI profile patterns, nevertheless maintained a statistically significant (and a practically important) edge over the Multiphasic reading powers even of clinicians who were working with the kind of population to which validity was being generalized. One of the things we ought to be trying is the joint utilization, in one function or table, of the most predictive kinds of life-history data *together with* our tests. Some of the shrinkage in transition to allied but different clinical populations might be taken care of by the inclusion of a few rather simple and objective facts about the patient such as age, education, social class, referral source, percentage of service-connected disability, and the like.

Hence, I agree with Dr. Loevinger's emphasis upon the long-term importance of constructing tests which will be conceptually embedded in the network of psychological theory, and therefore superior in cross-situational power; in the meantime we do not have such tests, and there is some reason to think that in making daily clinical decisions a standard set of decision problems and trait attributions can be constructed. Such empirical research (readily within present limitations of personnel and theory) could result in the near future in cookbook methods which would include approximate stipulations on those parametric modifications necessary for the main classes of clinical populations and for base rates, whether known or crudely estimated, in any given installation. I do not see anything statistically unfeasible about this, and I shall therefore continue to press for a serious prosecution of this line until somebody presents me with more convincing evidence than I have thus far seen that the clinical judge, or the team meeting, or the whole staff conference, is able somehow to surmount the limitations imposed by the inefficiency of the human mind in combining multiple variables in complex ways.

As for the long-term goal of developing construct-valid tests, maybe our ideas about the necessary research are insufficiently grandiose. Perhaps the kind of integrated psychometric-and-theory network which is being sought is not likely to be built up by the accumulation of a large number of minor studies. If we were trying to make a structured test scale, for instance, which would assess those aspects of a patient's phenomenology that are indicators of a fundamentally schizadaptive makeup, we would be carrying on an uphill fight against nature if we accepted as our criterion the rating of a second-year psychiatry resident on a seven-step "latent schizophrenia" variable! I would not myself be tempted to undertake the construction of an MMPI key for latent schizophrenic tendency unless I had the assurance that the classification or ordering of the patient population would be based upon a multiple attack taking account of all of the lines of evidence which would bear upon such as assessment in the light of my crude theory of the disease. *The desirability of a "criterion" considerably superior to what is routinely available clinically applies to the development of construct-valid genotypic measures even more than to criterion-oriented contexts.* Between such a hypothetical inner variable or state as "schizophrenic disposition" and almost any namable aspect of overt behavior, there is interpolated quite a collection of nuisance variables. In order to come to a decision regarding, for example, a certain subset of cases which are apparently "test misses" (or which throw subsets of items in the wrong direction and hence provide evidence that those items should be modified or eliminated) one has to have a sufficiently good assessment of the relevant nuisance variables to satisfy himself that the apparent test or item miss is a miss in actuality.

This brings me to what I have often thought of as the curse of clinical psychology as a scientific enterprise. There are some kinds of psychological test construction or validation in which it suffices to know a very little bit about each person, provided a large number of persons are involved (for example, in certain types of industrial, educational, or military screening contexts). At the other extreme, one thinks of the work of Freud, in which the most important process was the learning of a very great deal about a small number of individuals. When we come to the construction and validation of tests where, as is likely always to

113

be true in clinical work, higher order configurations of multivariable instruments are involved, we need to know a great deal about each individual in order to come to a conclusion about what the test or item should show regarding his genotype. However, in order to get statistical stability for our weights and to establish the reality of complex patterning trends suggested by our data, we need to have a sizable sample of individuals under study. So that where some kinds of psychological work require us to know only a little bit about a large number of persons, and other kinds of work require us to know a very great deal about a few persons, construct validation of tests of the sort that Loevinger is talking about will probably require that we know a great deal, and at a fairly intensive or "dynamic" level, about a large number of persons. You will note that this is not a reflection of some defect of our methods or lack of zeal in their application but arises, so to speak, from the nature of things. I do not myself see any easy solution to this problem.

I am sure that by now you are convinced of the complete appropriateness of my title. I am aware that the over-all tenor of my remarks could be described as somewhat on the discouraged side. But we believe in psychotherapy that one of the phases through which most patients have to pass is the painful one between the working through of pathogenic defenses and the reconstitution of the self-image upon a more insightful basis. The clinical psychologist should remind himself that medical diagnostic techniques frequently have only a modest degree of reliability and validity. I have, for instance, recently read a paper written by three nationally known roentgenologists on the descriptive classification of pulmonary shadows, which these authors subtitle "A Revelation of Unreliability in the Roentgenographic Diagnosis of Tuberculosis" (Newell, Chamberlain, and Rigler, 1954). I must say that my morale was improved after reading this article.

In an effort to conclude these ruminations on a more encouraging note, let me try to pull together some positive suggestions. Briefly and dogmatically stated, my constructive proposals would include the following:

1. Rather than decrying nosology, we should become clinical masters of it, recognizing that some of our psychiatric colleagues have in recent times become careless and even unskilled in the art of formal diagnosis.

2. The quantitative methods of the psychologist should be applied to the refinement of taxonomy and not confined to data arising from psy-

chological tests. (I would see the work of Wittenborn, 1955, and of Lorr and his associates, 1955, as notable beginnings in this direction.)

3. While its historical development typically begins with syndrome description, the reality of a diagnostic concept lies in its correspondence to an inner state, of which the symptoms or test scores are fallible indicators. Therefore, the validation of tests as diagnostic tools involves the psychiatrist's diagnosis merely as one of an indicator family, not as a "criterion" in the concurrent validity sense. Accumulation of numerous concurrent validity studies with inexplicably variable hit rates is a waste of research time.

4. Multiple indicators, gathered under optimal conditions and treated by configural methods, must be utilized before one can decide whether to treat interobserver disagreement as showing the unreality of a taxonomy or merely as diagnostic error.

5. We must free ourselves from the almost universal assumption that when we elucidate the motives and defenses of a psychiatric patient, we have thereby explained why he has fallen ill. As training analysts have observed for years, patients and "normals" tend to have pretty much the same things on their minds, conscious and unconscious.

6. The relative power, for prognosis and treatment selection, of formal diagnosis, non-nosological taxonomies based upon trait clusters, objective life-history factors, and dynamic understanding via tests, is an empirical question in need of study, rather than a closed issue. We must face honestly the disparity between current clinical practice and what the research evidence shows about the relatively feeble predictive power of present testing methods.

7. There is some reason to believe that quantitative treatment of life-history data may be as predictive as psychometrics in their present state of development. Research along these lines should be vigorously prosecuted.

8. It is also possible that interview-based judgments at a minimally inferential level, if recorded in standard form (for example, Q sort) and treated statistically, can be made more powerful than such data treated impressionistically as is currently the practice.

9. While maximum generalizability over populations hinges upon high construct validity in which the test's functioning is imbedded in the network of personality theory, there is a pressing interim need for empirically derived rules for making clinical decisions (that is, "clinical

115

cookbooks"). Research is needed to determine the extent to which such cookbooks are tied to specific clinic populations and how the recipes can be adjusted in moving from one population to another.

10. Perhaps there are mathematical models, more suitable than the factor-analytic one and its derivatives, for making genotypic inferences, and especially inferences to nosology. Investigation of such possibilities must be pursued by psychologists who possess a thorough familiarity with the intellectual traditions of medical thinking, a solid grasp of psychodynamics, and enough mathematical skill to take creative steps along these lines.

11. From the viewpoint of both patients' welfare and taxpayers' economics, the most pressing *immediate* clinical research problem is that of determining the incremental information provided by currently used tests, especially those which consume the time of highly skilled personnel. We need not merely validity, but incremental validity; further, the temporal factor—"Does the test tell us something we are not likely to learn fairly early in the course of treatment?"—should be investigated; finally, it is well within the capacity of available research methods and clinical facilities to determine what, if any, is the pragmatic advantage of a personality assessment being known in advance by the therapist.

12. In pursuing these investigations we might better avoid too much advertising of the results since neither psychiatrists nor government officials are in the habit of evaluating the efficiency of their own procedures, a fact which puts psychologists at a great propaganda disadvantage while the science is still in a primitive stage of development.

6

The Cognitive Activity
of the Clinician

SOMEBODY has described psychotherapy as "the art of applying a science which does not yet exist." Those of us who try to help people with their troubles by means of that special kind of conversation are uncomfortably aware of the serious truth behind this facetious remark. The clinical psychologist has been able to assuage some of his therapeutic anxiety, and to refurbish his sometimes battered self-image, by keeping one foot planted on what seemed like comparatively solid ground, namely, psychodiagnosis. In recent years, some clinicians have been making a determined effort to assess the validity of our currently fashionable diagnostic instruments, and the findings are not very impressive. The cumulative impact of validation studies is reflected, for example, in Garfield's excellent textbook (1957), where one does not need a highly sensitive third eye to discern a note of caution (or even pessimism?). E. L. Kelly finds that 40 percent of young clinicians state that they would not go into clinical psychology if they had it to do over again (personal communication). One suspects that at least part of this professional disillusionment springs either from awareness of the weaknesses in our psychodiagnostic methods or from the chronic intrapsychic (and interprofessional!) strain exacted of those who ward off such a confrontation. Who, for example, would *not* react with discouragement

AUTHOR'S NOTE: This paper first appeared in the *American Psychologist,* vol. 15, 1960; copyright 1960 by the American Psychological Association, Inc.

117

upon reading the monograph by Little and Shneidman (1959) where, in an unbiased and well-designed study, we find a very low congruency among interpretation of psychological test data, the test interpreters having been chosen as "experts" on four widely used instruments? Any tendency I felt to rejoice at the slight superiority of the MMPI over the three projective techniques with which it was competing was counteracted by the finding that my favorite test, like the others, does not do at all well when judged in absolute terms.

The cognitive activity of the clinician can be separated into several functions, which I have discussed in a recent paper (Meehl, 1959b— reprinted here as Chapter 5). Setting aside for the moment that special kind of cognitive activity which goes on within the therapeutic interview, we can distinguish three classes of functions performed by the psycho-diagnostician: *formal diagnosis, prognosis,* and *personality assessment* other than diagnosis or prognosis. This last may be divided, somewhat arbitrarily, into *phenotypic* and *genotypic.*

Quite apart from the validity of current techniques for performing these various cognitive functions, their pragmatic value is open to question. It is commonly believed that an accurate pretreatment personality assessment of his patient is of great value to the psychotherapist. It is not know to what extent, if at all, this is true. However, what do psychotherapists themselves have to say about it? Bernard C. Glueck, Jr., and I have recently collected responses from 168 psychotherapists (both medical and nonmedical, and representing a wide spectrum of orientations: e.g., Freudian, neo-Freudian, Radovian, Sullivanian, Rogerian, eclectic, "mixed") to a questionnaire dealing with 132 aspects of therapeutic technique. One of our items reads: "It greatly speeds therapy if the therapist has prior knowledge of the client's dynamics and content from such devices as the Rorschach and TAT." While the self-styled groups differ significantly in their response to this item (ranging from a unanimous negative among Rogerians to a two-thirds affirmative among George Kelly disciples), all groups except the last tend to respond negatively. The over-all percentage who believe that such prior knowledge of the client's personality greatly speeds therapy is only 17 percent. This low figure, taken together with the fashionable de-emphasis upon nosology and the feebleness of most prognostic studies, at least raises doubts about the practical value of our diagnostic contribution.

118

Although they do not bear directly upon this question, we have some other interesting results which suggest considerable skepticism among therapists about the significance of causal understanding itself in the treatment process. For example, 43 percent state that "Warmth and real sympathy are much more important than an accurate causal understanding of the client's difficulty." Over one-third believe that "Literary, dramatic, aesthetic, or mystical people are likely to be better therapists than people of a primarily scientific, logical, or mathematical bent." Four out of five believe that "The personality of the therapist is more important than the theory of personality he holds." About half believe that "Interpretation as a tool is greatly overrated at present." Two out of five go as far as to say that "Under proper conditions, an incorrect interpretation, not even near to the actual facts, can have a real and long-lasting therapeutic effect." Time does not permit me to give other examples of items which, in the aggregate, suggest minimization of the importance of the therapist's forming a "correct" picture of the client's psyche.

Setting aside the pragmatic question of the therapeutic value of assessment, let us look briefly at the inductive structure of the assessment process. The epistemological rock bottom is a single, concrete, dated slice or interval in the behavior flux, an "episode," identified by certain physical or social properties. Having observed one or more episodes of a given kind, we make an inductive inference about the strength of low-order *dispositions* which these episodes exemplify. Such dispositions are grouped into families, the justification for this grouping being, as Cattell (1946, 1950) has emphasized, some kind of covariation (although not necessarily of Type R) among the members of the disposition family. It is perhaps possible to formulate the clinician's decision-making behavior entirely in terms of such disposition classes. In such a formulation, clinical inference involves probabilistic transition from episodes to dispositions, followed by the attribution of further dispositions as yet unobserved. Ideally, such inferences would be based upon an extensive actuarial experience providing objective probability statements. Given a particular configuration of dispositions present in a patient, the statistical frequencies for all other dispositions of practical import would be known within the limits of observational and sampling errors. In practice, of course, this ideal is rarely achieved, the conditional probabilities being subjectively judged from clinical experience without the benefit of an actual tallying and accumulation of observations, and the probabilities being expressed in rough verbal form, such as "frequently" and "likely," rather than as numerical values.

I am still of the opinion (McArthur, Meehl, and Tiedeman, 1956; Meehl, 1954a; Meehl, 1956c, 1957—reprinted here as Chapters 3 and 4) that the practical utility of this approach has been insufficiently explored, and I think that many clinicians are unaware of the extent to which their daily decision-making behavior departs from such a model not by being qualitatively different but mainly by being less explicit and, therefore, less exact. However, we must recognize that a purely dispositional approach is not the *only* way of proceeding. An alternative, more exciting (and more congenial to the clinician's self-concept), is to view the clinician's cognitive activity as aiming at the assessment of hypothetical inner states, structures, or events which cannot be reduced to dispositions but which belong to the domain of theoretical entities, crude though the theory may be. Episodes and dispositions are here treated as "signs" or "indicators" of the postulated internal states. These states should not be spoken of as "operationally defined" in terms of the dispositions, because the logical relationship between propositions concerning theoretical entities and those describing dispositions is not one of equivalence, but merely one of degrees of confirmation. The inference *from* dispositions *to* states of theoretical variables is again only probabilistic, partly because statistical concepts occur within the causal model itself (i.e., probability appears, as in the other sciences, in the object language) and partly because the theoretical network is incomplete and imperfectly confirmed.

A fundamental contribution to the methodology of inference from multiple indicators is the "multitrait-multimethod matrix" of Campbell and Fiske (1959). These authors show that in order to support a claim of construct validity, we must take into account more kinds of correlational data than have been traditionally provided and that it is just as important for some correlations to be low as it is for others to be high. Consider two or more traits (e.g., dominance and sociability), each of which is allegedly measured by two or more methods (e.g., MMPI scores and peer-group ratings). Computing all possible intercorrelations, we construct a multitrait-multimethod matrix. The relationships within this matrix may or may not lend support to the claim of construct validity. The monotrait-heteromethod coefficients not only should be statistically significant and respectable in size, but should exceed both the heterotrait-heteromethod and heterotrait-monomethod coefficients. For example, if MMPI dominance and sociability correlate higher than does MMPI dominance with peer-group dominance or than MMPI sociability with peer-group sociability, we ought to be nervous about the relative contribution of methods factors versus traits under study. Campbell and Fiske point out that the individual differences literature is very weak in this respect, usually failing to provide the necessary data and, when it does, usually showing unimpressive results.

An interesting adaptation of the Campbell-Fiske technique arises if we substitute "persons" for "traits" and deal with Q correlations rather than R correlations. Suppose that a therapist provides us with Q-sort descriptions of two patients. From the MMPI profiles these patients are then Q sorted independently by two interpreters. This setup generates a modified Campbell-Fiske matrix of fifteen Q correlations, in which the validity diagonals (i.e., heteromethod-mono*patient* coefficients) represent how similarly the same patient is perceived by the therapist and the two MMPI readers; the monomethod-heteropatient and heteromethod-heteropatient values reflect the projections, stereotypes, and other idiosyncratic sorting biases of the therapist and of the two interpreters, the extent to which such stereotypes are shared by all three, and the unknown true resemblance of the particular patient pair. Robert Wirt and I have been running a series of such matrices, and thus far our results are as unencouraging as those of the Little and Shneidman study. I have decided to spare you the figures, faintly hoping that the pairs thus far completed will turn out to be atypically bad.

The situation is not much improved by selecting a small subset of "high-confidence" items before Q correlating. One disadvantage of Q sort is that it requires the clinician to record a judgment about every trait in the deck. The technique has the advantage that it presents the judge with a standard set of dispositions and constructs and therefore gets judgments which he is able to make but would often fail to make in producing a spontaneous description. But for this advantage in coverage we have to pay a price. Such a situation is clinically unrealistic: whether we are starting with test data, history, or interview impressions, the particular facets which stand out (whether high or low) will not be the same for different patients. It may be that the meager results of recent validation studies are attributable in part to the calculation of hit frequencies or Q correlations over the entire range of traits, only a minority of which, variable in composition, would willingly be judged by the clinician on any one patient.

I cited earlier the statistic that only one psychotherapist in six believes that he is greatly helped in the treatment process by having advance knowledge of the patient's psychodynamics. One relevant consideration here is the rate at which the psychotherapist's image of his patient converges to a stable picture. John Drevdahl, Shirley Mink, Sherman Nelson, Murray Stopol, and I have been looking into this question. So far, it seems that the therapist's image of his patient crystallizes quite rapidly, so that somewhere between the second and fourth therapeutic hour it has stabilized approximately to the degree permitted by the terminal sort-resort reliabilities. Let me demonstrate a couple of typical results. Figure 1 shows the Q correlations between Stopol's phenotypic sort after the twenty-fourth hour and his successive sorts after the first, second, fourth, eighth, and sixteenth hours. "S_t" indicates correlation of his stereotype with twenty-fourth-hour sort. "Rel" is sort-resort reliability. (The phenotypic and genotypic ratings are made separately.) Figure 2 shows results for the genotypic pool. I do not mean to suggest that the therapist's perception at the end of twenty-four hours is "the criterion," which would involve a concept of validation that I reject (Cronbach and Meehl, 1955—reprinted here as Chapter 1; see pp. 8–11, 16–22 above). But presumably his perception after twenty-four contacts is more trustworthy than after only one. Or, if we (a) assume that some information gained early is subsequently lost by forgetting, erroneous revisions, and the like; (b) take as our standard of comparison the average value of ratings over all six sortings; and (c) treat this as a kind of "best combined image," the essential character of the situation remains as shown.

Now this state of affairs presents any psychological test with a difficult task. If, after two to four hours of therapeutic interviewing, the therapist tends to arrive at a stable image of the patient which is not very different from the one he will have after twenty-four contacts, and if that final image is pretty accurate, the test would need to have very high validity before we could justify the expenditure of skilled psychological time in giving, scoring, interpreting, and communicating it.

When we first began this convergence study, our primary interest was in the pragmatic utility of the MMPI. One way to consider validity (which makes more practical sense than the conventional validation

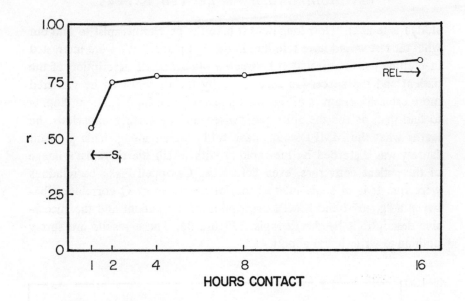

Figure 1. Q correlations between therapist's sort at 24 contacts and earlier sorts (phenotypic pool; $N = 182$ items; Stopol)

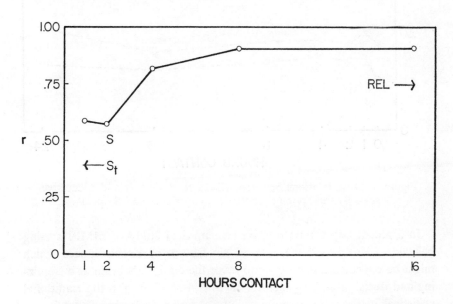

Figure 2. Q correlations between therapist's sort at 24 contacts and earlier sorts (genotypic pool; $N = 113$ items; Stopol)

123

study) is to ask: "How long does it take the psychotherapist to find out what the test would have told him in the first place?" We were interested in plotting the Q correlation between a blind MMPI description of the patient and the successive sorts done by the therapist as he gathered more extensive samples of the latter's behavior during treatment, hoping to find that, as the therapist gets "wised up" by further interviews, he learns what the MMPI would have told him all along. This pleasant fantasy was disturbed by the rapidity with which the therapist's image of the patient converges, even before the Campbell-Fiske correlations were run. It is of some interest to plot the curve of Q correlation between a "good" blind MMPI description of the patient and the successive descriptions by the therapist (Figure 3). These results are surely nothing to write home about!

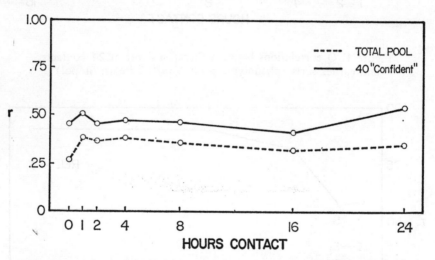

Figure 3. Q correlations between MMPI reader's sort and successive sorts by therapist (phenotypic pool; Meehl and Stopol)

In a recent paper reporting on an empirical study of MMPI sorting behavior (Meehl, 1959a) I listed six factors or circumstances which might be expected theoretically to favor the clinician's brain as a cognizing and decision-making instrument in competition with the traditional statistical methods of combining data. Among these six factors is one in which I have a particular interest, I suppose partly because it lends itself more readily to quantitative study than do some of the others.

This factor is the presumed ability of the clinician to react on the basis of higher order configural relations (Meehl, 1954a, pp. 130–134; Horst, 1954) by virtue of the fact that a system of variables can be graphically represented as a profile; and thereafter, given extensive clinical experience with a particular instrument, the clinician can respond to the visual gestalt. This he could do by *exemplifying* a complex mathematical function which neither he nor anyone else had as yet succeeded in *formulating*. The search for that function could take place in the context of studying the generalization and discrimination of complex visual forms. I recommend to your attention the recent work of Paul J. Hoffman on this subject, some of which has been reported (1958a, 1958b, 1959). Hoffman has undertaken a mathematical analysis of the rating behavior of judges who are presented with multivariable profiles, and the application of his formulas should teach us a great deal about the clinician's cognitive activity.

Comparing the impressionistic judgment of a group of Minnesota clinicians on the amount of "psychotic tendency" revealed by MMPI profiles with six statistical methods of treating the profiles, I found that the pooled judgment of twenty-one clinicians was significantly better (against the diagnostic criterion) than the linear discriminant function. In fact, there was a significant tendency (although slight) for even the *individual* clinicians to do a better job than the linear discriminant function. However, the best cross-validative results displayed by any method of sorting these profiles thus far tried utilizes a very complex set of configural rules developed by Grant Dahlstrom and myself (Meehl and Dahlstrom, 1960). Table 1 shows the results of applying these rules to

Table 1. Concurrent Validity of Meehl-Dahlstrom Rules
in Eight Cross-Validation Samples

Sample	N	H%	M%	I%	H/(H + M)	P
A*	92	55	16	28	.77	<.001
B*	77	45	29	26	.61	<.05
C	103	49	16	35	.75	<.001
D	42	40	21	38	.65	nonsig.
E*	181	45	18	36	.71	<.001
F	166	47	20	33	.70	<.001
G	273	63	12	25	.84	<.001
K*	54	78	5	17	.93	no test
Total group	988	53	17	30	.76	.001

* Essentially uncontaminated samples.

almost a thousand cases from eight clinics over the United States. These rules were concocted by a combination of clinical experience with statistical checking; and, while relatively crude and surely failing to extract all of the profile information, they are more efficient at this than a linear combination of scores, the pooled judgments of twenty-nine MMPI readers, or the judgment of the best of twenty-nine. Without knowing the form and constants of the mathematical function relating probability of psychosis to the MMPI variables, we cannot answer the question "How much of the information contained in the profile is extracted by the clinician?" One may plot probability of psychosis as a function of the clinician's placement of profiles on an eleven-step subjective scale of degree (or confidence) of psychoticism. Figure 4 shows probability of psychosis as a function of impressionistic profile placement by the best and worst clinician, and the pooled judgment of a group of twenty-nine. Figure 5 shows hit rate (whether neurotic or psychotic) as a function of the amount of consensus among twenty-nine judges.

While our data do indicate that the clinician's judging behavior with respect to the psychoticism variable is significantly configural, the *amount* of departure from a linear, additive model does not appear to be very great. For many years, skeptical statisticians have been pointing out to us clinicians that there is more conversation about nonlinear functions than there is actual demonstration of such and, anyway, that the value of departures from linearity and additivity involved in clinical judgments is likely to be attenuated, if not completely washed out, by the clinician's assignment of nonoptimal weights and the unreliability invariably involved in the impressionistic use of multivariate data.

Lykken, Hoffman, and I plan to utilize some of the MMPI psychoticism data for the kinds of analysis the latter has suggested, but in the meantime I have applied one of Hoffman's formulas to a portion of these data. He suggests that, if we treat the clinician's quantitative sorting as the dependent variable, the multiple R of this variable upon the profile scores should differ from unity only because of the clinician's unreliability, provided his sorting behavior follows a linear model. The multiple R of the eleven-step psychoticism ratings for my four best clinicians, when divided by the square root of their reliabilities (Hoffman's "complexity" formula), varies from .871 to .975, with a mean of .942, indicating that the departure of their judging behavior from a linear model is small. It is also interesting that the *inter*sorter reliability

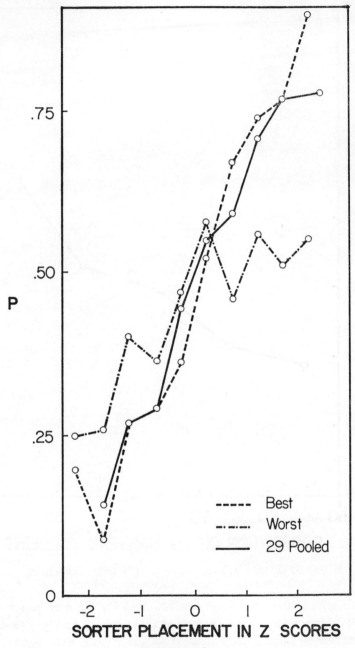

Figure 4. Probability of psychosis as function
of MMPI profile placement by sorters

127

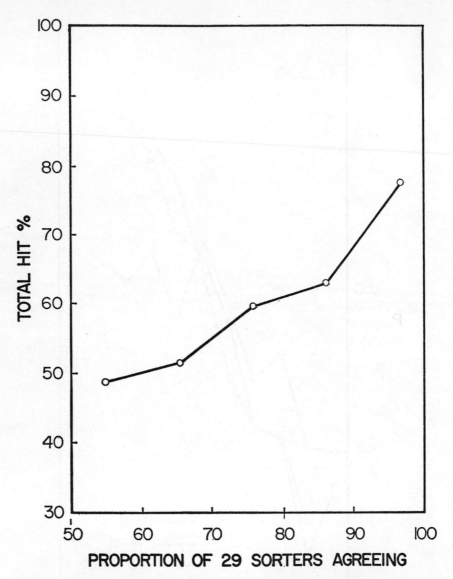

Figure 5. Hit rate as function of MMPI sorter consensus,
dichotomous judgment (neurosis-psychosis)

(Horst's generalized coefficient) reaches .994 for the four best sorters
and .987 for the four worst. Whatever these MMPI readers are doing
when asked to judge psychoticism from the profile, they seem to be
doing it in very much the same way.

Let me turn next to a brief account of an exploratory study which was
a dismal failure and which I am still trying to figure out. All told, there

now exist almost 200 different scoring keys for the MMPI item pool, ranging all the way from "dependency" to "baseball talent" and derived by a variety of methods (including factor analysis, face validity, and criterion keying). I thought it might be interesting to treat the patient's MMPI behavior more like the psychoanalyst than like the factor analyst: namely, to overdetermine the psychology of the patient by scoring him on a large number of these scales, in spite of their redundancy. Imagine two patients who produce identical profiles when scored on a very large number of partially overlapping but distinguishable variables. One might hope, except for the intrinsic defects of *coverage* in the MMPI item pool, that such a pair of individuals would be, so to speak, pinpointed in personality space as very close together. In practice it is impossible to find identical (or even nearly identical) profiles as the number of scored dimensions is increased, but perhaps one could get an estimate of this extreme by extrapolating interpatient similarities from lesser degrees of profile resemblance.

Selecting a sample of twenty female outpatients rated by staff psychiatrists or psychologists in connection with a study on the new ataraxic Mellaril (Fleeson, Glueck, Heistad, King, Lykken, Meehl, and Mena, 1958), we calculated the interviewer rating Q correlations for all possible pairs, thus generating an interpatient resemblance matrix of 190 elements. Turning then to the MMPI (by which the clinical raters were, of course, uncontaminated) and eliminating scales of fewer than ten or more than eighty items, we set up random sets of ten scales after defining the first set of ten as the basic profile of clinical scales commonly used. The Cronbach-Gleser distance measure was then computed on the MMPI profiles for the same 190 pairs. Thus we had a matrix of interpatient resemblances as clinically described by skilled interviewers through Q sorts and a corresponding matrix of MMPI profile similarity indices. A *series* of matrices of this latter kind was then generated by progressively extending the profile, adding successive blocks of ten randomly chosen scales. Thus, the first MMPI matrix was based upon the interpatient distance measures for the usual ten scores, the second one upon twenty scores (the usual ten plus ten randomly chosen), the third one on thirty scores, and so forth up to a profile of 160 variables! The idea, of course, was that through this procedure we would be squeezing all of the blood out of the psychometric turnip and that a second-order correlation (apologies to the statisticians) between the

129

corresponding elements of the two matrices would show a steady rise.

It would have been very nice had the asymptote of this intermatrix coefficient, when plotted as a function of the number of MMPI variables entering into the distance measure, approached a very high value. That is, if you measure—however unreliably and redundantly—a huge mass of variables (schizoid trend, recidivism, dominance, defensiveness, baseball talent, dependency, control, ego strength, use of repression, tendency to homesickness, academic potential, etc.), then the psychological resemblance between two patients will be closely related to their profile similarity on this extended list of MMPI scores. It turned out that there was no problem of curve fitting, for the simple reason that the intermatrix resemblances began at zero for the first ten scales and remained at zero, without the slightest tendency to increase as we included further blocks of scales in computing the distance measures. We know from a good deal of evidence that neither the MMPI nor the clinical Q sorts are quite *that* bad, and I am at a loss to understand these results. My suspicion is that they arise from inadequacies of the distance measure itself, and further analysis of the data is being undertaken with this hypothesis in mind. I still think that it was an interesting idea.

Leaving profile pattern interpretation, I should like to consider one more topic briefly. One of the most important problems in clinical psychology is deciding what kind of language communicates the largest amount of information about a patient. Most clinical practice today is predicated upon the assumption that useful statements about the patient can best be formulated (or at least inferentially mediated) by a theoretical language. The power of theoretical discourse in the other sciences makes this predilection understandable, and the characteristic Allport-Vernon-Lindzey profiles of clinical psychologists reflect strong theoretical interest. However, we learn in undergraduate physics that in order to apply theoretical constructs to the solution of practical problems (specifically, to predict the subsequent course of a particular physical system), one must fulfill two conditions. First, he must possess a reasonably well-developed theory. That is, he must know the laws that systems of the given kind obey. Second, he must have a technology, a set of measuring instruments, for determining the initial and boundary conditions of the particular system under study. To the extent that either, or both, of these conditions are not fulfilled, predictions arrived at by theoretical inference will be untrustworthy. I do not see how any-

130

one taking an objective view of the enterprise could claim that we fulfill *either,* let alone both, of these conditions in clinical psychology today. For this reason, in spite of my own personal interest in theoretical questions, I remain among that minority who persist in skepticism about the pragmatic utility of theoretical constructions in daily clinical decision making.

Suppose, however, that some kind of theoretical discourse is to be used; which of the several kinds of theoretical sublanguages is most economical? As a pilot study in connection with a Ford Foundation project now going on at Minnesota, I collected some preliminary data which you may find of interest. Twenty psychotherapists were asked to describe a patient whom they had had in treatment for at least twenty-five hours, using the 182-item phenotypic pool which generated the curves previously shown. They also described the patient in terms of the 113-item genotypic pool. Although the latter pool was not constructed in any systematic way with respect to theoretical orientation, having been built for a different purpose, one can identify five relatively homogeneous subsets of genotypic items as follows: 25 Murray needs, 14 areas of conflict, 13 mechanisms of defense, 10 value-orientation components, and 7 items referring to dimensions of psychiatric nosology. After calculating the 190 interpatient Q correlations based upon each of these subpools, we may ask how well the pattern of interpatient resemblances in the phenotype is reproduced by the genotypic matrix. Unfortunately, I have not been able to find a statistician who will tell me how to do a significance test on such data, but the coefficients obtained are shown in Table 2. It is remarkable, I think, that the 13 defense mechanisms do about as well in reproducing the 182-item

Table 2. Correlations between Interpatient P Matrix and G Matrices Based on Various Subpools*

Variable	r
P (182 items) vs. entire G pool (113 items)	.59
P vs. 13 defense mechanisms	.52
P vs. 25 Murray needs	.22
P vs. 7 nosological components	.22
P vs. 10 value dimensions	.03
P vs. 14 conflict areas	−.03
P vs. all 69 G items in above subpools	.45

* $_{20}C_2$ patients rated; $N = 190$ coefficients.

phenotypic matrix as does the entire genotypic pool consisting of almost ten times as many items. We hope that with a more systematic coverage of the domain the Ford project will give us some definite information about this question.

I have presented some samples of research currently in progress at Minnesota which, while somewhat heterogeneous and difficult to pull together, all treat of what we see as pragmatically important aspects of the clinician's cognitive activity. In order to place any confidence either in the theoretical constructs we employ in discussing patients or in the instrument-interpreter combinations we use to assess them, studies of convergent and discriminative validity must be carried out. The Campbell-Fiske multitrait-multimethod matrix, or the multiperson-multimethod variant of it, should be useful for this purpose. It seems obvious that even adequate and sophisticated studies of construct validity must be supplemented by data upon the *rate* at which the clinician acquires information from various sources. Since the commonest justification for expenditure of psychometric time is the utility to the therapist of "advance knowledge" (especially of the genotype), the skepticism expressed by our sample of psychotherapists, taken in combination with the convergence curves for the therapist's perception of his patient, put this widely held belief badly in need of experimental support. An important aspect of such data, presumably rather specific to various populations and clinical instruments, is that of differential convergence rates among items. There are probably certain attributes for which a test's validity is insufficient to justify a marked departure from the base rates or mean rating of the given clinical population, and others for which the therapist tends to be in error early in the game and to converge to the truth rather slowly in contrast to the test. I would predict that an example of this is MMPI scale 6, which is a rather weak scale when used as an exclusion test, but which, when elevated, turns out almost invariably to be right. I have had patients in treatment whose paranoid potential did not manifest itself until fifty or seventy-five sessions, by which time I had concluded (erroneously) that the MMPI was giving me a false positive.

As has been pointed out by many clinicians, lacking adequate clinical cookbooks (Meehl, 1956c—see Chapter 3 above) we have in practice to treat our instruments as instrument-interpreter combinations. I believe we can say upon present evidence that no one interpreter succeeds in extracting all of the information contained in a profile and that the development of objective configural methods of profile analysis (of which the Meehl-Dahlstrom rules are a primitive example) is a task of great importance. David Lykken and I are currently engaged in a study comparing more complex functions—such as a second-degree polynomial having squares and cross-products—with clinical judgment and the Meehl-Dahlstrom rules. I am betting on the last-named, because— while nonoptimally weighted—they do at least tap configural effects involving interactions up to the sixth order.

Finally, the question of what is the most economical language to employ in describing a patient remains open, although it appears that there are many practitioners who are not sufficiently aware that this problem exists.

I look forward to the next decade of research in clinical psychology with a certain ambivalence. We are asking more sensible questions and being more critical of our procedures; and several research techniques are now available, and in wide use, which should give us some pretty clear answers. The reason for my ambivalence (and I regret that in the role of prophet I have to sound like Jeremiah) is that the evidence already available suggests that the outcomes will look pretty gloomy. My advice to fledgling clinical psychologists is to construct their self-concept mainly around "I am a researcher" or "I am a psychotherapist," because one whose self-concept is mainly "I am a (test-oriented) psychodiagnostician" may have to maintain his professional security over the next few years by not reading the research literature, a maneuver which has apparently proved quite successful already for some clinicians. Personally, I find the cultural lag between what the published research shows and what clinicians persist in claiming to do with their favorite devices even more disheartening than the adverse evidence itself.

Psychologists cannot administer shock treatment or pass out tranquilizers, and I do not know of any evidence that we are better psychotherapists than our psychiatric colleagues. If there is anything that justifies our existence—other than the fact that we come cheaper—it is that we think scientifically about human behavior and that we come from a long tradition, going way back to the very origins of experimental psychology in the study of human error, of being critical of ourselves as cognizing organisms and of applying quantitative methods to the outcomes of our cognitive activity. If this methodological commitment

133

is not strong enough to compete with the commitments clinicians have to particular diagnostic instruments, the unique contribution of our discipline will have been lost. I can mobilize some enthusiasm for the next ten years within the field: while I expect discouraging findings at the level of practice, from the standpoint of the sociology of professions and the history of ideas, the developments should be very interesting to watch.

7

Schizotaxia, Schizotypy, Schizophrenia

IN THE COURSE of the last decade, while spending several thousand hours in the practice of intensive psychotherapy, I have treated—sometimes unknowingly except in retrospect—a considerable number of schizoid and schizophrenic patients. Like all clinicians, I have formed some theoretical opinions as a result of these experiences. While I have not until recently begun any systematic research efforts on this baffling disorder, I felt that to share with you some of my thoughts, based though they are upon clinical impressions in the context of selected research by others, might be an acceptable use of this occasion.

Let me begin by putting a question which I find is almost never answered correctly by our clinical students on Ph.D. orals, and the answer to which they seem to dislike when it is offered. Suppose that you were required to write down a procedure for selecting an individual from the population who would be diagnosed as schizophrenic by a psychiatric staff; you have to wager $1000 on being right; you may not include in your selection procedure any behavioral fact, such as a symptom or trait, manifested by the individual. What would you write down? So far as I have been able to ascertain, there is only one thing you could

AUTHOR'S NOTE: This paper was delivered as the presidential address to the Seventieth Annual Convention of the American Psychological Association, St. Louis, September 2, 1962. It appeared first in the *American Psychologist,* vol. 17, 1962; copyright 1962 by the American Psychological Association, Inc.

135

write down that would give you a better than even chance of winning such a bet—namely, "Find an individual X who has a schizophrenic identical twin." Admittedly, there are many other facts which would raise your odds somewhat above the low base rate of schizophrenia. You might, for example, identify X by first finding mothers who have certain unhealthy child-rearing attitudes; you might enter a subpopulation defined jointly by such demographic variables as age, size of community, religion, ethnic background, or social class. But these would leave you with a pretty unfair wager, as would the rule "Find an X who has a fraternal twin, of the same sex, diagnosed as schizophrenic" (Fuller and Thompson, 1960, pp. 272–283; Stern, 1960, pp. 581–584).

Now the twin studies leave a good deal to be desired methodologically (Rosenthal, 1962); but there seems to be a kind of "double standard of methodological morals" in our profession, in that we place a good deal of faith in our knowledge of schizophrenic dynamics, and we make theoretical inferences about social learning factors from the establishment of group trends which may be statistically significant and replicable although of small or moderate size; but when we come to the genetic studies, our standards of rigor suddenly increase. I would argue that the concordance rates in the twin studies need not be accepted uncritically as highly precise parameter estimates in order for us to say that their magnitudes represent the most important piece of etiological information we possess about schizophrenia.

It is worthwhile, I think, to pause here over a question in the sociology of knowledge, namely, why do psychologists exhibit an aversive response to the twin data? I have no wish to argue *ad hominem* here— I raise this question in a constructive and irenic spirit, because I think that a substantive confusion often lies at the bottom of this resistance, one which can be easily dispelled. Everybody readily assents to such vague dicta as "Heredity and environment interact," "There need be no conflict between organic and functional concepts," "We always deal with the total organism." But it almost seems that clinicians do not fully believe these principles in any concrete sense, because they show signs of thinking that *if* a genetic basis were found for schizophrenia, the psychodynamics of the disorder (especially in relation to intrafamilial social learnings) would be somehow negated or, at least, greatly demoted in importance. To what extent, if at all, is this true?

Here we run into some widespread misconceptions on what is meant

136

by *specific etiology* in nonpsychiatric medicine. By postulating a "specific etiology" one does *not* imply any of the following:

1. The etiological factor always, or even usually, produces clinical illness.

2. If illness occurs, the particular form and content of symptoms is derivable by reference to the specific etiology alone.

3. The course of the illness can be materially influenced only by procedures directed against the specific etiology.

4. All persons who share the specific etiology will have closely similar histories, symptoms, and course.

5. The largest single contributor to symptom variance is the specific etiology.

In medicine, not one of these is part of the concept of specific etiology, yet they are repeatedly invoked as arguments against a genetic interpretation of schizophrenia. I am not trying to impose the causal model of medicine by analogy; I merely wish to emphasize that *if* one postulates a genetic mutation as the specific etiology of schizophrenia, he is not thereby committed to any of the above as implications. Consequently such familiar objections as "Schizophrenics differ widely from one another" or "Many schizophrenics can be helped by purely psychological methods" should not disturb one who opts for a genetic hypothesis. In medicine, the concept of specific etiology means the sine qua non—the causal condition which is necessary, but not sufficient, for the disorder to occur. A genetic theory of schizophrenia would, in this sense, be stronger than that of "one contributor to variance," but weaker than that of "largest contributor to variance." In analysis of variance terms, it means an interaction effect such that no other variables can exert a main effect when the specific etiology is lacking.

Now it goes without saying that "clinical schizophrenia" as such cannot be inherited, because it has behavioral and phenomenal contents which are learned. As Bleuler says, in order to have a delusion involving Jesuits one must first have learned about Jesuits (1911 as reprinted 1950). It seems inappropriate to apply the geneticist's concept of "penetrance" to the crude statistics of formal diagnosis—if a specific genetic etiology exists, its phenotypic expression in *psychological* categories would be a quantitative aberration in some parameter of a behavioral acquisition function. What could possibly be a genetically determined functional parameter capable of generating such diverse behavioral outcomes, including the preservation of normal function in certain domains?

The theoretical puzzle is exaggerated when we fail to conceptualize at different levels of molarity. For instance, there is a tendency among organically minded theorists to analogize between catatonic phenomena and various neurological or chemically induced states in animals. But Bleuler's masterly *Theory of Schizophrenic Negativism* (1912) shows how the whole range of catatonic behavior, including diametrically opposite modes of relating to the interpersonal environment, can be satisfactorily explained as instrumental acts; thus even a convinced organicist, postulating a biochemical defect as specific etiology, should recognize that the causal linkage between this etiology and catatonia is indirect, requiring for the latter's derivation a lengthy chain of statements which are not even formulable except in molar psychological language.

What kind of behavioral fact about the patient leads us to diagnose schizophrenia? There are a number of traits and symptoms which get a high weight, and the weights differ among clinicians. But thought disorder continues to hold its own in spite of today's greater clinical interest in motivational (especially interpersonal) variables. If you are inclined to doubt this for yourself, consider the following indicators: Patient experiences intense ambivalence, readily reports conscious hatred of family figures, is pananxious, subjects therapist to a long series of testing operations, is withdrawn, and says, "Naturally, I am growing my father's hair."

While all of these are schizophrenic indicators, the last one is the diagnostic bell ringer. In this respect we are still Bleulerians, although we know a lot more about the schizophrenic's psychodynamics than Bleuler did. The significance of thought disorder, associative dyscontrol (or, as I prefer to call it so as to include the very mildest forms it may take, "cognitive slippage"), in schizophrenia has been somewhat deemphasized in recent years. Partly this is due to the greater interest in interpersonal dynamics, but partly also to the realization that much of our earlier psychometric assessment of the thought disorder was mainly reflecting the schizophrenic's tendency to underperform because uninterested, preoccupied, resentful, or frightened. I suggest that this realization has been overgeneralized and led us to swing too far the other way, as if we had shown that there really *is* no cognitive slippage factor present. One rather common assumption seems to be that if one can demonstrate the potentiating effect of a motivational state upon cognitive slippage, light has thereby been shed upon the etiology of schizophrenia. Why are we entitled to think this? Clinically, we see a degree of cognitive slippage not found to a comparable degree among nonschizophrenic persons. Some patients (e.g., pseudoneurotics) are highly anxious and exhibit minimal slippage; others (e.g., burnt-out cases) are minimally anxious with marked slippage. The demonstration that we can intensify a particular patient's cognitive dysfunction by manipulating his affects is not really very illuminating. After all, even ordinary neurological diseases can often be tremendously influenced symptomatically by emotional stimuli; but if a psychologist demonstrates that the spasticity or tremor of a multiple sclerotic is affected by rage or fear, we would not thereby have learned anything about the etiology of multiple sclerosis.

Consequent upon our general assimilation of the insights given us by psychoanalysis, there is today a widespread and largely unquestioned assumption that when we can trace the motivational forces linked to the content of aberrant behavior, then we understand why the person has fallen ill. There is no compelling reason to assume this, when the evidence is mainly our dynamic understanding of the patient, however valid that may be. The phrase "why the person has fallen ill" may, of course, be legitimately taken to include these things; an account of how and when he falls ill will certainly include them. But they may be quite inadequate to answer the question "Why does X fall ill and not Y, granted that we can understand both of them?" I like the analogy of a color psychosis, which might be developed by certain individuals in a society entirely oriented around the making of fine color discriminations. Social, sexual, economic signals are color mediated; to misuse a color word is strictly taboo; compulsive mothers are horribly ashamed of a child who is retarded in color development, and so forth. Some color-blind individuals (not all, perhaps not most) develop a color psychosis in this culture; as adults, they are found on the couches of color therapists, where a great deal of *valid* understanding is achieved about color dynamics. Some of them make a social recovery. Nonetheless, if we ask, "What was basically the matter with these patients?" meaning, "What is the specific etiology of the color psychosis?" the answer is that mutated gene on the X chromosome. This is why my own therapeutic experience with schizophrenic patients has not yet convinced me of the schizophrenogenic mother as a specific etiology, even though the picture I get of my patients' mothers is pretty much in accord with the familiar one.

139

There is no question here of accepting the patient's account; my point is that *given* the account, and taking it quite at face value, does not tell me why the patient is a patient and not just a fellow who had a bad mother.

Another theoretical lead is the one given greatest current emphasis, namely, *interpersonal aversiveness.* The schizophrene suffers a degree of social fear, distrust, expectation of rejection, and conviction of his own unlovability which cannot be matched in its depth, pervasity, and resistance to corrective experience by any other diagnostic group.

Then there is a quasi-pathognomonic sign, emphasized by Rado (1956; Rado and Daniels, 1956) but largely ignored in psychologists' diagnostic usage, namely, *anhedonia*—a marked, widespread, and refractory defect in pleasure capacity which, once you learn how to examine for it, is one of the most consistent and dramatic behavioral signs of the disease.

Finally, I include *ambivalence* from Bleuler's cardinal four (1911 as reprinted 1950). His other two, "autism" and "dereism," I consider derivative from the combination of slippage, anhedonia, and aversiveness. Crudely put, if a person cannot think straight, gets little pleasure, and is afraid of everyone, he will of course learn to be autistic and dereistic.

If these clinical characterizations are correct, and we combine them with the hypothesis of a genetic specific etiology, do they give us any lead on theoretical possibilities?

Granting its initial vagueness as a construct, requiring to be filled in by neurophysiological research, I believe we should take seriously the old European notion of an "integrative neural defect" as the only direct phenotypic consequence produced by the genic mutation. This is an aberration in some parameter of single-cell function, which may or may not be manifested in the functioning of more molar CNS systems, depending upon the organization of the mutual feedback controls and upon the stochastic parameters of the reinforcement regime. This neural integrative defect, which I shall christen *schizotaxia,* is all that can properly be spoken of as inherited. The imposition of a social learning history upon schizotaxic individuals results in a personality organization which I shall call, following Rado, the *schizotype.* The four core behavior traits are obviously not innate; but I postulate that they are universally learned by schizotaxic individuals, given any of the actually existing social reinforcement regimes, from the best to the worst. If the interpersonal regime is favorable, and the schizotaxic person also has the good fortune to inherit a low anxiety readiness, physical vigor, general resistance to stress, and the like, he will remain a well-compensated "normal" schizotype, never manifesting symptoms of mental disease. He will be like the gout-prone male whose genes determine him to have an elevated blood uric acid titer, but who never develops clinical gout.

Only a subset of schizotypic personalities decompensate into clinical schizophrenia. It seems likely that the most important causal influence pushing the schizotype toward schizophrenic decompensation is the schizophrenogenic mother.

I hope it is clear that this view does not conflict with what has been established about the mother-child interaction. If this interaction were totally free of maternal ambivalence and aversive inputs to the schizotaxic child, even compensated schizotypy might be avoided; at most, we might expect to find only the faintest signs of cognitive slippage and other minimal neurological aberrations, possibly including body image and other proprioceptive deviations, but not the interpersonal aversiveness which is central to the clinical picture.

Nevertheless, while assuming the etiological importance of mother in determining the course of aversive social learnings, it is worthwhile to speculate about the modification our genetic equations might take on this hypothesis. Many schizophrenogenic mothers are themselves schizotypes in varying degrees of compensation. Their etiological contribution then consists jointly in their passing on the gene *and* in the fact that being schizotypic, they provide the kind of ambivalent regime which potentiates the schizotypy of the child and raises the odds of his decompensating. Hence the incidence of the several parental genotypes among parent pairs of diagnosed proband cases is not calculable from the usual genetic formulas. For example, given a schizophrenic proband, the odds that mother is homozygous (or, if the gene were dominant, that it is mother who carries it) are different from those for father, since we have begun by selecting a decompensated case, and formal diagnosis as the phenotype involves a potentiating factor for mother which is psychodynamically greater than that for a schizotypic father. Another important influence would be the likelihood that the lower fertility of schizophrenics is also present, but to an unknown degree, among compensated schizotypes. Clinical experience suggests that in the semicompensated range, this lowering of fertility is greater among males, since many schizotypic women relate to men in an exploited or exploitive sexual way, whereas the male schizotype usually displays a marked deficit in heterosexual aggressiveness. Such a sex difference in fertility among decompensated cases has been reported by Meyers and Goldfarb (1962).

Since the extent of aversive learnings is a critical factor in decompensation, the inherited anxiety readiness is presumably greater among diagnosed cases. Since the more fertile mothers are likely to be compensated, hence themselves to be relatively low anxiety if schizotaxic, a frequent parent pattern should be a compensated schizotypic mother married to a neurotic father, the latter being the source of the proband's high-anxiety genes (plus providing a poor paternal model for identification in male patients, and a weak defender of the child against mother's schizotypic hostility).

These considerations make ordinary family concordance studies, based upon formal diagnoses, impossible to interpret. The most important research need here is development of high-validity indicators for compensated schizotypy. I see some evidence for these conceptions in the report of Lidz and co-workers, who in studying intensively the parents of fifteen schizophrenic patients were surprised to find that "minimally, 9 of the 15 patients had at least one parent who could be called schizophrenic, or ambulatory schizophrenic, or clearly paranoid in behavior and attitudes" (Lidz, Cornelison, Terry, and Fleck, 1958, p. 308). As I read the brief personality sketches presented, I would judge that all but two of the probands had a clearly schizotypic parent. These authors, while favoring a "learned irrationality" interpretation of their data, also recognize the alternative genetic interpretation. Such facts do not permit a decision, obviously; my main point is the striking difference between the high incidence of parental schizotypes, mostly quite decompensated (some to the point of diagnosable psychosis), and the zero incidence which a conventional family concordance study would have yielded for this group.

Another line of evidence, based upon a very small sample but exciting because of its uniformity, is McConaghy's report (1959) that among nondiagnosed parent pairs of ten schizophrenics, subclinical thought disorder was psychometrically detectable in at least one parent of every pair. Rosenthal (1962) reports that he can add five tallies to this parent-pair count, and suggests that such results might indicate that the specific heredity is dominant, and completely penetrant, rather than recessive. The attempt to replicate these findings, and other psychometric efforts to tap subclinical cognitive slippage in the "normal" relatives of schizophrenics, should receive top priority in our research efforts.

Summarizing, I hypothesize that the statistical relation between schizotaxia, schizotypy, and schizophrenia is class inclusion: All schizotaxics become, *on all actually existing social learning regimes,* schizotypic in personality organization; but most of these remain compensated. A minority, disadvantaged by other (largely polygenically determined) constitutional weaknesses and put on a bad regime by schizophrenogenic mothers (most of whom are themselves schizotypes), are thereby potentiated into clinical schizophrenia. What makes schizotaxia etiologically specific is its role as a *necessary* condition. I postulate that a non-schizotaxic individual, whatever his other genetic makeup and whatever his learning history, would at most develop a character disorder or a psychoneurosis; but he would not become a schizotype and therefore could never manifest its decompensated form, schizophrenia.

What sort of quantitative aberration in the structural or functional parameters of the nervous system can we conceive to be directly determined by a mutated gene, and to so alter initial dispositions that affected individuals will, in the course of their childhood learning history, develop the four schizotypal source traits: cognitive slippage, anhedonia, ambivalence, and interpersonal aversiveness? To me, the most baffling thing about the disorder is the phenotypic heterogeneity of this tetrad. If one sets himself to the task of doing a theoretical Vigotsky job on this list of psychological dispositions, he may manage part of it by invoking a sufficiently vague kind of descriptive unity between ambivalence and interpersonal aversiveness; and perhaps even anhedonia could be somehow subsumed. But the cognitive slippage presents a real roadblock. Since I consider cognitive slippage to be a core element in schizophrenia, any characterization of schizophrenic or schizotypic behavior which purports to abstract its essence but does not include the cognitive slippage must be deemed unsatisfactory. I believe that an adequate theoretical account will necessitate moving downward in the pyramid of the sciences to invoke explanatory constructs not found in social, psychodynamic, or even learning theory language, but instead at the neurophysiological level.

Perhaps we don't know enough about "how the brain works" to theorize profitably at that level; and I daresay that the more a psychologist knows about the latest research on brain function, the more reluctant he would be to engage in etiological speculation. Let me entreat my physiologically expert readers to be charitable toward this clinician's premature speculations about how the schizotaxic brain might work. I feel partially justified in such speculating because there are some well-attested general truths about mammalian learned behavior which could almost have been set down from the armchair, in the way engineers draw block diagrams indicating what kinds of parts or subsystems a physical system *must* have, and what their interconnections *must* be, in order to function "appropriately." Brain research of the last decade provides a direct neurophysiological substrate for such cardinal behavior requirements as avoidance, escape, reward, drive differentiation, general and specific arousal or activation, and the like (see Delafresnaye, 1961; Ramey and O'Doherty, 1960). The discovery in the limbic system of specific positive reinforcement centers by Olds and Milner in 1954, and of aversive centers in the same year by Delgado, Roberts, and Miller, seems to me to have an importance that can scarcely be exaggerated; and while the ensuing lines of research on the laws of intracranial stimulation as a mode of behavior control present some puzzles and paradoxes, what *has* been shown up to now may already suffice to provide a theoretical framework. As a general kind of brain model let us take a broadly Hebbian conception in combination with the findings on intracranial stimulation.

To avoid repetition I shall list some basic assumptions first but introduce others in context and only implicitly when the implication is obvious. I shall assume that:

When a presynaptic cell participates in firing a postsynaptic cell, the former gains an increment in firing control over the latter. Coactivation of anatomically connected cell assemblies or assembly systems therefore increases their stochastic control linkage, and the frequency of discharges by neurons of a system may be taken as an intensity variable influencing the growth rate of intersystem control linkage as well as the momentary activity level induced in the other systems. (I shall dichotomize acquired cortical systems into "perceptual-cognitive," including central representations of goal objects, and "instrumental," including overarching monitor systems which select and guide specific effector patterns.)

Most learning in mature organisms involves altering control linkages between systems which themselves have been consolidated by previous learnings, sometimes requiring thousands of activations and not necessarily related to the reinforcement operation to the extent that perceptual-to-instrumental linkage growth functions are.

Control linkage increments from coactivation depend heavily, if not entirely, upon a period of reverberatory activity facilitating consolidation.

Feedback from positive limbic centers is facilitative to concurrent perceptual-cognitive or instrumental sequences, whereas negative center feedback exerts an inhibitory influence. (These statements refer to initial features of the direct wiring diagram, not to all long-term results of learning.) Aversive input also has excitatory effects through the arousal system, which maintain activity permitting escape learning to occur because the organism is alerted and keeps doing things. But I postulate that this over-all influence is working along with an opposite effect, quite clear from both molar and intracranial experiments, that a major biological function of aversive-center activation is to produce "stoppage" of whatever the organism is currently doing.

Perceptual-cognitive systems and limbic motivational control centers develop two-way mutual controls (e.g., discriminative stimuli acquire the reinforcing property; "thoughts" become pleasantly toned; drive-relevant perceptual components are "souped-up").

What kind of heritable parametric aberration could underlie the schizotaxic's readiness to acquire the schizotypic tetrad? It would seem, first of all, that the defect is much more likely to reside in the neurone's synaptic control function than in its storage function. It is hard to conceive of a general defect in storage which would on the one hand permit so many perceptual-cognitive functions, such as are tapped by intelligence tests, school learning, or the high-order cognitive powers displayed by some schizotypes, and yet have the diffuse motivational and emotional effects found in these same individuals. I am not saying that a storage deficit is clearly excludable, but it hardly seems the best place to look. So we direct our attention to parameters of control.

One possibility is to take the anhedonia as fundamental. What is *phenomenologically* a radical pleasure deficiency may be roughly identi-

145

fied *behaviorally* with a quantitative deficit in the positive reinforcement growth constant, and each of these—the "inner" and "outer" aspects of the organism's appetitive control system—reflects a quantitative deficit in the limbic "positive" centers. The anhedonia would then be a direct consequence of the genetic defect in wiring. Ambivalence and interpersonal aversiveness would be quantitative deviations in the balance of appetitive-aversive controls. Most perceptual-cognitive and instrumental learnings occur under mixed positive and negative schedules, so the normal consequence is a collection of habits and expectancies varying widely in the intensity of their positive and negative components, but mostly "mixed" in character. Crudely put, everybody has *some* ambivalence about almost everything, and everybody has *some* capacity for "social fear." Now if the brain centers which mediate phenomenal pleasure and behavioral reward are numerically sparse or functionally feeble, the aversive centers meanwhile functioning normally, the long-term result would be a general shift toward the aversive end, appearing clinically as ambivalence and exaggerated interpersonal fear. If, as Brady believes, there is a wired-in reciprocal inhibiting relation between positive and negative centers, the long-term aversive drift would be further potentiated (i.e., what we see at the molar level as a sort of "softening" or "soothing" effect of feeding or petting upon anxiety elicitors would be reduced).

Cognitive slippage is not as easy to fit in, but if we assume that normal ego function is acquired by a combination of social reinforcements and the self-reinforcements which become available to the child through identification, then we might say roughly that "everybody has to learn *how* to think straight." Rationality is socially acquired; the secondary process and the reality principle are slowly and imperfectly learned, by even the most clearheaded. Insofar as slippage is manifested in the social sphere, such an explanation has some plausibility. An over-all aversive drift would account for the paradoxical schizotypic combination of interpersonal distortions and acute perceptiveness of others' unconscious, since the latter is really a hypersensitivity to aversive signals rather than an over-all superiority in realistically discriminating social cues. On the output side, we might view the cognitive slippage of mildly schizoid speech as originating from poorly consolidated second-order "monitor" assembly systems which function in an editing role, their momentary regnancy constituting the "set to communicate." At this level, selection

146

among competing verbal operants involves slight differences in appropriateness for which a washed-out social reinforcement history provides an insufficiently refined monitor system. However, if one is impressed with the presence of a pervasive and primary slippage, showing up in a diversity of tests (cf. Payne, 1961) and also on occasions when the patient is desperately trying to communicate, an explanation on the basis of deficient positive center activity is not too convincing.

This hypothesis has some other troubles which I shall merely indicate. Schizoid anhedonia is mainly interpersonal, i.e., schizotypes seem to derive adequate pleasure from esthetic and cognitive rewards. Secondly, some successful psychotherapeutic results include what appears to be a genuine normality of hedonic capacity. Thirdly, regressive electroshock sometimes has the same effect, and the animal evidence suggests that shock works by knocking out the aversive control system rather than by souping up appetitive centers. Finally, if the anhedonia is really general in extent, it is hard to conceive of any simple genetic basis for weakening the different positive centers, whose reactivity has been shown by Olds and others to be chemically drive specific.

A second neurological hypothesis takes the slippage factor as primary. Suppose that the immediate consequence of whatever biochemical aberration the gene directly controls were a specific alteration in the neurone's membrane stability, such that the distribution of optional transmission probabilities is more widely dispersed over the synaptic signal space than in normals. That is, presynaptic input signals whose spatiotemporal configuration locates them peripherally in the neurone's signal space yield transmission probabilities which are relatively closer to those at the maximum point, thereby producing a kind of dedifferentiation or flattening of the cell's selectivity. Under suitable parametric assumptions, this synaptic slippage would lead to a corresponding dedifferentiation of competing interassembly controls, because the elements in the less frequently or intensely coactivated control assembly would be accumulating control increments more rapidly than normal. Consider a perceptual-cognitive system whose regnancy is preponderantly associated with positive-center coactivation but sometimes with aversive. The cumulation of control increments will draw these apart; but if synaptic slippage exists, their difference, at least during intermediate stages of control development, will be attenuated. The intensity of aversive-center activation by a given level of perceptual-cognitive system

147

activity will be exaggerated relative to that induced in the positive centers. For a preponderantly aversive control this will be reversed. But now the different algebraic sign of the feedbacks introduces an important asymmetry. Exaggerated negative feedback will tend to lower activity level in the predominantly appetitive case, retarding the growth of the control linkage; whereas exaggerated positive feedback in the predominantly aversive case will tend to heighten activity levels, accelerating the linkage growth. The long-term tendency will be that movement in the negative direction which I call *aversive drift*. In addition to the asymmetry generated by the difference in feedback signs, certain other features in the mixed-regime setup contribute to aversive drift. One factor is the characteristic difference between positive and negative reinforcers in their role as strengtheners. It seems a fairly safe generalization to say that positive centers function only weakly as strengtheners when "on" continuously, and mainly when they are turned on as terminators of a cognitive or instrumental sequence; by contrast, negative centers work mainly as "off" signals, tending to inhibit elements while steadily "on." We may suppose that the former strengthen mainly by facilitating post-activity reverberation (and hence consolidation) in successful systems, the latter mainly by holding down such reverberation in unsuccessful ones. Now a slippage-heightened aversive steady state during predominantly appetitive control sequences reduces their activity level, leaves fewer recently active elements available for a subsequent Olds-plus "on" signal to consolidate, whereas a slippage-heightened Olds-plus steady state during predominantly aversive control sequences (a) increases their negative control *during* the "on" period and (b) leaves relatively more of their elements recently active and hence further consolidated by the negative "off" signal when it occurs. Another factor is exaggerated competition by aversively controlled sequences, whereby the appetitive chains do not continue to the stage of receiving socially mediated positive reinforcement, because avoidant chains (e.g., phobic behavior, withdrawal, intellectualization) are getting in the way. It is worth mentioning that the schizophrenogenic mother's regime is presumably "mixed" not only in the sense of the frequent and unpredictable aversive inputs she provides in response to the child's need signals, but also in her greater tendency to present such aversive inputs *concurrently* with drive reducers—thereby facilitating the "scrambling" of appetitive-and-aversive controls so typical of schizophrenia.

The schizotype's dependency guilt and aversive overreaction to offers of help are here seen as residues of the early knitting together of his cortical representations of appetitive goals with punishment-expectancy assembly systems. Roughly speaking, he has learned that to want anything interpersonally provided is to be endangered.

The cognitive slippage is here conceived as a direct molar consequence of synaptic slippage, potentiated by the disruptive effects of aversive control and inadequate development of interpersonal communication sets. Cognitive and instrumental linkages based upon sufficiently massive and consistent regimes, such as reaching for a seen pencil, will converge to asymptotes hardly distinguishable from the normal. But systems involving closely competing strengths and automatized selection among alternatives, especially when the main basis of acquisition and control is social reward, will exhibit evidences of malfunction.

My third speculative model revives a notion with a long history, namely, that the primary schizotaxic defect is a quantitative deficiency of inhibition. (In the light of Milner's revision of Hebb, in which the inhibitory action of Golgi Type II cells is crucial even for the formation of functionally differentiated cell assemblies, a defective inhibitory parameter could be an alternative basis for a kind of slippage similar in its consequences to the one we have just finished discussing.) There are two things about this somewhat moth-eaten "defective inhibition" idea which I find appealing. First, it is the most direct and uncomplicated neurologizing of the schizoid cognitive slippage. Schizoid cognitive slippage is neither an incapacity to link nor an unhealthy overcapacity to link; rather it seems to be a defective *control* over associations which are also accessible to the healthy (as in dreams, wit, psychoanalytic free association, and certain types of creative work) but are normally "edited out" or "automatically suppressed" by those superordinate monitoring assembly systems we lump together under the term "set." Second, in working with pseudoneurotic cases one sees a phenomenon to which insufficient theoretical attention has been paid: namely, these patients cannot turn off painful thoughts. They suffer constantly and intensely from painful thoughts about themselves, about possible adverse outcomes, about the past, about the attitudes and intentions of others. The "weak ego" of schizophrenia means a number of things, one of which is failure of defense; the schizophrenic has too ready access to his own id, and is too perceptive of the unconscious of others. It is tempting to read

149

"failure of defense" as "quantitatively deficient inhibitory feedback." As mentioned earlier, aversive signals (whether exteroceptive or internally originated) must exert both an exciting effect through the arousal system and a quick-stoppage effect upon cortical sequences which fail to terminate the ongoing aversive signal, leading the organism to shift to another. Suppose the gene resulted in an insufficient production (or too rapid inactivation) of the specific inhibitory transmitter substance, rendering all inhibitory neurones quantitatively weaker than normal. When aversively linked cognitive sequences activate negative limbic centers, these in turn soup up the arousal system normally but provide a subnormal inhibitory feedback, thereby permitting their elicitor to persist for a longer time and at higher intensity than normal. This further activates the negative control center, and so on, until an equilibrium level is reached which is above normal in intensity all around, and which meanwhile permits an excessive linkage growth in the aversive chain. (In this respect the semicompensated case would differ from the late-stage deteriorated schizophrenic, whose aversive drift has gradually proliferated so widely that almost any cognitive or instrumental chain elicits an overlearned defensive "stoppage," whereby even the inner life undergoes a profound and diffuse impoverishment.)

The mammalian brain is so wired that aversive signals tend to produce stoppage of regnant cognitive or instrumental sequences without the aversive signal having been specifically connected to their controlling cues or motivational systems. E.g., lever pressing under thirst or hunger can be inhibited by a shock-associated buzzer, even though the latter has not been previously connected with hunger, paired with the discriminative stimulus, or presented as punishment for the operant. A deficient capacity to inhibit concurrent activity of fringe elements (aversively connected to ambiguous social inputs from ambivalent mother) would accelerate the growth of linkages between them and appetitive systems not hitherto punished. Sequential effects are here especially important, and combine with the schizophrenogenic mother's tendency not to provide differential cues of high consistency as predictors of whether aversive or appetitive consequences will follow upon the child's indications of demand.

Consider two cortical systems having shared "fringe" subsystems (e.g., part percepts of mother's face). When exteroceptive inputs are the elicitors, negative feedback from aversive centers cannot usually produce stoppage; in the absence of such overdetermining external controls, the relative activity levels are determined by the balance of facilitative and inhibitory feedbacks. "Fringe" assemblies which have already acquired more aversive control, if they begin to be activated by regnant perceptual-cognitive sequences, will increase inhibitory feedback; and being "fringe" they can thereby be held down. The schizotaxic, whose aversive-feedback stoppage of fringe-element activity is weakened, accumulates excessive intertrial Hebbian increments toward the aversive side, the predominantly aversive fringe elements being more active and becoming more knit into the system than normally. On subsequent exteroceptively controlled trials, whenever the overdetermining stimulus input activates predominantly aversive perceptual-cognitive assemblies, their driving of the negative centers will be heightened. The resulting negative feedback may now be strong enough that, when imposed upon "fringe" assemblies weakly activated and toward the appetitive side, it can produce stoppage. On such occasions the more appetitive fringe elements will be retarded in their linkage growth, receiving fewer Hebbian increments. And those which do get over threshold will become further linked during such trials to the concurrent negative center activity. The result is twofold: a retarded growth of appetitive perceptual-cognitive linkages; and a progressive drawing of fringe elements into the aversive ambit.

"Ambiguous regimes," where the pairing of S^+ and S^- inputs occurs very unpredictably, will have a larger number of fringe elements. Also, if the external schedule is dependent upon regnant appetitive drive states as manifested in the child's instrumental social acts, so that these are often met with mixed S^+ (drive-relevant) and S^- (anxiety-eliciting) inputs, the appetitive and aversive assemblies will tend to become linked, and to activate positive and negative centers concurrently. The anhedonia and ambivalence would be consequences of this plus-minus "scrambling," especially if the positive and negative limbic centers are mutually inhibitory but here deficiently so. We would then expect schizotypic anhedonia to be basically interpersonal, and only derivatively present, if at all, in other contexts. This would in part explain the schizotype's preservation of relatively normal function in a large body of instrumental domains. For example, the acquisition of basic motor and cognitive skills would be relatively less geared to a mixed input, since "successful" mastery is both mechanically rewarded (e.g., how to open a door) and also interpersonally rewarded as "school success,"

151

etc. The hypercathexis of intellect, often found even among nonbright schizotypes, might arise from the fact that these performances are rewarded rather "impersonally" and make minimal demands on the reinforcing others. Also, the same cognitive and mechanical instrumental acts can often be employed both to turn on positive center feedback and to turn off negative, an equivalence much less true of purely social signals linked to interpersonal needs.

Having briefly sketched three neurological possibilities for the postulated schizotaxic aberration, let me emphasize that while each has sufficient merit to be worth pursuing, they are mainly meant to be illustrative of the vague concept "integrative neural defect." I shall myself not be surprised if all three are refuted, whereas I shall be astounded if future research shows no fundamental aberration in nerve-cell function in the schizotype. Postulating schizotaxia as an open concept seems at first to pose a search problem of needle-in-haystack proportions, but I suggest that the plausible alternatives are really somewhat limited. After all, what does a neuron do to another neuron? It excites, or it inhibits! The schizotypic preservation of relatively normal function in selected domains directs our search toward some minimal deviation in a synaptic control parameter, as opposed to, say, a gross defect in cell distribution or structure, or the kind of biochemical anomaly that yields mental deficiency. Anything which would give rise to defective storage, grossly impaired transmission, or sizable limitations on functional complexity can be pretty well excluded on present evidence. What we are looking for is a quantitative aberration in synaptic control—a deviation in amount or patterning of excitatory or inhibitory action—capable of yielding cumulative departures from normal control linkages under mixed appetitive-aversive regimes; but slight enough to permit convergence to quasi-normal asymptotes under more consistent schedules (or when massive repetition with motive-incentive factors unimportant is the chief basis for consolidation). The defect must generate aversive drift on mixed social reinforcement regimes, and must yield a primary cognitive slippage which, however, may be extremely small in magnitude except as potentiated by the cumulative effects of aversive drift. Taken together these molar constraints limit our degrees of freedom considerably when it comes to filling in the neurophysiology of schizotaxia.

Leaving aside the specific nature of schizotaxia, we must now raise the familiar question whether such a basic neurological defect, however subtle and nonstructural it might be, should not have been demonstrated hitherto? In reply to this objection I shall content myself with pointing out that there are several lines of evidence which, while not strongly arguing *for* a neurological theory, are rebuttals of an argument presupposing clear and consistent *negative* findings. For example: Ignoring several early European reports with inadequate controls, the literature contains a half-dozen quantitative studies showing marked vestibular system dysfunction in schizophrenics (Angyal and Blackman, 1940, 1941; Angyal and Sherman, 1942; Colbert and Koegler, 1959; Freeman and Rodnick, 1942; Leach, 1960; Payne and Hewlett, 1960; Pollack and Krieger, 1958). Hoskins (1946) concluded that a neurological defect in the vestibular system was one of the few clear-cut biological findings in the Worcester studies. It is of prime importance to replicate these findings among compensated and pseudoneurotic cases, where the diffuse withdrawal and deactivation factor would not provide the explanation it does in the chronic, burnt-out case (cf. Collins, Crampton, and Posner, 1961). Another line of evidence is in the work of King (1954) on psychomotor deficit, noteworthy for its careful use of task simplicity, asymptote performance, concern for patient cooperation, and inclusion of an outpatient pseudoneurotic sample. King himself regards his data as indicative of a rather basic behavior defect, although he does not hold it to be schizophrenia-specific. Then we have such research as that of Barbara Fish (1961) indicating the occurrence of varying signs of perceptual-motor maldevelopment among infants and children who subsequently manifest clinical schizophrenia. The earlier work of Schilder and Bender along these lines is of course well known, and there has always been a strong minority report in clinical psychiatry that many schizophrenics provide subtle and fluctuating neurological signs of the "soft" variety, if one keeps alert to notice or elicit them. I have myself been struck by the frequent occurrence, even among pseudoneurotic patients, of transitory neurologiclike complaints (e.g., diplopia, localized weakness, one-sided tremor, temperature dyscontrol, dizziness, disorientation) which seem to lack dynamic meaning or secondary gain and whose main effect upon the patient is to produce bafflement and anxiety. I have seen preliminary findings by J. McVicker Hunt and his students in which a rather dramatic quantitative deficiency in spatial cognizing

153

is detectable in schizophrenics of above-normal verbal intelligence. Research by Cleveland (1960; Cleveland, Fisher, Reitman, and Rothaus, 1962) and by Arnhoff and Damianopoulos (1964) on the clinically well-known body-image anomalies in schizophrenia suggests that this domain yields quantitative departures from the norm of such magnitude that with further instrumental and statistical refinement it might be used as a quasi-pathognomonic sign of the disease. It is interesting to note a certain thread of unity running through this evidence, which perhaps lends support to Rado's hypothesis that a kinesthetic integrative defect is even more characteristic of schizotypy than is the radical anhedonia.

All these kinds of data are capable of a psychodynamic interpretation. "Soft" neurological signs are admittedly ambiguous, especially when found in the severely decompensated case. The only point I wish to make here is that *since* they exist and are at present unclear in etiology, an otherwise plausible neurological view cannot be refuted on the ground that there is a *lack* of any sign of neurological dysfunction in schizophrenia; there is no such lack.

Time forces me to leave detailed research strategy for another place, but the main directions are obvious and may be stated briefly: The clinician's Mental Status ratings on anhedonia, ambivalence, and interpersonal aversiveness should be objectified and preferably replaced by psychometric measures. The research findings on cognitive slippage, psychomotor dyscontrol, vestibular malfunction, body image, and other spatial aberrations should be thoroughly replicated and extended into the pseudoneurotic and semicompensated ranges. If these efforts succeed, it will be possible to set up a multiple-sign pattern, using optimal cuts on phenotypically diverse indicators, for identifying compensated schizotypes in the nonclinical population. Statistics used must be appropriate to the theoretical model of a dichotomous latent taxonomy reflecting itself in otherwise independent quantitative indicators. Family concordance studies should then be run relating proband schizophrenia to schizotypy as identified by this multiple indicator pattern. Meanwhile we should carry on an active and varied search for more direct neurological signs of schizotaxia, concentrating our hunches on novel stimulus inputs (e.g., the stabilized retinal image situation) which may provide a better context for basic neural dysfunction to show up instead of being masked by learned compensations or imitated by psychopathology.

In closing, I should like to take this unusual propaganda opportunity to play the prophet. It is my strong personal conviction that such a research strategy will enable psychologists to make a unique contribution in the near future, using psychological techniques to establish that schizophrenia, while its content is learned, is fundamentally a neurological disease of genetic origin.

8

Mixed-Group Validation: A Method for Determining the Validity of Diagnostic Signs without Using Criterion Groups

A MEDICAL PRACTITIONER discovers a sign that he believes will distinguish between patients who will survive lockjaw and patients who will not. A psychologist discovers a sign that he believes will distinguish between schizophrenic and nonschizophrenic adults. An educator discovers a sign that he believes will distinguish between students who will be successful in graduate school and those who will not.

In all the above examples, the diagnostician is concerned with a universe of people that can be exhaustively divided into two types (survivors and nonsurvivors, schizophrenics and nonschizophrenics, successful students and unsuccessful students); let these types be labeled X and Y ($Y = $ not-X). In all the examples, the diagnostician has discovered some sign, label it x, that he thinks may distinguish between X-type individuals and Y-type individuals. "Type" is used here in a very general sense—almost synonymous with "class" or "category." A stricter meaning of "type" (e.g., Cattell, 1957, pp. 364–381) is not required in the present context.

AUTHOR'S NOTE: This paper was written in collaboration with Robyn Mason Dawes, then of the Veterans Administration Hospital, Ann Arbor, and the University of Michigan. It first appeared in the *Psychological Bulletin*, vol. 66, 1966; copyright 1966 by the Psychological Association, Inc.

The statements in this paper are those of the authors and do not necessarily reflect the views of the Veterans Administration. My work on this problem was supported in part by grants from the Ford Foundation and the National Institute of Mental Health, United States Public Health Service (Research Grant M-4465).

The problem of validating the sign x is the problem of finding some method for determining $p(x/X)$ and $p(x/Y)$—the probability that an X-type individual shows sign x and the probability that a Y-type individual shows sign x. This paper presents what we believe to be a new method for determining these probabilities.

The standard method for determining $p(x/X)$ and $p(x/Y)$ is *criterion-group validation*. The diagnostician obtains a group of X-type people and a group of Y-type people; the incidence of sign x among the X-type people yields $p(x/X)$; the incidence of sign x among Y-type people yields $p(x/Y)$. Obtaining such (pure criterion) groups is full of difficulties, which will be discussed later (not the least of which is that, in many cases of interest, the diagnostician would have to wait many years in order to determine who is an X-type and who is a Y-type). What we wish to point out is that it is not necessary to have such groups in order to obtain $p(x/X)$ and $p(x/Y)$; the desirability of having such groups is discussed later.

Consider a *mixed group* consisting of a set containing people of both type X and type Y. Consider, moreover, that we know the proportion of X-type individuals in the group, *even though we do not know specifically who is an X-type and who is a Y-type*. Labeling our group as Number 1, we may write this proportion as $p_1(X)$; similarly, $p_1(Y) = 1 - p_1(X)$ is the proportion of type Y individuals in the group. Let $p_1(X)$ be termed the *base rate* of X in Group 1.

Now consider $p_1(x)$, the proportion of sign x in Group 1. Term this the *sign rate* of x in Group 1.

Since X-types and Y-types are mutually exclusive and exhaustive, $p_1(x) = p_1(xX) + p_1(xY)$; that is, the sign rate in Population 1 is equal to the proportion of people in Population 1 who are type X and who show sign x plus the proportion in Population 1 who are type Y and who shown sign x.

But $p_1(xX) = p(x/X)p_1(X)$; that is, the proportion of people who are type X and who show sign x is equal to the proportion of people who are of type X multiplied by the probability that a type X individual shows sign x. It is assumed that this conditional probability is independent of the population (see section 3).

Similarly, $p_1(xY) = p(x/Y)p_1(Y)$; and substituting in the original equation we obtain:

[1] $p_1(x) = p(x/X)p_1(X) + p(x/Y)p_1(Y).$

We have assumed that we know $p_1(X)$; then, since $p_1(x)$ may be observed empirically, the only unknowns in the above equations are $p(x/X)$ and $p(x/Y)$.

Consider, now, a second mixed group with a *different* base rate $p_2(X)$ and a sign rate $p_2(x)$. As above:

[2] $p_2(x) = p(x/X)p_2(X) + p(x/Y)p_2(Y).$

Equation 2 has the same unknowns as equation 1. Moreover, the two equations are independent. For if the vector $[p_1(x), p_1(X), p_1(Y)]$ were a multiple of the vector $[p_2(x), p_2(X), p_2(Y)]$, the condition that both $p_1(X) + p_1(Y)$ and $p_2(X) + p_2(Y)$ must equal 1 would be violated. Therefore, the two equations may be combined and solved for $p(x/X)$. The solution is:

[3] $$p(x/X) = \frac{[p_1(x)p_2(Y) - p_2(x)p_1(Y)]}{[p_1(X)p_2(Y) - p_2(X)p_1(Y)]}.$$

Equation 3 yields the desired information necessary for validating the sign x; $p(x/Y)$ may be trivially obtained from equation 1 or 2 once $p(x/X)$ is obtained from equation 3.

We conclude that it is not necessary to observe the incidence of x in two pure criterion groups to determine $p(x/X)$; the incidence of x in any two (distinct) groups with known and different base rates yields the same information. We shall refer to validation making use of equation 3 as *mixed-group validation*.

One special case should be mentioned here, because it is counterintuitive (at least for some researchers). A brief glance at equation 3 shows that if $p_1(x)$ were to be equal to $p_1(X)$ and $p_2(x)$ were to be equal to $p_2(X)$, then $p(x/X)$ would be 1. In other words, if the sign rate matched the base rate in the two populations, then the sign would be perfectly valid. Again, this is true of *any* two populations. (Since perfect signs are never found in the field of psychology, the above conclusion might be restated as No matter what the sign, its rate cannot match the base rate in any two populations.)

Another special case is that in which the sign rate does not differ in two populations with differing base rates. In this case, the sign is totally useless. That is, if $p_1(X) \neq p_2(X)$ yet $p_1(x) = p_2(x)$, then $p(x/X) = p(x/Y) = [p_1(x) = p_2(x)]$. This conclusion may be confirmed from equation 3 by substituting $[1 - p_1(Y)]$ for $p_1(X)$ and $[1 - p_2(Y)]$ for $p_2(X)$ in the denominator of the fraction; the denominator then reduces to $p_2(Y) - p_1(Y)$. The numerator in the case where $p_1(x) = p_2(x)$ is equal to $p_1(x)[p_2(Y) - p_1(Y)]$. Hence, so long as $p_2(Y) \neq p_1(Y)$, the fraction reduces to $p_1(x)$. However, if $p(x/X) = p_1(x)$, and $p_1(X) \neq 0,1$, the sign x is by definition independent of the type X; $p(x/X)$ will equal $p(x/Y)$.

Finally, it must be pointed out that criterion-group validation is just that special case of mixed-group validation in which $p_1(X) = p_2(Y) = 1$ and $p_2(X) = p_1(Y) = 0$; then equation 3 reduces to $p(x/X) = p_1(x)$.

The Bootstraps Phenomenon

One particular property of mixed-group validation should be mentioned before discussing its practical advantages: the base rates in mixed groups may be determined from a sign with little validity, while a sign would have to be perfect if it were to be used for establishing pure criterion groups.

Since the sign validated from two mixed groups may be more valid than the sign used to obtain these groups, we refer to the resulting validation as a "bootstraps" operation. Suppose, for example, we had a sign x' of poor validity; say, $p(x'/X) = .60$ and $p(x'/Y) = .40$. If we were to take a population in which $p(X) = p(Y) = .50$, and if we were to divide this population into those who showed sign x' and those who did not, we would then have two subpopulations, one of which would have a base rate of X of .60, the other of which would have a base rate of X of .40. If, then, another sign x showed a sign rate of .60 in the first subpopulation and a sign rate of .40 in the second subpopulation, we could conclude that *sign x has perfect validity*. Yet, it was *validated on* a sign with little validity. Of course, most signs x will not be perfectly valid, but their degree of validity, as determined from equation 3, is entirely independent of the degree of validity of sign x', when sign x' is used as a criterion for determining the base rates in two mixed groups.

Cronbach and Meehl (1955—reprinted here as Chapter 1), in their article on construct validity in psychology, have pointed out the bootstraps phenomenon. They argued that, in practice, a psychological test may be validated on a test of lesser validity. The conclusions presented here give a precise mathematical explication of how this phenomenon works, at least in one class of validation contexts. Moreover, the fact that one may determine the validity of signs from mixed groups argues for the essential merit of the construct-validity approach.

The Assumption that $p(x/X)$ Does Not Vary from Population to Population

This assumption is undoubtedly an approximation to the state of nature, and sometimes a rather poor one. However, the assumption's validity is not germane to the distinction between mixed-group validation and criterion-group validation. If $p(x/X)$ varies greatly from population to population, the attempt to obtain a single value for it from criterion-group validation is just as suspect as the attempt to obtain a single value for it from mixed-group validation. If $p(x/X)$ varies slightly, we see no reason why its value as determined from mixed-group validation should be any further from its mean (or median, or modal) value than should its value as determined from criterion-group validation. (The problem of sampling error will be discussed in the last section of this paper; the reader should be forewarned, however, that we are not experts on distribution theory, and we will not derive precise estimates of the variance of $p(x/X)$ using the mixed-group method—or the criterion-group method, for that matter.)

Advantages of Mixed-Group Validation

The most obvious advantage of mixed-group validation is that it allows the immediate estimate of sign validity in investigations in which the category to which an individual belongs cannot be determined until some time after the observation of whether or not the person displays the sign whose validity is of interest. Typical of such studies are those that attempt to discover signs of mortality associated with a given disease or (physical or mental) syndrome. If the investigator uses criterion-group validation, he must wait after observing which people show the sign until every person in his sample can be classified. If he uses mixed-group validation, he can determine the sign validity if he is able to find two groups with known base rates among his subjects.

Consider, for example, the problem of the psychologist who is at-

160

tempting to discover signs associated with future suicide. He can only classify a given subject as suicidal or nonsuicidal after the subject is dead, because one cannot be sure a subject will not commit suicide until he has died from some other cause (or is physically incapacitated to the point he cannot commit suicide, even though he may wish to). If the psychologist is to use criterion-group validation in determining the validity of the signs he is studying, he must wait until every last subject is dead. Aside from the problem that it is highly likely that some of his subjects will outlive him, the psychologist is faced with all sorts of demands for results now. If the psychologist feels compelled to use criterion-group validation, he is likely to give up, or not begin the project in the first place. On the other hand, he can use mixed-group validation, because there is extensive sociological literature on the differential suicide rates among various social groups, and he can make use of this literature in determining the base rates of suicide among various subpopulations in his sample. He can then validate any sign he is investigating by using equation 3.

It is generally recognized that studies involving classification based on future events are becoming extremely important, especially in medicine. Medicine has advanced to the point that one of its major concerns is the prevention, as opposed to the cure, of disease (see DeBakey, 1964). Prevention can be effective only if it is known who is likely to suffer some disease *in the future* and who is not. The validation of present signs for predicting future illness is therefore a pressing concern. The mathematics of this paper demonstrate that such studies need not take the form of "follow-up studies," in which people with various signs (e.g., heavy smoking) are classified on the basis of their health over a number of years after the sign is observed. Rather, the extensive statistical literature on prevalence rates may be used to determine sign validity here and now—by equation 3.

Another, but not so obvious, advantage of mixed-group validation is that it allows us to determine the validity of signs associated with categories that are "open concepts." An example will best illustrate this point. Suppose a psychologist has an "open concept" of schizophrenia. That is, he doesn't have a precise idea of what he means by the term, but he feels the term has meaning; he doesn't have an operational definition of "schizophrenia," but he does not wish to abandon the concept, which is loosely, approximately specified by a set of observable

161

indicators of unknown relative weight ("validities"). Without a precise operational definition, he cannot say with certainty whether each given subject he studies is, or is not, a schizophrenic. Hence, he cannot use criterion groups to determine the validity of a sign he wishes to study. He can, however, use mixed-group validation if he is willing to estimate the base rates of schizophrenia in two different populations. It might be asked how he is able to estimate base rates when he cannot state precisely who is and who is not schizophrenic; and an answer to this question would involve a long argument on the virtues of open concepts—particularly for "beginning" sciences—as opposed to pure operational concepts. This argument is not presented here since it is not central to the method of mixed-group validation. (But see Meehl, 1965a.)

The Problem of Sampling Error

Equation 1 is just as valid whether one is dealing with a universe or a sample from that universe. Hence, any sample deviation of $p_1(x)$ from the universe $p_1(x)$ is due to the fact the sample values of $p_1(X)$ or $p(x/X)$ or $p(x/Y)$ differ from the universe values of $p_1(X)$, $p(x/X)$, or $p(x/Y)$.

It would be difficult to determine how the sample values of $p(x/X)$ and $p(x/Y)$ differ from the universe values for these probabilities because these probabilities are what is solved for in equation 3. On the other hand, it can be easily seen that the sample value of $p_1(X)$ may differ from the universe value. One is sampling from a mixed universe with proportion $p_1(X)$ of people who are type X, and one happens to get proportion $\hat{p}_1(X)$ in the sample.

To determine how such a discrepancy would affect an investigator's estimate, we must begin by assuming that $p(x/X)$ and $p(x/Y)$ are constant from population to population. (As pointed out previously, this assumption is also made in criterion-group validation.) Suppose, further, that the proportion of people of type X in Population 1 in the investigator's sample is $\hat{p}_1(X)$ and the proportion in Population 2 is $\hat{p}_2(X)$; whereas, the investigator supposes these proportions are $p_1(X)$ and $p_2(X)$ (the universe values). The *actual value* of $p(x/X)$ is equal to

$$\frac{[p_1(x)\hat{p}_2(Y) - p_2(x)\hat{p}_1(Y)]}{[\hat{p}_1(X)\hat{p}_2(Y) - \hat{p}_2(X)\hat{p}_1(Y)]}$$

But the value the investigator estimates, label it $p^*(x/X)$, is

$$\frac{[p_1(x)p_2(Y) - p_2(x)p_1(Y)]}{[p_1(X)p_2(Y) - p_2(X)p_1(Y)]}$$

The difference between true and estimated values simplifies to

[4] $p(x/X) - p^*(x/X) = \dfrac{[p_1(x) - p_2(x)][\hat{p}_1(Y)p_2(Y) - \hat{p}_2(Y)p_1(Y)]}{[p_2(Y) - p_1(Y)][\hat{p}_2(Y) - \hat{p}_1(Y)]}.$

Various examples can be worked out from this formula by the investigator who is interested in knowing how mistaken he might be in his estimate of $p(x/X)$; of course, he will have to start with some idea of how much his sample values, $\hat{p}_1(X)$ and $\hat{p}_2(X)$, might differ from the universe values.

We have not developed any analytic expression for the error of estimate more general than equation 4. This equation may, however, serve as the basis for one further conclusion: In general, the validity of a sign x will be underestimated if and only if the investigator overestimates the differences between his two groups, and it will be overestimated if and only if the investigator underestimates.

This conclusion is supported as follows: Without loss of generality, we may suppose that x is associated with X (not Y) and that Population 1 has a higher base rate of X than Population 2. Then, the factor $[p_2(Y) - p_1(Y)]$ will be positive, and unless the investigator's sample proportions go in the opposite direction from the universe proportions, $[\hat{p}_2(Y) - \hat{p}_1(Y)]$, and $[p_1(x) - p_2(x)]$ as well, will be positive. Therefore, it follows from equation 4 that $p(x/X) - p^*(x/X)$ will be positive, that is, the investigator will *underestimate* the validity of sign x, if and only if the factor $[\hat{p}_1(Y)p_2(Y) - \hat{p}_2(Y)p_1(Y)]$ is positive. *In general,* this latter condition will be true when $\hat{p}_1(Y) > p_1(Y)$ and $\hat{p}_2(Y) < p_2(Y)$, which is the case when there are fewer X's in Sample 1 than the investigator believes and more in Sample 2—that is, when he has overestimated the difference between Groups 1 and 2.

The limiting case occurs when the investigator believes he has pure criterion groups, but actually has mixed groups; in this case, the investigator will *always* underestimate the validity of his sign—provided it has any validity at all.

Another consideration relevant to the problem of sampling error is that the denominator of equation 3 may be written as $p_2(Y) - p_1(Y)$

163

or, equivalently, as $p_1(X) - p_2(X)$. The error in estimating this difference will increase as these probabilities approach .50, because the variance of a difference between two independent quantities is equal to the sum of their variances, and the variance of a probability increases monotonically as the probability approaches .50. Therefore, the more the base rates approach .50 (i.e., the greater the "mixture" in the mixed groups), the larger the sample the investigator should use.

Conclusion

In the above discussion, the word "sign" has been used as a generic term. A "sign" can refer to anything from a particular symptom to a summary score on a heterogeneous personality inventory. Moreover, all signs have been treated as if they are either present or absent; the problem of *determining* (what constitutes) a sign has been ignored. If, for example, we suspect that subjects' scores on a given personality inventory might be useful signs, we must determine optimal "cutting points" on this inventory. While a variant of the method of mixed-group validation can probably solve this cutting-point problem, it has not yet been developed. (But see Meehl, 1965a.) Finally, treatment of the sampling problem has been cursory.

The purpose of this paper was to present the basic logic of the method of mixed-group validation, not to explore all of its many ramifications.

9

What Can the Clinician Do Well?

IN THE PREFACE to the book *Clinical versus Statistical Prediction* (1954a) I wrote that students reacted to my lectures on prediction as to a projective technique. Many psychologists have responded to the book in the same way. I am therefore going to take this opportunity to repeat, with refinement and clarification, the statement of my essential position.

First of all, I am puzzled by the extent to which both statisticians and clinicians perceive the book as an attack upon the clinician. On the contrary, my position was, and is, that the clinician performs certain unique, important, and unduplicable functions, in some of which he has literally no competition. I think the book states this very clearly. (I hope it's true, since I occupy almost one-third of my time and earn a sizable part of my income in clinical work!) But in current practice, clinicians spend a good deal of time and energy performing functions at which there is neither theoretical nor empirical reason for supposing them to be efficient. My position is not, therefore, one of being "for" or "against" the clinician, or proposing to eliminate him. I cannot understand, for example, how my friend Bill Hunt could possibly read me as viewing ". . . the exercise of clinical judgment as a necessary evil" rather than,

AUTHOR'S NOTE: This paper was read at the symposium "Clinical Skills Revisited," American Psychological Association Convention, Cincinnati, Ohio, September 4, 1959. It first appeared in Douglas N. Jackson and Samuel Messick, eds., *Problems in Human Assessment* (New York: McGraw-Hill, 1967); copyright 1967 by McGraw-Hill.

as for him, ". . . a fascinating phenomenon with a genuine predictive potential"(Hunt, 1959, p. 177). Two full chapters of my book, and portions of two others, were devoted to analyzing (and defending!) the clinician's nonformalized judging and hypothesizing behavior, and I should have thought that my own fascination with the phenomenon was quite apparent.

However, I did want to influence clinical practice toward a more optimal utilization of skilled time, by removing the clinical judge from loci in the decision process where he functions ineffectively, thereby both (a) improving predictive accuracy and (b) freeing the clinician's time for other activities, whether cognitive or manipulative, in which he is efficient or unique.

Some feel that it was a disservice to formulate the problem in terms of opposition or competition, as clinical "versus" statistical prediction. Reading their discussions as sympathetically as my own bias permits, I remain persuaded that a pragmatically meaningful decision problem, involving a comparison between two distinguishable procedures, does exist. Discussions which have appeared during the last five years do necessitate some reformulations but, although I may be overly identified with my original position, I cannot regard them as fundamental. Given a set of data on a patient, and given the pragmatic necessity to make a certain decision, *either* one may combine these data, or selected portions thereof, in a formalized, mechanical, clerical fashion (of which the regression equation is only one example, perhaps not the most powerful); *or* he may invite a clinician, or a staff conference, to think and talk about these data and come to a decision. Now no one contends that the individual decisions resulting from these two methods of combining data will always coincide. This would be theoretically preposterous; and there is, of course, a massive body of experience to the contrary. In those numerous instances in which they *fail* to coincide, one must act in some way. If he acts in accordance with the decision provided by the clerical procedure, he has countermanded the judgment of the clinician or staff conference. If he acts in the other way, he has countermanded the statistical formula. *I have yet to see any cogent, or even plausible, criticism of this fundamental point, which was made clear by Sarbin fifteen years ago* (Sarbin, 1942). It is thoroughly misleading to speak of Sarbin or Meehl as fomenting a controversy, or as having set two procedures in "needless opposition" to each other. They *are in* daily opposition, mani-

166

fest or covert; their opposition is an immediate logical consequence of a simple, undisputed fact: namely, that the human judge and the statistical clerk correlate less than 1.00 when required to make diagnoses, prognoses, or decisions from a given body of information. Nothing is gained by adopting a hysteroid, "sweetness-and-light" attitude, akin to Mr. Dooley's definition of democracy as a situation in which "everybody is equally better."

There has been an overemphasis upon the chapter in which I surveyed the then available empirical studies, some readers reacting with glee to the box score, and others stressing the fact that these studies are not ideal, as I also emphasized in summarizing them. Personally, I consider that chapter to be almost the least important part of the book. On the other hand, no detailed, rigorous analyses or criticisms of the *theoretical* and *methodological* considerations raised in the book have appeared. I am at a loss to know whether this is because everybody agrees with me, or because these considerations are mistakenly thought to be irrelevant. I am convinced that the *formal* arguments on the actuarial side are very powerful, and they ought not to be thus airily dismissed or bypassed.

Well, what can the clinician do well? However well or badly he does certain things, he alone can do them, and therefore it is administratively justifiable to occupy his time with them. He can, for instance, observe and interview the patient, functions which are not eliminable by any kind of statistics. He can *be* a person himself in relation to the patient, with all that this means for the helping process. He can construct hypotheses and carry out research to test them. Every hour saved out of those innumerable and interminable staff conferences and team meetings in which some clinicians seem to delight (you know, there are clinics where the average weekly hours of interstaff contacts exceed those of staff-patient contacts!) can be devoted to seeing patients and doing research.

Among decisions which can, in principle, be arrived at by either a formalized or a judgmental method, I would now state the generalized clinical-statistical issue something like this: "Given a population of patients, with variable information on each; and a population of judges, with variable information on each; and a decision task imposed upon us pragmatically; *then,* at *which* points in the total decision-making process should we use *which judges*; and at which *other* points should a non-judgmental ('formal,' tabular, graphical, statistical, clerical, 'mechanical') operation be employed?"

It astounds me that, in spite of my having very carefully distinguished between *type of data* (i.e., psychometric or nonpsychometric) and *method of combining data* (i.e., judgmental or formalized), numerous writers have continued to perpetuate the old confusion between these two; several have even quoted me as maintaining that tests are better predictors than nontest data! This is a remarkable projective distortion, especially since I am extremely skeptical myself about the predictive power of the available tests in the personality field. I have held for some years that life-history and "mental status" variables are probably superior to existing tests, a superiority which I expect to become clear as actuarial methods of combining these nonpsychometric data are more widely utilized.

In answering the general question for a given prediction problem, we must include the utilities of the several outcomes of right and wrong decisions, the cost (monetary and otherwise) of the alternative decision methods, and the distribution of hit frequencies. "Equal hits" means "equal predictive success" only if hits are equally important whichever kind they are; and "equal predictive success," in turn, means "equal efficiency" only if one predictive method costs no more than the other.

The formulation is generalizable over all of the clinician's cognitive activity, whether predictive, postdictive, or diagnostic. Some have argued that the clinician doesn't "merely predict," but tries to influence the course of events, so that the problem posed is of little practical importance. This argument is philosophically naive. Selecting a certain line of action in order to influence the course of events is itself justified by implicative statements of the form, "If procedure X is carried out, the patient will respond in manner Y." And this, of course, is a prediction whether realized or counterfactual. A related error is made by those who have suggested that the clinician doesn't predict directly, but decides, upon the data he has, what additional data he needs before predicting. Not to act at a given moment in time, but to collect additional data of a specified kind is, of course, itself a decision; and is, like other decisions, rational or irrational, depending upon the probabilities and utilities involved.

In reporting a recent empirical study I listed six factors or circumstances theoretically favoring clinical prediction (Meehl, 1959a). Although that list was not presented as exhaustive, I have not yet come across any examples, either factual or armchair, falling outside these six rubrics:

1. *Open-endedness:* It often happens that the predictive task is not presented in the form of a prespecified criterion dimension or exhaustive set of categories, but rather as an open-ended question where the very content of the prediction has to be produced by the predictor.

2. *Unanalyzed stimulus-equivalences:* Sometimes the scanning and classifying of the data, including the recognition of a certain fact or pattern as relevant, cannot proceed by explicit rules because the operative "rules" are laws of our mental life as yet unknown or incompletely known. Perceptual gestalts, psychological similarities in physically dissimilar events, analogical and primary-process thinking, and similar inexplicit psychic processes are available to the predictor because he, being human, exemplifies laws which he may not be able to report because research has not yet elucidated them.

3. *Empty cells:* From time to time the prediction situation presents special cases in which a factor or configuration is highly relevant but has not occurred even in the course of very extended actuarial experience. In such cases the human judge must spontaneously notice the special circumstance and assign to it an estimated weight. In extreme instances such rare factors must be treated as "stop" items, being allowed to countermand an otherwise strong prediction reached by the formal (mathematical) procedure.

4. *Theory mediation:* When a prediction can be made by the use of hypothetical mental constructs whose laws (usually very imperfectly known) are in such general form as to permit a variety of structural-dynamic arrangements *in concreto,* the predictive process is not straightforward because hypothesis building is a creative, synthetic act for which automatic rules cannot be written. The $fact_1 \rightarrow fact_2$ sequence can always (in principle) be reduced to an actuarial generalization holding between members of the large (but finite) set of combinations and hence can be treated formally; whereas the $fact_1 \rightarrow construct \rightarrow fact_2$ sequence cannot always be thus formalized. The extreme case of this situation is the rare one in which the clinician actually invents new nomothetic *constructs* (as distinguished from thinking up new concrete exemplifications of familiar ones) in formulating a particular case. Freud's early analyses exemplify this case.

169

5. *Insufficient time:* In some predictive situations (e.g., interpretive psychotherapy) the pragmatic context requires that the prediction, to be of any use, must be reached in a very short time, even a matter of seconds, after the relevant data appear. A therapist cannot put his patient in cold storage while he, the therapist, runs off a *P*-technique factor analysis on a twenty-eight-variable correlation matrix derived from the patient's verbal productions during the preceding thirty minutes. Even if every office of the ten thousand skilled therapists in the U.S.A. were somehow provided with a high-caliber electronic computer, the time required for coding and feeding would make this science-fiction fantasy an inadequate solution.

6. *Highly configured functions:* Suppose that a configural relationship exists between a set of predictor variables and a criterion, but that the function is not derivable on rational grounds. We have to approximate this unknown optimal formula by empirical methods. Multivariable tests such as the Strong, MMPI, and Rorschach provide familiar instances of the problem. Clinicians skilled in the use of these devices find it helpful to have the several scores expressed graphically as a psychogram or profile, and this practice is not merely a matter of convenience in reading. Typically the clinician reports that his inferences from the profile are based partly upon discriminations he has learned to make among the various "patterns" which arise in an extended clinical experience. Usually these patterns are grouped into categories or types, but the clinician recognizes the existence of numerous intermediate forms so that the underlying function is presumably continuous. What seems to be happening is that an unknown configured mathematical function is being approximately expressed through the graphical mode, utilizing the fact that differences and similarities of visual gestalten can be perceived without the percipient's knowing the underlying formula.

Each of these six presents its own special problems for research, and in most actual clinical judgments more than one is likely to be operative. Like Dr. Hoffman (1960), I have chosen to investigate the sixth factor empirically, although I would readily agree that it is theoretically the least interesting. It has, however, the advantage of being somewhat easier to subject to quantitative analysis, and sizable samples of such judgments are fairly easy to obtain.

Admittedly, a mere tally of the "box score" based upon heterogeneous studies comparing the efficiency of formal and judgmental methods of combining data is not as helpful, either for practical purposes or in giving us greater theoretical insight into the clinician's cognitive activity, as will be systematic studies of these six components as they appear at different stages of the total decision-making process. Where, in this chain of gathering facts and making inferences, is the skilled human judge indispensable? Where is he dispensable, but only with a loss in predictive accuracy? Where are his cerebrations inferior in their outcomes to the application of a formalized procedure, such as an actuarial table or mathematical equation? Many studies, in the several domains of predictive activity, will be needed to answer these questions.

However, since large amounts of time are being spent today making decisions by impressionistic, judgmental, and conversational methods (such as the staff conference), it is worthwhile to attempt a rough generalization on the relative power of the two methods over diverse predictive domains. I cannot agree with those who consider that such a box score is either meaningless or unimportant. By the latest count, there are thirty-five studies which permit a comparison between the human judge and a clerical, formalized procedure for combining information. Many of these studies are not based upon clinical data of a high order, either in quantity or quality. However, I must emphasize that *many of the studies do involve amounts and quality of data quite comparable to what are routinely available in most clinical and counseling situations and which are being applied daily by clinicians in making their judgments.* The shortage of skilled professional personnel, which is certain to be with us (and in fact to get worse) during the lifetime of everyone now alive, makes it thoroughly unrealistic to argue that no significant comparison can be made unless it involves the kind of workup that a wealthy patient in a plush mental hospital receives at fancy prices. I would further point out that it is a quite unjustified assumption, commonly made by critics of the box score, that "naturally," if the quality and quantity of the clinical data, and the professional competence of the clinicians, were deliberately picked as being of a very high order, the clinician *would* show up markedly better than a souped-up, configural statistical prediction system *utilizing the same top-quality data.* This may or may not be true; some of us are still patiently watching the journals for the evidence.

Of the thirty-five studies known to me, twelve deal with predicting outcome in some kind of training or schooling; eight with recidivism, delinquency, or parole violation; three with improvement of psychotics; three with psychiatric diagnosis, i.e., the attachment of a nosological label; three with the outcome of outpatient psychotherapy of neurotics; and five with personality description not covered by any of the preceding such as Q-sort characterization of a patient and aggression as inferred from the Rorschach. One study compares the two methods in organic medicine. If we define equal efficiency without regard for time and economics (a definition strongly biased against the statistical technique), we find twenty-three of the thirty-five studies showing a difference in favor of the statistical method, twelve studies showing approximate equality, and no study favoring the judgmental method. Of course from the social and economic viewpoint, this really means thirty-five studies on the actuarial side. The over-all picture has, therefore, not changed since 1954, except that the proportion of "equal" outcomes has somewhat decreased.

I think that it is time for those who resist drawing any generalization from the published research, by fantasying what *would* happen if studies of a different sort *were* conducted, to do them. I claim that this crude, pragmatic box score *is* important, and that those who deny its importance do so because they just don't like the way it comes out. There are very few issues in clinical, personality, or social psychology (or, for that matter, even in such fields as animal learning) in which the research trends are as uniform as this one. Amazingly, this strong trend seems to exert almost no influence upon clinical practice, even, you may be surprised to learn, in Minnesota!

In the single study of medical diagnosis, it was found that a linear discriminant function combining the results of two biochemical tests did as well in differentiating types of jaundice as did internists who, in addition to these two tests, had available a large mass of other information, and averaged between three and four hours going over each patient's material! Some psychoclinicians oppose the actuarial method on the ground that physicians have been practicing medicine for centuries without it. This argument completely mystifies me, since, with the exception of this one study, no comparison of the two methods in organic medicine has ever been made. The frequency of erroneous diagnoses in medicine is well known, and it is hard to imagine why anyone familiar with organic medicine would give such an argument any weight.

There are physicians who have begun to apply statistical techniques, the mathematics of decision theory, and electronic computers to medical diagnosis. Those psychologists who use the analogy with medicine counteractuarially would be well advised to wait until we find out what happens there. It would be ironic indeed (but not in the least surprising to one acquainted with the sociology of our profession) if physicians in nonpsychiatric medicine should learn the actuarial lesson from biometricians and engineers, while the psychiatrist continues to muddle through with inefficient combinations of unreliable judgments because he has not been properly instructed by his colleagues in clinical psychology, who might have been expected to take the lead in this development.

I understand (anecdotally) that there are two other domains, unrelated to either personality assessment or the healing arts, in which actuarial methods of data combination seem to do at least as good a job as the traditional impressionistic methods: namely, meteorology and the forecasting of security prices. From my limited experience I have the impression that in these fields also there is a strong emotional resistance to substituting formalized techniques for human judgment. Personally, I look upon the "formal-versus-judgmental" issue as one of great generality, not confined to the clinical context. I do not see why clinical psychologists should persist in using inefficient means of combining data just because investment brokers, physicians, and weathermen do so. Meanwhile, I urge those who find the box score "35:0" distasteful to publish empirical studies filling in the score board with numbers more to their liking.

10

High School Yearbooks: A Reply to Schwarz

IN A RECENT CONTRIBUTION to the *Journal of Abnormal Psychology,* Schwarz (1970) criticized the methodology of an archival study by Barthell and Holmes (1968) on grounds which are of general interest to social scientists, and which I have treated elsewhere (Meehl, 1969a, 1969b, expanded in 1970a).[1] The paper by Barthell and Holmes provides a beautiful example, in the area of psychopathology, of a *major* unsolved problem in nonexperimental social science research, and my present purpose is to call it forcefully to the attention of readers of the psychopathology literature. With the substantive merits of Barthell and Holmes' investigation (e.g., how much light it sheds on the schizophrenia question), I am not here concerned. I shall also set aside some psychometric issues, for example, bearing of base-rate values (Meehl and Rosen, 1955—reprinted here as Chapter 2) upon causal interpretations, that would be important in an adequate over-all assessment of their particular application of archival method.

Barthell and Holmes found that retrofollowed schizophrenic and (hospitalized) psychoneurotic patients had been less socially participant in high school than a control group. The archival measure employed was number of "activities" listed for each student in the high school year-

AUTHOR'S NOTE: This paper first appeared in *Journal of Abnormal Psychology,* vol. 77, 1971; copyright 1971 by the American Psychological Association.
[1] I am indebted to my colleague Thomas J. Bouchard for calling the Schwarz and Barthell-Holmes articles to my attention.

book. A control case was identified as the student whose picture was adjacent to the (subsequently) schizophrenic student's.

Schwarz argued that this method "lacked crucial and customary precautions in the selection of a control group [because] the basic question is whether a random sample [which Schwarz allows theirs arguably to be] is an adequate control group" (p. 317), which Schwarz holds it is not. Assuming *arguendo* that "customary" precautions would have included a matching on other variables than sex and race, are these customary precautions "crucial," as Schwarz alleged? I do not wish to assert dogmatically that they are not; but it is far from clear that they are, regardless of how "customary" they may be. Let me emphasize that I do not fault Schwarz, who expresses the current social science consensus. If he were idiosyncratic in his methodological assumptions, I should not think it proper to take up space with the present paper, which is longer than the papers of Schwarz and Barthell and Holmes combined.

Schwarz believes that Barthell and Holmes should have shown that their preschizophrenics and controls did not differ in intelligence, academic achievement, or social class. He suspects (and cites supporting literature) that a random sample of non-preschizophrenics would differ on one or more of these nuisance variables from the preschizophrenic group. If so, he thinks, the data should be reanalyzed "incorporating either statistical or classificatory controls for that variable" (p. 318). My first heretical query to Schwarz is, "Why?" My second (contingent) query is, "If so, *how much?*"

I shall consider only social class, which is on present evidence the most likely of the three to be a schizophrenia correlate. (Any reader who sees the point will find it easy to apply it, mutatis mutandis, to the other two, although the intelligence variable presents additional difficulties associated with systematic psychometric error.) Why should social class be "held constant," "controlled," or "corrected for" in an archival study of the kind Barthell and Holmes did? The received view, which Schwarz (quite pardonably) accepts without questioning, is that *if* a variable Z (= social class) is a correlate of two behavioral variables X (= high school activity) and Y (= subsequent schizophrenia), *then* its "influence" must be removed. Presumably this is because, in the absence of such statistical control, the observed XY-correlation is somehow spurious or artifactual. These are my terms, not Schwarz's. I can't use his words for what is wrong, as he does not use any, that is, he

175

does not *say* explicitly what is wrong. It is fascinating testimony to the grip of the received tradition that Schwarz *nowhere states* precisely what is "wrong" with the zero-order XY correlation reported, from the interpretative standpoint. He *takes it for granted*—as almost everyone does, apparently—that any difference between patients and controls on a nuisance-variable Z that is a correlate of X and Y constitutes, ipso facto, a defect in experimental design. All he says about it is that the two groups differ, apparently deemed a sufficient objection. That is the ubiquitous and unexamined principle I wish to challenge.

Let us set aside a purely "predictive" view of the Barthell-Holmes study, since their discussion indicates, albeit unclearly, a *causal-theoretical* orientation (e.g., the locution "precipitating factor" is applied to social isolation in their abstract). Predictively, of course, an XY-relationship is what it is, and the value of a zero-order correlation as a basis of forecasting is not liquidated by what happens when we calculate, say, a partial $r_{XY\cdot Z}$ (although we may be concerned even there with the validity-generalization problem in a new practical context where the Z variance is greatly reduced—will r_{XY} in that population hold up?). The point is: statistical techniques like analysis of covariance, partial correlation, and casewise matching in "constructing" samples are almost always aimed at unscrambling a *causal* question. The reason we worry about the "influence" of a nuisance variable like social class is that we want our investigation to shed light on what influences what, and the presence of nuisance variables in the system is believed to complicate matters interpretively. I certainly do not wish to deny that it complicates matters; on the contrary, my complaint to Schwarz is that he makes them less complicated than they are, by presupposing the role of social class as a nuisance variable must lie solely on the *causal input* side. This we do not know, and I for one do not believe it. Further, there are causal chains with social class as an input variable in which its influence is mediated by social isolation as a penultimate link, in which case statistical suppression of the shared variance would mask a real effect of the kind Barthell and Holmes want to study.

Let us assume with Schwarz that in the (somewhat ill-defined) population of high school seniors sampled by Barthell and Holmes, both low social class and low social participation are associated with a higher probability of subsequently developing schizophrenia. (Throughout this paper, I neglect both sampling errors and trend size, that is, is the relation large enough to have *either* practical or theoretical significance? Most "statistically significant" correlations in this field are, of course, too small to possess either, and hence are worthless either clinically or scientifically, but that is a topic for another paper!) Thinking in terms of genetic, social, and psychological influences, what are some of the plausible causal chains that might underlie such correlations? Consider these possibilities:

1. Lower class students have less money to spend, hence join fewer activity groups, hence suffer more social isolation, which isolation helps precipitate schizophrenia.

2. Lower class students are perceived by peers as lower class, hence snobbishly rejected from activity groups *on a class basis,* hence suffer more social isolation, which . . .

3. Lower class students tend to acquire less competent social skills in home and neighborhood, hence tend to be peer-rejected (but not on an explicit *class basis*), hence . . .

4. Lower class children tend to be the victims of dyshygienic child-rearing practices, hence develop more battered self-concepts, exaggerated social fear, pathogenic defense systems, etc.—personality attributes that raise the odds of subsequent schizophrenia. These attributes also lead them to be lower social participators.

5. The genes predisposing to schizophrenia are polygenes contributing to anxiety-proneness, social introversion, low dominance, low energy level, low persistence, etc. These genetic factors tend to produce lesser social competence in the preschizophrenics, reflected in their low participation. But they received these genes from their ancestors, in whom these same genes tended to produce lesser social competence in our competitive, extraverted, energetic, work-oriented American culture (see footnote 17 in Meehl, 1970a).

6. While schizoidia is a Mendelizing (dominant) trait, uncorrelated with social class, whether a schizotype remains compensated or not (Gottesman and Shields, 1972; Heston, 1966, 1970; Hoch and Polatin, 1949; Meehl, 1962—reprinted here as Chapter 7, 1964, 1972b—reprinted here as Chapter 11; Rado, 1956, 1960; Rado and Daniels, 1956) depends upon (a) polygenes as in 5 above; (b) bad child-rearing practices as in 4 above; and (c) "accidental" stresses in adult life (e.g., foreclosed mortgage). Since a, b, and c are all correlates of parental family's social class, the incidence of (clinically diagnosable) schizo-

phrenia is higher for lower class schizotypes. And since both a and b influence social participation in high school, variables X and Z will be correlated.

This list of six hypothetical causal chains is merely illustrative (although I myself find all six eminently reasonable guesses, on what we now know). The reader will, given these examples, find it easy to cook up another half-dozen defensible chains. I need hardly add that those chains listed are not incompatible, but could (I think, probably do) operate conjointly to generate the observed correlations. For a set of helpful diagrams delineating the ways in which causal arrows can account for correlations, see Kempthorne (1957, p. 285).

Which among the six chains, if operative in pure form, would require an archival researcher to "control" social class, on pain of wrongly interpreting an XY correlation that is "spurious" or "artifactual"? I submit it is not clear that *any* of them would, or, assuming some would, to what *extent* shared components of variance should be suppressed. The substantive theory of interest, that social isolation is a *precipitator* of schizophrenia, is harmonious with Chains 1, 2, and 3, these three chains differing in their *earlier* linkages between social class and the personality traits involved, but sharing the feature that the penultimate link is social isolation (however induced). Chain 4 does not fit the authors' precipitator hypothesis, but neither does it generate a spurious XY correlation. On the Chain 4 interpretation, the personality dispositions that predispose to schizophrenia "validly" overlap with those conducive to low high school participation; there is nothing spurious about the relationship, which is an even more intimate one than direct causal influence, to wit, identical elements. To what extent the self-maintained social isolation of a schizotype should be conceived as a *causal agent* rather than a *dispositional-sampling precursor* depends upon the unknown psychodynamic details of schizophrenic decompensation. But it is hardly conceivable that it would always be one and never the other. The impression one forms during intensive psychotherapy of borderline cases, whatever the therapists' etiological bias, is that these processes are typically characterized by marked feedback and autocatalytic features.

In Chains 5 and 6, social isolation is not literally a precipitant, but it is an indirect, low-validity *indicator* of the same causal influence that gives rise to schizophrenia. To control for social class would be misleading because it would suppress statistically the set of valid causal factors (genes) that are responsible not only for both "output" variables (social participation and subsequent schizophrenia) but also for the nuisance variable (social class of parental family). This error, neglecting the possibility of *any* genetic influence upon social class, thereby taking it as axiomatic that social class functions solely on the causal "input" side, is undoubtedly the commonest methodological vice in contemporary social science research, so much so that Jensen (1969, p. 221) labels it the "sociologist's fallacy" (*his* language, not mine!). In Chains 5 and 6, we see that it would be grossly misleading to treat the *XY* relation as somehow "spurious" when uncorrected for *Z*, since the schizophrenia and participation variables are *psychologically* related; yet this perfectly respectable nonspurious relationship does not tend to support the Barthell-Holmes "precipitator" view. Hence a social class control imposed for incorrect reasons might nevertheless facilitate correct interpretation!

Suppose that Barthell and Holmes had concocted matched pairs with social class as the basis of matching. Since (on Schwarz's assumptions) both schizophrenia and social participation are class correlates, either the resulting sample of preschizophrenics will be atypical (higher class than usual), or the controls will be more lower class than usual, or both. (The usual result of case-matching on even a few variables is marked reduction in both variance and *N* due to the constraints imposed in finding a "statistical twin"; see, for example, Chapin, 1955). What question would Barthell and Holmes then be asking and answering? Presumably: Do high school students who later develop schizophrenia but who differ from the average preschizophrenic by coming from higher social class backgrounds show less social participation than a nonrandom sample of *non*-preschizophrenic controls selected for having somewhat lower class backgrounds than students generally? Maybe the answer to this funny question is scientifically interesting, but it is unclear to me why it would be.

Of course my six causal-chain examples, while perfectly conceivable, and, as I think, plausible, were chosen with pedagogical intent, to make the point. I am not so foolish as to dispute the existence of spurious correlations, although I find that language misleading and prefer to speak of "incorrect interpretations" of correlations. My view is that unless a correlation arises from errors of sampling, measurement, or computation, it is not spurious. (There is a sense in which even the paradigm case of "spurious index correlation" ought not to be labeled spurious, since, after all, it *does* tell us how well one index can be predicted from the other.) Surely there are plausible causal chains in which failure to control social class would tempt an archival researcher to grossly erroneous inferences? Of course there are, as witness the following:

7. Lower class students, having less money to spend, cannot afford to participate in as many social activities as middle class and upper class students. While this may distress some of them, it does not engender a pathogenic social isolation (i.e., has no causal role as a schizophrenia-precipitator in their post-school adult life). But the economic stresses and status frustrations they suffer as adults act (upon predisposed individuals) to precipitate schizophrenia. Hence the correlation found by Barthell and Holmes arises.

8. Polygenes contributory to schizophrenia in the subjects were contributory to lesser social competence in their parents, hence to their lower social class. Independently of student personalities, class snobbery in high school tends to "keep out" these students from certain social activities, although this exclusion exerts no appreciable pathogenic influence.

In Chain 7, the nuisance variable *produces* the correlation, but its influence on schizophrenia rate is not mediated by any social isolation link in the causal chain, nor is there any sharing of *psychological* links between the terminal branches, unlike that in Chains 1–5 and, perhaps Chain 6. In Chain 8, the nuisance variable *produces* one effect and *reflects* the causal antecedent (genes) of the other. In both chains, the correlational evidence for a theory involving a pathogenic role of social isolation cannot be properly interpreted unless the nuisance variable's "statistical influence" is removed. We note that whether social isolation is conceived strictly as a *pathogenic agent* or more loosely as a *psychological precursor* (i.e., perhaps partly pathogenic and partly dispositional) of schizophrenia makes no difference in these last two chains: either interpretation is erroneous, the nuisance variable here having served a *truly* "nuisance" role in the statistical system.

Contemplation of all eight hypothetical chains suffices to disabuse one of the easy notion that controlling social class is at least "playing it safe," the commonest response I get from students and colleagues when I raise these questions. It is obvious that in Chains 1, 2, and 3, for example, if the "control" of social class were to liquidate Barthell and

Holmes' original finding, the received methodology would lead us to conclude wrongly. We would say: "Since—when proper controls exist—there is no correlation between low high school activity and subsequent schizophrenia, the substantive theory of interest (isolation as a precipitator) is discorroborated." But that would be a mistaken inference, for any of these three chains. One cannot label a methodological rule as playing it safe when it is likely to produce pseudofalsifications, unless we have a strange philosophy of science that says we want wrongly to abandon good theories so as to avoid temporarily betting on false ones!

Of course Schwarz may reply, "I will amend my criticism thus: Barthell and Holmes should have reported *both* corrected and uncorrected trends. Given Meehl's arguments, I will not insist that their reported correlations are 'wrong' or 'spurious,' or that the 'corrected' relationships are the 'true' ones. But surely we know more if we have both to think about?" With this I cheerfully agree. Insofar as I understand it, that is the line of thought behind path analysis. More generally, it is the rationale of all multivariate methods, where the more variables we put into the hopper, and the more we antecedently know about each one's causal role, the better able we are to interpret the total pattern of correlations. It goes without saying that statistical manipulations cannot provide an automatic "inference-machine," but the tendency in social science is to treat control of nuisance variables in that way. Whether the number and nature of the five variables under discussion is such that we would know *importantly* more with respect to the task of causal interpretation is, I submit, impossible to say.

This is not the place to develop the theme further. Whether the revived interest in such old techniques as path analysis (Werts and Linn, 1970) will result in a general solution is not presently foreseeable, although I incline to doubt it. Simon and Rescher (1966) have presented a highly general formal analysis which, if I understand them correctly, suggests (proves?) that *no* statistical method can do the job. My sole aim in this paper is to call attention to the methodological mistake, repeated by Schwarz but in the best company of "establishment" social science, of assuming that social class and similar nuisance variables should always be "controlled" in archival research. Whether they should or not depends upon one's causal presuppositions, which in this kind of research are usually as problematic as the substantive theory being tested, sometimes more so.

181

11

Specific Genetic Etiology, Psychodynamics, and Therapeutic Nihilism

DR. ERLENMEYER-KIMLING [guest editor of the issue of the journal in which this paper originally appeared, an issue devoted to "Genetics and Mental Disorders"] has assigned to me one of the most difficult and unrewarding of scholarly tasks, to wit, expounding the obvious. My feeling is that if a clinician or behavior scientist needs the clarifications of this paper, it can only be because he is so ideologically committed that he will be psychologically unable to receive them. For the others it will be just one more exposition of "what every informed and sophisticated person knows." But I accepted the job, so I shall do my best, endeavoring to keep in mind Gide's all-too-true comment that "It has all been said before, but you must say it again, since nobody listens."

The Problem: Theoretical Integration

I am reliably informed, by Dr. Erlenmeyer-Kimling (and others who get about the country more than I do), that some psychologists and psy-

AUTHOR'S NOTE: This paper originally appeared in the *International Journal of Mental Health*, vol. 1, 1972; copyright 1972 by the International Arts and Sciences Press, Inc., White Plains, N.Y.

I am indebted to the Carnegie Corporation for support of my summer appointment as professor in the Minnesota Center for Philosophy of Science, and to Dr. Irving I. Gottesman for suggestions on improving this manuscript.

chiatrists persist in rejecting the strong evidence for genetic factors in the etiology of schizophrenia (Gottesman and Shields, 1968, 1972; Heston, 1966, 1970; Jackson, 1960; Kety and Rosenthal, 1968). I know that many clinicians and social scientists either ignore or "explain away" the evidence for genetic factors as co-determiners of other behavior disorders, and even of intelligence, temperament, and "personality" traits generally—evidence that is already considerable and accumulating at an accelerated rate (Manosevitz, Lindzey, and Thiessen, 1969). Clinicians typically react negatively to genetic formulations on the ground that a genetic emphasis contradicts what we know about psychodynamics; that, as a corollary, it makes psychological intervention (e.g., psychotherapy, behavior modification, milieu therapy, vigorous combating of the hospitalization syndrome) theoretically incomprehensible or pragmatically useless; and, finally, that the over-all result would be the development among professionals of a malignant therapeutic nihilism. Since no informed person in my immediate academic vicinity advances such arguments, I find them puzzling. It is hard to answer an argument whose structure one does not understand.

I take it for granted, as a practicing psychotherapist interested in behavior genetics, that some day—perhaps sooner than we had dared to hope even a decade ago—there will exist at least the broad outlines of a truly *integrated theory* of schizophrenia. By the locution "integrated theory" I do not mean such clichés as "Every organism has a heredity and an environment." Nor do I mean the kind of perfunctory nod to "psychological stresses" given by nondynamically trained psychiatrists of the old school (are there really any left?), or the equally perfunctory nod to "constitutional factors" by those of the opposite persuasion. It is time for us to stop being biotropes or sociotropes. This stuff is perhaps all right for after-dinner speeches, but a truly integrated theory of schizophrenia will formulate the interactions between genetically determined dispositions of the individual and his social learning regime. That is, such a theory will specify *what it is* that is inherited, i.e., what parameters of the nervous system are aberrant as a result close in the causal chain to the gene or genes; what the *genetic model* (Mendelizing, polygenic?) is; and *how* the combination of aversive social learnings in the early developmental history, plus the precipitating stressors acting on the adult end product of these aversive learnings, results (as I assume) in the psychodynamics, the phenomenology, and the clinical symptomatology of the disorder. (Note I say stress*ors*—environmental events or situations that produce *stress* in the disposed individual.)

I would not require that a genuinely integrated theory explain *everything* about schizophrenia, a preposterous demand, which we do not customarily make of any theory in the biological or social sciences. At this stage of our knowledge, it is probably bad strategy to spend time theorizing about small effects, low correlations, minor discrepancies between studies, and the like. The "big facts" about schizophrenia should hold the spotlight; and it is methodologically healthy—if not overdone—to "sit loose" with respect to the host of small empirical puzzles. Some of the argumentation one reads could be analogized to a medical geneticist's fretting over his current inability to explain, say, a correlation of .30 between gout and income, or the higher male rate of clinical nephritis in rheumatic fever.

Being a neo-Popperian in the philosophy of science, I am myself quite comfortable engaging in speculative formulations completely unsubstantiated by data (Bunge, 1964; Lakatos, 1968; Lakatos and Musgrave, 1970; references in Meehl, 1970c; Popper, 1959; Schilpp, in press). I am not an inductivist. To "justify" concocting a theory, all one needs is a problem, plus a notion (I use a weak word advisedly) of how one might test one's theory (= subject it to the danger of refutation). Better, in the light of recent historical studies, one might settle for an even more tolerant demand: A theorist may properly be expected to indicate what notions he has about tests of his theory, given such-and-such *other* things he would need to know, but does not at present know (cf. Meehl, 1970c). Therefore, I shall not hesitate to use my own speculative theory of schizophrenia as an example of what a genuinely integrated theory *would* look like (Meehl, 1962—reprinted here as Chapter 7; 1964). It may have low verisimilitude; but it is an integrated theory. The substantive verisimilitude of this theory is of no interest to me here, nor should it be to the reader.

Genome-Environment Interaction: Discouraged Mice, Color-Blind Men

Let us begin not with schizophrenia, but with the mouse. Suppose I subject a sample of laboratory mice to a somewhat complicated experimental regime in the operant conditioning chamber ("Skinner box"—

see Skinner, 1938; also Ferster and Skinner, 1957; Honig, 1966). When the mouse presses the lever, he sometimes receives a food pellet, sometimes not (intermittent schedule); lever pressing is sometimes followed —unpredictably and sometimes noncontingently—by delivery of a painful electric shock to the mouse's feet. Suppose we assign the parameters of these positive and negative reinforcing schedules so they differ greatly from one mouse to another. At the end of our experiment, we find that a rather small proportion (say, 1 percent) of the large initial sample of mice (chosen at random from within our laboratory colony) have become either so thoroughly extinguished on the food-reward schedule or so intimidated by the shock schedule, or both (usually both), that they no longer press the lever with sufficient frequency to maintain life were the box their sole means of obtaining food.

Being expert learning theorists, we understand in great detail what has happened to these unfortunate mice, including the quantitative aspects of the patterns of positive and negative reinforcement that are more *likely* to yield this "bad" result. In the light of that understanding, we are able to make fairly effective psychological interventions by suitable changes in the schedule. Our methods are so effective that even completely discouraged mice can be, under sufficiently ingenious and patient Skinner-box "treatment," brought to pressing the lever again and getting enough food to stay alive. In a few instances we are able, over a long period of time, to bring them back to "normal," so that they behave very much like mice that have never been shocked or extinguished, although we do notice that even these "cured" cases persist in showing a somewhat greater tendency to slip into hopeless and aversively controlled behavior if they have a run of bad luck or if we reintroduce the shock, however briefly and weakly. Admittedly there are some theoretical puzzles remaining (e.g., why is it that mouse number 5 has ended up in the massively discouraged group whereas mouse number 7, whose schedule and initial sequence of responses and inputs were hardly distinguishable from mouse number 5's, did not reach this sorry end state?). But except for these puzzles, we have a fairly complete understanding of *what* was learned, *how* it was learned, and what some of the ways are in which we can *help the mouse to unlearn* what we taught him by this scrambled regime of rewards and punishments. We have, in other words, a fairly satisfactory sociology and psychodynamics of the phenomenon "massive Skinner-box discouragement in the mouse."

Now comes some scoundrel of a behavior geneticist with surprising information. He first reminds us that although our box-behavior theory is quite impressive, and the application of its principles to treating the discouraged mice was fairly successful, we have been de-emphasizing a big statistical fact, to wit, that only a small minority of the mice (1 percent) became *this badly* discouraged. He now tells us that our laboratory population consisted (unbeknownst to us) of two homozygous mouse strains, and that practically every one of the massively discouraged mice belongs to a minority strain that previous research has shown to have pronounced genetic loadings for "high anxiety" and "rapid food-extinguishability." How, as rational minds, should we receive this information? Should we be threatened by it as learning theorists, or discouraged by it as mouse clinicians? Clearly not. *The learning theory is just as well supported by the facts relating the regimes to the outcomes as it was before. And whatever "therapeutic" efficacy was demonstrated for reconditioning the lever pressing and extinguishing conditioned anxiety is just as good as it was before.* Nothing we understood about how the mouse learns and unlearns food-getting behavior or shock-avoiding behavior, and the delicate interplay between these two in the various regimes imposed, is *in the least* disharmonious with a *parametric* finding concerning individual differences. In fact, our new information really serves to fill out our causal understanding, because it explains what had been mysterious, namely, why we can find quite a few mouse pairs whose schedules, and whose initial behavior sequences on those schedules, were substantially indistinguishable, but which did not end up in the same state.

Readers unfamiliar with the behavior genetics literature might consult, for a fascinating and persuasive example of this interaction between genetic dispositions and learning experiences, the classic study by Freedman (1958), in which the following two conclusions are clearly shown: (1) how some dogs react to food "temptation" when the human experimenter leaves the room depends greatly on their socialization experiences with humans when they were puppies, and (2) there are genetic strain differences in the effect of these socializing experiences, e.g., the Basenji does not form a good canine conscience under either social regime, whereas the Shetland sheepdog forms what Freud would call a very harsh superego! For further examples, see Manosevitz, Lindzey, and Thiessen (1969) and references cited therein. My own (jaded) view is that by combining theoretical considerations with the evidence now available, we could properly conclude that whether or not a given experiment on different genetic strains detects a (strain × experience) interaction depends almost wholly upon (a) construct validity of the measures, (b) efficacy of the operations, and (c) statistical power of the design and sample size. *Genes will always make a difference if one does the experiment right.* I suggest that further research aimed merely to show that "strains differ" is a waste of time. But I admit that this opinion stems partly from my belief that the null hypothesis is (quasi-) always false (Badia, Haber, and Runyon, 1970; Lykken, 1968; Meehl, 1967a; Morrison and Henkel, 1970).

Returning to psychopathology, in lecturing to clinical psychology students (who usually suffer from the sociotrope-biotrope conflict), I have found the fantasy of a "color neurosis" pedagogically helpful. To quote an earlier paper of mine,

There is no contradiction between classifying a patient as belonging to a certain taxonomic group and attempting concurrently to understand his motivations and his defenses. Even if a certain major mental disease were found to be of organic or genetic origin, it would not be necessary to abandon any well-established psychodynamic interpretations. Let me give you an analogy. Suppose that there existed a color-oriented culture in which a large part of social, economic, and sexual behavior was dependent upon precise color discriminations. In such a culture, a child who makes errors in color behavior will be teased by his peer group, will be rejected by an overanxious parent who cannot tolerate the idea of having produced an inferior or deviant child, and so on. One who was unfortunate enough to inherit the gene for color blindness might develop a color neurosis. He might be found as an adult on the couch of a color therapist, where he would produce a great deal of material which would be historically relevant and which would give us a picture of the particular pattern of his current color dynamics. But none of this answers the question "What is fundamentally the matter with these people?"—that is, what do all such patients have in common? What they have in common, of course, is that defective gene on the X chromosome; and this, while it does not provide a *sufficient* condition for a color neurosis in such a culture, does provide the *necessary* condition. It is in this sense that a nosologist in that culture could legitimately argue that "color neuroticism" is an inherited disease [Meehl, 1959b—reprinted here as Chapter 5].

Philosophical Excursus: Orders of Dispositions

Clinicians would have less trouble assimilating these relationships, which are complex only with respect to their mathematics and the number of

187

causal chains involved, but are conceptually rather simple, if they would familiarize themselves with some elementary philosophical notions about dispositions (see, for example, Broad, 1933; Carnap, 1936–37, 1956; Pap, 1958a, 1958b, 1962; Sellars, 1958). The world consists of four kinds of entities—structures, events, states, and dispositions. There are *orders* of dispositions, a disposition of order k being, roughly, the tendency to acquire a disposition of order $(k - 1)$. For example, "magnetic" is a first-order disposition, and "magnetizable" is a second-order disposition. (Thus, iron is magnetizable, since it can be made magnetic.) If a nonmagnetizable substance can be transmuted so as to be magnetizable, that possibility corresponds to a third-order disposition. The basic idea is, of course, older than modern analytic philosophy, being found explicitly in Aquinas, and in Aristotle before him.

At the molar level (Littman and Rosen, 1950; Tolman, 1932) of behavior and experience, what the genes provide is dispositions. Most of these dispositions are of higher order than the first; that is to say, they are *dispositions to develop capacities* to acquire abilities to acquire achievements, these last being dispositions of the first order. For example, a child with the PKU genotype has fourth-order dispositions to develop defective intellectual capacities unless his phenylalanine intake is restricted, and to develop normal capacity under proper dietary regime. His intellectual *capacity* (say, "first, big factor") is a third-order disposition to acquire numerous second-order dispositions, such as the *ability* to learn algebra or English, knowing algebra or English being first-order dispositions.

But obviously, this child's *learning* of algebra, or his preference for certain stylistic features in speaking English, has a complicated social learning history. An adequate account of either would include reference to his self-concept, his unconscious fantasies, his identification with his professor father or his sonata-writing mother, and the like. None of these experiential factors is a mere "frill" on genetic explanation. On the contrary, to understand his English-speaking behavior or why he prefers geometry to algebra it is imperative to determine in detail (as we did with the study of our Skinner-box mice, or as we do in treating a patient on the couch) which kinds of experiences, *in which sequence,* resulted in his now having such-and-such mental content, linked with such-and-such drives, affects, defenses, etc.

The fact remains that a PKU child's disposition ("ability") to learn arithmetic depends upon the nonrealization of a (pathological) third-order disposition ("incapacity"), which nonrealization, in turn, depends upon an adequate biochemical assessment of a fourth-order (pathological) disposition of genetic origin.

Philosophical confusion about orders of dispositions is responsible for the naive view that "If schizophrenia has a specific genetic etiology, we can't do anything about it. But psychotherapy does help. Ergo, it cannot have a genetic basis." It is hard for me to believe that psychotherapists persist in saying this. But I have heard it myself; and I am told that in some parts of the country it is commonly heard. Schizophrenia is a complicated collection of learned social responses, object cathexes, self-concepts, ego weaknesses, psychodynamisms, etc. These are dispositions of first or second order. They are *not* provided by our genes. They are acquired by social learning, especially learning involving interpersonal aversiveness. Assume the mutated gene (a structure) causes an aberrant neurohumor that directly alters signal selectively at the synapse (Meehl, 1962—see Chapter 7 above). Then the gene is a *structure;* the gene-controlled synthesis of an abnormal substance (or failure to make a certain substance) is an *event;* the altered synaptic condition is a *state;* and the result of that state's existing at the billions of CNS synapses is an altered parameter of CNS function, i.e., a *disposition*. But this disposition is a disposition of at least third (perhaps fourth or fifth) order with respect to those molar dispositions that are the subject matter of clinical psychiatry and psychoanalysis. Hence an individual's being characterized by a certain genotype is a disposition of still higher order, because (presumably) the synaptic disposition itself is not an absolutely *necessary* consequence of the first link of the gene's action, since it could be avoided if we knew how to supplement the brain's inadequate supply of magic substance X, or how to provide a related molecule that would bring the parameters of CNS function back to the "normal" base.

Etiology and Healing

In the diagram on page 190 (which I consider, as the caption says, of *minimum* complexity for even a *sketch* of an integrated theory of schizophrenia) the reader can discern that at all levels except the very bottom one, a systematic alteration in the social-reinforcement schedule, whether

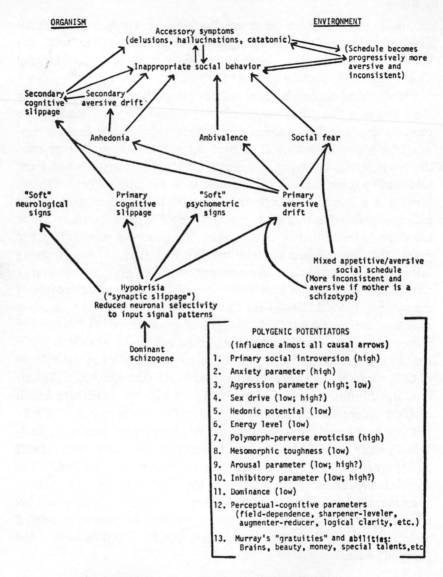

Figure 1. Causal chains in schizophrenia,
minimum complexity (Meehl, 1966)

190

in the early developmental stages (preferable, of course, as psycho-dynamic prophylaxis) or in the adult decompensated case (as by milieu therapy, behavior modification, or psychotherapy) can influence the causal arrows. There is nothing—I repeat, *nothing*—about the postula-tion of a dominant schizogene as the first link in the causal chain that requires me as a psychotherapist to deny what I know about the psycho-dynamics and phenomenology of the schizophrenic patient, to believe that he is "hopeless," or to play down the importance of family and social factors in determining who falls ill, how ill he becomes, what his "content" emphasizes, or how hard it is to help him back to mental health. What scientific or philosophical reason could a genetically knowledgeable clinician have for thinking that a disposition is more (or less) "real" than the process of its actualization, or the causal events that in fact actualized it? Dispositions, structure, states, events— all are real, as real as can be. It is our undergraduate education in coarse and slovenly mental habits that does us in when we try to think clearly about these matters.

Of course, any psychotherapist who believes that under his gentle ministrations patients with clear-cut cases of clinical schizophrenia have become "just like anybody else" will find it hard to accept a causal diagram even as complicated as mine. But I have never met a psycho-therapist who made such a preposterous claim; and I must say, in all frankness, that I would not believe him if he did. (Most psychotherapists would not be so rash as to say this even for the "good, healthy neurotic"!) But I am convinced, as convinced as those psychotherapists who resist assimilating the growing body of genetic data, that I have benefited most of my schizoid or schizophrenic patients—which, theoretically, I should, given my high score on the Whitehorn-Betz A-B scale of the Strong Vocational Interest Blank and a profile pattern resembling that of therapists "good with schizophrenics" (Whitehorn and Betz, 1954, 1960; but see also Betz, 1967; Campbell, Stevens, Uhlenhuth, and Johansson, 1968; McNair, Callahan, and Lorr, 1962).

I rather suspect one reason most psychoclinicians do not feel re-assured about therapeutic nihilism when presented with such familiar "optimistic" examples as diabetes, gout, and PKU is that what they have in mind is psychotherapy, not chemotherapy or dietary therapy. That is why I hope my mouse example and color-neurosis example are pedagogically more illuminating and reassuring than the examples from

191

internal medicine. But I must confess that antihereditarian clinicians do show a sound intuition here, given their ideology. I would view modification by chemical methods of the critical CNS parameter as, in an important sense, a more *basic* therapeutic intervention than psychotherapy. To say that chemical methods do not "get at the root of the problem," one of the current clichés of my profession (in which prescribing Stelazine is analogized to "giving aspirin for a brain tumor"), begs the question. What one considers the "root of the problem" depends upon his causal model.

Most persons do *not* become schizophrenic under the impact of a battle-ax mother. Suppose we conjecture that a few do so because they have something wrong with their brains on a biochemical basis. Then, although I myself would prefer to steer clear of dangerous metaphors like "What is the root of the problem?" (since a sophisticated causal analysis cannot easily assign different "importance" to the *actualizing of a disposition* by mother's behavior and the *disposition itself* given by the gene!), I suppose one might view the biochemical aberration as *in some sense* more "rootlike." Philosophical analysis could lead one to say, if pressed, that an innate disposition is more "rootlike" than the subsequent condition for its actualization—*especially when the actualizing condition is common, but the disposition is rare.* We have, permitting a nomic notation with a causal arrow, where D = schizoid disposition, C = actualizing condition (= battle-ax mother), and R = reaction (= clinical decompensation = schizophrenia),

$$D = (C \rightarrow R),$$

and the further fact that, in a specified population of organisms, the probabilities of these three stand in the relation:

$$P(R) < P(D) \ll P(C).$$

I am in rather good company here:

I will digress for a moment to ask if you know what is meant by a causal therapy. That is how we describe a procedure which does not take the symptoms of an illness as its point of attack but sets about removing its *causes*. Well, then, is our psychoanalytic method a causal therapy or not? The reply is not a simple one, but it may perhaps give us an opportunity of realizing the worthlessness of a question framed in this way. Insofar as analytic therapy does not make it its first task to remove the symptoms, it is behaving like a causal therapy. In another respect, you may say, it is not. For we long ago traced the causal chain back through the repressions to the in-

192

stinctual dispositions, their relative intensities in the constitution and the deviations in the course of their development. Supposing, now, that it was possible, by some chemical means, perhaps, to interfere in this mechanism, to increase or diminish the quantity of libido present at a given time or to strengthen one instinct at the cost of another—this then would be a causal therapy in the true sense of the word, for which our analysis would have carried out the indispensable preliminary work of reconnaissance. At present, as you know, there is no question of any such method of influencing libidinal processes; with our psychical therapy we attack at a different point in the combination—not exactly at what we know are the roots of the phenomena, but nevertheless far enough away from the symptoms, at a point which has been made accessible to us by some very remarkable circumstances. [Freud, 1917 as reprinted 1963, pp. 435–436.]

Another passage from the master of psychodynamics, showing (as usual) how much clearer a thinker he was than some of his American epigones, is the following:

I take this opportunity of defending myself against the mistaken charge of having denied the importance of innate (constitutional) factors because I have stressed that of infantile impressions. A charge such as this arises from the restricted nature of what men look for in the field of causation: In contrast to what ordinarily holds good in the real world, people prefer to be satisfied with a single causative factor. Psychoanalysis has talked a lot about the accidental factors in aetiology and little about the constitutional ones; but that is only because it was able to contribute something fresh to the former, while, to begin with, it knew no more than was commonly known about the latter. We refuse to posit any contrast in principle between the two sets of aetiological factors; on the contrary, we assume that the two sets regularly act jointly in bringing about the observed result. Δαίμων καὶ Τύχη [Endowment and Chance] determine a man's fate—rarely or never one of these powers alone. The amount of aetiological effectiveness to be attributed to each of them can only be arrived at in every individual case separately. These cases may be arranged in a series according to the varying proportion in which the two factors are present, and this series will no doubt have its extreme cases. We shall estimate the share taken by constitution or experience differently in individual cases according to the stage reached by our knowledge; and we shall retain the right to modify our judgment along with changes in our understanding. [Freud, 1912 as reprinted 1958, p. 99, footnote 2.]

See also the beautifully clear dispositional formulation in Freud's reply to Löwenfeld's criticism of the anxiety neurosis (Freud, 1895 as reprinted 1962).

Confining ourselves to psychotherapeutic interventions, however, we cannot really think that treatment choice is more effective when it is based upon erroneous causal understanding such as leads to the adoption of unrealistic therapeutic goals. (I say treatment *choice* because it is possible, perhaps even likely, that *treatment* may sometimes be qualitatively superior because the psychotherapist is under optimistic illusions.) I entertain the dark suspicion that many (most?) of the interminable analyses currently taking place among the well-heeled of our society are partly attributable to the adoption of unrealistic therapeutic goals by patient and analyst, that is, both trying to make a silk purse out of a sow's ear—which sometimes means trying to make a "good, healthy neurotic" out of a schizotype (Mcehl, 1965b). The delivery of mental health care services will, in my opinion, become more rational and economically sound, especially given the terrible scarcity of skilled personnel, as our assessment techniques (and the ancillary contribution of the psychotropic drugs) become less hit-and-miss than at the present time.

How to Think about Entities, and How Not To

One intellectual disorder that is endemic to my profession (and, strangely enough, also prevalent among psychiatrists, whose medical training should help them know better) is the habit of dissolving these complicated questions by incantation, using catchphrases such as "disease entity" or "medical model." (I actually had the experience of a psychiatrist's explaining to me patiently and gently at a cocktail party, "You know, Paul, we really shouldn't think of schizophrenia like mumps or measles." *I* need *this* kind of instruction?) I have not found such talk in the least clarifying to my own thought, and I observe that it consistently muddles the thinking of others. Those who talk and write this way almost never bother to explain rigorously just what the "medical model" or "disease-entity concept" consists of. It would be a salutary exercise for them to attempt such an explication, perhaps confining themselves to well-known, nonpsychiatric diseases whose etiology and pathology are not in dispute. They would find, in short order, that *there is actually no clearly formulable "disease-entity" model,* even in neurology or internal medicine. One can discern nothing obviously common—in the postulated causal structure, in the statistical relations between signs or symptoms and the defining etiology, and in the approach to prophylaxis and treatment—among the following conditions, all of which are recognized "disease entities": Huntington's Disease, pellagra, measles, rheumatoid arthritis, subacute bacterial endocarditis, congenital aneurysm, idiopathic epilepsy, general paresis, dementia senilis, obesity, diabetic gangrene, appendicitis, gout, cerebral fat embolism following bone-crushing trauma. So far as I have been able to ascertain, no general systematic conceptual clarification has been done within organic medicine on the metaquestion "When does a disease entity *exist?*" That being so, tossing around phrases like "the medical model" or "the disease-entity concept" in the field of behavior genetics can hardly be expected to clarify anything much.

In analyzing the problem of a *taxonomic entity* (I am not myself the least bit interested in the label "disease," or the perennial trade-union hassling over whether mental disorder is "illness"), there are four *kinds* of questions to be explored if this is to be an intellectually responsible enterprise rather than the burblings of a cliché artist. They are:

1. *Philosophical-methodological:* Here we struggle with metatheoretical problems concerning contextual or "implicit" definition, reduction sentences, counterfactuals, open concepts, operationism, the logic of inexact concepts, the distinction between stipulations and assertions, frame analyticity, orders of dispositions, and the like. The literature on dispositions and counterfactuals is considerable, and mostly not helpful to the biological or social scientist (see, for example, footnote 12 in Meehl, 1970a). On the very important problem of open concepts, the "ordinary language" movement in contemporary philosophy—at last, thankfully, becoming moribund—has exerted a particularly malignant effect by discouraging young philosophers from constructive attempts at rigorous formulation of a metatheory of loose concepts. The reader may perhaps best be referred to Black (1937, 1970), Campbell and Fiske (1959), Carnap (1936–37), Copilowish (1939), Cronbach and Meehl (1955—reprinted here as Chapter 1), Hempel (1939, 1952, 1965—Chapters 6–7), Kaplan (1946), Loevinger (1957), Meehl (1959b—reprinted here as Chapter 5), Pap (1953, 1958b—Chapter 11, "Reduction and Open Concepts," probably the best single treatment), and Robinson (1950). I do not suggest that formal, technical expertise in the philosophy of science is necessary to a behavior geneticist; that would be absurd. I *do* say that some of our current hangups arise partly from methodological misconceptions that are "philosophical" in nature, although the arguments are not put in the logician's terminology.

Space limitations forbid my showing this here, but I have in preparation a general methodological paper on open concepts and testability that utilizes examples from psychiatric taxonomy and behavior genetics. To whet the reader's appetite, I adumbrate that presentation.

In almost any discussion of research strategy or data interpretation, one will hear plausible statements like the following: "You cannot study the genetics of schizophrenia until agreement exists on a *definitive* set of diagnostic signs." "To add a new symptomatic indicator to the list constituting a syndrome, or to justify a shift in the diagnostic weights within the received list, either (a) is an arbitrary redefinition or (b) requires nonsymptomatic criteria to validate it." "To rediagnose a case because its subsequent clinical course disconfirms expectation is an arbitrary act (or, 'circular')." "To say that 'true schizophrenia' refers to the genetically determined cases and all others are phenocopies is viciously circular." "We cannot assign differential diagnostic weights to the elements of a syndrome unless we have an external criterion, as in neuropathology." "Since all classifications are arbitrary anyway, and mental patients differ from normal persons in ways that exist in all degrees, it makes no scientific sense to ask whether an entity like schizophrenia 'really exists,' and the use or avoidance of this concept is a matter of preference only." "It is inadmissible to explain a given symptom as caused by a disease D unless we can define the term 'D' independently of its symptoms. Otherwise we would be mixing empirical relationships and meaning stipulations." "Any diagnostic cutting score on a continuous indicator variable will be arbitrary, a matter of semantics or convenience." "I can find you a so-called 'schizophrenic' who is more similar symptomatically to some manic-depressives than to most schizophrenics, which proves there is no such entity as schizophrenia." "To speculate that a particular person has the disposition to schizophrenia even though he has survived the morbidity risk period without becoming clinically schizophrenic is scientifically meaningless."

None of these familiar remarks is expressed in technical philosophese; but they are all methodological in nature. *And they are all erroneous.* The last one, for example, imposes a criterion of empirical meaningfulness whose grave disadvantages were already shown by Carnap more than three decades ago (Carnap 1936–37, pp. 461–463)—when the philosophy of science was far more "operational" and "positivistic" than today. I doubt one could find a single contemporary logician or historian of science who would accept the remark quoted.

2. *Causal structures and variables:* A metatheoretical taxonomy of causal factors and a metataxonomy of causal relations (such as "necessary but not sufficient condition," "interaction effects," "threshold effects") are badly needed. In medicine, we recognize several broad etiologic classes, such as deficiency diseases, autoimmunity diseases, diseases due to microorganisms, hereditary-degenerative diseases, developmental anomalies, diseases due to trauma, diseases due to toxins, and psychosomatic disorders. I am preparing for publication elsewhere the beginnings of an analysis of the concept "specific etiology," which appears to have half a dozen distinguishable and equally defensible meanings (e.g., sine qua non, critical threshold, uniformly most powerful factor) that might be useful under various circumstances. See the stimulating papers by Dalén (1969), Murphy (1964), and Wender (1967). Readers prejudiced against nosology might look at footnote 10 in Meehl (1970b) and footnote 19 in Livermore, Malmquist, and Meehl (1968).

3. *Formalism:* We need a formalism adequate to express the epistemic relationships of 1 above and the inferred ontological relationships of 2 above (see Cleave, 1970; Goguen, 1969; and Kaplan and Schott, 1951). There has been little need to do this in other branches of the healing arts, although, for all we know, some problems in internal medicine *might* have been solved more rapidly had its practitioners and researchers possessed a higher average level of logical and mathematical know-how. The logicians' references just cited may or may not represent approaches to the hazy-concept problem that are directly useful to the behavior-genetic theoretician. I incline to think they do not; but they should at least serve to disabuse psychiatric readers of the idea that the problem is a simple one or susceptible of easy, off-the-cuff "solutions." It is both refreshing and disturbing to read about the *methodological* conflicts that agitated internal medicine during the nineteenth century, when its state of scientific development was, alas, already more advanced than that of clinical psychiatry or psychodynamics today. One can discern some remarkable analogies between their disputes and ours, sometimes to the point of identical language (see Faber, 1923, and the fascinating book by Carlson, 1966).

4. *Statistical search technique:* Current problems in taxonomic and typological classification systems are often approached without adequate formulation of steps 1, 2, and 3, but considerable ingenuity and creativeness have been manifested in recent years by workers in several disci-

plines. The classic general treatment is by Sokal and Sneath (1963). See also Cattell (1968) and Dahlstrom (1972). Dr. Bernard Rimland (personal communication) informed me three years ago that a computer-engineer of his acquaintance was collecting published and unpublished taxonomic search methods and had located over fifty at that time. I heard a score or more new ones described at the 1970 meeting of the Classification Society. The more methods, the better, since it is a tough problem; and we should adopt Chairman Mao's motto to "Let a hundred flowers bloom." (For my own groping efforts, see Meehl, 1965a, 1968, 1970d, and Meehl, Lykken, Burdick, and Schoener, 1969.) However, one might suggest that ideally the statistical search techniques appropriate for the testing of taxonomic hypotheses (which, of course, include the hypothesis of Mendelizing genetic determiners) should flow quasi-deductively from the preceding philosophical, causal, and mathematical formulations 1, 2, and 3.

This is difficult to do, and an adequate job will require the pooled conceptual resources of a variety of methodological and substantive disciplines ranging from the philosophy of science (mainly prophylactic, not positively helpful) through statistics, mathematics, and computer science to developmental psychology, learning theory, behavior genetics, psychodynamics, and descriptive clinical psychiatry. Psychologists and psychiatrists who try to discuss whether there is such a "thing" as schizophrenia without having even a superficial acquaintance with classification theory, mathematics, statistics, psychometrics, behavior genetics, or history of medicine seem to me rather like people who would try to perform ophthalmic surgery with their bare hands.

Recently I delivered an invited lecture at the first meeting of the newly formed North American Branch of the Classification Society (Meehl, 1970d). I spent two days being highly stimulated and illuminated by the conversations and lectures of a group of first-class intellects (whose disciplines ranged from astronomy through botany and entomology to personnel psychology) struggling with the difficult, obscure, recondite, subtle, technical problems of taxonomy. On returning to my office in Minneapolis, I found on my desk an issue of a psychological journal containing one more pedestrian, pseudosophisticated snow-job attacking the "medical model." My reaction was not even one of irritation; rather, I was *embarrassed* for my profession. I asked myself, "What would these scientific men, with whom I had just spent two days working on problems of taxonomy—of which specific genetic etiology is one of the most important—do if they were to read this pretentious 'analysis' produced for the consumption of psychological readers?" I could imagine their saying, "Well, Meehl, so *that's* how you solve difficult conceptual problems in psychology, is it? When you are confronted with the question whether there is or is not an entity 'schizophrenia,' you do not have to ask yourself hard questions like 'What is an entity? What is a disease? What is a species or taxon?' You do not have to ask yourself: 'What is the logical and mathematical formalism appropriate to a specific causal postulation?' or 'What is the appropriate statistical search technique arising from causal theory T expressed in formalism F?' 'If the number of variables in a provisional indicator set is only one or two orders of magnitude less than the number of organisms studied, how do we minimize the danger of seeing a typology where none exists?' 'Are cut-and-try computer-search approaches on huge samples a better bet than analytically derived taxonomic methods?' All you have to do in psychology is engage in a kind of la-de-da, dilettante, cocktail-party conversation to make all these tough conceptual problems go away." Well, they won't. But even to understand the difficulties of the problem, one must get past the kind of undergraduate mistake this brief paper has, one more time, attempted to prevent or cure.

12

MAXCOV-HITMAX: A Taxonomic Search Method for Loose Genetic Syndromes

AT THIS WRITING it is no longer possible for an informed person, unless he is an environmentalist fanatic, to believe that everyone is born with an equal biological talent for developing schizophrenia, the only important difference between schizophrenics and others arising from their social learning experiences. Two monumental investigations alone would suffice to make such a view completely untenable (Heston, 1966, 1970; Gottesman and Shields, 1968, 1972). I think it is time for those of us interested in behavioral genetics to suspend debate with radical environmentalists, calmly recognizing that there are ideologies in science (as in politics and religion) which are, for all practical purposes, temporarily resistive to the influence of counterevidence. (See Barber, 1961; Kuhn, 1970; Lakatos and Musgrave, 1970; and the writings of Feyerabend cited on pp. 229–230 therein; but see also Nash, 1963. A fascinating account of the interplay among geneticists between fact and speculation, "rigor" and "looseness," and the fine line between dogmatism and fruitful theoretical tenacity is to be found in Carlson, 1966.) The research task is no longer to find out whether genes have

AUTHOR'S NOTE: This paper is an expansion of an invited lecture delivered at the first convention of the Classification Society (North American Branch), Battelle Memorial Institute, Columbus, Ohio, April 9, 1970. I am indebted to the Carnegie Corporation for support of a summer appointment as professor in the Minnesota Center for Philosophy of Science, and to my colleague Dr. Irving I. Gottesman for suggestions on improving the manuscript.

something to do with schizophrenia, or to convince those who have been brainwashed by American "dynamic psychiatry" and social science doctrine. We should pass on to what is now the scientifically important question, to wit, "Just *what* is inherited and *how* is it transmitted?" (Heston, 1970; Meehl, 1972b—reprinted here as Chapter 11.) It is worth mentioning, however, that determining the mode of inheritance might have an impact even upon the most rabid environmentalist, since the making of successful statistical point-predictions for a syndrome or pathognomonic sign based on, say, a dominant gene theory would constitute pretty strong corroboration. Thus, if the DZ twins, ordinary sibs, and parents of carefully diagnosed schizophrenics showed an incidence $\simeq$ $\frac{1}{2}$, grandparents, uncles, aunts, and half-sibs $\simeq$ $\frac{1}{4}$, and cousins $\simeq$ $\frac{1}{8}$, of a quasi-pathognomonic sign of "schizoidia" (= schizoid tendency, schizoid disposition, schizotypy; see Rado, 1956, 1960; Rado and Daniels, 1956; Meehl, 1962—reprinted here as Chapter 7; Meehl, 1964; Heston, 1970), not only would such a finding argue against a polygenic model (with which it is statistically inconsistent— although the inconsistency may be very hard to detect with unreliable measures, small or moderate size samples, and "unlucky" threshold values, as shown by Edwards, 1960; see also Edwards, 1963, 1969; Falconer, 1965; Murphy, 1964; Dalén, 1969); it would indirectly go against an environmental model, not because such findings are incompatible—they cannot be since the environmental theory generates no point-predictions!—but because in the usual scientific sense a "strong" theory which makes point-predictions is preferable to a weak theory which, while not *refuted* by certain empirical point-values, is incapable of generating them. Putting it another way, since the pure social learning view of schizophrenia does not imply any such point-predictions, a rational man could hardly say that a successful prediction of the point-values 1, $\frac{1}{2}$, $\frac{1}{4}$, and $\frac{1}{8}$ for MZ twins, first-, second-, and third-degree relatives respectively was a sheer coincidence, or that a complex social learning model happens mysteriously to generate precisely the same fractions as flow from a dominant gene hypothesis. (See, for the methodological point involved, Platt, 1964; Lykken, 1968; Meehl, 1967a, 1970a and references, especially to Sir Karl Popper, cited therein.) Problem: Is it somehow possible to generate numerical point-predictions—as contrasted with mere directional significance tests—so as to yield "difficult hurdles" and "strong inference" in the Popper-Platt sense, despite the open-concept (Pap, 1953, 1958b, Chapter 11) status of a loose syndrome?

Clean corroborations would ideally utilize a pathognomonic sign for identifying the schizotype or, lacking that, a set of symptoms each sufficiently strong that a clear identification of the syndrome is possible when they are taken as a group. It seems rather improbable on any plausible theory of schizophrenia that such a pathognomonic sign or sign pattern will be discovered, unless it is biochemical or, possibly, neurological. It can hardly be anticipated that any such sign or sign pattern will be found at the level of molar behavior studied by either psychiatric or psychometric techniques. And if we deal, as we probably will, with so-called "soft" neurological signs—such as experienced clinicians (going back to Kraepelin, Bleuler, and Schilder) have often noted even in the nonpsychotic schizotype—we will be dealing with a loose cluster of highly fallible indicators rather than anything pathognomonic or quasi-pathognomonic.

As I view the current research situation in the genetics of schizophrenia, this constitutes our main methodological hangup. Most investigators now realize that research relying on formal diagnoses of schizophrenia will probably not enable us to pass much beyond the statement "Genes have a lot to do with this disorder." We would like to substitute a high-confidence diagnostic criterion that an individual relative of a schizophrenic proband is or is not a schizotype. But even that may not be attainable for a while yet. The next best thing would be probability numbers associated with fallible sign patterns, which also—like pathognomonic signs or quasi-infallible syndromes—generate specific point-predictions for a Mendelian model. At the risk of exaggeration, but with the hope of saving some taxpayer money, I would say that very little further research on schizophrenia genetics is likely to be illuminating until a better means of identifying the clinically compensated or semicompensated schizotype is available. My behavior geneticist colleague Professor Irving Gottesman keeps needling me about my theory of schizophrenia, which was published a decade ago (Meehl, 1962—reprinted here as Chapter 7), saying, "Meehl, you have an interesting theory but your time has run out for testing it." Other than the feeble defense that there ought to be a place for a theoretical psychologist as there is for a theoretical physicist, a more honest reason for my failure to publish empirical evidence for or against my theory is that *I have not known how to test it*. And I am not interested in adding one more article to the vast and dismal literature of schizophrenia research, most of which, in my opinion, does not tend appreciably to confirm anything (except that this is a complicated disorder, and that psychologists are not very clever about devising "strong inference" methods).

Consider the theory that schizoidia is determined by a dominant gene. I avoid mentioning the penetrance, for reasons which are better given after I explain my statistical method. How might we go about estimating the probability that a particular individual carries the gene, relying on a loose cluster of highly fallible phenotypic indicators? (I use the neutral term "indicator" because not all indicators in the psychological domain are "sick" or pathological enough to be called "symptom," and they are not sufficiently valid to be called "sign" (*Dorland's Medical Dictionary*, 1965; Cronbach and Meehl, 1955—reprinted here as Chapter 1; Meehl and Rosen, 1955—reprinted here as Chapter 2; Meehl, 1959b—reprinted here as Chapter 5). It is imperative, in thinking about the methodological problem, to recognize that there is not presently available any diagnostically definitive touchstone, sign, symptom, or trait which we know how to measure reliably. Even what I view—following Bleuler—as the sine qua non of the disease entity, to wit, thought disorder or "cognitive slippage," will not do for genetic research purposes. There are certain clinical manifestations of cognitive slippage which can be used as quasi-infallible *inclusion* tests, i.e., pathognomonic when present. But these are too deviant to be employed safely as *exclusion* tests, and we do not have any psychometric or clinical device for assessing subtle, subclinical, episodic cognitive slippage of the kind we are accustomed to detect during intensive psychotherapy of schizoid patients, including those that rarely or never show diagnosably psychotic degrees of decompensation. We have therefore a beautiful example of a "bootstraps" problem (Cronbach and Meehl, 1955) in which we start with a fallible set of indicators of unknown relative weights (Meehl, 1959b) and somehow end up assigning weights on the basis of the internal statistical relationships of the elements in this cluster. We have no "acceptable criterion" in the traditional sense. In other words, we have a problem akin to the classical problems of factor analysis, cluster analysis, latent structure analysis, and the like. A schizophrenia theorist or investigator who hasn't reached at least this stage of sophistication is not in the ball park (I would say he's hardly in the league). It goes without saying (among geneticists) that one of the strongest evidences of a "successful bootstrapping" operation is resultant conformity of family statistics to a strong genetic model—although one finds psychologists who (with undergraduate canniness) view such arguments as "circular." That the business of a scientific theory is to "carve nature at its joints" is, I trust, not something one must take time defending to professional readers.

How do we decide which indicators belong in the provisional indicator set? We have to decide this on the basis of some combination of clinical experience, previous research evidence—relying upon formal diagnosis merely as a means of "getting our foot in the door"—and, we hope, at least the sketch of a theory. Thus, for example, in attempting to assess the frequency of schizotypy among the relatives of schizophrenic probands, I would certainly include one or more neurological indicators, such as subclinical Romberg sign, a tendency to past pointing, kinesthetic aberration, or paradoxical influence of alcohol upon post-rotatory nystagmus. Why would I see such "soft" neurological signs as good candidates for an indicator set? First, because clinicians have often found such soft neurological signs and transitory subjective neurological "complaints" among patients diagnosed as schizophrenic or schizotypic on other grounds; second, because there is some research evidence to indicate that such signs have validity when the crude criterion is taken as diagnosed schizophrenia; and finally, because my speculative neurological hypothesis quasi-implies that if you are lucky or clever where you look, you *should* find soft neurological signs in schizotypes even when they are not psychotic.

In bootstrapping fallible indicators of schizotypy there are some special statistical problems which are less likely to arise in nonbehavioral genetics. We cannot, for instance, begin our bootstrapping operation by assigning initial weights on the basis of concurrent validity for diagnosable (psychotic or semipsychotic) schizotypes, because part of the reason we have such a serious diagnostic problem here is that these weights will be very different for the compensated case. It cannot even be excluded that in some instances an indicator might function backwards. For instance, in the "natural history of the disorder" we find clinically that a patient who succeeds in reducing his anxiety by consolidating a paranoid projection system may become more aggressive and extrapunitive than the average or normal person; whereas, before this defensive resolution, he would have been rated by peers, relatives, and even some professionals as being underaggressive. Nor can we safely assume such familiar statistical approximations as normal distribution or homogeneity of variances. One of the best established generalizations about the population of clinical schizophrenics is that they are more variable—both longitudinally (over time) and cross-sectionally (in the sense of individual differences)—than controls, a tendency presumably heightened when the population under study includes all schizotypes rather than only the subset decompensated to the point of receiving a formal psychiatric diagnosis of schizophrenia.

Consider a provisional indicator set of not less than three phenotypic variables, deliberately chosen on the basis of the criteria above, plus plausible grounds for hoping that they will be pair-wise uncorrelated (or approximately so) within the postulated latent taxa. So I am making the same assumption as in Lazarsfeld's latent structure analysis, that the observed correlation between the indicators is almost wholly attributable to the influence of the latent taxa. This assumption need not remain an "assumption" in the technical sense of the statistician, i.e., something we postulate without having any means of testing it on the data (as, for instance, the psychometric assumption underlying an arbitrary normalized transformation of test scores). The assumption itself can be a statistical hypothesis subject to refutation, and I have developed a group of "consistency" tests which should help us decide whether the intrataxon independence assumption is being grossly violated (Meehl, 1965c, section 9; Meehl, 1968, section g). Further, we can raise the odds that this independence condition will be approximately fulfilled, at least close enough for the use of the proposed bootstraps method. First, we may rely on theoretical considerations, such as that indicators sampling different behavioral domains or different neurological systems—having, so to speak, very little "qualitative phenotypic similarity or overlap"—ought to be relatively independent. Second, we can ascertain the empirical correlation between the indicators within a group of normals (where the base rate of schizotypy can be safely taken as so low as not to be capable of generating a correlation) as well as among diagnosed schizophrenics, and then extrapolate to the working hypothesis that if a pair of indicators is uncorrelated *within* the schizophrenic group and *within* the normal group, it will

205

probably not be *markedly* correlated among nonpsychotic schizotypes found in the "normal" population or in a mixed psychiatric population with an erroneous (nonschizoid) diagnosis. Third, in the case of psychometric indicators such as scores on a personality inventory or a "mental status" checklist (Meehl, 1964) or rating scale, we can employ item-analytic procedures to reduce the intrataxon correlation, which we will be willing to do at the expense of sacrificing some amount of validity. I cannot yet make any general statement about the robustness of my method with respect to this assumption of zero intrataxon correlation, although I have some numerical examples (e.g., Meehl, 1965c, section 13) as well as some empirical data on one taxonomic problem, suggesting that a Pearson r running up to .30 or .40 may not be too damaging.

An illustrative example of such a provisional indicator set would be (a) a psychometric measure of subclinical cognitive slippage based upon intransitive ("irrational") choice behavior (Braatz, 1970); (b) a measure of the paradoxical effect of alcohol ingestion upon post-rotatory nystagmus (Angyal and Blackman, 1941); (c) a patient's score on a structured personality inventory measuring (by self-report) the phenomenology of pleasure deficit (Rado's *anhedonia*; see Rado, 1956, 1960; Rado and Daniels, 1956). These three kinds of behavior are sufficiently different in the kind and level of dysfunction tapped that one would be surprised to find them appreciably correlated either in a normal population or in a clinical population of non-schizoid psychiatric patients from which organic brain disease, mental deficiency, and grossly psychotic cases had been excluded. So we have here three tentative indicators of schizotypy which we have plausible reasons to hope are relatively independent except as they are influenced by the hypothesized dominant schizogene.

I want to emphasize how little we know by way of commencing our bootstraps operation even if we assume the above. We do not know the relative validity of these three indicator variables, and we cannot estimate it by relying on cases of diagnosed schizophrenia. Putting this more generally, we do not know what the means and variances, or even the distribution forms, of the indicator variables are within the postulated latent taxa. We cannot safely assume that the distributions are homogeneous in variance, or that they are normal. (As a matter of fact, if we extrapolate from research on diagnosed schizophrenics there

is good reason to think they will not satisfy either of these assumptions.)
Finally, we do not know the base rate P of schizotypy in a population at
high risk, such as the first-degree relatives of diagnosed schizophrenic
probands, or in a mixed psychiatric population. For readers unfamiliar
with the diagnostic situation in psychiatry I should mention that not
only is this very important parameter P unknown, but we cannot even
begin with a plausible estimate of it for bootstrapsing purposes. This is
because competent and seasoned clinicians, holding differing views
about schizophrenia, assign markedly different indicator weights to the
clinical phenomena. One can find boarded psychiatrists or clinical psychologists who, when asked "What is the base rate P of schizophrenia
(or latent schizophrenia, or subclinical schizophrenia) in a general outpatient psychiatric population?" will give estimates ranging from a low
of 10 percent—particularly if they are British or Continental psychiatrists whose conception of schizophrenia is rather close to Kraepelin's
dementia praecox—to a high of 90 percent (I have actually heard this
figure from a very capable psychiatrist trained by Rado). And nobody is
presently in a position to refute either of these extreme values. So we
start out with very little tentative knowledge and a large amount of ignorance. It might seem impossible to get anywhere bootstrapsing from
such feeble foundations, but unless I have made a mistake, I think we
can do it. The very inadequacy of our antecedent information is reassuring, because it frees us of the obligation to show that our proposed
bootstrapsing method is highly precise, that it leads to maximum likelihood estimates, that the sampling errors are very small, or to provide
analytical derivations of random sampling distribution functions for the
consistency tests. The point is that when you know this little, even a
rather crude method, so long as it seems to check out on real data (as
in the example I shall present later) and to be reasonably robust on
Monte Carlo study, may legitimately be employed. I may say that I
find some statisticians puzzling in this respect, because they seem to
me to be saying, in effect, that if a proposed method does not lead to
elegant mathematical answers or to studentized sampling distributions
derivable analytically, the method isn't even worth exploring. But
meanwhile they themselves seem often to be making assumptions about
the latent situation or the state of prior knowledge which are unrealistic
in the behavior genetics of psychoses and neuroses. My view is that one
is better off with approximate methods that are realistic in the research

context *and help to answer an important question* than with "precise" methods for which the assumptions and input information are not fulfilled, or which answer uninteresting questions, e.g., "Is the null hypothesis false?" (See, in this connection, Badia, Haber, and Runyon, 1970; Morrison and Henkel, 1970.) When I first presented this paper at a meeting of the newly formed Classification Society, I experienced trepidation over the fact that I had no analytical derivations of exact sampling distributions for the statistics proposed. It was surprising and reassuring to discover that the mathematicians, statisticians, and computer experts who there presented new taxonomic search methods rarely had any such either, and were strangely freewheeling about it.

So we have three quantitative variables x, y, and z of unknown relative weight, of unknown variance and distribution function, and we do not even have a base rate (in this context, gene frequency) for the taxon of interest. We hypothesize that each indicator has some moderate to high construct validity (Cronbach and Meehl, 1955—see Chapter 1 above; Campbell and Fiske, 1959; Loevinger, 1957) and that the indicators are uncorrelated pair-wise within the schizoid taxon and outside it. As to distribution form, we hypothesize that while perhaps skew or leptokurtic or platykurtic, each indicator variable is at least unimodal within the two groups. I note in passing that even this weak assumption may actually be false for schizotypy, there being some evidence to suggest a bimodality when we mix schizophrenics of the paranoid and nonparanoid subgroups.

Consider one of the three indicators z, which I shall call, for reasons which will be apparent in a moment, the "input indicator." This does not mean "input" in the causal sense, but simply input in the context of our search technique. We therefore imagine the latent situation, the state of nature as known to Omniscient Jones but not to the investigator, as in Figure 1. These are unrelativized frequency functions rather than probability-density functions, so the ordinates and areas reflect the different base rates P, Q.

Suppose the clinician or researcher, being ignorant as he is of the parameters of these latent frequency functions, draws an arbitrary cut on the abscissa, dividing the manifest (mixed taxa) empirical distribution, and labels patients falling above this cut as "indicator positive." The area under the upper distribution lying above this cut represents the "valid positives," that is, the cases classified by the cut as schizo-

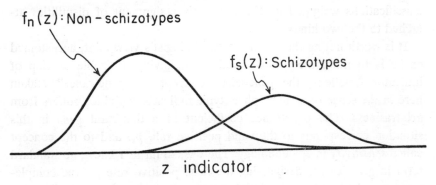

$f_n(z)$: Non - schizotypes

$f_s(z)$: Schizotypes

z indicator

Figure 1. The latent situation

types who are in fact members of the schizotypal latent taxon. The *proportion* of the schizotypal distribution falling above that cut we label the "valid positive rate," symbolized by p_s. Note that this rate is not the proportion of indicator positives that are in fact schizotypes, but the proportion of true schizotypes who are correctly identified as such by the cut, i.e., the denominator of this rate p_s is the true schizotype base frequency N_s. Similarly the proportion of cases in the lower (non-schizotype) distribution lying above that cut we designate as the "false positive rate," symbolized by p_n.

For any such fallible indicator, i.e., any indicator in which the two indicator functions overlap, shifting the cut results in an improvement in one of these rates at the expense (worsening) of the other. By moving the cut downward we increase the proportion of schizotypes correctly so labeled (i.e., p_s rises) for which we pay the price of an increase in the false positive rate p_n. If we wish to reduce the false positive rate p_n, we have to move the cut upward, which identifies fewer of the true schizotypes and therefore gives us a reduction in the valid positive rate p_s. The "optimal" cut depends therefore not only upon the character of the two probability functions but upon the base rate P (proportion of true schizotypes in the mixed population under study). For a discussion of the practical clinical problems arising from this state of affairs see Meehl and Rosen (1955—Chapter 2 above). For purely research purposes, as in testing a dominant-gene hypothesis, the optimal cut is one that minimizes the misclassifications; for clinical purposes, however, it may not be total misclassifications we desire to minimize but misclassifications weighted by the clinician's assignment of disutilities attached to the two kinds of errors.

It is worth noting that from the psychologist's viewpoint, accustomed as he is to moderate or low validities involving a sizable overlap of indicator functions, the geneticist's concept of "penetrance" (taken here in the sense of a single phenotypic indicator variable) suffers from arbitrariness. The penetrance coefficient of a dominant gene in this situation corresponds to the valid positive rate p_s, and to the concept called *sensitivity* in epidemiology. There is, so far as I know, no standard term in genetics for designating the false positive rate p_n, the complement of which, $(1 - p_n)$, is labeled *specificity* by the epidemiologist. From the psychometric standpoint, penetrance is a derivative concept, the geneticist's *expressivity* being the fundamental one. That is to say, what I would call the *expressivity function* is nonarbitrary, being a mathematical fact about the state of nature for a given genome-cum-environment joint distribution characterizing a specified population. We may not know at a given stage of research what that function is, but we know that such a function exists in the state of nature and is not arbitrary, whereas penetrance, except in the case where the distributions are nonoverlapping (penetrance of 100 percent), is an arbitrary function of the sliding cut. By increasing the proportion of false positives, i.e., by lowering the cut, we increase the penetrance of the gene with respect to a given indicator variable. It is my understanding that in the case of fallible indicators, what geneticists tend to do is to choose a cutting score more or less arbitrarily rather than to optimize the cut (like an industrial psychologist) in the light of the base rate P. For example, in considering the palm lines associated with Mongolism, a cutting score of 57° in maximum atd angle is set as aberrant, following Penrose (1954). In our notation, this cut on a quantitative indicator variable yields $p_s = .80$ for Mongols, $p_n = .07$ to $.09$ for the general population, and $p_n = .14$ to $.16$ for mothers and sibs of Mongols (Stern, 1960, pp. 471–472). (Are these last all "false positives," and, if so, why do they run almost double the general population $(+)$ rate?) Strictly speaking, the optimality of a cut at 57° would depend upon these parameters, the base rate P of the Mongol karyotype, and the research or clinical context. One may of course choose some suitably low value of false positives and treat the errors as essentially negligible, such as the 5 percent or 1 percent point on the lower frequency function; this is satisfactory for most clinical and research purposes in other branches of pathological genetics, where we typically deal with the combination of high-validity indicators and minuscule base rate P. But in research on such a loose syndrome as schizotypy, and one with a high gene frequency, a less arbitrary procedure is desirable.

Calling a "hit" a schizotype falling above the cut or a nonschizotype falling below the cut, the total correct classifications (taking account of the base rate P, i.e., the gene frequency in a high-risk population) is given by

[1] $\quad H_t = H_n + H_s = F_n(z) + [N_s - F_s(z)]$, where $F_n(z)$

$$= \int_{-\infty}^{z} f_n(z)dz; \; F_s(z) = \int_{-\infty}^{z} f_s(z)dz$$

and to maximize the total hits yielded by cutting a single-indicator variable we set the derivative of this sum at zero

[2] $\quad F'_n(z) - F'_s(z) = 0$

[3] $\quad f_s(z) = f_n(z)$

which means that the optimal cut for minimizing total errors occurs at the abscissa value below the intersection of the two frequency functions, i.e., where the ordinates f_s and f_n are equal. This is intuitively obvious from the geometry of Figure 1. I shall designate that abscissa value the *hitmax cut on z*. But of course we do not know the latent frequency functions f_s, f_n. Can we locate the hitmax cut on z by studying the behavior of the other two indicators (x, y)? Intuitively, on our provisional assumption that the variables of the indicator set are pair-wise uncorrelated within taxa, it is obvious that any observed correlation—I am neglecting sampling error throughout this paper—will be attributable to the existence of taxon mixture. That is, if we had a subpopulation consisting wholly of schizotypes, or one consisting wholly of non-schizotypes, the correlation (or, as will be more convenient to work with, the covariance) of an indicator pair would be zero. If we were to examine various subpopulations composed of varying mixtures of the two latent taxa, it is intuitively obvious that the observed covariance of two indicators will increase with the amount of taxon mixture, and will be a maximum when the taxon mixture is a maximum, i.e., in the subpopulation composed equally of schizotypes and non-schizotypes. Algebraically, we write the general expression for the covariance of a

211

mixed population for two indicator variables x and y, where $p =$ proportion of schizotypes, $q = 1 - p$,

[4] $\quad cov(xy) = pcov_s(xy) + qcov_n(xy) + pq(\bar{x}_s - \bar{x}_n)(\bar{y}_s - \bar{y}_n)$

The components of this total mixed-taxon manifest covariance $cov(xy)$ are then the weighted intrataxon covariances plus a term whose size depends upon the "validities" of the two indicators, represented by the differences of the latent means, and the product pq representing the amount of mixture. On the assumption of zero intrataxon covariance, the first two terms drop out and the expression for the observed covariance of x and y reduces to

[5] $\quad cov(xy) = pq(\bar{x}_s - \bar{x}_n)(\bar{y}_s - \bar{y}_n)$

If there were some way to arrange a series of subpopulations beginning with a "pure" population composed solely of non-schizotypes and running through a series of subpopulations in which the proportion of schizotypes increases steadily until we reach a value $p = \frac{1}{2}$, and thereafter a series of populations in which the proportion of schizotypes increases beyond $\frac{1}{2}$ until we get to a subpopulation which is also "pure," consisting only of schizotypes, the manifest (xy) covariance would be seen to begin at zero, increase to a maximum, then to decline again to zero. Taking the product of the latent means $(\bar{x}_s - \bar{x}_n)(\bar{y}_s - \bar{y}_n) = K$ as fixed—ignoring sampling fluctuations—the quantity $cov(xy) = Kpq$ will be maximized for the subpopulation in which the taxa are equally represented, that is, where $p = q = \frac{1}{2}$. That the product pq is greatest for diagnostic symmetry $(p = q)$ corresponds to the intuitive notion that if two indicator variables are correlated solely because of the latent taxa, they will correlate most when the population is "most mixed" taxonomically.

But of course we do have a way of ordering a series of subpopulations in this fashion, namely, we can order them on the basis of our third indicator variable z. Since if one considers the sequence of class intervals on z arranged by taking successive slabs of patients on the mixed frequency function $f_t(z) = [f_s(z) + f_n(z)]$ of Figure 1, at the low end of this distribution all of the cases in the class intervals of z are non-schizotypes; at the upper tail all of them are schizotypes; and in the middle we have varying amounts of mixture, the greatest mixture occurring in the interval surrounding the hitmax cut on z. So our search proccdure, taking indicator z as the input variable and the indicator pair (x, y) as output variables, consists simply in calculating the (xy) covariance for each z interval from low to high, and looking for its maximum. Since this is the core idea of the method, I have tentatively christened it "MAXCOV-HITMAX."

With a respectable sample, the orderly behavior of the (xy) covariance as a function of the position of each subsample on the z indicator tends of course to corroborate the postulated latent model. One can employ some kind of moving average, or—as my research assistant did in an effort to improve the method—fit a function (he fitted a parabola) to the plot of the covariances, although (strangely enough) this determination of the hitmax cut by finding the analytic maximum of a fitted curve did not improve validity.

Locating the hitmax cut on z is intrinsically useful, especially since it can be checked by an independent method that relies, however, on a somewhat stronger model, postulating approximate intrataxon normality (Meehl, Lykken, Burdick, and Schoener, 1969). But in locating the hitmax cut on z by maximizing the (xy) covariance, we have meanwhile obtained the latter's numerical value, and this permits us to make a further inference which is powerful for our bootstraps operation. Taking the product of the latent mean differences as a constant, that is $K = (\bar{x}_s - \bar{x}_n)(\bar{y}_s - \bar{y}_n)$, we have in the hitmax interval on z the relation

[6] $cov_{hz}(xy) = Kp_h q_h = \frac{1}{4}K$

and since the quantity $cov_{hz}(xy)$ is an observed value (that is, the mixed-taxon (xy) covariance obtained on the cases lying in the hitmax interval of z), we solve for the product of the latent means on the output indicators $= K$.

Knowing K, since on the assumption of zero intrataxon (xy) covariance the relation of equation 5 holds within each of the z intervals, we can write the general expression for any z interval,

[7] $Kp^2{}_z - Kp_z + cov_z(xy) = 0$

a quadratic in the variable $p =$ proportion of schizotypes in that z interval. For each of the z intervals we can plug in the observed (xy) covariance for that z interval and solve the resulting quadratic for p. Multiplying p_i in each z interval by the observed frequency n_i for that interval gives us an estimate of the latent frequency of schizotypes n_{si}

within the interval, so that in effect the series of solutions of this quadratic over the z range draws us the unknown latent frequency functions $f_s(z)$ and $f_n(z)$. Summing the values n_{si} and n_{ni} over all z intervals gives us the latent total taxon frequencies N_s and N_n, and dividing these by our total N yields the unknown base rates P and $Q = 1 - P$.

We can then choose a different indicator of the set, say y, and repeat the process above using y as the input variable and $cov(xz)$ as the output variable; similarly we can choose the remaining indicator x as input and plot $cov(yz)$ as output. Agreement between the results of these procedures (on both the base rates obtained and the latent means) provides consistency tests for the adequacy of our idealization.

Suppose we conclude on this basis that the postulated latent taxonomic model is reasonably satisfied and our estimates are consistent enough to be relied upon as a bootstrapsed approximation. We have determined hitmax cuts on each of the three indicators of the set, and for each indicator cut we have estimated the valid and false positive rates P_s and P_n characteristic of the population under study, keeping in mind that these hitmax cuts and the resulting hit rates are not invariant over clinical populations having different base rates. We can now employ Bayes' Theorem to calculate the inverse probability that a patient belongs to the schizotypal taxon. That is, consider a patient who falls above the hitmax cut on indicators x and y but below the hitmax cut on indicator z. What is the probability that he is a schizotype? We write

$$[8] \qquad p(S_c/x^+y^+z^-) = \frac{Pp_{sx}p_{sy}q_{sz}}{Pp_{sx}p_{sy}q_{sz} + Qp_{nx}p_{ny}q_{nz}}$$

so that for each of the eight possible sign patterns $(+++)$, $(++-)$, $(+-+)$, . . . $(--+)$, $(---)$, there is a Bayes' Theorem probability computable for patients showing that specified sign pattern. Even if each of the three indicators taken singly has only moderate validity (corresponding to "low penetrances" of the sort that make geneticists skittish about invoking the concept) we can subject a Mendelian hypothesis such as dominance to a fairly rigorous empirical test because, while we do not know with high confidence for each individual patient, or each relative of a known schizophrenic proband, whether *he* is or is not a schizotype, we can assign probability values to this taxonomic classification; and this possibility leads to the generation of point-predictions for various sign patterns arising in first-, second-, and third-degree relatives of schizophrenic probands.

Not being a mathematical statistician I have not attempted to derive random-sampling distributions of these statistics analytically, and I am informed by my local experts that it would not be possible to do much along these lines without imposing greater constraints upon the latent model than I wish to do. I am therefore engaged in a large-scale Monte Carlo investigation of this question. Unfortunately my only sufficiently large mass of empirical psychometric data (our Minnesota files on MMPI records) is currently unavailable to me, being in the process of careful diagnostic screening and rescoring before being put on computer tapes. But I have conducted one empirical investigation of the method on real data, employing a genetic problem that is known to be taxonomic and where we have an infallible criterion, to wit, biological sex, and working with psychological indicators very remote in the causal chain from the XX and XY genotypes. Taking three highly fallible psychometric indicators of sex, consisting of three item-analyzed masculinity-femininity scales derived from the MMPI item pool, and pretending that we do not know the indicator functions or the base rates, we applied the method on a sample of 1105 psychiatric patients with a true male base rate $P = .39$, which yielded an estimated base rate $P' = .36$, gratifyingly close to the true value; and application of Bayes' Theorem to the eight sign patterns—classifying each patient as male or female depending upon whether the inverse probability of taxon membership was greater or less than ½—yielded 85 percent hits.

I have developed about a half-dozen alternative methods of locating the hitmax interval and some nine consistency tests of the latent model. As an example of one of these consistency tests, suppose we apply equation 5 to the *total* manifest distribution, plugging in the estimated base rates and the estimated latent means for each of our three indicator pairs. Then the three grand covariances can be calculated relying on the estimated latent quantities as follows:

[9] $\quad cov_t(xy) = PQ(\bar{x}_s - \bar{x}_n)(\bar{y}_s - \bar{y}_n)$
[10] $\quad cov_t(xz) = PQ(\bar{x}_s - \bar{x}_n)(\bar{z}_s - \bar{z}_n)$
[11] $\quad cov_t(yz) = PQ(\bar{y}_s - \bar{y}_n)(\bar{z}_s - \bar{z}_n)$

It may also be possible to work with situations in which the intrataxon covariances depart from zero too much to take this as an adequate approximation. (So far as locating the hitmax cut is concerned, equation 4 shows that a weaker assumption suffices, namely, that the intrataxon

215

covariances are at least equal, if not zero. But the next step, estimating K, cannot be taken on this basis.) By beginning with the zero intrataxon covariance assumption and making initial estimates of the latent parameters, we draw an arbitrary cut (say, at the median) on each indicator, write the complete equation 4 for the case of non-zero intrataxon covariance, solve these two equations (one based upon the observed subsample lying above the median cut and the other on the cases lying below it) for the two intrataxon covariances as unknowns, plug these values into the grand equation, and recycle until the system settles down. Our results on the sex-classification data do not, perhaps surprisingly, indicate that this iterative procedure improves validity appreciably. I have done some rough paper-and-pencil computations which suggest that the method may be fairly robust under departures from the assumption of zero intrataxon covariance, but this question is obviously in need of thorough Monte Carlo or analytic investigation.

A major limitation of the method is the sizable sample required; but I should point out that the validities of new indicators can be estimated on considerably smaller samples, once we have obtained estimates on old indicators (such as personality test data) available in larger numbers from clinical files. In fact, I have shown elsewhere (Meehl, 1965c; see also Dawes and Meehl, 1966—reprinted here as Chapter 8; Dawes, 1967; for a criticism see Alf and Abrahams, 1967; an improvement which amounts to a consistency test is given by Linn, 1967) that if we were so clever or lucky as to hit upon a neurological or biochemical indicator v that was quasi-infallible in tracing the schizogene, the fact of its quasi-infallibility could be inferred with confidence. We could do this by showing that there exists an optimal cut on v such that the observed rates of cut positives $p^+(v)$ could be made to conform to the Bayes' Theorem-estimated schizotype rates in the cells of a table defined by the sign patterns on psychometric indicators (x, y, z) of only moderate validity. This result, which I call (because of its paradoxical character) the "Super-Bootstraps Theorem," permits us to begin with file data on indicators of only moderate validity, such as personality test scores or psychiatric behavior ratings. Such indicators are many steps removed (in the causal chain of polygenic and environmental factors) from the gene of interest, but the statistics enable us to locate and validate neurological and biochemical indicators which, being much closer to the gene action, manifest a much higher "penetrance." Numerical example:

216

Suppose the base rate of schizotypy in a mixed psychiatric population to have been estimated at $P = .40$ employing the MAXCOV-HITMAX method, with hitmax cuts on each of three indicators yielding symmetrical hit rates $p_s = q_n = .70$, which is pretty fallible but presently achievable (e.g., the MMPI schizoid scale 8 has a concurrent validity better than this, against fallible diagnosis as criterion). The eight sign patterns would then provide Bayes' Theorem estimates for latent schizotype rates ranging from $p(S_c/x^+y^+z^+) \simeq .83$ to $p(S_c/x^-y^-z^-) \simeq .05$ over the eight cells of an inverse probability table. A new indicator v can now be cut at arbitrary values and the discrepancy of the (v^+) rates from the Bayes' rates per cell tabulated. We choose the cut v_c that minimizes these cell-value disparities. If that optimal v cut achieves a very close fit (ideally, a fit within sampling and psychometric errors) we conclude that v_c is quasi-pathognomonic. Short of such good luck, however, we may be able to infer that the construct validity of v when optimally cut is extremely high—better than that of bootstraps indicators x, y, z singly or jointly.

Not being a geneticist, I am properly hesitant to suggest modifications in genetic terminology, although I have been so rash as to employ the term "potentiator" for designating any of an open class of (presumably polygenic) variables that, in my theory of schizophrenia, increase the probability of a schizotype's decompensating to the extent that he becomes clinically diagnosable as "schizophrenic." My Minnesota colleagues have tried to convince me that the available terminology (e.g., "epistasis," "modifier") suffices to cover what I label "potentiators," and I have no wish to clutter up the language of behavior genetics by a superfluous neologism. But I should perhaps say a few words about why I hesitate to employ the received terminology in expositing my own theory. Perchance such an explanation, even if my terminological proposal is deemed unnecessary, may highlight some methodological issues that have not as yet received sufficient attention. In what follows, I presuppose that any theory of schizophrenia possessing respectable verisimilitude (Popper, 1959, 1962; Lakatos, 1968) will be *at least* as complex, causally and statistically, as that shown in a diagram I prepared for another paper (Meehl, 1972c; see page 190 above). (As a clinician, I find it quite impossible to suppose that temperamental parameters of anxiety, rage, social introversion, dominance, sexual constitution, energy, and the like—all of which have heritable components in humans

217

as well as infrahuman mammals—should be *irrelevant* to whether a schizotypal individual remains clinically compensated. I am therefore puzzled by those psychologists who find the increased incidence of *non*-schizoid psychopathology among the relatives of schizophrenics a big surprise, suggestive of old-fashioned "neuropathic diathesis" concepts. *Psychodynamically, how could it be otherwise?*) It is this causal complexity that gives rise to the taxonomic search problem discussed in the present paper. Every time we add another link in the causal chain, whether that link is a non-schizo-specific polygenic influence (e.g., anxiety proneness) or an environmental parameter (such as schizophrenogenic mother, lower social class, or a cruel husband) we lower the probability linkage between the postulated dominant schizogene and the behavioral indicator relied on for diagnosis. Furthermore, we are almost certainly dealing with such causally complicated relations as (a) correlated initial and boundary conditions, (b) subject-selected learning experience, (c) social feedback loops, (d) autocatalytic psychological processes, (e) critical junctures in "divergent" causality (Langmuir, 1943; London, 1946), and (f) intrinsically unpredictable "contingency factors" (Horst, 1941). For a methodological discussion of these see Meehl (1970a).

The same semantic doubts that generate my reluctance to employ the geneticist's standard term *modifier* for fear of mishandling it in a situation as complicated as schizophrenia also lead me to wonder whether the word *penetrance* is appropriate. This latter issue is important because one finds that geneticists are troubled by a causal model which would lead to a rather low penetrance coefficient for clinical schizophrenia taken as the phenotypic expression of a dominant gene. My hunch is that we are somewhat misled by taking as our paradigm a neurological disorder such as Huntington's Disease or any of the large number of Mendelizing forms of mental deficiency, where one conceives of the clinical *disease* entity as, so to speak, the "expected outcome" of the genotype of interest, and its absence in some individuals as a kind of "exception" which is a candidate for special explanation. We know, for instance, that in order to fit a strict dominant gene model for Huntington's Disease, one must extend the risk period up to age seventy or more, and we do not get fully 100 percent penetrance even then. I suggest that these paradigm cases lead us astray when we think about schizophrenia, and we should rather think of the "usual," "typical," "to-be-expected" result of the schizogene's presence as being the subtle, subclinical, non-social neurological syndrome I postulate and label "schizotaxia." We then think of the individual with that fundamental neurological disposition as acquiring, by a complicated process of social learning, the personality structure, dynamics, and mental content that Rado designates "schizotypal." Finally, we postulate that some unknown proportion (considerably less than one-half) of schizotypes decompensate to the point that they *would* be clinically diagnosable under careful study; and only a fraction of these latter are actually formally diagnosed, so that they show up in the files available to most investigators (Heston, 1970).

To see how serious this problem is, I may perhaps be permitted to invoke my own clinical experience in the private practice of psychotherapy. Using an earlier form of the present taxonomic search method, combining the MMPI with therapy-based judgments quantified in my Schizotypal Checklist (Meehl, 1964), I concluded that a little less than half of the therapy patients I had carried over a ten-year period were schizotypal, amounting to some two dozen in number. For many of these I had very high confidence in the schizotypal diagnosis. For quite a few of them there had occurred, in the course of intensive psychotherapy, micropsychotic episodes (Hoch and Polatin, 1949) which, *had they come to the attention of any clinician,* would have led him to agree with me that the patient was (at least transitorily) "schizophrenic," whatever might be our disagreements upon etiological theory. For example, most of these patients had experienced episodes of body-image aberration, hallucinatory and delusional phenomena, severe thought disorder, and the like. The point of this story for present purposes is that at the time I surveyed my clinical files, not one of these two dozen (almost certainly schizoid) patients had ever been formally diagnosed as schizophrenic, or even as schizoid, in any clinic or hospital (cf. Peterson, 1954). Hence, if they had been under statistical study as the relatives of some officially labeled schizophrenic proband, they would have all been discordant! (Two of them have since been hospitalized and diagnosed schizophrenic, however.) This argument may appear to the reader to prove too much. However, these patients were selected by me as sufficiently intact (and in several cases, thereby misdiagnosed) to be suitable for outpatient treatment by myself as a nonphysician. They are therefore a selected sample; but the main point of the story remains, to wit, that here we have two dozen people who were psychometrically and clinically schizotypal, and the majority of whom had experienced transitory acute schizophrenic phenomena, but who were not down on any medical, educational, or social agency's record as "schizophrenic."

Since I am a neo-Popperian in my philosophy of science, I do not mind going out on a limb in the absence of adequate "inductive evidence"; so I will record my prophecy that the "clinical penetrance" of the dominant schizogene is less than 20 percent, and possibly as low as 10 percent. (I am well aware that some geneticists consider such penetrance values to be methodologically sinful; and that is one reason why I do not like to use the word here.) Taking as a rough base rate of diagnosed schizophrenia the usual figure of around 1 percent, this means that I am taking the prevalence of schizotypes, who carry the dominant gene, to be as high as 5 percent of the population. This is a pretty steep figure if we take Mendelizing "mental defects" as our model; but I remind my geneticist friends that diagnosed schizophrenia itself has a *huge* incidence by their usual standards (as compared to disorders like Huntington's, Turner's, Tay-Sachs', PKU, and so forth). I guess I am saying, as a confessed nonexpert speaking to the experts, "Perhaps we should not be too surprised if this entity turns out to have some quantitative oddities; we already have reason to see it as kind of special." I have elsewhere suggested that the schizoid disposition is more analogous to something like ordinary (and very common) red-green color blindness, i.e., a kind of capacity defect whose "psychological" consequences develop as a result of complex social learning processes (Meehl, 1959b —reprinted here as Chapter 5; 1962—reprinted here as Chapter 7; 1972c—reprinted here as Chapter 11).

I can illustrate my reluctance about whether the terms *modifier* and *penetrance* would be used here sufficiently like their traditional meaning by an analogy which some might think is farfetched, but which I view as misleading only because it is too simple! Consider diabetes, which is admittedly a genetic disorder (although its mode of inheritance is still in dispute). Suppose that a particular carrier of the diabetic genotype has also inherited a heavy loading of anxiety-parameter polygenes, as well as the gene or genes that (on some views) are relatively specific for alcoholism (i.e., that lead the individual to experience that very powerful reinforcing effect of the alcohol molecule, and therefore tend to lead to overconsumption and addiction, even if the subject is otherwise not under any unusual degree of psychological or social stress). As a result of his alcoholic tendencies, the patient maintains poor foot hygiene. Also, one night when he is intoxicated, he traumatizes his big toe. He doesn't pay any attention to this, and as a result he develops diabetic gangrene, a common phenomenon but one observed in only a small minority of younger, well-controlled diabetics. The gangrene necessitates that his leg be amputated. This he unconsciously construes, owing to an intense unresolved Oedipus complex (having nothing at all to do with his diabetic tendencies, but related to his anxiety proneness and his hysteroid seductive mother) as a major castration experience. As a result of this symbolic castration, he becomes deeply depressed. Now as a clinician interested in behavior genetics, I do not find anything the least bit farfetched or implausible about that causal chain. But surely it would be a misleading use of the geneticists' language to say that the genes for anxiety proneness or alcoholic addictiveness—in spite of the very important role they played in the development of this particular patient's troubles—were "modifiers" or "epistatic" with respect to the diabetic gene! And it would also seem rather strange use of the geneticist's terminology to count the percentage of individuals in whom such a sequence had happened, and then to label that numerical value the "penetrance." If the patient had a seductive mother and a terrifying father, which combined to yield such a strong Oedipus complex and, hence, such an exaggerated susceptibility to the castrative meaning of a leg amputation, I cannot imagine that a geneticist would want to refer to those environmental factors as influencing the "expressivity" of the diabetic genotype, would he?

If I had some competence in genetics, I would examine a collection of medical and nonmedical examples involving complicated feedback loops and effects upon behavior, with an eye to formulating some sort of methodological distinction between the kind of polygenic influence that sticks rather closely to the original meaning of *modifier,* as contrasted with the kind of situation I have just described, for which I have employed the word *potentiator.* For instance, in the case of schizophrenia, suppose one holds—as I do—that some of the "soft" neurological signs are fairly close in the causal chain to the schizogene, and that there may be some perceptual and psychometric signs, unfortu-

221

nately also "soft" statistically, that are almost equally close. Polygenic systems affecting microstructural features of the CNS and altering the probability that a schizotaxic individual would show a particular "soft" neurological sign (e.g., subclinical Romberg) would seem to be appropriately labeled *modifier*. Similarly, if there are genetic determiners for some of the perceptual-cognitive differences that psychologists study (e.g., the augmenter-reducer dimension in the kinesthetic aftereffect) it would not seem an overly stretched usage to apply the term *modifier*. But when we get to such a causally remote link in the chain as whether a patient projects hostile delusional material, and explain this partly on the basis that he is a mesomorph and partly on the basis that he has inherited a high rage parameter (completely independent genetically of the schizogene), one begins to feel that "modifier" is no longer the right word. We have to face the fact that clinical schizophrenia, except in its subtle and still-disputed neurological features, is a collection of socially learned behaviors. We do not need any further research to be able to say that. We need only ask, "What are the behavior dispositions sampled in deciding that a patient is schizophrenic?" They are, without exception, learned social responses, having a learned motivational, affective, and cognitive *content*. And this is just not the sort of thing involved in something like Huntington's Disease. As Bleuler (1911 as reprinted 1950) said sixty years ago in his classic work, a person cannot have a delusion concerning Jesuits unless he has learned about Jesuits. In that sense, the psychodynamically oriented clinician who insists that schizophrenia is not biologically inherited but socially learned is obviously (but not illuminatingly) correct.

Addendum (July 1972)

Subsequent to the presentation of this paper at the Classification Society's meeting, the large-scale Monte Carlo runs then projected have been completed and partially analyzed for major trends of prime interest. Detailed results will be reported elsewhere (see Golden and Meehl, 1973a, 1973b, and papers now in preparation for submission to a psychometric or statistical journal). To avoid further delay in publishing the present volume, I here confine myself to summarizing our main interpretations of the results to date:

1. The MAXCOV-HITMAX method yields highly accurate estimates of

the unknown latent taxon's base rate P, typically with an error about that of the standard error of a proportion for each sample size.

2. Joint satisfaction of the three or four best consistency tests practically assures an adequate numerical approximation by the state of nature to the idealized latent structure.

3. The method is gratifyingly robust, leading to accurate parameter estimates even when intrataxon indicator correlations depart markedly from the idealized $r = 0$.

4. Only a "malicious" combination of highly adverse latent circumstances (e.g., extreme inequality of intrataxon variances, marked indicator skewness, base-rate asymmetry $P \ll Q$, small sample size, large and unequal intrataxon covariances) seems capable of yielding bad parameter estimates *without clear warning* (*by consistency tests*) *that this is happening*. Even for these far-out "bad luck" combinations, we have reason to conjecture that an optimal configural use of the consistency tests may yet succeed in reducing the inferential danger to a negligible threat.

5. Application of the method to some further "real data" (U.K. psychiatric ratings) strongly suggests that it works much better than the leading "cluster method" contender.

6. A related but nonredundant method, MAXDIFF-HITMAX, which locates the hitmax cut on indicator x by searching for the maximum difference between means of indicator y calculated above and below a sliding x cut (i.e., we assign x_c such that $[\bar{y}_{(x > x_c)} - \bar{y}_{(x < x_c)}] = \text{Max}$), is as good as MAXCOV-HITMAX, perhaps better. This procedure (see Meehl, 1965a, section 9d, pp. 29–30; Meehl, 1968, section 2b, pp. 9–23) can be powerfully combined with an "item-iterative" approach, in which the taxonomic parameters p_s and p_n of individual MMPI items are estimated in a first approximation, then used to improve the hitmax cut location and to eliminate "bad-acting" items, and continuing to recycle until consistency tests are well satisfied by the surviving items. Since MAXCOV-HITMAX and MAXDIFF-HITMAX rely on largely independent search principles, good numerical agreement between final base-rate estimates and item-parameter values tends strongly to corroborate both (a) the latent structure postulated and (b) the numerical values thus converged upon.

7. Commencing with an item pool composed of only 20 percent moderately valid items and 80 percent "garbage" items (for separating

sexes), the methods lead to liquidation of the poor items and accurate estimates of the (p_s, p_n) psychometric parameters of the retained valid items.

8. Despite the cautionary remarks in text concerning sample size, it now appears that much smaller samples (e.g., as few as 100 patients in the taxon and 100 extrataxon) can, under favorable circumstances, yield values having 95 percent accuracy for the major latent parameters sought.

9. My conclusion, now becoming fairly firm on the growing body of Monte Carlo and real-data evidence to date, is that the Classification Society paper was, if anything, overcautious. It appears that a remarkably powerful approach exists here, deserving thorough exploration in a variety of taxonomic research problems.

13

Why I Do Not Attend
Case Conferences

I HAVE FOR MANY YEARS been accustomed to the social fact that colleagues and students find some of my beliefs and attitudes paradoxical (some would, perhaps, use the stronger word *contradictory*). I flatter myself that this paradoxicality arises primarily because my views (like the world) are complex and cannot be neatly subsumed under some simpleminded undergraduate rubric (e.g., behavioristic, Freudian, actuarial, positivist, hereditarian). I find, for example, that psychologists who visit Minneapolis for the first time and drop in for a chat with me generally show clinical signs of mild psychic shock when they find a couch in my office and a picture of Sigmund Freud on the wall. Apparently one is not supposed to think or practice psychoanalytically if he understands something about philosophy of science, thinks that genes are important for psychology, knows how to take a partial derivative, enjoys and esteems Albert Ellis, or is interested in optimizing the prediction of behavior by the use of actuarial methods! I maintain that there is no unresolvable conflict between these things, but do not propose to argue that position here.

On the local scene, one manifestation of this puzzlement has come frequently to my attention and, given its nature, I think it likely that for each time I hear the question there are numerous other occasions when it is raised. In substance, the puzzle—sometimes complaint—among our graduate students goes like this: "Dr. Meehl sees patients on the campus

225

and at the Nicollet Clinic, averaging, so we are told, around a dozen hours a week of psychotherapy. With the exception of a short period when he was APA president, he has been continuously engaged in the practice of psychotherapy for almost thirty years. It is well known that he not only thinks it important for a psychologist to work as a responsible professional with real-life clinical problems but, further, considers the purely 'theoretical' personality research of academic psychologists to be usually naive and unrealistic when the researcher is not a seasoned, practicing clinician. When he taught the introductory assessment course, the lectures were about evenly divided between rather abstract theoretical and methodological content (such as 'What is the nature of a phenotypic trait, considered as a class of related dispositions?' 'What precisely do we mean by the phrase *disease entity*?' 'What is *specific etiology*?') and practical, down-to-earth material (such as 'How do you handle a patient's questions about yourself?' 'What do you do with the patient who in the initial interview sits passively expecting you to cross-examine him?' 'How do you assess the severity of a depression, especially with respect to suicidal potential?' 'How do you tell the difference between an acting-out neurotic and a true psychopath?'). He took the trouble to become a (non-grandfathered) diplomate of ABPP although in his academic position this had little advantage either of economics or of status. When he was chairman of the Psychology Department he had a policy of not hiring faculty to teach courses in the clinical and personality area unless they were practitioners and either had the ABPP diploma or intended to get it. He has been an (unsuccessful) advocate of a special doctorate in clinical psychology, the Ps.D., which would dispense with some of the medieval academic requirements for the Ph.D. degree and would permit a much more intensive and diversified clinical training for persons aiming at full-time work as practitioners in the profession. Meehl lists himself in the Yellow Section of the phone book and is a member of such outfits as the American Academy of Psychotherapists, the American Academy of Psychoanalysis, and the Institute for Advanced Study in Rational Psychotherapy. On all these counts, it seems evident that Meehl is 'clinically oriented,' that his expressed views about the importance of professional practice are sincere rather than pro forma. It is therefore puzzling to us students, and disappointing to us after having been stimulated by him as a lecturer, to find that he almost never shows up in the clinical settings where we take our clerkship and internship. We never see Dr. Meehl at a case conference. Why is this?"

This understandable puzzlement was the precipitating cause of my writing the present paper, partly because it becomes tiresome to explain this mystery repeatedly to baffled, well-meaning students, but also because responding to the puzzlement provides an occasion for some catharsis and, I hope, for making a constructive contribution to the field. Accordingly the first portion of the paper will be highly critical and aggressively polemic. (If you want to shake people up, you have to raise a little hell.) The second part, while not claiming grandiosely to offer a definitive solution to the problem, proposes some directions of thinking and "experimenting" that might lead to a significant improvement over current conditions.

The main reason I rarely show up at case conferences is easily stated: The intellectual level is so low that I find them boring, sometimes even offensive. Why the level of a psychiatric case conference is usually so mediocre, by contrast with conferences in internal medicine or neurology —both of which I have usually found stimulating and illuminating—is not known, and it is a topic worthy of research. I do not believe my attitude is as unusual as it may seem. I think I am merely more honest than most clinical psychologists about admitting my reaction. Witness the fact that the staff conferences in the Medical School where I work are typically attended by only a minority of the faculty—usually those who *must* be there as part of their paid responsibility, or who have some other special reason (such as invitation) for attending a particular one. If the professional faculty found them worthwhile, they wouldn't be so reluctant to spend their time that way. Pending adequate research on "What's the matter with the typical case conference," I present herewith some clinical impressions by way of explanation, and some constructive suggestions for improvement. My impressionistic list of explanations constitutes the "destructive criticism" portion of this paper.

Part I: What's Wrong?

1. *Buddy-buddy syndrome.* In one respect the clinical case conference is no different from other academic group phenomena such as committee meetings, in that many intelligent, educated, sane, rational persons seem to undergo a kind of intellectual deterioration when they gather around a table in one room. The cognitive degradation and feck-

227

less vocalization characteristic of committees are too well known to require comment. Somehow the group situation brings out the worst in many people, and results in an intellectual functioning that is at the lowest common denominator, which in clinical psychology and psychiatry is likely to be pretty low.

2. *"All evidence is equally good."* This absurd idea perhaps arises from the "groupy," affiliative tendency of behavioral scientists in "soft" fields like clinical, counseling, personality, and social psychology. It seems that there are many professionals for whom committee work and conferences represent part of their social, intellectual, and erotic life. If you take that "groupy" attitude, you tend to have a sort of mush-headed approach which says that everybody in the room has something to contribute (absurd on the face of it, since most persons don't usually have anything worthwhile to contribute about anything, especially if it's the least bit complicated). In order to maintain the fiction that everybody's ideas are worthwhile, it is necessary to lower the standards for what is evidential. As a result, a casual anecdote about one's senile uncle as remembered from childhood is given the same group interest and intellectual respect that is accorded to the citation of a high-quality experimental or field-actuarial study. Or a casual impression found in the nurses' notes is given the same weight as the patient's MMPI code. Nobody would be prepared to defend this rationally in a seminar on research methods, but we put up with it in our psychiatric case conferences.

3. *Reward everything—gold and garbage alike.* The tradition of exaggerated tenderness in psychiatry and psychology reflects our "therapeutic attitude" and contrasts with that of scholars in fields like philosophy or law, where a dumb argument is *called* a dumb argument, and he who makes a dumb argument can expect to be slapped down by his peers. Nobody ever gives anybody negative reinforcement in a psychiatric case conference. (Try it once—you will be heard with horror and disbelief.) The most inane remark is received with joy and open arms as part of the groupthink process. Consequently the educational function, for either staff or students, is prevented from getting off the ground. Any psychologist should know that part of the process of training or educating is to administer differential reinforcement for good versus bad, effective versus ineffective, correct versus incorrect behaviors. If *all* behavior is rewarded by friendly attention and nobody is ever non-

reinforced (let alone punished!) for talking foolishly, it is unlikely that significant educational growth will take place.

A corollary of the "reward everything" policy with respect to evidence and arguments is a substantive absurdity, namely, everyone is right—or at least, nobody is *wrong*. The group impulse toward a radical democratization of qualifications and opinions leads almost to denying the Law of Noncontradiction. A nice quotation from the statistician M. G. Kendall is apposite: "A friend of mine once remarked to me that if some people asserted that the earth rotated from East to West and others that it rotated from West to East, there would always be a few well-meaning citizens to suggest that perhaps there was something to be said for both sides and that maybe it did a little of one and a little of the other; or that the truth probably lay between the extremes and perhaps it did not rotate at all" (Kendall, 1949, p. 115).

4. *Tolerance of feeble inferences (e.g., irrelevancies)*. The ordinary rules of scientific inference, and reliance upon general principles of human development, which everybody takes for granted in a neurology staff conference, are somehow forgotten in a psychiatric case conference. This is perhaps due to the fact that the psychiatrist has had to learn to live with the sorry state of his specialty after having had training in the more scientific branches of medicine, with the result that once having learned to live this way, he assumes that the whole set of rules about how to think straight have to be junked, so that logic, statistics, experiments, scientific evidence, and so on don't apply. I have heard professionals say things in a psychiatric staff conference which I am certain they would never have said about a comparable problem in a conference room one floor below (neurology service). Example: In a case conference involving a differential diagnosis between schizophrenia and anxiety reaction in a pan-anxious patient that any well-read clinician would easily recognize as a classical case of the Hoch-Polatin "pseudoneurotic schizophrenia" syndrome (Hoch and Polatin, 1949; Meehl, 1964) the psychiatrist presiding at the conference argued that the patient was probably latently or manifestly schizophrenic. He argued thus partly because—in addition to her schizophrenic MMPI profile—she had a vivid and sustained hallucinatory experience immediately preceding her entry into the hospital. She saw a Ku Klux Klansman standing in the living room, in full regalia, eying her malignantly and making threatening gestures with a knife, this hallucination lasting for several

229

minutes. Since hallucinations of this sort are textbook symptoms of a psychotic break in ego function (reality testing), it seemed pretty clear to the presiding psychiatrist (and myself) that this would have to be considered evidence—not dispositive, but pretty strong—for our schizophrenic diagnosis as against the anxiety-neurosis alternative. At this point one of the nurses said, "I don't see why Dr. Koutsky and Dr. Meehl are laying emphasis upon this Ku Klux Klansman. After all, I remember having an imaginary companion when I was a little girl." Now suppose that this well-meaning nurse, whose remark was greeted with the usual respectful attention to "a contribution," had been attending a case conference on the neurology service. And suppose that in attempting a differential diagnosis of spinal cord tumor the presiding neurologist had offered in evidence the fact that the patient was incontinent of urine. It would never occur to this nurse to advance, as a counterargument, the fact that she used to wet her pants when she was a little girl. (If she did advance such a stupid argument on neurology, my colleague Dr. A. B. Baker—who has "standards"—would tromp on her with his hobnail boots, and she would never make *that* mistake again.) But somehow when she gets into a psychiatric case conference she undergoes a twenty-point decrement in functional IQ score, so as to forget how to distinguish between different degrees of pathology or between phenomena occurring at different developmental levels. Equating a childhood imaginary companion with an adult's experiencing a clear and persisting visual hallucination of a Ku Klux Klansman is of course just silly—but in a psychiatry case conference no one would be so tactless as to point this out.

5. *Failure to distinguish between an inclusion test and an exclusion test.* In a differential diagnosis between schizophrenia and manic-depressive psychosis, a psychology trainee argues against schizophrenia on the ground that the patient does not have delusions or hallucinations with clear sensorium. Of course this is just plain uninformed, because delusions and hallucinations are among Bleuler's "accessory" symptoms, present in some schizophrenics but not all, and they are *not* part of the indicator family that "defines" the disease (Bleuler, 1911 as reprinted 1950). Some American clinicians (not I) would hold that delusions and hallucinations with clear sensorium are so rare in uncomplicated manic depression that when *present* they could be used as a quasi-exclusion test against that diagnosis. But since many schizophrenics—not only

borderline cases of "pseudoneurotic schizophrenia" but those cases known in the present nomenclature as "schizophrenia, chronic undifferentiated" and "schizophrenia, acute episode" and "schizophrenia, simple type"—are without these particular accessory symptoms, the trainee's argument is without merit. Psychodynamically, delusions and hallucinations are among the so-called restitutional symptoms of the disorder, as contrasted with the regressive ones. Depending upon the form and stage of the disease, restitutional symptoms may or may not be in evidence. That delusions and hallucinations with unclouded sensorium are absent in many schizophrenics is not an idiosyncratic clinical opinion of mine. It is a theory found in all of the textbooks, it is in the standard nomenclature, it is in Kraepelin and Bleuler, who defined the entity "schizophrenia." There is no justification for utilizing the *absence* of these accessory symptoms as an exclusion test. Neither semantic nor empirical grounds exist for this practice. But when I point this out forcefully, the trainee looks at me as if I were a mean ogre.

6. *Failure to distinguish between mere consistency of a sign and differential weight of a sign.* Once the differential diagnosis has been narrowed to two or three nosological possibilities, it is inappropriate to cite in evidence signs or symptoms which are nondifferentiating as between them. This is so obvious a mistake that one thinks it would never happen; but some clinicians do it regularly. In distinguishing *between* a sociopathic personality, an acting-out neurotic delinquent, and a garden-variety "sociological" criminal, it is fallacious to argue that the patient was a marked underachiever or a high school dropout, in spite of high IQ, as grounds for a diagnosis of sociopathic personality, because, whereas this sign is a correlate of the sociopathic diagnosis, we have now narrowed the nosological range to three possibilities, each of which is a correlate of academic underachievement, so that this sign has lost its diagnostic relevancy at this stage of the investigation. This illustrates one of the generic features of case conferences in psychiatry, namely, the tendency to mention things that don't make any difference one way or the other. The idea seems to be that as long as something is true, or is believed to be true, or is possibly true, it is worth mentioning! In other medical specialties in order to be worth mentioning the statement must not only be true but be *differentially* relevant, i.e., it must argue for one diagnosis, outlook, or treatment, rather than another.

7. *Shift in the evidential standard, depending upon whose ox is being*

231

gored. A favorite tactic of case conference gamesmanship is to use a "double standard of morals" on the weight of the evidence. When you are putting your own diagnostic case, you permit indirect inferences (mediated by weak theoretical constructions and psychodynamic conclusions); then when the other fellow is making his case for a different diagnosis, you become superscientific and behavioristic, making comments like "Well, of course, all we actually know is the *behavior.*" You *don't really* know "the behavior" in the sense it is usually discussed in the staff conference, since even phenotypic characterizations are almost invariably summary-type statements with a large component of sampling inference at least involved. Further, to this sampling inference we usually conjoin theory-mediated inferences, relying on extrapolations from other contexts as justification for weighting some sources of data more heavily than others. As a result this superbehaviorism is not even intellectually honest.

The opposite of this ("simpleminded") error is, of course, the failure to connect theoretical constructs with behavioral data, actual *or possible.* This is the error of the "muddleheaded." Projective tests lend themselves particularly well to this, since trends, forces, and structures that are *latent* (a perfectly legitimate metaconcept) cannot be operationally defined, hence offer unusual temptation for a muddlehead to use them without regard for any kind of corroborative evidence, direct or indirect, tight or probabilistic.

8. *Ignorance* (*or repression*) *of statistical logic.* A whole class of loosely related errors made in the clinical case conference arises from forgetting (on the part of the psychologist) or never having learned (in the case of the psychiatrist and social worker) certain elementary statistical or psychometric principles. Examples are the following:

a. *Forgetting Bayes' Theorem.* One should always keep in mind that there is a relationship between prior probability (e.g., the base rate P of a certain diagnosis or dynamic configuration in the particular clinic population) and the increment in probability contributed by a certain diagnostic symptom or sign. If the prior probability is extremely low, you don't get very much mileage out of a moderately strong sign or symptom. On the other hand, when the prior probability is extremely high, you get mileage out of an additional fact, but you don't really "need it much," so to speak. The considerations advanced by Meehl and Rosen (1955—reprinted here as Chapter 2) apply in a clinical

232

case conference just as strongly as they do in a research design involving psychometrics.

b. *Forgetting about unreliability when interpreting score changes or difference scores* (e.g., on subtests of the WAIS). Despite the mass of adverse research and psychometric theoretical criticism of the practice of overinterpreting small difference scores on unreliable subtests (which are of doubtful validity for the alleged noncognitive traits anyway!), one still hears this kind of "evidence" pressed in case conferences. Who cares whether the patient "did well on the Block Design subtest but seemed to enjoy it less than Picture Arrangement"?

c. *Reliance upon inadequate behavior samples for trait attribution.* Sometimes the inadequacy is *qualitative,* in the sense that the context in which the behavior was sampled is in some way unusual or atypical for the population or for this particular individual; more commonly, the error is simply one of believing that you can estimate the proportion of white marbles in an urn after sampling only a couple of marbles. This error is particularly serious because in addition to the numerical smallness of the samples of behavior adduced as the basis for trait attribution, we have almost no control over the conscious or unconscious selection factor that has determined which behavior chunk was noticed, was remembered, and is now reproduced for tendentious purposes. It is obvious that over a period of several hours or days of unsystematic observation, practically any human being is likely to emit at least a few behaviors which can be subsumed under almost any trait in the phenotypic or genotypic lexicon.

d. *Inadequate consideration of whether and when the (fact → fact) linkage is stronger or weaker than the (multiple-fact → diagnosis → fact) linkage.* It seems there are some cases in which the best way to infer to a certain fact, whether postdictive or predictive, is by relying upon its correlation with certain other relatively atomistic facts with which, from previous experience or research, the inferred fact is known to be correlated. In other cases it appears that a set of facts which qualitatively does not seem related to the fact of interest is related to it rather strongly because this first set of facts known to us converges powerfully upon a taxonomic decision (whether formal diagnosis, environmental mold, personality "type," or dynamic configuration). When that taxonomic decision has been made with high confidence, certain other individual atomistic facts or dispositions may follow with reasonably high confidence. It is a mistake to assume, without looking into the matter, that one or the other of these approaches is "obviously" the way to proceed most powerfully. (Cf. Meehl, 1960—reprinted here as Chapter 6.)

e. *Failing to understand probability logic as applied to the single case.* This disability is apparently endemic to the psychiatric profession and strangely enough is also found among clinical psychologists in spite of their academic training in statistical reasoning. There are still tough, unsolved philosophical problems connected with the application of frequencies to individual cases. But we cannot come to grips with those problems, or arrive at a pragmatic decision policy in staff conferences, unless we have gotten beyond the blunders characteristically enunciated by clinicians who are not familiar with the literature on this subject from Lundberg (1941) and Sarbin (1942) through Meehl (1945a, 1954a, 1956a, 1956b, 1956c—reprinted here as Chapter 3, 1957—reprinted here as Chapter 4, 1959a, 1959b—reprinted here as Chapter 5, 1960 —reprinted here as Chapter 6, Meehl and Dahlstrom, 1960) to recent contributors like Goldberg (1968, 1970), Sawyer (1966), Kleinmuntz (1968, 1969), Einhorn (1970, 1972), Pankoff and Roberts (1968), Marks and Sines (1969), Alker and Hermann (1971), Mirabile, Houck, and Glueck (1971); see also footnote 4 in Livermore, Malmquist, and Meehl, 1968 (at page 76), and footnotes 8 and 9 in Meehl, 1970b (at pp. 8–9), and references cited thereat. The vulgar error is the cliché that "We aren't dealing with groups, we are dealing with this individual case." It is doubtful that one can profitably debate this cliché in a case conference, since anyone who puts it quite this way is not educable in ten minutes. He who wishes to reform the thinking in case conferences must constantly reiterate the elementary truth that if you depart in your clinical decision making from a well-established (or even moderately well-supported) empirical frequency—whether it is based upon psychometrics, life-history material, rating scales or whatever— your departure may save a particular case from being misclassified predictively or therapeutically; but that such departures are, prima facie, counterinductive, so that a decision *policy* of this kind is almost certain to have a cost that exceeds its benefits. The research evidence strongly suggests that a policy of making such departures, except very sparingly, will result in the misclassifying of other cases that would have been correctly classified had such nonactuarial departures been forbidden; it also suggests that more of this second kind of misclassification will occur than will be compensated for by the improvement in the first kind (Meehl, 1957—reprinted here as Chapter 4). That there are occasions when you should use your head instead of the formula is perfectly clear. But which occasions they are is most emphatically *not* clear. What *is* clear on the available empirical data is that these occasions are much rarer than most clinicians suppose.

9. *Inappropriate task specification.* Nobody seems very clear about which kinds of tasks are well performed in the case conference context and which would be better performed in other ways. There are some cognitive jobs for which it seems doubtful that the case conference is suitable. I myself think that the commonest form of this mistake is the spinning out of complicated psychodynamics which are explained in terms of the life history and which in turn are used to explain the present aberrant behavior, on evidence which is neither quantitatively nor qualitatively adequate to carry out such an ambitious enterprise (assuming, as I believe, that the enterprise is sometimes feasible in the present state of psychology). Any psychologist who has practiced long-term, intensive, "uncovering" psychotherapy knows that there are psychodynamic puzzles and paradoxes which remain in his mind after listening to fifty or a hundred hours of the patient's productions. Yet this same psychotherapist may undergo a strange metamorphosis when he enters the case conference context, finding himself pronouncing (sometimes rather dogmatically) about the psychodynamics of the presented patient, on the basis of ten minutes' exposure to the patient during the conference, plus some shoddy, scanty "material" presented by the resident and social worker (based in turn upon a relatively small total time of contact with the patient and interviewing that *on the psychotherapist's own usual criteria* would be considered "superficial").

Part of the difficulty here lies in American psychiatry's emphasis upon psychodynamics at the expense of nosology. A case conference *can* be, under some circumstances, an appropriate place to clarify the nosological or taxonomic issue—provided that the participants have bothered to learn some nosology, and that the clinicians mainly concerned with the patient have obtained the relevant clinical data. But since diagnosis is devalued, the prestigious thing to do is to contribute psychodynamic ideas to the conference, so we try to do that, whether or not the quality and quantity of the material available to us is adequate to such an enterprise, which it usually isn't.

10. *Asking pointless questions.* Participants in a case conference frequently ask questions the answers to which make no conceivable difference, or only the most negligible difference, to the handling of the case. I have often thought that the clinician in charge of the case conference should emulate a professor of law from whom I took a course in equitable remedies, David Bryden. When a law student advanced a stupid argument about the case being discussed, he would respond with a blank stare and the question "And therefore?" This would usually elicit some further response from the student (attempting to present the next link in an argumentative chain), but this shoring-up job would in turn be greeted by the same blank stare, the same inquisitorial "And therefore?" I daresay Professor Bryden made the law students nervous; but he also forced them to *think.* I suspect that one who persisted in asking the question "And therefore?" every time somebody made a half-baked contribution to the case conference would wreak havoc, but it might be an educational experience for all concerned.

11. *Ambiguity of professional roles.* When the conference is not confined to one of the three professions in the team, there may arise a sticky problem about roles. For example, in mixed-group conferences I note a tendency to assume that the psychologist's job should be to present the psychometrics and that he is only very gingerly and tentatively to talk about anything else. I think this attitude is ridiculous. I can conduct a diagnostic interview or take a history as well as most psychiatrists, and nonpsychometric data are just as much part of my subject matter as they are of the psychiatrist's. Similarly, if a physician has developed clinical competence in interpreting Rorschachs or MMPI profiles or practicing behavior modification, I listen to what he says without regard to trade-union considerations. By the same token, if I discern that a patient walks with the "schizophrenic float" or exhibits paranoid hypervigility or sociopathic insouciance, I feel free to offer this clinical observation in evidence.

12. *Some common fallacies.* Not all of these fallacies are clearly visible in case conferences, and none of them is confined to the case conference, being part of the general collection of sloppy thinking habits with which much American psychiatry is infected. I have given some of them special "catchy" names, admittedly for propaganda purposes but also as an aid to memory.

a. *Barnum effect.* Saying trivial things that are true of practically all

236

psychiatric patients, or sometimes of practically all human beings—this is the Barnum effect. It is not illuminating to be told that a mental patient has intrapsychic conflicts, ambivalent object relations, sexual inhibitions, or a damaged self-image! (Cf. Meehl, 1956c—reprinted here as Chapter 3; Sundberg, 1955; Tallent, 1958; Forer, 1949; Ulrich, Stachnik, and Stainton, 1963; and Paterson in Blum and Balinsky, 1951, p. 47, and Dunnette, 1957, p. 223.)

b. *Sick-sick fallacy* ("pathological set"). There is a widespread tendency for people in the mental health field to identify their personal ideology of adjustment, health, and social role, and even to some extent their religious and political beliefs and values, with freedom from disease or aberration. Therefore if we find somebody very unlike us in these respects we see him as being sick. The psychiatric establishment officially makes a point of never doing this and then proceeds to do it routinely. Thus, for example, many family psychiatrists have a stereotype of what the healthy family ought to be; and if anybody's family life does not meet these criteria, this is taken as a sign of pathology. Other stereotypes may exist in connection with the "genital character," the person who "fulfills his potential," and so on. Don't let this one pass by, saying that we already know about it! We *do* know about it "officially," but the point is that many people in the mental health field are not very clear about the question in their own thinking. Example: Despite the Kinsey research, some psychiatrists of sexually conservative tastes are likely to overinterpret forms of sexual behavior such as cunnilingus or fellatio as symptomatic of psychopathology, even though the data indicate that mouth-genital contacts have occurred in the *majority* of members of Kinsey's "sophisticated" classes. In my opinion it is almost impossible to say anything clinically significant about a patient on the basis of a history of cunnilingus or fellatio unless one knows a good deal about the motivations. That is to say, it is the motivational basis and not the act which is clinically relevant.

c. *"Me too" fallacy* (the unconsidered allegation that "anyone would do that"). This is the opposite of the overpathologizing "sick-sick" fallacy, and one might therefore suppose that clinicians fond of committing the "sick-sick" fallacy would be unlikely to commit the "me too" fallacy. I have no quantitative data on this, but my impression is that the same clinicians have a tendency to commit both. Perhaps the common property is not conservatism or liberalism in diagnosing pathology but mere sloppy-headedness. The sloppy-headed clinician unconsciously selects, in terms of his personal biases and values, which things he is going to look upon as "terribly sick" and which things he is going to look upon as "perfectly okay" (normal). The example I gave earlier of the nurse who tried to mitigate the diagnostic significance of a patient's visual hallucination by telling us that as a child she had imaginery companions is an example of the "me too" fallacy, although it is compounded with various other errors, such as false analogy and the failure to take developmental stages into account.

I was first forcibly struck with the significance and seductiveness of the "me too" fallacy when I was a graduate student in clinical training. One of my first diagnostic workups was with a girl in late adolescence (a classic Cleckley psychopath: Cleckley, 1964) who was brought in for evaluation on a district court order. She had a considerable history of minor acting out in the form of truancy, impulsive behavior, and running away from home; but the problem which brought her in was that she had "in a fit of pique" hit her foster mother over the head with a lamp base, as a result of which the foster mother sustained a fracture and concussion. One important thing to assess, from the standpoint of the court's inquiry, was the extent to which the patient could exert behavioral control over her impulses. In the 1940's, the patients on our psychiatric service did not have continuous access to their cigarettes but could only smoke at certain times. One of the times when everybody was allowed to come to the nurses' cage to get a cigarette was, let us say, at 3:00 P.M. This particular patient came to the cage around a half hour early and said she wanted her cigarette. The charge nurse told her kindly but firmly that it wasn't quite time yet. The patient insisted that she wanted a cigarette right now and that she didn't want to wait a half hour. The nurse repeated that it wasn't time yet but that she could have a cigarette at 3 P.M. Whereupon the patient began pounding with her fists on the nurse's cage and then flung herself on the floor where she kicked and screamed like a small child having a tantrum. When this episode was discussed in the weekly conference with the junior medical students, the student physician told Dr. Hathaway, the clinical psychologist presiding at the conference, that he didn't see any point in "making a lot out of this tantrum" because, "after all, anybody might act the same way under the circumstances." The dialogue continued thus:

DR. HATHAWAY: "How do you mean 'under the circumstances'?"

MEDICAL STUDENT: "Well, she wanted a cigarette and it's kind of a silly rule."

DR. HATHAWAY: "Let's assume it's a silly rule, but it is a rule which she knows about, and she knows that the tantrum is probably going to deprive her of some privileges on the station. Would you act this way under the circumstances?"

MEDICAL STUDENT: "Sure I would."

DR. HATHAWAY: "Now, think a moment; *would* you, really?"

MEDICAL STUDENT (thoughtful): "Well, perhaps I wouldn't, actually."

And of course he wouldn't. Point: If you find yourself minimizing a recognized sign or symptom of pathology by thinking, "Anybody would do this," think again. *Would* just anybody do it? Behavioristically speaking, what is the actual objective probability of a mentally healthy person behaving just this way? Or, from the introspective point of view, would you *really* do or say what the patient did? Obviously it is *not* the same to say that you might feel an impulse or have a momentary thought similar to that of the patient. The question is, in the case of cognitive distortions, whether you would seriously entertain or believe the thought; or, in the case of overt acting-out conduct, whether you would act out the impulse, having experienced it. You will find that many times, when your initial tendency is to mitigate the symptom's significance in this way, a closer look will convince you that the behavior or belief is actually a serious aberration in reality testing or normal impulse control.

d. *Uncle George's pancakes fallacy.* This is a variant of the "me too" fallacy, once removed; rather than referring to what anybody would do or what you yourself would do, you call to mind a friend or relative who exhibited a sign or symptom similar to that of the patient. For example, a patient does not like to throw away leftover pancakes and he stores them in the attic. A mitigating clinician says, "Why, there is nothing so terrible about that—I remember good ole Uncle George from my childhood, *he* used to store uneaten pancakes in the attic." The proper conclusion from such a personal recollection is, of course, not that the patient is mentally well but that good ole Uncle George—whatever may have been his other delightful qualities—was mentally aberrated. The underlying premise in this kind of fallacious argument seems to be the notion that none of one's personal friends or family could have been a psychiatric case, partly because the individual in question was not hospitalized or officially diagnosed and partly because (whereas other people may have crazy friends and relatives) *I* obviously have never known or been related to such persons in my private life. Once this premise is made explicit, the fallacy is obvious.

e. *Multiple Napoleons fallacy* (the Doctrine of Unreal Realities). This is the mush-headed objection that "Well, it may not be 'real' to us, but it's 'real' to him." (This arises partly from the relativism cultivated by American education or, at a more sophisticated level, from extreme instrumentalism in one's philosophy of science.) It is unnecessary to resolve the deep technical questions of realism and instrumentalism before one can recognize a distinction between reality and delusion as clinical categories. So far as I am aware, even Dewey, Vaihinger, and Heidegger would allow that a man who believes he is Napoleon or has invented a perpetual-motion machine is crazy. If I think the moon is made of green cheese and you think it's a piece of rock, one of us must be wrong. To point out that the aberrated cognitions of a delusional patient "seem real to him" is a complete waste of time. Furthermore, there is some research evidence and considerable clinical experience to suggest that the reality feeling of delusions and hallucinations does differ at least quantitatively, and some investigators allege even qualitatively, from the reality feeling of normal people or from that of the patient regarding familiar nondistorted objects. Thus the statement "It is reality to him," which is philosophically either trivial or false, is also clinically misleading. Nevertheless I have actually heard clinicians in conference invoke this kind of notion on quasi-philosophical grounds, as if to suggest that since nobody knows for certain what reality is, we have no justification for invoking the distinction between the real and the imaginary in assessing a patient.

f. *Crummy criterion fallacy.* It is remarkable that eighteen years after the publication of Cronbach and Meehl's "Construct Validity in Psychological Tests" (1955—reprinted here as Chapter 1) and fourteen years after the beautiful methodological development by Campbell and Fiske (1959) and a philosophical treatment by Meehl which has been widely reprinted (1959b—reprinted here as Chapter 5; see also Loevinger, 1957), many clinical psychology trainees (and some full professors) persist in a naive undergraduate view of psychometric validity. (I mention "contemporary" writers—the point about construct validity was made clearly enough by several authors cited in the Cronbach-Meehl paper, and by the great Spearman, whom we unaccountably failed to mention. It reflects on the shoddy state of psychology that a *graduate* student recently asked me, "Who is this Spearman?") Repeatedly in a clinical case conference one finds psychologists seeing their task as "explaining away" the psychometrics rather than "explaining them" in the sense of genuinely integrating them with the interview, life-history, and ward-behavior material on the patient. It rarely occurs to anyone to feel that he must explain away the intelligence test: the psychiatrist has come to recognize that a successful "bootstraps operation" (Cronbach and Meehl, 1955—see p. 11 above) has been achieved in the measurement of intellect. We do not ordinarily say, "The social worker thought Johnny was dumb, but he has a WISC IQ of 160; isn't it a shame that the test missed again!" But if an MMPI profile indicates strongly that the patient is profoundly depressed or has a schizoid makeup, this psychometric finding is supposed to agree with the global impression of a first-year psychiatric resident, and if it doesn't the psychologist typically adopts a posture of psychometric apology. Now this is silly. Even from the armchair, we start with the fact that an MMPI profile represents the statistical distillation of 550 verbal responses which is considerably in excess of what the clinician has elicited from the patient in most instances, even assuming that the clinician knows how to combine the information he does elicit in an optimal fashion—a proposition at least arguable. Surely there are cases where the psychometrics disagree with the interviewer's clinical impression and yet are at least as likely to be correct as the interviewer, particularly if he is a relatively fresh practitioner in the early stages of his clinical training.

The methodological point is so obvious that it is almost embarrassing to explain it, but I gather it is still necessary. Point: If a psychometric device has been empirically constructed and cross-validated in reliance upon the average statistical correctness of a series of clinical judgments, including judgments by well-trained clinicians as well as ill-trained ones, there is a pretty good probability that the score pattern reflects the patient's personality structure and dynamics better than does the clinical judgment of an individual contributor to the case conference—even if he is a seasoned practitioner, and a fortiori if he is a clinical fledgling. The old-fashioned concept of the "criterion," which applies literally in *forecasting* contexts (such as predicting how much life insurance a person will sell from the insurance salesman key of the SVIB), is not the only appropriate model for the clinical case conference except when we are explicitly engaged in pragmatic forecasting tasks (e.g., predicting whether the patient will be a continuer or a dropout in outpatient psychotherapy, predicting whether he will respond favorably to Stelazine or EST). It is necessary to be clear about the clinical *task*. Sometimes the clinical task is comparable to the task of the industrial or military psychologist or the educational psychologist trying to select applicants for engineering school who will not flunk out. Most of the time, however, the (alleged) purpose of the clinical case conference is to attain a psychodynamic, nosological, and etiological understanding of the individual patient. I do not enter here into the controversy whether this is an achievable or socially defensible goal, which it may or may not be. The point is that it is the tacitly understood function of much (not all!) of the discussion that goes on in the case conference; given that, it is inappropriate to treat the psychometrics in the same way that we treat them when we have a problem of pure concurrent or predictive validity in the traditional sense.

An MMPI profile is a behavior sample which has been analyzed and summarized in quasi-rigorous fashion on the basis of very extensive clinical experience. This extensive clinical experience has operated first in the construction of the item pool, then in construction and cross-validation of the scales, and then in the development of the various actuarial interpretative cookbook systems. If a patient was diagnosed "reactive depression" by the resident, appears mainly depressed when he is interviewed in the case conference, but has a clearly schizophrenic MMPI supported by some bad schizophrenic F— responses, contamination, and the like on the Rorschach, I cannot imagine why a psychologist would take the simplistic position that his "psychological Wassermann" has failed. If the aim of psychometrics is to help us infer the psychodynamic equivalent of pathology in organic medicine—and that is surely one of its main aims when it is used in a sophisticated way—what the analogy suggests is that there will be, from time to time, discrepancies between what we are prone to infer from the brief interview contact and what Omniscient Jones knows about the psychological innards of the patient.

I don't mean to suggest that we accept the psychometrics as criterion in the old-fashioned sense, which would equally be a mistake. The point is that there *is* no criterion in the traditional sense, and it is preposterous that one still has to explain this to full professors. We do not know the psychological states and processes from which the various kinds of clinical behavior arise. We *infer* them from a variety of lines of evidence. Our problem is that of the detective (or theory builder!) who is trying to put together different kinds of data to form a more or less coherent picture of unknown latent and historical situations to which he does not have direct operational access. That being so, the task of explaining an apparent discrepancy between the resident's opinion or the impression we get in a case conference and what the MMPI or Rorschach tells us is a much more complicated intellectual job than it seems generally thought to be. As I pointed out in "Some Ruminations on the Validation of Clinical Procedures" (Meehl, 1959b—reprinted here as Chapter 5), giving a Rorschach or an MMPI in order to predict the verbal behavior of the psychiatrist (dynamically or diagnostically) is pointless. It's a waste of the patient's time and the taxpayer's money. If all I want to do is forecast what the psychiatrist will say about the patient's diagnosis or dynamics, it is obvious that the easiest way to do that is to walk down the hall and ask him! A psychometric instrument is not a parlor trick in which, for some strange (union-card?) reason, you keep yourself from having access to easily available information about a patient for the fun of seeing whether you can guess it instead of getting it directly. The psychologist who doesn't understand this point is not even in the ball park of clinical sophistication. To "validate" a test, in any but the crudest sense of initial investigation to determine whether the test has anything going for it at all, a sophisticated thinker realizes that one must use a criterion that is qualitatively and quantitatively superior to what is regularly available in a clinical workup. We validate the Wassermann against the pathologist's and bacteriologist's findings, *not* against the general practitioner's impression after a ten-minute hearing of the presenting complaints. Validation studies that take as the criterion the nosological label or the psychodynamic assessment which one gets on the basis of a couple of interviews are almost always a waste of time. The statements we infer about the patient from psychometrics ought to have attached to them a probability that arises from qualitatively and quantitatively *better* data than we routinely have from the nonpsychometric sources in the ordinary clinical workup. If we don't have that, it is doubtful how much point there is in giving the test in the first place. If a patient has a schizophrenic MMPI and Rorschach but does not appear schizophrenic when interviewed in staff, the *proper* questions are: "What are some of the things we might have looked for more skillfully to elicit data on the schizoid disposition that the psychometrics indicate are almost certainly present?" "What can be inferred about the psychological defense system of a patient who manages to look like a case of simple depression when he is actually a latent schizophrenic?" "What speculations would we have about discrepancies of this kind?" "What kinds of research might we carry out in order to check these speculations?" "Are there identifiable subclasses of psychometric/interview discrepancies for which the psychometrics are likely to be correct, and others for which the reverse obtains?" I do not assert that one *never* hears these important metaquestions asked in the case conference; but you can attend a hundred conferences without hearing them raised a dozen times.

g. *"Understanding it makes it normal"* (and, if legal or ethical issues are involved, "acceptable"). This is a psychiatric variant of the ethical notion that understanding behavior makes that behavior ethically permissible or "excusable." I once heard a clinical psychologist say that it was "unimportant" whether a defendant for whom I testified was legally insane, since his homicide was "dynamically understandable" in either case. (The defendant and both counsel, benighted nonpsychologists they, felt it *was* important whether a man is called a murderer and he is put in prison for twenty years or whether he is considered insane and is discharged from the state security hospital after his psychosis lifts.) As for T. Eugene Thompson, the St. Paul lawyer who cold-bloodedly murdered his wife to get a million dollars from life insurance, this psychologist argued that "I suppose if I knew enough about T. Eugene Thompson, like the way his wife sometimes talked to him at breakfast, I would understand why he did it." I gather that this psychologist (a Ph.D.!!) believes that if T. Eugene Thompson's wife was sometimes grumpy in the morning, he was entitled to kill her.

h. *Assumption that content and dynamics explain why this person is abnormal.* Of all the methodological errors committed in the name of dynamic psychiatry, this one is probably the most widespread, unquestioned, and seductive. The "reasoning" involved is simple. We find ourselves in possession of two sorts of facts about a person. The first kind of fact, present by virtue of his being a patient, is that he has mental or physical symptoms, or characterological traits, that are pathological in some accepted sense of that term.

244

This is not the place rigorously to define "pathological," for a beautiful discussion of which see the wise treatment by my colleague William Schofield (1964). For present purposes, it will suffice to say that behavior pathology is roughly defined by some (subjectively) weighted combination of marked statistical deviations from biological and cultural norms, on dimensions and in directions involving (1) subjective distress (anxiety, depression, rage, inadequacy feeling, dissatisfaction, boredom, and the like), (2) medical complaints, symptoms, or concerns, (3) impairment of educational, economic, sexual, or "social" performance, and (4) distorted appreciation of reality, external or internal. It will not usually be the case that any of these aberrations taken alone suffices to define pathology, although there are exceptions involving extreme degrees. For example, no matter how well adjusted socially, economically self-sufficient, and subjectively comfortable a person may be, if he is firmly convinced that he is Napoleon he is pathological ipso facto. It is regrettable, from the standpoint of philosophical cleanness, but the semantic situation must be honestly faced: our conception of psychopathology almost always involves some *mixture* of statistical deviation, "health" or "adjustment" evaluations, and notions of adequate ego function (reality testing and executive competence).

The point is that the individual under study in a clinical case conference comes to be there, unless there has been some sort of mistake (e.g., wrong party in a marriage is the "patient"), because he is psychologically aberrated, i.e., he has psychiatric or medical symptoms, gross social incompetence (delinquency, economic dependency), or extreme deviations in characterological structure. It does not seem useful to define "psychopathology" in solely statistical terms (is absolute pitch, an IQ = 160, or long-sustained sexual performance pathological?). Yet statistical deviations on selected dimensions considered relevant to "health," "social adaptation," "gratification," "effectiveness," and "reality appraisal" seem somehow involved. A down-playing of statistical rarity, in contrast to the work of Schofield cited above, can be found in Fine (1971, pp. 2–6; see also footnote 11 in Livermore, Malmquist, and Meehl, 1968, and citations therein).

The second kind of fact about the person is not true of him by virtue of his being a "patient," but is true of him simply because he is a human being—namely, he has conflicts and frustrations; there are areas of life in which he is less than optimally satisfied, aspects of reality he tends to distort, and performance domains in which he is less than maximally effective. There is nobody who can honestly and insightfully say that he is always efficient in his work, that he likes everyone he knows ("lie" item on MMPI L scale!), that everybody finds him a fascinating person, that he is idyllically happy in his marriage and his job, that he always finds life interesting rather than boring, that he never gets discouraged or has doubts about "whether it's all worth the trouble," and the like. If you examine the contents of a mental patient's mind, he will, by and large, have pretty much the same things on his mind as the rest of us do. If asked whether there is something that bothers him a lot, he will not emphasize his dissatisfaction with the weather. The seductive fallacy consists in *assuming,* in the absence of a respectable showing of causal connection, that this first set of facts, i.e., the medical, psychological, or social aberrations that define him as a patient, *flows from* the second set, i.e., his conflicts, failures, frustrations, dissatisfactions, and other facts which characterize him as a fallible human being, subject like the rest of us to the human condition. Example: A patient has paranoid delusions that people do not appreciate his merits. He had a father who favored his older brother. One (nonclassical) psychodynamic conclusion is that his present aberrations are mainly attributable to this bit of childhood family dynamics. I do not mean to say that this cannot happen or to deny that sometimes it does. It may be, for all I know, that this inference is true more often than not. By and large, the research literature on retrospective data for persons who have become mentally ill shows only rather weak (and frequently inconsistent) statistical relations between purportedly pathogenic background factors and mental illness (e.g., Schofield and Balian, 1959; Frank, 1965; Gottesman and Shields, 1972). Even those antecedent conditions which do show some association are ambiguous concerning causal interpretation because one does not have any scientific way of determining to what extent the life-history datum—almost always a perception by or of the patient in some interpersonal relation—was itself a reflection of personality aberrations in the "pre-patient" which led siblings, parents, teachers, or peer group to behave differently toward him at an early age. (See, for example, the fascinating study comparing mothers' attitudes toward normal, schizophrenic, and brain-damaged offspring by Klebanoff, 1959.) I do not object to speculating whether a certain event in the patient's past or a certain kind of current

246

mental conflict *may* have played an important role in producing his present pathological behavior or phenomenology. I merely point out that most of the time these are little more than speculations, whereas the tradition is to take almost any kind of unpleasant fact about the person's concerns or deprivations, present or historical, as *of course* playing an etiological role.

It is worthwhile to distinguish two forms of the mistake in connection with current psychological conflicts or frustrations. The grosser error is to attribute a causal role to an intrapsychic or situational evil when, in the eyes of Omniscient Jones, it has no connection whatever with the presented psychopathology. Thus, for example, a paranoid patient has been out of work for some time due to fluctuations in the economic cycle, and while the development of his paranoid mentation has proceeded quite independently of this unemployment, we assign a causal role to his being out of a job. Sometimes this is done even if the paranoid content itself bears no clear relationship to the alleged situational stressor. But even when it does, the inference remains highly problematic. If I feel put upon by my social environment, I will naturally look around for the most plausible cognitive content in harmony with this feeling; and the fact that I was fired from my job recently is a suitable candidate.

The other form of the mistake is less serious because, philosophically speaking, the alleged factor is really a factor, but its quantitative role is not assigned in a sophisticated manner. These are cases in which a certain factor *does* enter the causal chain eventuating in the pathological symptom which makes the individual classifiable as a mental patient, but it is a factor shared by a very large number—let us say the vast majority—of "normal" persons; and it does not exist in a greater quantitative degree in the patient than it does in the rest of us. The question then arises, why is this particular individual a patient when the rest of us are not? Most often the clarification of such situations lies in the distinction between a genetic or early-acquired disposition and a psychological (environmental) event or condition that appears in the logician's formula as the antecedent term of that disposition. (See Meehl, 1972b—reprinted here as Chapter 11.) Strictly speaking, a *disposition* and *the event that constitutes the realization of its antecedent* count equally as causes. The person can be said to actualize the consequent of the disposition *because* his environment actualizes the antecedent and

247

because he had the disposition [antecedent → consequent] to begin with, owing to his biological heredity or childhood history. However, when we ask, in a medical or social setting, "What is the matter with this individual?" we do not usually intend to ask, "What is the complete, detailed causal analysis of all the causal chains that converge upon his diagnosably aberrated state as we now see it?" That would be a legitimate question, of course. But it is *not* what we are ordinarily asking when we ask the etiological question "Why?" What we ordinarily have in mind by our etiological "Why?" is "What does this person have, or what befell him, that makes him different from those who have not developed clinical psychopathology?" That means we are looking for the *differentiating* causal agent, the thing which is true of him and not of the others who have remained "healthy." Whether that differentiating agent, picked out of the total causal confluence by our clinical interests, should more properly be the disposition or the realized antecedent term of the disposition depends primarily upon the relative frequencies of the two in the population. If many, perhaps most, persons experience the realization of the antecedent term of the disposition but do not become aberrated because they do not have the disposition to begin with, then the disposition is what is specifically abnormal in this person and should usually be the focus of our clinical and theoretical interest.

The clearest examples of the distinction between the two cases (that is, between a rare disposition whose antecedent is so commonly realized that the antecedent is considered normal and a rarely realized antecedent of a disposition so common that the disposition is called normal) are from medical genetics. In order for a child to develop the PKU syndrome, it is not sufficient that he have a mutated gene at a particular locus, and it is not sufficient that his diet contain phenylalanine. However, the conjunction [mutated gene + dietary phenylalanine] is, given the set of "normal developmental conditions" necessary for the organism to survive at all, jointly necessary and sufficient for PKU (clinical) disease. Why then do we consider this disease hereditary? Obviously, because normal children have considerable phenylalanine in their diet, and the reason they do not develop PKU is that they do not have the mutated gene, i.e., they do not have the disposition. Since the phenylalanine dietary intake is common, PKU is extremely rare, and the reason for its rarity lies in the extreme rarity of the disposition [phenylalanine intake → PKU disease], we use the common-language term "cause" to designate the genetic mutation, i.e., the source of the rare disposition. Comparable examples are diabetes (normal dietary intake of sugar), gout (normal dietary intake of certain nitrogenous food-stuffs), allergies (e.g., normal dietary intake of buckwheat), and the like. And on the other side, the "cause" of lead poisoning or scurvy is taken to be an anomalous dietary intake (excess of lead or deficiency of ascorbic acid), but these are realizations of dispositions that consti-tute the norm.

There are some circumstances in which, population frequency aside, our choice between the disposition and the realized antecedent as the culprit depends on other contextual parameters, notably therapeutic interest. It may be useful to concentrate our attention upon that which can be changed, irrespective of its rarity. But it is worth noting that in the case of PKU, although we cannot change the child's genes and we can manipulate his diet, any knowledgeable person would unhesitatingly answer the question "Is PKU a genetic disease?" affirmatively. The only basis I can see for this preferential assignment of causality—since a disposition and its actualized antecedent are equally causal in the philo-sophical sense—is the matter of frequency, i.e., what is the statistically aberrant condition? Expressed in nomic notation, with a genetic (or other constitutional or early-acquired disposition) as 'D,' the antecedent activation condition of the disposition as 'C,' and the resulting disease outcome of the combination as 'R,' the disposition may be written:

$$D = [C \rightarrow R]$$

In our ordinary medical and sociological usage of the term *cause*, with rare exceptions, what we consider is the set of population probabilities $p(D)$, $p(C)$, and $p(R)$. If the relation among these probabilities is

$$p(C) \gg p(D) > p(R)$$

we identify the (rare) disposition as the cause; whereas if

$$p(D) \gg p(C) > p(R)$$

we instead identify the (rare) actualized antecedent of the disposition as the cause. There is no harm in this selective use of *cause* on the basis of rarity, so long as we are philosophically clear about the situation as thus spelled out. The research tasks in medicine, psychology, criminol-ogy, etc., are often profitably put in terms of directing our interest and identification of the cause in this sense of statistical rarity, since one of the first things we want to know is what it is specifically that is the matter with these individuals, i.e., in what respect do they differ from others who have not fallen ill, have not become delinquent or economically marginal, or whatever.

i. *Hidden decisions.* In practical decision making about patients, it is undesirable to deceive ourselves about those "hidden decisions" that we might challenge were they made explicit, especially that important class of decisions forced upon us by a variety of economic and social factors not presently within our institutional or professional control. An unforced hidden decision is exemplified by the research showing that lower class patients are more likely to receive pills, shock, or supportive therapy than are middle and upper class patients, who are more likely to receive intensive, uncovering, long-term psychotherapy—the latter being, by and large, more congenial to the interests and self-concepts of most practitioners. While this was anecdotally apparent to many of us before it was well documented by Hollingshead and Redlich (1958; see also Myers and Schaffer, 1954), some had supposed that the decision to treat proletarians in a different way hinged almost wholly upon economic considerations. We now know that other factors are also operative, since the social-class correlations persist when economics is substantially eliminated (as at Veterans Administration or other free clinics, graduated-fee community clinics, and the like). These other factors, which should have been obvious to any middle class WASP psychotherapist by introspection, include social-class "cultural compatibility," verbal fluency, conceptual intelligence, the tendency to think psychologically, lesser reliance on somatization (with epinosic gains), less preference for acting-out extrapunitive mechanisms over intropunitive guilt-laden mechanisms, a reality situation that provides some gratification and is modifiable in the nongratifying domains, and the like. Schofield (1964) has described the modal psychotherapist's "ideal patient" as the YAVIS syndrome (young, attractive, verbal, intelligent, and successful).

These YAVIS preferences aside, no practitioner, with or without systematic quantitative research on the sociology of the mental health professions, could be unaware that whether a patient receives a certain kind of treatment—never mind its merits—may hinge negligibly on his objective psychological appropriateness for it, depending instead upon factors of income, geography, available personnel, and the like. It is important in thinking administratively (one may often say also *ethically*)

250

about the selection of patients for psychotherapy and the assignment of personnel, to face squarely the social fact that even in the affluent society our situation with respect to hours available of professionally skilled time really does present a different situation from that prevailing in other branches of the healing arts. I do not wish to defend the current status of delivery of *non*-mental health care in the United States, which is generally perceived as unsatisfactory. But there are some important quantitative differences between the situation pertaining to psychology and that pertaining to organic disease. Admittedly an indigent patient with a brain tumor may have a significantly lower probability of diagnosis partly because he does not wish to spend money to see a physician about early symptoms, partly because of "social incompetence" traits that show up in caring for one's health (as in all other areas—a social fact that one is not supposed to mention, but is documented by statistical data from prepaid group health care plans). Furthermore, anyone who has gone through (anonymously, not as the "professor" or "doctor" he is) the outpatient department of a charity hospital (something that should be annually required of hospital administrators!) can attest that the underprivileged patient is kept waiting a longer time, is treated with less courtesy and sympathy by paramedical professionals (sometimes scandalously so), is often dealt with rather more high-handedly by the physician, and the like. But despite these conditions, for which there is no excuse, it remains true that the indigent patient, once diagnosed, will not go untreated for his operable brain tumor just because he is poor or because he lives a hundred miles away from the nearest competent neurosurgeon; whereas it is a statistical fact, *not* changeable by some sort of ethical decision or act of will on our part, that the majority of psychiatric patients will not get intensive, long-term psychotherapy (assuming that were the ideal method of treatment for them), money or no money, socially conscious clinic administrator or not, because there are just not enough psychotherapists around.

I have noted in discussion with fellow professionals, and very much in the classroom, that those predictive and prognostic problems that press upon us the clinical-actuarial issue (Meehl, 1954a; Sawyer, 1966) are sometimes rejected with considerable moral indignation, on the plausible-sounding ground that we should not be predicting (fallibly!) who will respond favorably to psychotherapy, since everybody has a

251

right to it; that we ought to provide it for all comers, even if it happens that their actuarial odds are sometimes rather low for significant improvement. Unfortunately for the clientele but fortunately for the argument, we need not debate the merits of that ethical position—with which I personally have considerable sympathy—because it is a literal, physical impossibility to satisfy this demand, even if all clinical, counseling, and school psychologists, psychiatrists, social workers, clergymen, marriage counselors, and other "mental healers" avoided all teaching and research, and could manage to go without any sleep, recreation, or family life. The situation in psychotherapy is not like the brain tumor, appendicitis, or pernicious anemia situation; it is, regrettably, closer to the situation of a shortage of surgeons or blood plasma in a military field hospital (where overpressed surgeons may literally have to make the decision who shall live and who shall die) or to that of a public health official who runs into a shortage of plague serum during an epidemic of plague. It is not a question of unethically deciding to withhold maximum-intensity psychological treatment from some in favor of others. That decision is already made for us by the sheer logistics of the situation. The point is that we are, willy-nilly, going to withhold intensive psychotherapy from the great majority of persons who come in for some sort of medical or psychological help. Consequently the *character* of our ethical dilemma is fixed. We are not confronted with the problem *whether* to treat some patients intensively and not others. Our present ethical dilemma is whether to assign treatment and nontreatment (or kinds of treatments) in a random fashion or by some selection procedure which improves the average long-term outcome. I cannot think that anyone with a clear head would argue for random assignment (except for research purposes), but I have come across all sorts of strange arguments in this world. In any case, whatever ethical considerations we may raise about the utilization of skilled professional personnel in the foreseeable future, and whatever conclusion we may reach (or agree to disagree on), at least we should keep in mind the fact of hidden decisions.

j. *The spun-glass theory of the mind*. Every great intellectual and social movement seems to carry some "bad" correlates that may not, strictly speaking, follow *logically* from society's acceptance of the "good" components of the movement but that *psychologically* have a tendency to flow therefrom. One undesirable side effect of the mental hygiene movement and the over-all tradition of dynamic psychiatry has been the development among educated persons (and here I do not refer only to professionals but to many persons who get an undergraduate degree in a variety of majors) of what I call the "spun-glass theory of the mind." This is the doctrine that the human organism, adult or child (particularly the latter), is constituted of such frail material, is of such exquisite psychological delicacy, that rather minor, garden-variety frustrations, deprivations, criticisms, rejections, or failure experiences are likely to play the causative role of major traumas. It is well known among psychotherapists that part of the chronic, free-floating guilt feelings of the educated American woman is her fear that she is not a perfect mother because she is not always 100 percent loving, giving, stimulating, and accepting toward her children. (There is more than a mild suspicion in my mind that some child therapists are ideological "parent haters," drawn to the field by their own parent-surrogate hang-ups.) Some psychotherapists—myself included—actually find it necessary to *undo* the educational and social impact of the mental hygiene movement in women of this sort.

I would do myself a disservice as a clinical practitioner to let these toughminded comments go unqualified. I have a clock on my desk which makes it unnecessary to glance surreptitiously at my wristwatch —one need not hold the spun-glass theory of the mind to notice that checking how close one is to the end of the hour can sometimes have a distinctly adverse effect on patients (particularly schizotypes who, more often than not, react to it as a rejection experience). I offer this minor clinical example to show that I do not here defend a clumsy, insensitive, bull-in-a-china-shop approach to the human psyche. After all, part of the reason people come to psychotherapists is that we offer tact, sensitivity, and empathy beyond that provided by the patient's nurturing environment and by his present family and work group.

Nevertheless, even in one's relations with the patient, it is possible to have a countertherapeutic effect because of subscribing to the spun-glass theory of the mind. The concept of extreme psychic fragility is likely to be truer for the schizotype than for most other kinds of patient, for example. Yet a therapist's *super*-delicacy, flowing from the spun-glass theory of the mind, can boomerang in working with some schizotypes. If, for instance, the therapist is so frightened by the concept "schizophrenia" that he regards it as a kind of psychic cancer, and therefore tends to react skittishly to some of its major symptoms (e.g., confused thinking, body-image aberrations, reality distortion), he may find himself trying to humor the patient, as "lunatics" are handled in the funny papers, even though all the books and lectures have taught him that this humoring maneuver cannot be successfully carried out. The schizotypic patient, with his hyper-acute perception of others' thoughts and motives—especially when aversive to himself—perceives this therapeutic double-talk as a form of insincerity and feels that the therapist is fooling him while pretending to be honest with him, as, in the patient's view, other people have done in the past. Such an experience confirms the schizotype's deep-seated mistrust, as well as aggravating his cognitive confusions about "what reality is."

The most preposterous example of the spun-glass theory of the mind that has come to my attention illustrates it so beautifully that I can close this portion of my discussion with it. Thirty years ago, when I was an advanced graduate student in Dr. Hathaway's therapy seminar, live-mike interviews were piped in so the staff and students in the class could discuss the therapeutic technique demonstrated. One day we were scheduled to hear an interview by a social worker who (as I had already inferred from other facts) was thoroughly imbued with the spun-glass theory of the mind. The interviewee was a pre-adolescent male with a prostitute mother and a violent, drunken father, living in marginal economic circumstances in a high-delinquency neighborhood, the child having been rejected by his parents, his peer group, and the teachers in his school. His acting-out tendencies and morbid fantasies were such that he was seen on the inpatient child psychiatry service; this session was to be his last interview before discharge, although the social worker planned to continue seeing him with lower density on an outpatient basis. The therapy was considered a success. Shortly before the seminar was scheduled to be held, the social worker informed Dr. Hathaway that she really could not go ahead with the interview as planned, having just learned that the microphone (concealed in a lamp base) was in a different room from the office in which the child was accustomed to being interviewed. She felt that to interview him in this "strange situation" ($=$ different office) might have a traumatic effect and undo the successful achievements of the therapy. This is the spun-glass theory of the mind with a vengeance. Here is this poor little urchin about to be returned to his multiply pathogenic environment, presumably with his psyche properly refurbished by the interviews so that he will be able to maintain himself in the harsh outside world; yet, despite the "successful" psychotherapy, he is still so fragile that these therapeutic achievements could be liquidated by having an interview in a different office! I submit that the best way to describe that combination of views is that it is just plain silly.

k. *Identifying the softhearted with the softheaded.* While there is surely no logical connection between having a sincere concern for the suffering of the individual patient (roughly, being "softhearted") and a tendency to commit logical or empirical mistakes in diagnosis, prognosis, treatment choice, and the like (roughly, being "softheaded"), one observes clinicians who betray a tendency to conflate the two. Because of my own longtime interest in the clinical-actuarial issue, this is the domain of clinical decision making where the tendency to think and act in terms of the unspoken equation [softhearted = softheaded] has come forcibly to my attention. Given space limitations, its somewhat peripheral relevance, and a firm intention to revise my 1954 monograph (Meehl, 1954a) on the clinical-statistical issue, I shall not reiterate the old arguments—to which, I may say, there have been remarkably few amendments or rebuttals—in the discussion here. But two arguments commonly heard in case conferences bring out the point so beautifully that I cannot resist the impulse to discuss them briefly. One is the old argument that rejects even a strong actuarial prediction concerning the instant patient on the ground that we are concerned not with groups but with this particular individual. Now all predictions about the consequences of clinical action (including inaction, "waiting to see what happens"—often the physician's tactic in accordance with the ancient medical maxim *primum non nocere*) are inherently probabilistic in nature. For one who explicitly recognizes this inherently probabilistic character (even when, as rarely, $p = .99$) of *all* our clinical inferences, the advice to defy our formalized actuarial experience in decision making about the single patient before us amounts to saying that the unformalized inductive inferences of the clinician should be trusted in preference to the formalized probability inferences of a regression equation or an actuarial table. I said in 1954, and have repeated in subsequent publications (Meehl, 1954b, 1956b, 1957—reprinted here as Chapter 4, 1959a, 1960—reprinted here as Chapter 6, 1965c, 1967b—reprinted here as Chapter 9, 1970c, 1972b), that there are individual instances in which this counteractuarial choice is correct. But I have also pointed out, and have as yet seen no persuasive rebuttal, that it is very rarely the preferred action and that a policy that permits it frequently is indefensible. Permitting a weak or moderately strong clinical inference to countervail a well-supported actuarial backlog of data on patients resembling the immediate case in a researched set of predictively powerful respects will lead, in the long run, to an increase in erroneous clinical decisions. Some clinicians still do not see that this question is itself one of the questions that is answered, "in the average sense," by the now numerous (over seventy-five) empirical investigations of the clinical-actuarial controversy.

What befalls the softheaded clinician in his admirable desire to be softhearted (i.e., to be most helpful to this particular patient) is that he fears the very real possibility—which the actuarial data themselves express in terms of the error rate—that he will treat the patient non-optimally through reliance on actuarial experience. I empathize intensely with his existential predicament; I have often felt it acutely myself as a practitioner. But I must insist that he is wrong. In thinking thus, he fails to take two considerations into account. The first is that by departing from the recorded actuarial expectations in reliance upon lower validity informal clinical inferences, he is probably *not* doing the best thing for the immediate case. He thinks (or feels) that he is—but he is probably not. Secondly, should it turn out that by this counteractuarial departure he *has* in fact done the best thing for the particular patient, he will have achieved this individually desirable result by applying a decision policy that (according to the studies) will lead him to mispredict for other patients, who are also individual human beings with presumably as much claim upon his ethical concerns as the one currently before him. In the absence of some showing that we have a kind of superordinate method—whether actuarial or clinical in nature—for discriminating before the fact which are the cases that will be better handled by counteractuarial decisions and which should be left where the table puts them, such a policy is not ethically defensible, regardless of how good it makes us feel.

As to the stock argument that we are not concerned with probabilities, frequencies, or group trends but with the unique individual before us, I do not really know how to add to what I have said, with others before and since, on this vexed issue. There are admittedly some profound unresolved problems, still in dispute among statisticians and logicians, concerning the logical reconstruction of "rational decision" under these circumstances (see, for example, the excellent discussion by Hacking, 1965). But, so far as I am aware, the technical debates among the experts concern the logical reconstruction of the matter, rather than being disputes concerning what a reasonable man would be well advised to do. In teaching our first-year clinical assessment class—where one invariably hears students who offer this "single case" objection to actuarial decision methods in the clinic—I have found it helpful to consider the following hypothetical example (I like this example because it really puts the student on the "existential knife-edge," where he himself is the "patient," and the issue is one of life or death): Suppose I place before you two revolvers. I show you that one of them is loaded with five live shells, having a single empty chamber; the other has five empty chambers and a single live shell. I am, let us say, a sadistic decision-theorist in charge of a concentration camp in which you are an inmate, and I tell you that you are forced to play a single game of Russian roulette with one of these two revolvers. You are not going to have to repeat it. In your ordinary life you are not in the habit of playing Russian roulette. You have never done so before, and you are firmly determined never to do it again. If you avoid blowing your brains out, I promise to release you from the camp. In the other eventuality, we leave the probable outcome to your theology. Which revolver would you choose under these circumstances? Whatever may be the detailed, rigorous, logical reconstruction of your reasoning processes, can you honestly say that you would let me pick the gun or that you would flip a coin to decide between them?

I have asked quite a few persons this question, and I have not yet encountered anybody who alleged that he would just as soon play his single game of Russian roulette with the five-shell weapon. *But why not?* Suppose I am told, by a "softheaded" clinician, "Well, but you are only going to do it once, it is a *unique event,* we are not talking about groups or classes or frequencies—we are talking about whether *you,* Regents' Professor Paul Everett Meehl, that unique human individual, live or die in the next couple of minutes. What do you *care* about probabilities and such, since this choice will never be presented to you again?" I have not found anybody willing to apply such nonactuarial reasoning to the Russian roulette case. Point: We should apply to the unique patient before us the same kind of rational decision rule that we would insist upon applying if our own life were hanging in the balance.

Despite what I take to be the irrefutability of this two-revolver argument, I can sometimes work myself into the frame of mind of a soft-headed clinician by putting his favorite query, "Do *you* want to be treated as a mere tally mark in an actuarial table?" No, I do not want to be "treated as a *mere* tally mark." But I put it to you, dear reader, that the seductiveness of this appeal lies in a confusion between thinking about my physician's personal concern for my welfare—which I value as highly as anybody else—and trusting him to "bet on the best horse" in my behalf. As a matter of fact, one thing I happen to like about my physician is his tendency (noted appreciatively by other faculty patients of his who are not in the statistics business) to cite statistics when considering whether a certain painful or expensive diagnostic procedure or a certain therapeutic regime is worth trying. I cannot convince myself that it would be a charitable act on my physician's part to think fuzzily about my diagnosis or treatment as a result of his "feeling sympathetic" toward me. Hence I do not think I have a "double standard of morals" that depends upon whether I am considering myself as clinical decision maker or as patient. Whether my physician decides for me, or, as is usually more appropriate—and I would say this also for the psychiatric patient—helps me to decide, I prefer that he act on the principle of Thomas Aquinas that charity is not a state of the emotions but a state of the rationally informed will, i.e., that charity consists of willing the other person's good. On this philosophic basis, it is a *pseudo*charitable act, given the presently available evidence, for a psychiatrist to withhold EST from a patient with classical psychotic depression on the ground that there is something about deliberately inducing a cerebral storm by pushing that button which offends his human sensibility (a feeling I share). By the same token, the psychoanalytic therapist must learn to dissolve resistances rather than timidly playing along with them; an RET practitioner must be able to point out to a proud, educated, intellectualizing patient that he is operating irrationally on a postulate which is unrealistic and self-defeating (tactless though such a confrontation would be in most ordinary human relationships); a behavior modifier must be able to stick to a reinforcement schedule; and the surgeon must not be afraid to shed blood.

It should not require mentioning, but to forestall any possibility of

258

misunderstanding I shall state explicitly, that all of the foregoing discussion is predicated upon the assumption that a clinical case conference sometimes eventuates in decisions "for" or "about" the patient. Consider the clearly psychotic patient who constitutes a danger to himself or others and whose ego function is so grossly impaired that his relatives (acting through the agency of the state) have placed certain decisions in our hands. One can raise fundamental philosophical questions about such a patient's autonomy in considering the justification of civil commitment (see Livermore, Malmquist, and Meehl, 1968) and if one concludes against current practice, he may have an ethical obligation to refuse to participate in some case conferences, at least in their decision-making aspects. But aside from the involuntary commitment issue, if we do not believe it is a legitimate professional function to decide anything, or even (by advice or by the presentation of relevant information to the patient or his relatives) to help decide anything, then most of the discussion above concerning *how* to decide becomes pointless.

1. *Neglect of overlap.* This one is so trite and has become so much a part of standard elementary instruction in applied statistics that I would have little justification in mentioning it were it not for the almost incredible fact that respectable journals in clinical psychology and psychiatry still persist in publishing articles on the validity of clinical instruments which give no indication that either the author or the journal editor ever heard of the overlap problem. Partly as a result of this "academic" perpetuation of error, case conferences—which usually operate several notches lower in the hierarchy of scholarliness than scientific journals—continue to make the mistake. I suppose the statistics professors are right in their opinion that the primary villainous influence was the unfortunate semantic choice (by whom?) decades ago of the term "significant" in referring to an obtained group difference that cannot plausibly be attributed to random-sampling fluctuations. I am not concerned here with *theoretical* (causal-structure) inferences, commonly made from refutations of the null hypothesis, for a discussion of which see the excellent collection by Morrison and Henkel (1970). The question before us here is the *pragmatic application* of a statistically significant difference, taken for present purposes as being nonproblematic from the statistician's standpoint. The point is that various psychological tests, rating scales, symptom checklists, and the like are unashamedly proposed for clinical use on the basis of "statistical significance" with

little or no attention paid to the overlap of the clinical populations it is desired to discriminate (assuming that we were to treat the sample statistics not only as establishing a "significant difference" but as infallible estimators). I have repeatedly observed that reminders to faculty and students of the truism that statistical significance does not mean practical importance fail of effect when presented *in abstracto*. At the risk of seeming utterly trivial I shall therefore present a single, simplified numerical example that I hope will carry more pedagogical punch. Suppose I have devised the Midwestern Multiplastic Tennis-Ball Projection Test which I allege to be clinically useful in discriminating schizophrenics from anxiety-neurotics. I set aside the terrible complexities of assessing construct validity for this type of problem, assuming for simplicity that we treat the construct validity as approximately equivalent to a concurrent validity (Cronbach and Meehl, 1955—Chapter 1 above) when the latter has been established on two groups of patients in whose formal diagnoses we are entitled to have much more confidence than we would have on the basis of routine clinical workup (see point f above, "crummy criterion fallacy"). Despite the Fisherian emphasis upon small samples, given our aim to obtain reasonably solid conclusions about the psychometric characteristics of these populations for future use, we would probably be somewhat uncomfortable (if not, we should be!) with sample sizes barely large enough to squeak out a respectable power in refuting the null hypothesis with a t test. So let us suppose that we have run the Midwestern Multiplastic Tennis-Ball Projection Test on a carefully diagnosed sample of 100 schizophrenics and 100 anxiety-neurotics. And let us suppose we succeed in achieving a "statistically significant difference" between the two groups at the $p = .01$ level (about par for the course in most journal articles of this sort). To make the computations easy, I shall assume the standard deviations to be equal, and, as indicated above, I shall treat the obtained values as if they were parameters. A little arithmetic applied to these assumptions shows that the ratio of the mean difference $\bar{d}$ to each patient group's standard deviation is approximately .37 which, assuming equal base rates in the clinical population, locates the "hitmax cut" (Meehl, 1973 —Chapter 12 above) midway between the two means, i.e., about .18 sigma units above the mean of the lower frequency distribution and .18 sigma units below the mean of the upper distribution. Entering normal curve tables we find that clinical application of this optimal cutting score

260

to the dichotomous diagnosis would yield around 57 percent "hits," i.e., a measly 7 percent improvement over what we could achieve by flipping pennies. From my perusal of the current clinical literature I think it not an unfair exaggeration to say that a considerable number—perhaps the majority—of all psychometric differentiators urged upon us for clinical use are close to worthless. A scientific cost accounting of their role in the decision-making process would usually not justify the expense to the patient (or the taxpayer) in the use of skilled clinical time required to administer and score the instrument and to present it in evidence at the case conference.

The conclusion is obvious. We ought to stop doing this sort of silly business, and we should constantly reiterate this elementary point when we note that it has been forgotten by clinicians in the case conference. Also it would be salutary—and would cut down on the garbage found in clinical periodicals—if editors *insisted* that several standard overlap measures be included in every manuscript submitted for publication in which a clinical instrument is purportedly validated or seriously proposed as a device worthy of further exploration. These might be Tilton's overlap, statements of percentages of valid positives attainable by cutting at certain standard percentiles or sigma points on the other distribution (e.g., the median, the 75th percentile, the 90th percentile, the 99th percentile), and, for most clinical problems worth arguing about, an indication of how much employing the hitmax cut on the proposed instrument would be better than "playing the base rate" (Meehl and Rosen, 1955—Chapter 2 above) for various base-rate values.

m. *Ad hoc fallacy*. On this I shall say little at this point because my constructive suggestions for improving the quality of clinical case conferences in Part II below are devoted heavily to this problem. Like the preceding statistical mistake, the ad hoc fallacy is one that everybody "officially" knows about and recognizes as a source of error, but we find it so tempting that we frequently commit it anyway. The ingenuity of the human mind in "explaining" things, the looseness of the theoretical network available to us in the present stage of clinical psychology, and the absence of a quasi-definitive criterion (comparable to the pathologist's report in internal medicine) of what the truth about the patient really is, all combine to make it easy for us to cook up plausible-sounding explanations, after the available relevant evidence is in, of why the patient is the way he is. The only solution to this problem that is

261

likely to be successful, because it will go beyond mere exhortation and provide quasi-objective differential reinforcement to the verbal behavior of the clinical conferees, is some method that introduces a *predictive* (epistemologically speaking, hence including *postdictive*) element that is now largely lacking. The possibilities that occur to me as reasonably toughminded, not unduly artificial in the pragmatic clinical context, feasible in terms of time and money, and sufficiently enjoyable so that staff can be induced to bear their share of the increased burden, are developed in Part II below.

n. *"Doing it the hard way."* By this I mean employing some clinical instrument or procedure, such as a time-consuming projective test, to ascertain something that documents in the patient's social record or an informant could tell one in a few minutes. I have witnessed tedious and tenuous discussions aimed at making inferences concerning, say, why the patient is an academic underachiever, when nobody had taken the trouble to get in touch with the school and find out how the staff viewed the disparity between his measured intelligence and his academic performance, how the peer group accepted him, what temporal trends showed up in his cumulative record (e.g., teacher ratings), whether he ever was seen by the school counselor, and so on. There are some types of cases in which such failure to look at the record may be especially misleading, such as the clever and ingratiating psychopath who can sometimes fool even a moderately experienced clinician and can completely bamboozle a beginner. Clinicians prone to the [softhearted = softheaded] equation described above, reason, in effect, "Why, this friendly, tousle-headed thirty-five-year-old lad is very cooperative and forms a good relationship with me; I am sure he couldn't have been sticking switchblades into old ladies." In the differential diagnosis between an "unlucky" normal, an acting-out neurotic, a hard-core psychopath, and a solid-gold professional con man, the Rorschach, TAT, and MMPI (or, for that matter, even a short Mental Status interview) may be less illuminating than the school record, a social agency's file, or the police blotter. (See, in this connection, Meehl, 1970a, pp. 10–13.)

In considering psychometrics on their validity, we should try to think clearly about the *role* of our tests in the particular clinical situation. For what purpose are the tests being given? (Of course in thinking about this question, a psychologist who is not clear about the distinctions between content, concurrent, predictive, and construct validity is not up to the task's demands.) You have to make up your mind *why* you are bothering to give an intelligence test or an MMPI or a TAT. I cannot myself imagine doing so for the purpose of postdicting delinquency, social withdrawal, economic dependency, overdrinking, and the like; but many clinicians seem to view that pointless guessing game as their psychometric task. Just as treating a personality test as a means of predicting some other professional's impressionistic opinion from non-psychometric data is "doing it the hard way," so postdicting a relatively objective fact about the patient's life history is a wasteful exercise in psychometric muscle flexing.

o. *Social scientist's anti-biology bias.* Associated with the spun-glass theory of the mind (as one of the undesirable side effects of the mental hygiene and dynamic psychiatry movements in this country) is a deep, pervasive, and recalcitrant prejudice among psychologists, sociologists, and psychiatrists against biological factors in abnormality. This bias often correlates with a diffuse and fact-blind rejection of biologically oriented treatment procedures. Thus many clinical psychologists are anti-drug, anti-genetic, and anti-EST in their attitudes. Articles and books on psychopathology have been written by eminent and brilliant men (e.g., Thomas Szasz) which not only fail to *refute* the considerable (and rapidly growing) data on genetic determiners of human and animal behavior, including the major psychoses, but—as in the case of Dr. Szasz—do not so much as *mention* in a footnote the existence of such data (see, for example, Erlenmeyer-Kimling, 1972; Gottesman and Shields, 1972; Heston, 1972; Manosevitz, Lindzey, and Thiessen, 1969; and Rosenthal, 1970). One wonders, in reading his writings, whether he is literally unaware of the research on the genetics of schizophrenia; or, if he is aware of it, why he considers it acceptable scholarship to leave the nonprofessional reader in complete darkness about the fact that a scientific controversy exists. For many psychotherapists, everything that is wrong with anybody is attributable either to having a battle-ax mother, being raised on the wrong side of the tracks, or having married the wrong mate. It is dangerous to be the parent or spouse of a mentally ill person because you will almost certainly get blamed for it, even if he was patently abnormal before you met him and his family tree abounds with food faddists, recluses, perpetual-motion inventors, suicides, and residents of mental hospitals. Part of this attitude springs from the two related ideas that if it were the case that

263

genes had something to do with aberrated behavior, then (1) psychotherapy could not "work," and (2) the psychodynamics we think we understand about mental patients would have to be abandoned. For what I hope is a clear refutation of that undergraduate mistake, see Meehl, 1972c—Chapter 11 above. There simply isn't any contradiction, or even any "friction," between saying in a case conference, "This patient is a schizotype, the specific etiology of which I hypothesize is a dominant gene that produces a specific kind of integrative neural deficit (see Meehl, 1962—Chapter 7 above)" and saying, "This patient's paranoid delusions are restitutional symptoms, forms of miscarried repair the dynamic meaning of which is the patient's effort to reinvest cathexis in social objects." If a clinician thinks that these two statements are incompatible, it merely shows that he is a muddleheaded thinker and needs to take an undergraduate course in genetics plus, perhaps, a little philosophy of science to get clear about dispositions and actualization of their antecedents. Reading Freud will help too.

p. *Double standard of evidential morals.* One common way in which the anti-biological prejudices of the preceding subsection are maintained against contrary evidence is by shifting the standards of evidential rigor depending upon whose ox is being gored. Having been drawn into psychology as a teen-ager by my reading of Menninger, Adler, and Freud, and preferring psychoanalytic therapy (when the patient is appropriate) because it is more theoretically interesting and gives me what I believe to be a deeper causal understanding of the individual, I cannot perceive myself as being a hardnosed, super-rigorous, compulsively operational type of psychologist—although I am aware that the impact of some of my writings on the special problem of prediction has been that other psychologists often view me in this stereotyped way. As mentioned in the introductory section, I have found myself in a strange position vis-à-vis my colleagues: the typical (non-Minnesota) cliniker perceives me as excessively critical and objective, whereas my local psychonomic brethren find it odd that I should be seriously interested in the interpretation of dreams. This is not the place to develop that paradox at length, but in discussing the double standard of evidential morals I must say something about it. I think that one big error committed by psychologists who insist upon sorting other psychologists into boxes like "humanistic" and "scientific" or "dynamic" and "behaviorist" is the failure to distinguish between two sorts of statements.

The first sort of statement is the kind that you might be willing to bet money on, act upon in your personal affairs, rely upon in making decisions concerning a patient—questions on where you place your bets when forced, even though you may be acutely conscious of the fact that you cannot develop the evidence for your choice (when on the existential knife-edge) in a rigorous fashion. The writings on personalistic probability exemplify this (Savage, 1954; Hacking, 1965; Levi, 1967; Raiffa, 1968). There is a difference—but not an inconsistency—between saying, "Lacking coercive evidence, I am prepared, until further notice, to bet that Gallumpher will place in the third," and saying, "It can be shown by rigorous mathematical analysis that the prediction of Gallumpher's placing in the third is the best decision." Consider, for example, psychoanalytic theory. I classify myself as a "60 percent Freudian." I consider that the two men who have contributed most to our understanding of behavior in the first half of the twentieth century are Sigmund Freud and B. Frederic Skinner. I find it a little hard to imagine a conversation between these two geniuses, although I would love to have heard one. But the point is that I can decide, on the existential knife-edge—*required* by the pragmatic context to make decisions willy-nilly—to play it Freudian or Skinnerian, without supposing I can make a rigorous scientific case that my decision is the right one. There is a distinction between what we believe (on the best evidence available, and given the social fact that we *must* decide) and what we would think as pure scientists, which might very well cause us to abstain from any decision until more and better evidence becomes available.

I have no objection if professionals choose to be extremely rigorous about their standards of evidence, but they should recognize that if they adopt that policy, many of the assertions made in a case conference ought not to be uttered because they cannot meet such a tough standard. Neither do I have any objection to freewheeling speculation; I am quite willing to engage in it myself (e.g., I have published some highly speculative views concerning the nature of schizophrenia: Meehl, 1962—Chapter 7 above, 1964, 1972c—Chapter 11 above). You can play it tight, or you can play it loose. What I find objectionable in staff conferences is a tendency to shift the criterion of tightness so that the evidence offered is upgraded or downgraded in the service of polemical interests. Example: A psychologist tells me that he is perfectly confident that psychotherapy benefits psychotic depressions (a question open on available data), his reason being that his personal experience shows this. But this same psychologist tells me that he has never seen a single patient helped by shock therapy. (Such a statement, that he has never seen a *single patient* helped by shock therapy, can only be attributed to some sort of perceptual or memory defect on his part.) When challenged with the published evidence indicating that shock is a near specific for classical depression, he says that those experiments are not perfect, and further adds, "You can prove anything by experiments." (Believe it or not, these are quotations!) I confess I am at a loss to know how I can profitably pursue a conversation conducted on these ground rules. He is willing (1) to rely upon *his* casual impressions that psychotherapy helps patients, (2) to deny *my* casual impression that shock treatment helps patients, but (3) to reject the controlled research on the subject of electroshock—which meets considerably tighter standards evidentially than *either* his clinical impressions or mine—on the grounds that it is not perfectly trustworthy. It is not intellectually honest or, I would argue, clinically responsible thus to vary your tightness-looseness parameter when evaluating conflicting evidence on the same issue.

I am well aware of a respectable counterargument to these construct-validity considerations, the substance of which is the following: Whatever may be the philosophical or mathematical reconstruction for the idea of construct validity (and the rebuttal is sometimes offered by psychologists who are sophisticated about construct validity as a *theoretical* metanotion), in the pragmatic context whatever we say in the case conference must ultimately come down to some practical decision of a predictive nature. It can even be argued that postdictive, content, and concurrent validity interests—and, a fortiori, construct-validity interests—are defensible in this setting only in reliance upon some relation they have to predictive validity, because the aim of the conference is to decide what to *do* for the patient; this "do" of course includes proposing treatment alternatives to him, making prognostic statements to a referring social institution (court, school), advising the family about the odds on a regime requiring major financial outlay, and the like. In substance, the argument is that whatever the theoretical merits of other kinds of validity, or their technological value over the long run (e.g., improving psychometric instruments through better insight about the construct), in the context of clinical case conferences the *only* kind of validity that counts is predictive validity. There is much to be said for this line of thought, and no reader familiar with my writings on the actuarial prediction problem would expect me to be unsympathetic to it. And I want to reiterate that there are numerous specific decision-making tasks that do have this pure predictive validity form. Example: A court puts to the professional staff a list of specific forecasting questions, for example, "If the defendant stands trial, will he be able to function well enough cognitively so that his counsel can provide him with an adequate defense?" "This hitherto law-abiding person committed an act of violence under unusual circumstances; if, following your presentence investigation, the court releases him on probation, is he likely to commit acts dangerous to himself or others?" The test of any construct's value in such situations is obviously its predictive power.

Nevertheless, I cannot accept the anti–construct-validity argument when presented in its extreme (hyperoperational) form. My first reservation arises from the social fact that decision making on behalf of the patient or a social institution is not typically the sole function of a clinical case conference. I think it would be generally agreed that the conference is also intended to serve an educational function for the faculty and students attending it. We are supposedly trying to improve our decision-making skills as helpers and societal advisers, and to clarify our thoughts as teachers and researchers.

In that connection, the display—especially by prestigeful faculty figures—of inefficient decisional procedures must be viewed as countereducational as well as countertherapeutic for the patient. It is not, therefore, even a partial excuse for committing some of the methodological errors I am criticizing to say, "Well, Meehl, you are talking as though the only reason we meet in a clinical case conference is to make decisions about the patient. But we also meet for educational purposes." To the extent that the content of the discussants' contributions is predictive content, fallacies and nonoptimalities in that content, when allowed to go unchallenged or, worse, positively reinforced by group approval, presumably have the effect of indoctrinating our student clinicians with undesirable decision-making habits of mind. Hence the same features that make inefficient decision-making procedures undesirable from the standpoint of helping the individual patient make them undesirable as an educational practice.

The main point I wish to make concerning the educational functions of the conference is that while clinical comments advocating inefficient predictive methods cannot be justified on educational grounds, we are endeavoring to teach the students (and one another) several things in addition to how best to reach concrete clinical decisions about patients for treatment and social forecasting purposes. Admittedly the items in this list of nonpredictive pedagogical aims will differ somewhat from one teacher-professional to another, and I have no wish to impose my hierarchy of personal preferences upon others. I shall merely mention some of the main items that would surely be found in *some* competent persons' lists, without claiming completeness or attempting to argue the merits of the items fully. First, I take it that psychiatrists and clinical psychologists are typically interested in understanding the human person, despite the fact that this understanding does not always lead in any straightforward way to a specific practical decision concerning treatment. I know that this is true for me, and it seems pretty clearly true for many of my colleagues and students. Psychological curiosity is unquestionably among the motives inducing some able minds to enter the profession, and the gratification of *n Cognizance* is for many professionals among the important rewards that keep them going in the face of what is often a somewhat discouraging level of satisfaction of our *n Nurturance*. While some clinicians come fairly close to being pure behavioral engineers, others are more like psychological physicists, the vast majority of us being somewhere in between, characterized by a mixture—sometimes leading to uncomfortable role conflicts—of the wish to *heal,* the wish to *control,* and the wish to *understand.*

I have heard it argued, by extreme representatives of the "tough-minded" end of the tough-tender continuum, that even from the purely theoretical standpoint (setting aside practical relevance in treating the immediate case) this aim to understand cannot be distinguished from the predictive one, since "the purpose of scientific theories is to predict and control." Aside from an element of dogmatism displayed in imposing such a pure instrumentalist view of theoretical science, with which it is possible for a rational man to disagree philosophically, I would emphasize that *some* pragmatically useless inferences may serve epistemologically as corroborators and refuters of nomothetic psychological theories (or their explanatory application to the idiographic material). Such "useless" inferences, when sound, can contribute to the satisfaction of psychological curiosity without contributing to our role as helpers of patients and social forecasters.

Several kinds of concurrent and postdictive validity illustrate this point. I may, for instance, formulate a construction about the patient's personality by integrating, in the course of the conference discussion, a couple of subtle signs (manifested by the patient when presented in staff conference) with certain aspects of the psychometrics. Relying on this tentative psychodynamic construction, I am led to a probabilistic prediction concerning his ward behavior, which the participant nursing staff then confirms. Assuming that I have not committed any of the methodological errors herein discussed, and that the base rate of my ward-behavior "prediction" (actually postdictive or concurrent validation) is low enough so that its correctness—given the small evidential "prior" p in Bayes' Formula—counts as a strong corroborator; then I have probably learned (and taught) something about this patient's mind and, indirectly, about the verisimilitude of the nomothetic network mediating my inference. But the specificity of treatment in our field is not such that corroborating (in a moderate degree) a particular inference (e.g., this patient has rigid reaction formations against his oral-dependent impulses) must lead directly to a concrete prescription for treatment. The same is, of course, often true for construct-validity-mediated inferences susceptible of confirmation by the patient's psychotherapist.

Again, consider a postdiction which would be, I suppose, largely useless for our helping aim. Suppose I am interested in the theory of depression and entertain the speculation, based partly upon my clinical experience and partly upon quantitative research, that there are at least four, and possibly as many as seven, kinds of depression. Deciding among these for the immediate case *may* have treatment implications; e.g., neurotic depressions and depressions secondary to schizoid anhedonia do not react favorably to EST. But among some of my other speculative depression types, I am not aware of any therapeutic indications. Thus, for example, I believe there is such a state as "rage-depression," and that it even has characteristic somatic complaint aspects not found as frequently in the other varieties, such as the patient's presenting complaint that his head feels as if it had a pressure on it or in it, or as if it were about to explode. These patients also, I believe, are more likely to manifest bruxism. I would contrast this syndrome with object-loss depression, and would distinguish both from the very common reactive depressions attributable (as Skinner pointed out in 1938) to a prolonged extinction schedule. I speculate that childhood (even adolescent?) object loss predisposes genetically vulnerable persons to subsequent object-loss depression, and the reason it does not show up consistently but only as a statistically significant trend in retrospective studies of depression-prone individuals is that it characterizes only this subgroup (Malmquist, 1970; Beck, Sethi, and Tuthill, 1963; Beck, 1967, Chapter 14). I am not concerned here with arguing the merits of these speculations. The point is that on the basis of the evidence presented in conference, I might be interested in a (quite useless!) postdiction of childhood object loss, whereas in another depressed patient, I might be moved by the way the patient describes his head as feeling as if it were about to explode, together with some violent Rorschach content and some "aggressive" MMPI signs, to inquire whether, according to the patient's wife, he had a tendency to grind his teeth when asleep.

These examples serve also to illustrate the research-stimulus function of the case conference. From the standpoint of research strategy, it may be rational for a research-oriented clinician to find in bits and pieces of concurrent and postdictive validity encouragement to embark upon a research project, although their probabilistic linkage to pragmatically important dispositions of the patient might be too weak to justify reliance upon them in handling the immediate case.

Finally, there is a simple point about construct validity (whether the construct involved is nosological, dynamic, or "historical") that is easy to overlook when our mental set as clinicians emphasizes the importance of predictive statements. A narrowly operational view of the relations between behavioral dispositions (phenotypic, with a minimum of theoretical construction) demands that we have direct evidential support for what would turn out to be an unmanageably huge collection of pair-wise dispositional statistical linkages. If one were to list, in a huge catalog, all of the first-order descriptive traits, signs, symptoms, psychometric patterns, and life-history facts dealt with in psychiatry, it is hardly conceivable that such a list would contain fewer than several hundred elements. Even if we were to prune the list mercilessly—eliminating all elements having (1) marginal reliability, (2) base rates very close to zero or one, or (3) too highly correlated with others having nearly identical "content," and then finally (4) throwing out anything that we had little or no clinical or research basis for believing was appreciably correlated with anything else we cared about—I find it hard to suppose that such a list would contain fewer than, say, 100 variables. First-order predictions among all these pair wise, if based upon directly researched empirical linkages, would therefore require investigation of 10,000 correlations. But suppose that one investigator finds that bruxism, complaint of exploding headache, and certain MMPI and Rorschach signs cluster as a syndrome which, while "loose," is good enough to provide construct validity for the dynamic nosological entity "rage-depression." And suppose that another investigator, also interested in rage-depression but not familiar with these indicators, reports that patients he and a colleague independently classified as rage-depression (from Mental Status plus psychotherapy evidence plus precipitating situation) respond especially well to a particular antidepressant drug but do badly on Dexamyl. Then, pending the monster study of 10,000 pairwise correlations between everything and everything, clinicians who read these two articles can begin prescribing that specific antidepressant for patients showing the syndrome of bruxism, aggressive psychometrics, and exploding headache.

The same line of reasoning applies to the teaching of diagnostic, dynamic, and etiological factors. Presumably one justification for having case conferences instead of just sending all of the residents and psychology trainees to the library is our belief that certain things can be best taught with dramatic punch in the real-life clinical situation. I do not know whether that generally accepted pedagogic principle has been quantitatively researched in medicine, but the psychiatric and clinical psychology conference has accepted the tradition from other branches of medicine, and I am willing here to presuppose it. You can "tell" a resident or psychology trainee that many schizophrenic patients are baffling and frustrating to the therapist, and elicit adverse countertransference reactions not because the therapist has been technically mishandling the case—although he may now begin to do so!—but because the schizotype is prone to "testing" operations on persons he would like to trust but dare not. You can also state in a lecture that some schizophrenic patients have a special way of walking (I will not try to describe it verbally here) which I refer to as the "schizophrenic float." A fledgeling therapist, mistreating a pseudoneurotic schizophrenic as a "good healthy neurotic," comes into the conference hurt and puzzled by the patient's ambivalent testing operations. The schizophrenic float is called to the therapist's attention by his conference neighbor (who spots it as the patient walks in), and the student therapist has a chance to observe it as the patient leaves the conference room. This resident or psychology trainee will have formed a vivid connection in his clinical thinking that it is likely he will never forget. However, such a linkage need not be formed on the same patient, although it's better that way. If the senior staff succeed in convincing the resident in this week's conference that the reason for his countertransference troubles lay in the patient's being a pseudoneurotic schizophrenic, and next week he sees some other student's patient showing the schizophrenic float as he walks into the room, that pair of experiences will perhaps do almost as well.

13. *Antinosological bias.* It is common knowledge that American psychiatry and clinical psychology, the former under psychodynamic influence and the latter under both psychodynamic and learning theory influence, have an animus against formal "diagnosis." The status of formal nosological diagnosis in American theory and practice warrants detailed treatment, and I am preparing such a discussion of theory and research literature for presentation elsewhere. I shall therefore confine myself here to a mere listing of some of the current clichés, with brief critical comments upon each but without attempting an adequate exposition of the argument or—when decent empirical data exist—detailed survey of the research findings. There are, of course, good reasons for being skeptical about diagnostic rubrics, and even more skeptical about their current application in a psychiatric tradition that de-emphasizes training in diagnostic skills. But it is regrettable to find that the majority of beginning graduate students in clinical psychology "know" that "mere diagnostic labels" have no reliability or validity, no theoretical significance, no prognostic importance, and no relevance to treatment choice. They "know" these things because they were told them dogmatically in undergraduate abnormal psychology classes. They typically react with amazement, disbelief, and resentment to find a psychologist who bluntly challenges these ideas. If you want to be a diagnostic nihilist, you should be one in an intellectually responsible way, for scientific reasons rather than from bobbysoxer antidiagnostic propaganda. On the current scene, antidiagnostic prejudices of the familiar kinds (four of which I consider here) have recently been bolstered by a new ideological factor,

to wit, the tendency of many students to *politicize everything*. A professor can (perhaps) discuss the helium nucleus or the sun's temperature without finding himself shortly involved in a debate on women's liberation, police brutality, Indochina, "establishment" bourgeois values, or the black ghetto. But psychiatric diagnosis is one of those topics that are reflexly politicized by many of our students.

Herewith, then, a brief summary of the usual antidiagnostic arguments, and my objections to each:

a. "Formal diagnoses are extremely unreliable." If it were empirically shown that formal diagnoses are extremely unreliable, it would remain an open question whether they are unreliable because (1) the diagnostic constructs do not refer to anything that really exists (i.e., there *is* no typology or taxonomy of behavior aberration that "carves nature at its joints,"), or (2) differential diagnosis of behavior disorders is unusually difficult, or (3) it is not unusually difficult but many clinicians perform it carelessly and uninformedly. One ought not, after all, be astounded to find that American psychiatrists and psychologists, educated in an antinosological tradition in which they have been taught that diagnosis is of no importance (and consequently never exposed to the classic nosological writings in the European tradition), have been presented with professional models of senior staff who do not take diagnosis seriously, and have not been differentially reinforced for good and poor diagnostic behavior, are unable to do it well!

It is not true that formal nosological diagnosis in psychiatry is as unreliable as the usual statements suggest. If we confine ourselves to major diagnostic categories (e.g., schizophrenia versus nonschizophrenia, organic brain syndrome versus functional disorder, and the like), if we require adequate clinical exposure to the patient (why would anyone in his right mind conduct a study of diagnostic rubrics based upon brief outpatient contact?), and if we study well-trained clinicians who take the diagnostic process seriously, then it is not clear that interclinician diagnostic agreement in psychiatry is worse than in other branches of medicine. (A colleague responds with "That's true, but medical diagnoses are completely unreliable also." I am curious what leads this colleague, given his "official" classroom beliefs, to consult a physician when he is ill? Presumably such an enterprise is pointless, and taking your sick child to a pediatrician is wasted time and money. Do any of my readers *really* believe this?) For instance, as to the diagnostic dichotomy schizophrenia versus nonschizophrenia, one study—based upon a very large N—shows the interjudge reliability to equal that of a good individual intelligence test (Schmidt and Fonda, 1956). I do not mean to suggest that the various interjudge reliability studies are consistent, which they are not (see, for example, Rosen, Fox, and Gregory, 1972, Table 3-1, p. 46); nor do I assert that the evidence on this question is adequate at present. I merely point out that the majority of psychologists and psychiatrists in this country persist in reflexly repeating the dogma "Diagnosis is very unreliable" without paying due attention to the diagnostic circumstances and personnel involved in various studies, or telling us how unreliable something has to be before it is "very unreliable." The spectacle of a clinical psychologist spitting on formal psychiatric diagnostic labels on grounds of unreliability, meanwhile asking us to make clinical decisions on the basis of Rorschach interpretations, can only be described as ludicrous. For an excellent survey and sophisticated criticism of the empirical research on diagnostic interjudge reliability, plus some impressive new data on the subject, see Gottesman and Shields (1972, Chapter 2). I need hardly add that the errors criticized in this paper are presumably a major source of diagnostic unreliability, so that their reduction would yield an improvement (I predict a big improvement) over typical reported coefficients.

b. "We should be interested in understanding the patient rather than labeling him." This muddleheaded comment may be given additional controversial power by describing a taxonomic rubric as a "pigeonhole," whereby a clinician who diagnoses his patients or clients is adjudged guilty of "putting people into pigeonholes"—a manifestly wicked practice, the wickedness being immediately apparent from the very words, so no further argument is required. *Res ipsa loquitur!*

It should not be necessary to explain to sophisticated minds that whether "labeling" in the nosological sense is *part* of "understanding" the patient cannot be decided by fiat, but hinges upon the etiological content of the label. If the nosological label is a completely arbitrary classification corresponding to nothing in nature, then it is admittedly not contributory to our understanding the patient we are trying to help. And of course if that is its status, it is not contributory to anything (even epidemiological statistics) and shouldn't be engaged in. Anyone who uses formal nosological categories responsibly should, in consistency, believe that the rubrics mean something. (He need not, obviously,

274

believe that they *all* mean something.) A diagnostic label means something about genetics or salient conflicts or schizophrenogenic mothers or social-class factors or unconscious fantasies or preferred mechanisms of defense or aberrated neurochemistry or whatever; and these kinds of entities are aspects—frequently clinically relevant aspects—of an adequate "causal understanding." It is important to see that which *class* of theoretical entities is implied by the nosologic term still remains open after a methodological decision to permit nosological labels is made. To conflate the two questions—"Are there taxonomic entities in psychiatry?" and "Is aberrated behavior sometimes caused by germs, genes, or structural CNS conditions?"—is just dumb, but the conflation is well nigh universal in American clinical thinking. See, in this connection, Meehl, 1972c—Chapter 11 above; also footnote 19 (at p. 80) of Livermore, Malmquist, and Meehl, 1968; and footnote 10 (at p. 12) of Meehl, 1970b. The widespread habit of mentioning the "medical model" without having bothered to think through what it is (causally, statistically, and epistemologically) prevents an intellectually responsible consideration of complex taxonomic questions. An "organic" causal factor (e.g., vitamin deficiency) may be taxonomic or not; so also for a genetic causal factor (e.g., PKU mental deficiency is taxonomic, but garden-variety hereditary stupidity is not). On the other hand, a "nonorganic, nongenetic," purely social-learning etiology, while perhaps *usually* nontaxonomic, may sometimes be taxonomic. The schizophrenogenic mother has been so conceived by some. Suppose that Freud had been correct in his (pre-1900) opinion about the respective etiologies of hysteria and the obsessional neurosis. He held, on the basis of his early psychoanalytic treatment of these two groups of patients, and before his shattering discovery that much of his psychoanalytic reconstruction of their early childhood was fantasy, that the specific life-history etiology of hysteria consisted of prepubescent sexual (specifically *genital*-stimulation) experience in which the future patient was passive and in which fear or disgust predominated over pleasure. Whereas he thought that the obsessional neurosis had its specific life-history origin in prepubescent sexual experience in which the subsequent patient played an active (aggressive) role and in which pleasure predominated over the negative affects. Had this specific life-history etiology been corroborated by subsequent investigation, the diagnostic labels "hysteria" and "obsessional neurosis" would have carried a heavy freight of causal

275

understanding, and would have been truly taxonomic. It makes no difference what *kind* of etiology we focus on (social, genetic, biochemical, or whatever), so long as the label points to it.

The notion that subsuming an individual under a category or rubric somehow prevents us from understanding the causal structure of his situation is one which has been repeatedly criticized but with negligible effect. The methodological level at which such discussions are typically carried on in the American tradition is pathetic in its superficiality. So far as I can discern, most clinicians who talk about the subject in this way have never even asked themselves what they *mean* by saying that "There are no disease entities in functional psychiatry." To make such a negative statement significantly, one ought presumably to have some idea about what would be the case if there *were* "entities" in functional psychiatry. One cannot deal with complicated questions of this sort by a few burblings to the effect that schizophrenia is not the same kind of thing as measles. What kinds of causal structures (and resultant phenotypic correlations and clusterings) may conveniently be labeled as "real entities" is a metaquestion of extraordinary complexity. To think about it in an intellectually responsible way requires philosophical, mathematical, and substantive competence at a level possessed by very few psychiatrists or clinical psychologists. Much of what we have to think clearly about in connection with the nosology-dynamics problem is tied up with the genetic factors problem in psychodynamics (cf. Meehl, 1972c—Chapter 11 above).

c. "Formal diagnoses are prognostically worthless." This statement is just plain false as a matter of empirical fact. No one familiar with the published statistics, and for that matter no one who has kept his eyes and ears open around a mental hospital for a while, can deny—unless he has been brainwashed into a rabid antidiagnostic prejudice—that paranoid schizophrenia has a very different outlook from a nice clean hypomanic attack in a cyclothymic personality, or that a "reactive depression" (precipitated, say, by failing one's Ph.D. prelims) will run a shorter course (with or without psychotherapy or chemotherapy) than a textbook compulsion neurosis, or that a hard-core Cleckley psychopath (Cleckley, 1964) is likely to continue getting into trouble until he becomes old enough to "simmer down" or "burn out," or that a case of hypochondriasis has a very poor outlook. I find it strange that psychologists urge us to rely upon psychological tests (especially the low-validity projective methods) for predictive purposes when, so far as the record shows, they do not have as much prognostic power as does formal diagnosis *even when made sloppily as in this country.*

Consider such a life-or-death prognostic problem as suicide risk in patients suffering from psychotic depression. Despite Bayes' Formula, and the arguments advanced by my doctoral student and co-author Albert Rosen in his paper on suicide (Rosen, 1954; see also Meehl and Rosen, 1955—Chapter 2 above), in cases of psychotic depression the suicide risk figure is large enough to take into serious account. The usual estimates are that, before the introduction of EST and the anti-depressant psychotropic drugs, roughly *one psychotic depression in six managed to kill himself.* (This figure cannot, of course, be easily calculated from the usual epidemiologic "rate" value.) More recently, follow-up studies of psychotically depressed patients who had made a "clinical recovery" sufficient to be discharged from the hospital found that another 3–5 percent will commit suicide in the ensuing two or three years after discharge. Point: Suicide probability among patients with psychotic depression is approximately equivalent to death risk in playing Russian roulette. If the responsible clinician does not recognize a psychotically depressed patient as such, and (therefore) fails to treat him as having a suicide risk of this magnitude, what he is in effect doing is handing the patient a revolver with one live shell and five empty chambers. Considering the irreversibility of death as an event, and the disutility attached to it in our society's value system, I assume my readers will agree that a Russian roulette probability figure is nothing to treat cavalierly. *Any psychiatrist or psychologist who does not make a thorough effort to ascertain whether his patient has a psychotic depression rather than a "depressive mood"* (the most common single psychiatric symptom, found in a wide variety of disorders), *in order to determine whether the patient requires treatment as a suicide risk of this magnitude, is behaving incompetently and irresponsibly.*

I will add some punch to this statistical argument by relating an anecdote (it comes to me directly from the student clinician to whom it happened). I report it in the form of a dialogue between myself and the student. This student therapist (a "psychiatric assistant") is an extremely bright, highly motivated, and very conscientious Arts College senior with three majors (one of which is psychology) and an HPR = 3.80. I mention these facts as evidence that the student's ignorance

277

arises *not* from stupidity, lack of curiosity, poor motivation, or irresponsibility. It arises from the antinosological bias (more generally, the antiscientific, anti-intellectual attitudes) of his teachers and supervisors. The exchange goes as follows:

MEEHL: "You look kind of low today."

STUDENT: "Well, I should be—one of my therapy cases blew his brains out over the weekend."

MEEHL: "Oh, I'm sorry to hear that—that is a bad experience for any helper. Do you want to talk about it?"

STUDENT: "Yes. I have been thinking over whether I did wrong, and trying to figure out what happened. I have been his therapist and I thought we were making quite a bit of progress; we had a good relationship. But then he went home on a weekend pass and shot himself."

MEEHL: "Had the patient talked to you about suicide before?"

STUDENT: "Oh, yes, quite a number of times. He had even tried to do it once before, although that was before I began to see him."

MEEHL: "What was the diagnosis?"

STUDENT: "I don't know."

MEEHL: "You mean you didn't read the chart to see what the formal diagnosis was on this man?"

STUDENT: "Well, maybe I read it, but it doesn't come to my mind right now. Do you think diagnosis is all that important?"

MEEHL: "Well, I would be curious to know what it says in the chart."

STUDENT: "I am not sure there is an actual diagnosis in the chart."

MEEHL: "There *has* to be a formal diagnosis in the chart, by the regulations of any hospital or medical clinic, in conformity with the statistical standards of the World Health Organization, for insurance purposes, and so on. Even somebody who doesn't believe in diagnosis and wouldn't bother to put it in a staff note, must record a formal diagnosis on the face sheet somewhere. He has to put something that is codeable in terms of the WHO *Manual of the International Statistical Classification of Diseases, Injuries, and Causes of Death.*"

STUDENT: "Oh, really? I never knew that."

MEEHL: "Did you see this man when he first came into the hospital?"

STUDENT: "Yes, I saw him within the first week after he was admitted."

MEEHL: "How depressed did he look then?"

STUDENT: "Oh, he was pretty depressed all right. He was very depressed at that time."

MEEHL: "Well, was he psychotically depressed?"

STUDENT: "I don't know how depressed 'psychotically depressed' is. How do you tell a psychotic depression?"

MEEHL: "Hasn't anybody ever given you a list of differential diagnostic signs for psychotic depression?"

STUDENT: "No."

MEEHL: "Tell me some of the ways you thought he was 'very depressed' at the time he came into the hospital."

STUDENT: "Well, he was mute, for one thing."

MEEHL: *"Mute?"*

STUDENT: "Yes, he was mute."

MEEHL: "You mean he was not very talkative, or do you mean that he wouldn't talk at all?"

STUDENT: "I mean he wouldn't talk at all—he was mute, literally mute."

MEEHL: "And you don't know whether that tells you the diagnosis— is that right?"

STUDENT: "No, but I suppose that means he was pretty depressed."

MEEHL: "If he was literally mute, meaning that he wouldn't answer simple questions like what his name is, or where he lives, or what he does for a living, then you have the diagnosis right away. If the man is not a catatonic schizophrenia, and if you know from all the available evidence that he is some kind of depression, you now know that he is a psychotic depression. There is no such thing as a neurotic depression with muteness."

STUDENT: "I guess I didn't know that."

MEEHL: "Why was he sent out on pass?"

STUDENT: "Well, we felt that he had formed a good group relationship and that his depression was lifting considerably."

MEEHL: "Did you say his depression was *lifting?*"

STUDENT: "Yes, I mean he was less depressed than when he came in— although he was still pretty depressed."

MEEHL: "When does a patient with a psychotic depression have the greatest risk of suicide?"

STUDENT: "I don't know."

MEEHL: "Well, what do the textbooks of psychiatry and abnormal psy-

279

chology *say* about the time of greatest suicide risk for a patient with psychotic depression?"

STUDENT: "I don't know."

MEEHL: "You mean you have never read, or heard in a lecture, or been told by your supervisors, that the time when a psychotically depressed patient is most likely to kill himself is when his depression is 'lifting'?"

STUDENT: "No, I never heard of that."

MEEHL: "Well you have heard of it now. You better read a couple of old books, and maybe next time you will be able to save somebody's life."

The obvious educational question is, how does it happen that this bright, conscientious, well-motivated, social-service-oriented premed psychology major with a 3.80 average *doesn't know the most elementary things about psychotic depression,* such as its diagnostic indicators, its statistical suicide risk, or the time phase in the natural history of the illness which presents the greatest risk of suicide? The answer, brethren, is very simple: Some of those who are "teaching" and "supervising" him either don't know these things themselves or don't think it is important for him to know them. This hapless student is at the educational mercy of a crew that is so unscholarly, antiscientific, "groupy-groupy," and "touchy-feely" that they have almost no concern for facts, statistics, diagnostic assessment, or the work of the intellect generally.

d. "Diagnosis does not help with treatment." This is, of course, not a valid criterion for determining whether formal diagnoses have factual meaning, empirical validity, or interjudge reliability; that it is even thought to be so reflects the shoddy mental habits of our profession. But its conceptual implications aside, how much truth is there in the assertion, given the baselines of accuracy in treatment choice we generally have to live with in clinical psychology? I would be interested to learn that any psychological test, or any psychodynamic inference, has a treatment selection validity as high as the nosological distinction between the affective psychoses and other disorders with regard to the efficacy of one of the few near-specifics we have in psychiatry, to wit, EST. Even a much less specific treatment indication, the phenothiazines for schizophrenia, has, as I read the record, as good a batting average as psychometrics or psychodynamic inference (see, for example, Meltzoff and Kornreich, 1970; Bergin and Strupp, 1972).

As elsewhere in this paper, I have here the occasion to point out the problem of a "double standard of methodological morals." If somebody is superskeptical and superscientific and requires reliability coefficients regularly better than .90 before he will use a proposed category or dimension in clinical decision making, then he will have a hard time justifying formal psychiatric diagnosis even when it is made by well-trained diagnosticians. (He will also have to advocate that physicians abandon their pernicious habit of taking blood pressures!) But such a superskeptic ought not, in consistency, waste his or our time in a case conference gassing about the patient's family dynamics or his unconscious mechanisms or his Rorschach or TAT or MMPI—*because none of these, singly or collectively, can measure up to his strict methodological demands either.* The decrying of diagnosis by psychiatrists and psychologists in favor of psychodynamic understanding or psychologist's test interpretation would require a showing that these competing methods of prediction and treatment choice are superior to psychiatric diagnosis when each is being done respectably. So far as I have been able to make out, there is no such showing.

Part II: Suggestions for Improvement

The preceding discussion has admittedly been almost wholly destructive criticism, and I confess to having written it partly motivated by a need for catharsis. Being an oral-impatient character with a 99th percentile "theoretical" score on the Allport-Vernon-Lindzey Values, my boredom tolerance is regrettably low. I don't really mind it much when my colleagues or students ignore me or disagree (interestingly) with me— but I become irritated when they bore me. It is annoying to walk across campus to the hospital and find oneself treated to such intellectual delicacies as "The way a person is perceived by his family affects the way he feels about himself—it's a dynamic interaction," or "Schizophrenia is not like mumps or measles." However, having expressed some long-standing irks and, I hope, having scored a few valid points about what is wrong with most case conferences in psychiatry or clinical psychology, I feel an obligation to try to say something constructive. Not that I accept the pollyanna cliché that purely destructive criticism is inadmissible. This has always struck me as a rather stupid position, since it is perfectly possible to see with blinding clarity that something is awry without thereby being clever enough to know how to cure it. I do not know how to stop religious wars or structural unemployment or racial prejudice or delinquency or divorce or mental illness—but I am tolerably clear that these are undesirable things in need of amelioration. Whether the following proposals for improving the quality of clinical case conferences are sound, about which I have no firm opinion, does not affect the validity of the preceding critical analysis. I invite the reader who does not find himself sympathetic to my proposed solutions to look for alternative solutions of his own.

The first suggestion that comes to the mind of anyone whose training emphasized differential psychology (and I am old-fashioned enough to believe that trait analysis is still important) is an improvement in the intellectual caliber of the participants. Obviously this is not something one can go about accomplishing directly by administrative fiat. We can't pass an ordinance requiring of the cosmos that more people should have super-high IQ's! However, several top schools (Minnesota included) have in recent years opted for a marked reduction in size and goals of their Ph.D. clinical psychology training programs, which has permitted the imposition of tougher "scholarly standards." The social issues involved are vexatious and beyond the scope of this paper.

More difficult to assess quantitatively, and therefore more subject to my personal biases, is the question of value orientation, what "turns people on." In my graduate school days, those of my peers who went over to the University Hospitals to work on the psychiatric ward and with Dr. Hathaway on MMPI development were students having *both* a strong interest in helping real flesh-and-blood patients (not to mention the fun of wearing a white coat!) *and* intense cognitive hungers. While wanting to be clinicians, they were characterized by "intellectual passion"; they would all rate very high on *n Cognizance*. But most observers of the contemporary psychological scene agree with me that strong cognitive passions (and their reflection in highly scholarly achievement and research visibility) have, alas, a distinct tendency to be negatively associated with a preference for spending many hours per week in service-oriented, face-to-face patient contact. This anecdotal impression (noted by every psychologist I have asked) receives indirect quantitative support in the well-known negative correlations (many in the −.50's and −.60's, some in the −.80's) between "scientific" and "uplift" scores on the SVIB (Strong, 1943, Table 193, p. 716; Campbell, 1971, Table 2-4 on p. 36, Table 3-31 on p. 111); the weak "social" tendencies of Terman's gifted subjects as children and adults (Terman, 1925, p. 420; Burks, Jensen, and Terman, 1930, pp. 173–176; Terman and Oden, 1947, pp. 36–37; Terman and Oden, 1959, p. 10; see also Hollingworth, 1926, *passim*); Robert Thorndike's investigations of activity preferences and values of psychologists (Thorndike, 1954, 1955; see also Clark, 1957, pp. 85, 90–95, 112, 224–225; related are Shaffer, 1953, and Campbell, 1965). Highly creative professionals have been shown in several studies to be less "socially oriented" than uncreative controls (see, for example, Dellas and Gaier, 1970, and references cited therein). But this negative correlation between "social" and "cognitive" passions is very far from being perfect. Hence we can select, *if we have a rather small N of trainees in a program,* applicants falling in the (++) cell of a cognizance-nurturance fourfold table. However, when the N becomes very large, when the particular psychology department has a reputation for an "applied emphasis," and when the criteria of selection become somewhat less scientifically or intellectually oriented, then one finds an increasing number of trainees in the program who are really not "turned on" by the life of the intellect. These students, admirable as human beings and doubtless well-motivated healers, find themselves somewhat bored, and in some cases actively irked, by abstract ideas.

As I said above, I am somewhat old-fashioned in these matters. I believe there is no substitute for brains. I do not believe the difference between an IQ of 135—perfectly adequate to get a respectable Ph.D. degree in clinical psychology at a state university—and an IQ of 185 is an unimportant difference between two human beings (cf. McNemar, 1964). Nor do I believe a person, even if basically bright, can be intellectually *exciting* unless he is intellectually *excited.* It astonishes me that so many persons enter academic life despite having what, to all appearances, is a rather feeble capacity for becoming excited about ideas. This aspect of the case conference problem—the fact that many of its participants are not first-class intellects in either ability or values—is obviously not curable by any modification in format.

However, without being unkindly elitist, we might try to convey (gently but firmly) the message that if you don't have anything worthwhile to say, you should probably shut up. The current practice, based upon a kind of diffuse "T-group" orientation to case conferences, seems to assume that everybody should get into the act regardless of how bright he is or what he knows, either clinically or theoretically. I view this attitude as preposterous on the face of it. The plain fact is that what most people have to say about anything complicated is not worth listening to. Or, as my medical colleague Dr. Howard Horns put it in a lovely metaphysical witticism, "Most people's thoughts are worth their weight in gold." If it is argued that you can't prevent people who have nothing significant to contribute from talking without being cruel or discourteous, I submit that this is empirically false. I point to case conferences in other specialties like neurology and internal medicine, where, so far as I have observed, there is no social discourtesy or cruelty manifested by those in charge; but the general atmosphere is nevertheless one which says, in effect, "Unless you know what you are talking about and have reason to think that you are saying something really educational for the rest of us or beneficial to the patient, you would be well advised to remain silent. Mere yakking for yakking's sake is not valued in this club." I have rarely had to listen to trivia, confused mentation, plain ignorance, or irrelevancies when I have attended case conferences in internal medicine or neurology, or the clinicopathological conference on the medical service. If an atmosphere of decent intellectual scholarly standards can be created and maintained on those services, I cannot think it is impossible to approximate the same thing in clinical psychology and psychiatry.

Mention of the clinicopathological conference in medicine brings me to my tentative and sketchy suggestions for improving the *format* of the case conference, suggestions largely although not entirely independent of the two preceding (unchangeable?) factors. One of the main reasons why so much hot air is emitted and reinforced in the psychiatric conference has almost nothing to do with the intellectual competence of the participants, namely, the sad fact that nobody can be proved wrong in what he says because there are no even quasi-objective external criteria. As is well known, one of the great contributions of Dr. Richard Clarke Cabot in dreaming up the clinicopathological conference—reports on the conferences from the Massachusetts General Hospital still appear regularly and would be highly educational reading for clinical psychologists, to whom I recommend the collections (Castleman and Burke, 1964; Castleman and Dudley, 1960; Castleman and McNeill, 1967; Castleman and Richardson, 1969)—is that everybody is put on the spot. For instance, a distinguished, world-famous visiting professor of medicine might be asked, on the basis of the clinical material presented, to set up the differential diagnosis, to argue the pros and cons, to ask for additional data that may not have been presented in the first go-around, and finally to stick his neck out and make a guess about what the pathologist found postmortem. While pathology is not, strictly speaking, a definitive operational criterion in the logician's sense (as anyone can easily discover by attending a clinicopathological conference in, say, pediatrics and listening to the pathologists debate whether the blood-cell slides are or are not early leukemia of a certain kind), still, for many diseases, the pathological findings can be taken as quasi-criteria. No matter what kind of psychiatric and neurological symptoms a patient shows clinically, if he has a negative blood and spinal fluid Wassermann, if his cerebral cortex does not show characteristic paretic changes, and if his brain tissue is completely free of *Treponema pallidum,* then he does not have paresis. If all the neurologists had agreed "clinically" that he was paretic, the interesting questions in the conference then become "What did he have instead?" and "How were the clinicians led so badly astray?" Point: A clinicopathological conference in neurology or medicine is an educational experience for students and staff largely because there is a *right answer.* And one desirable fringe benefit of the existence of this quasi-criterial "right answer" is the non-reinforcement of foolish conversation. If you say something grossly stupid, you are almost certain to be found out when the pathologist enters the fracas at the end of the conference.

A diagnostic entity in organic medicine is quasi-defined by the conjunction etiology-cum-pathology. If there were microscopically and chemically indistinguishable tissue changes, from the standpoint of the pathologist working alone, producible by two different microorganisms (or by vitamin deficiencies, or by genetic mutations at two loci), they would be two different disease entities. So far as I am aware, this state of affairs is never strictly true. At least I have not come across any such in my reading of medicine, nor have my medical colleagues come up with any examples. The opposite case, of identical etiology (if etiology is identified with the specific etiological agents) but different pathology, is, of course, fairly common. Witness, for example, the numerous varieties of tuberculosis. The theoretical significance of a different bodily reaction to a particular invading organism is paralleled by great practical significance, since the physician does not treat tuberculous meningi-

285

tis, pulmonary tuberculosis, and tuberculous disease of the spine in precisely the same way. Of course when we expand the concept of etiology to mean both specific etiology and the predisposing, auxiliary, and precipitating causes (see, for example, Freud, 1895 as reprinted 1962), then the two different diagnoses can be separated (theoretically) into the same two taxa either on the basis of etiology or on the basis of pathology. Suppose that two patients' defensive reactions to invasion by an adequately infective number of microorganisms *Mycobacterium tuberculosis* do not succeed in preventing clinical involvement, but in one patient it takes the form of pulmonary tuberculosis and in the other patient the locus of tissue pathology is bone. In such an instance we must suppose that we have to deal with a *locus minoris resistentiae,* a disposition that must, strictly speaking, be counted as part of the "complete etiological equation." Hence a Utopian description of the etiological sequence as visualized by Omniscient Jones would distinguish the two cases just as clearly (specific etiology + dispositions of *locus minoris resistentiae*) as would the differential pathology (bone versus lung).

It is nevertheless a convenient simplification to distinguish pathology and etiology for many purposes, and I shall do so here. Figure 1 shows the situation in functional psychiatry by analogy to that in internal medicine. The diagram clarifies the core problem we face in setting up a reality-linked differential reinforcement schedule for the verbal behavior of participants in a clinical case conference. We do not *know* the pathology (character structure, psychodynamics, need/defense system, trait organization, basic temperamental parameters) of the patient; we only infer them, frequently with rather low degrees of probability and with marked disagreement among competent clinicians. But the situation is worse than it sounds. It is not merely a question (as it typically would be in internal medicine or neurology) about the *particulars* of the instant case, i.e., where this individual patient's pathology fits into the causal hyperspace of our received biochemistry, physiology, pathological anatomy, etc. In psychiatry there will be disagreements also about the nomothetic explanatory *system* that is admissible, to such an extent that at times there will be nearly zero overlap in the technical terminology between two clinicians. When we come to etiology, the situation is, if possible, worse still. One can find boarded psychologists and psychiatrists who believe that everyone is born with ab-

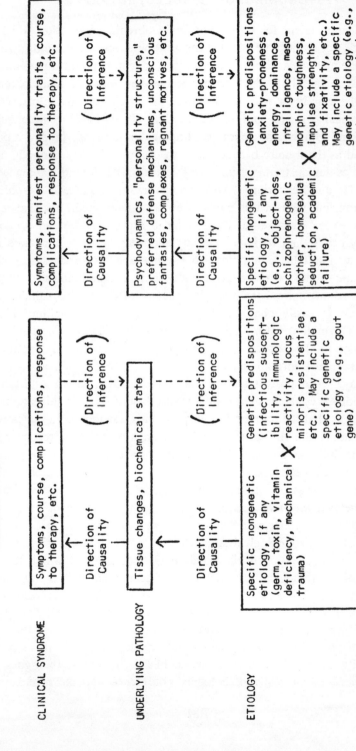

Figure 1. Clinical syndrome, underlying pathology, and etiology in organic disease entity and "functional" disease entity

solutely equal talent for developing schizophrenia (a position which I myself cannot see as now possible for a rational, informed mind); while others of equal professional qualifications (educational and experiential) may believe that both the occurrence and the form of schizophrenic disease lie wholly in genetic plus broadly constitutional factors, with psychological stresses and sociodynamics playing a negligible role. There is no Omniscient Jones psychopathologist whose biopsy report can stand as the umpire between such theoretical conflicts. Nobody can show slides demonstrating "superego lacunae." That fact, the absence of a definitive quasi-criterion, would seem to make insoluble the problem I am struggling with in this paper. Let us grant immediately that it is insoluble in the strict sense. But I want to argue that we can do considerably better than we have been, by adopting the unpopular medical model (with suitable adaptations to psychodiagnosis) and asking ourselves what would be the nearest equivalent to a pathologist's report.

The fundamental epistemological structure of the clinicopathological conference is easily characterized: It consists of withholding high-validity information, information that is quasi-definitive of the diagnosis, and requiring the participating clinicians to *infer* that high-validity, quasi-definitive information from other information which, at least in the average sense, possesses lower diagnostic validity. But this epistemic high validity is connected (as always) with the ontology, in this situation with the fact that the information in question is less remote in the causal chain than are the clinical symptoms, patient's complaints, response to treatment, hospital course, and so forth from the (definitive) pathological state cum etiological agent. That is, corresponding ontologically to causal closeness or intimacy (in some instances one could say "explicitly defined *meaning*") is something which, by virtue of its causal closeness, is also epistemologically "stronger" evidentially. In the limiting case, this epistemological strength is accepted as a criterion in the definitive sense mentioned above; although the extent to which this is true for the pathological examination of diseased tissue is easily exaggerated by psychologists. We withhold this high-validity information from the diagnosing clinician with the aim of sharpening his ability to make inferences from lower validity information, which he is often required to do in his clinical practice. Of course sometimes there is an artificiality about this in that we withhold information in the "guesstimate" phase of the clinicopathological conference that the clinician in his own practice might normally insist on having available before arriving at a decision. This element of artificiality is not considered too great a price to pay in order to attain the pedagogical aim of an objective criterion for differential reinforcement of inferential processes by a clinician diagnosing from presenting complaint, symptoms, signs, course, reaction to a therapeutic regime, and the like. I make this point because in searching for a realizable analogy to the epistemic circumstances of the clinicopathological conference when behavior disorder is the subject matter, one must be prepared for the objection that something artificial is being done. That is quite correct.

In addition to the epistemic factor of high validity deriving from the ontological factor of causal closeness, another influence tending to prevent case conferences in psychology or psychiatry from resembling a clinicopathological conference in medicine is the vagueness of the inferred statements, quite apart from the difficulty of ascertaining their truth. In a clinicopathological conference I might hazard the inference that the patient had an olfactory groove meningioma and I might be disappointed to learn that none such was found at autopsy, or that the patient was not operated on and the family refused permission for postmortem studies. The falsification of my inference, or the practical impossibility of checking it, does not arise from vagueness in the *meaning* of the expression "olfactory groove meningioma." *If* the tissue were available to the pathologist, whether or not the patient had an olfactory groove meningioma would be a question answerable with 99 percent certainty, whereas if I say that the patient has superego lacuna or (to use a once-favorite Rorschacher inference) has intrapsychic ataxia or—to gore Meehl's ox in a spirit of objectivity—that the patient is somewhat anhedonic, these expressions do not designate an even semiprecise state of affairs ontologically and therefore do not have a precise condition for their warranted assertability.

The rules of the game are so loose in psychiatry that it is interesting to speculate how far out, either in terms of conceptual vagueness or evidentiary weakness, one would have to go before his brethren called him on it. My teacher Dr. Starke Hathaway once mentioned that he was having so much trouble in one of his seminars in getting the psychiatry residents to adopt a critical posture, toward either the received doctrine or his own iconoclastic verbal productions, that he was about to go in and propound some absolute nonsense about the influence of sunspots

289

in schizophrenia, just to see whether they would rise to debate him or would dutifully note it down. There is in fact some quantitative evidence on this point (Goulett, 1965, pp. 8–9; cf. Goldsmith and Mandell, 1969), and all of us in the field of psychopathology at times permit ourselves utterances that, while perhaps not *utterly* devoid of empirical content, come about as close to it as one can find outside of Hegelian metaphysics.

We can formulate the psychiatric case conference problem thus, laying down conditions aimed at improvement but not unrealistically perfectionistic: We wish to divide the classes of information available at the time of the conference into two categories, the first category being available to the participant clinicians during their assessment process (including the conference discussion) and the second category being withheld from them until the end of the conference, presentation of this latter category of information being the differential reinforcement. In order for that division of information to serve its pedagogical function, we must meet three conditions:

1. The withheld information must be such that it will become reasonably clear ("objective") whether the statements inferred during the guesstimate phase of the conference are confirmed or refuted.

2. By and large, the statements belonging to the corpus of information withheld should themselves have an epistemologically privileged status in terms of the ontological structure, i.e., they should, in some sense that is defensible over the long run of patients, be closer to the underlying psychopathology/etiology than the evidentiary statements that are available in the guesstimate phase. While they cannot hope to have the status of the pathologist's report on a piece of biopsied or autopsied tissue, they should be analogous to it in the sense of being closer to that intrapsychic state of affairs that is nomologically definitive of the diagnostic entity or psychodynamic state.

3. This division of information on grounds of clearness and privileged evidentiary status must not do excessive violence to the ordinary clinical context. We are treating the participant clinicians as organisms whose behavior is being shaped up; we want to train them to do what they are going to do. Therefore while, in the interest of sharpening diagnostic skills by differential reinforcement, we may withhold some data that would normally be available at a comparable stage in the clinician's own

290

practice, the situation must not be so unlike that of ordinary clinical decision making as to be highly unrealistic.

Prima facie there are three sources of data theoretically capable of satisfying the first two of these conditions. First, we have the diagnostic, historical, and dynamic conclusions of the patient's therapist. In spite of a distressingly large element of subjectivity, these have merit in that they are based upon a larger sample of the patient's talk, gestures, fluctuations over time, response to probing, etc., than we have available when he is presented at the conference; and they are—unfortunately tied to the subjectivity—likely to be somewhat superior in quality to what we get in the case conference. But suppose it were seriously argued, as some hardnosed skeptics of my acquaintance would be willing to argue, that ten hours of psychotherapy is nearly worthless as a criterion of the truth about the patient's psychopathology. I cannot refute this skepticism. But then, by the same token, one would, in consistency, have to dismiss the conventional case conference enterprise in this field as fruitless. After all, if we think that *nothing* can be learned by observing and listening to a person talk and act in an interview, it is pointless to bring him into the conference to be interviewed by even the most able member of the professional staff. Second, we have the patient's behavior on the ward as observed by the ward personnel. It is a fairly objective fact that the patient refuses to take his medication, that he frequently approaches the nurses' cage with some sort of complaint, that he does not interact with other patients, that he sleeps soundly, and so forth. Third, whatever their intrinsic validity, the patient's psychometrics are a highly objective distillation of his responses to standard stimuli.

Each of these three information domains, which I shall label simply as "therapist ratings," "ward behavior," and "psychometrics," is likely to be qualitatively and quantitatively superior to what we can gather in the case conference. Further, it can be argued that to the extent that they cohere, they represent the closest we can come to a psychopathological equivalent of the pathologist's report in internal medicine. It is true that, with the exception of the psychometrics, the usual form in which these three data sources are available leaves much to be desired in the way of objectivity. But they do not have to be in the usual form, and part of my positive proposal is to modify that usual form in the direction of greater objectivity.

Consider first the psychotherapist's evaluation as a quasi-criterion. In order to reduce its vagueness, we require the psychotherapist to record his judgment in a standard format, such as the MHPA (Glueck, Meehl, Schofield, and Clyde, *Doctor's Sub-set, Forty Factors,* n.d.; Glueck, Meehl, Schofield, and Clyde, 1964; Glueck and Stroebel, 1969; Hedberg, Houck, and Glueck, 1971; Meehl, Lykken, Schofield, and Tellegen, 1971; Meehl, Schofield, Glueck, Studdiford, Hastings, Hathaway, and Clyde, 1962; Melrose, Stroebel, and Glueck, 1970; Mirabile, Houck, and Glueck, 1971). On the basis of such interviews, the psychotherapist has rated the patient on phenotypic variables (relatively close to behavior summaries), and the computer draws a factor profile. The same can be done for genotypic inferences by the therapist, although at present such profiles have not been developed for the MHPA genotypic pool. The obvious objection to taking this as a quasi-criterion is that although the therapist will have had a kind of clinical contact that is qualitatively superior to what we get at the case conference, and quantitatively he has had more hours than we have available, he may still be wrong, in the eyes of Omniscient Jones. There is no definitive answer to this objection, which is why I label it *quasi*-criterion. The best solution presently available, in my opinion, is to obtain independent ratings from a second skilled clinician who listens to tape recordings of the first clinician interviewing the patient. This suggestion may strike some readers as unrealistically burdensome for the staff, but it is not really so. There is evidence (Meehl, 1960—Chapter 6 above) to suggest that a psychotherapeutic interviewer's ratings converge rapidly toward the ratings he will be making after twenty-four hours of clinical contact, so that it would not usually be necessary for the second rating clinician to hear more than, say, two to four sessions of interviewing for present purposes. If this clinical job were performed solely for the purposes of the staff conference, it would be justifiable in the interest of better training; but of course carrying out such a rating task is itself a professional learning experience for the second judge and so can be defended on those grounds as well.

What do we do if the Q correlation between these two raters is low? The answer seems obvious to me: For most of our clinical case conferences, we would deliberately select those patients on whom there is satisfactory agreement between the two judges. Especially useful pedagogically would be patients on whom the two judges come to agree (convergence over time with more information) after poor agreement initially, presumably "hard" cases but not too hard to permit convergence given sufficient information.

From time to time, we would hold a staff conference on a patient where there was marked disagreement. In what follows I set aside that case and confine myself to the case in which there is a satisfactorily high Q correlation between the two independent raters. Some psychologists would argue that one should not infer validity from reliability, but this flat statement is misleading in some contexts. Reliability cannot prove validity, but it sometimes tends to support it. I urge that it does here— unless the enterprise is fruitless. (Nonpsychological example: If two surveying students independently come up with answers that a certain water tower is 847 feet from Stone X and is 200 feet high, this *does* tend to support the validity claim that these numbers are correct.) Ideally, if one were to set up a long-term program of improving the case conference along the lines suggested, it would be desirable to have a larger group of raters listening to the tapes or, better, a second interviewer making independent judgments on the basis of his own interview stimuli, together with a number of other raters listening to the tapes of this interviewer and the psychotherapist, Q correlating these ratings and arriving at an optimal statistical weight to be assigned. That is, we "calibrate" the (modal) therapist and (modal) tape listener on the basis of a larger number of expert clinicians, and use those statistical weights in future practice. The "best estimate" of the patient's characteristics is then a weighted sum of his therapist's judgments and the tape listener's judgments.

Predicting an MMPI profile seems like a rather silly thing to do, but it is really not. However, it is more realistic to predict not the profile itself but the modal Q-sort description of persons having the profile produced by the instant case. In order to bring this into coordination with the clinician's judgment, one must prepare an actuarial table such as the Marks-Seeman atlas (Marks and Seeman, 1963; Meehl, 1972b; Dahlstrom, Welsh, and Dahlstrom, 1972, pp. 307–339; Manning, 1971; Gilberstadt and Duker, 1965; Gilberstadt, 1970, 1972) and—again speaking ideally—one would want a large-scale investigation in which the MMPI-based description, the therapist's description, and the tape listener's descriptions were thrown into one statistical hopper to yield weights for the best available construct-valid characterization of patients.

Finally, the traditional nurses' notes in the chart and the informal comments of nurses and psychiatric aides are poor substitutes for a checklist or rating scale as a summary of the patient's ward behavior (Glueck and Stroebel, 1969; Rosenberg, Glueck, and Stroebel, 1967).

Adopting the preceding suggestions would, one hopes, result in a set of high–construct-validity statements about the patient, with which statements made by clinicians participating in a staff conference could be compared. It is hardly feasible to require the conference participants to make a Q sort, but this does not present an insuperable difficulty for comparative purposes. What we do is to specify a set of domain rubrics for the characterization of patients, such as ego function, adequacy of control system, suitability for interpretative psychotherapy, acting-out tendencies, indications for this or that psychotropic medication, major mechanisms of defense, Murray needs, affective tone, insight, and nosological category. A mimeographed sheet could be passed out at the beginning of the conference to remind participants of these major sectors of patient description. For each descriptive area it will be possible to ascertain whether one has made inferences that correspond to those reached by an optimal statistical weighting of the nurses' observations of ward behavior, the psychotherapist's and the tape listener's ratings, and the personality description actuarially derived from the MMPI profile.

On the question of artificiality, there is admittedly something unrealistic about the proposed sequence of informational input. However, it is not as unrealistic as one might think at first—less so than the conventional case conference, in some ways. In clinical practice, for example, one does not normally have the psychometrics available to him at the time of his initial contact with the patient. He takes the history, does a Mental Status, and begins an inquiry into the patient's personality difficulties. Obviously he does not normally have any nurses' notes. If it is objected that we arrive at our integrated picture of the patient from all of the data, the answer is that we can do this after these quasi-criterial variables have been presented toward the end of the conference. Objections to blind diagnosis from personality tests seem to assume that one must choose whether to read the personality test in the light of other information or without it. The fact of the matter is, of course, that one can read it both with and without the other evidence. (In my private office practice, and when I sit as a member of the State Hospital Review Board, I never look at MMPI profiles, if available, until *after* recording my interview impressions. The rationale is obvious: One set of "objective" numbers on a profile can infect my clinical impression, whereas infection going the other direction is impossible.) If it turns out that what the clinical staff concludes from the (selectively presented) life history plus the patient's behavior when interviewed in the conference is grossly out of line with the other data, this discrepancy should itself be a subject of discussion. The important point is that the inferences arrived at in the staff conference would include predictions about what the psychotherapists and the nurses and the MMPI said, and these agreements or discrepancies should constitute differential reinforcements for adequate versus inadequate clinical behavior by the participants. I may, of course, still think that I am right and that the MMPI is wrong; but it is a *fact* that I mispredicted the MMPI profile, or the personality profile based upon the MMPI.

While in this paper I am mainly concerned with the "intellectual" deficiencies that typically make clinical case conferences so boring, irksome, and educationally counterproductive, there are some practices of a procedural nature that help to make things dull, and need repair (whether or not my main suggestions for introducing a risky predictive element are acceptable to the reader). Since they are somewhat peripheral, I shall not develop argument at length but mainly list suggestions, with only the briefest summary of my reasons. Such a summary presentation will inevitably have a certain flavor of dogmatism about it.

When life-history material is presented (either initially, as in the currently accepted system, or later on, as in my suggested revision) it should be in documentary rather than oral form. It is preposterous that a roomful of highly paid faculty and busy psychiatric residents and graduate students in psychology should be forced to listen to somebody drone on about the fact that the patient's older brother died of appendicitis, that the patient had scarlet fever at age ten, that his uncle was a Swedenborgian, and the like. Even if the presentation of historical material were done more analytically and selectively than most residents or psychology trainees seem capable of doing, it would still be a terrible waste of time. There are certain kinds of basic "skeletal" data (geography, income, family's religion, organic illnesses, occupational history, educational progress, and the like) which there is no justification for presenting orally to the group in the precious conference time period.

One of the vices of the present system is that so much time is thus spent (frequently because of inadequate preparation plus the inefficient oral presentation of history material) that in a conference scheduled to last an hour and a half, by the time we are ready to see the live patient, whoever is in charge of the conference and interviewing the patient is so uncomfortably conscious of how little time remains that the interview is almost pro forma. I have sat through conferences in which the first hour was spent in oral presentation of a mélange of piddling and disconnected facts (including, say, that the patient had a great-uncle who died of cancer—the patient never having known his uncle); the patient then came in for ten minutes, leaving twenty minutes for a discussion of diagnosis, dynamics, and the treatment. This is simply absurd. For educational purposes (I am not here considering the sort of brief intake conference that many hospitals have on all new patients admitted since the previous morning) I think experience shows that no conference should be scheduled to run less than an hour and a half, and I myself would advocate two hours. Colleagues warn me that people's attention can't be held for two hours. I agree that you can't hold their attention with a bunch of poorly prepared third-raters doing a deadly presentation of meaningless material. But a variation in *who* is talking and *what* we are talking about, the difference between history and interview inputs, and especially the element of intellectual excitement generated by introducing elements of postdiction and prediction as I propose, should make it possible to hold people's interest for two hours. Most of us find we can run a two-hour seminar provided we run it right (that means, incidentally, not listening weekly to student literature reports!); and I therefore believe that two hours is feasible for good case conferences. Analogously to the seminar situation, anybody who has been around academia very long, and who remembers how he felt as a student, is aware that students do not much enjoy listening to each other. Admittedly student presentations serve an educational function for the presenter, although I see no reason for assuming that a first-year trainee, who has never attended any sort of conference before, is "ready" to begin his active learning process by presenting a case. In any event, we sacrifice a good deal of other students' valuable time when we force them to listen to an incompetent and boring presentation by somebody who really isn't ready to do it. At the very least, I would suggest an alternation of major responsibility for presentation by advanced students, faculty, and near beginners. I recognize that this is predicated on the old-fashioned idea that full professors with twenty years of teaching, research, and clinical experience should, on the average, be capable of serving as educational models for fledgeling clinicians. Perhaps that is not true in psychiatry. If it is untrue, I think we ought to let the taxpayer in on the secret. If everybody is about equal in brains, skill, and knowledge, the taxpayer's elected representatives should be allowed to make up their minds whether they really want to pay Professor Fisbee $30,000 a year for functions like participating in a case conference, inasmuch as he doesn't know anything that a junior medical student or a first-year graduate in psychology doesn't know! (I have the impression that there is an economic question here, and conceivably an ethical one, but this is not the place to develop that line of thought.)

In either the present or the revised system, one must allow sufficient time so that discussion of the diagnosis, dynamics, and treatment can be carried on at a respectable level of intellectual depth. Questions like "Is there such an entity as schizophrenia?" or "Should the construct 'sociopathic personality' be defined mainly by psychological-trait criteria, or by life-history criteria (such as delinquency and underachievement)?" cannot be discussed meaningfully in five minutes. Many important questions which would presumably be part of the function of a clinical case conference are far better left undiscussed than discussed in a superficial, dilettante fashion. Nothing is more offensive to a first-class intellect than to have to listen to third-raters converse about an intrinsically fascinating and complicated topic. I have sat through case conferences in which nothing even moderately interesting took place until only ten minutes remained to discuss it. Of course this suggestion involves not merely suitable changes in the procedural aspects, and an enforcement of constraints on the consumption of time in certain ways by the participating personnel, but also more refractory problems, including the need for the power elite of a particular department to recognize that there *is* a scholarly and intellectually exciting way to discuss complicated subjects. Of course if someone does not have much of anything going on in his head, and suffers an impoverishment of mental furniture (common in the field we are discussing), he will not even understand why it is silly to discuss certain topics in ten minutes.

297

Part III: Concluding Remarks

This paper is a polemic. If some of my judgments seem harsh, I remind the reader that a psychiatric case conference involves the welfare of patients and their families, that we deal with the physical or psychological pain, the "success" or "failure," the incarceration or liberty, the economic dependency, and sometimes the life or death, of human beings for whom we have accepted some measure of responsibility. It will have been apparent that I am deeply offended by the intellectual mediocrity of what transpires in most case conferences; but this personal reaction is of only autobiographical interest. The ignorance, errors, scientific fallacies, clinical carelessness, and slovenly mental habits which I have discussed above are not merely offensive "academically." They have—sometimes dramatically—an adverse impact upon human lives. When a student therapist tells me that a patient he was treating went home on a weekend pass and blew his brains out, and I find out upon thorough exploration that this almost straight-A student (with high motivation and lofty ethical standards) *did not even know the patient's chart diagnosis,* I am not animated by sentiments of esteem or charity toward those responsible for this student's classroom instruction and clinical supervision. Furthermore, the taxpayer is shelling out some pretty fancy salaries for the professionals who conduct case conferences. One need not be a disciple of Ayn Rand to share her distaste for incompetence. I freely admit that a major component of my attack is a claim that the case conferences I have attended have been unrewarding to me largely because of the low level of competence—*both scientific and clinical*—of most participants.

But I hope to have said something more than this, something "constructive." I have tried to indicate that we face some special methodological difficulties in the psychiatric and psychological fields, difficulties so complicated and recalcitrant as to present major problems even for first-class scientists and practitioners. However, in order for those problems to be solved or ameliorated, it is first necessary to clean out the Augean stables—a thankless task, and one not calculated to win me any popularity contests. I have written bluntly and forcefully—no doubt some will think arrogantly—for which I herewith tender whatever apologies are due. I confess that I do not suffer fools gladly. But aside from the cathartic effect of writing this polemic, which expresses the accumulated frustration and irritation of hundreds of hours of being subjected to this dismal business off and on for thirty years, before I quit entirely I cannot emphasize too strongly that part of the social and intellectual tradition of American psychiatry and clinical psychology tending to perpetuate the counterproductive mental habits described above is precisely this "buddy-buddy" syndrome which forbids anyone to call attention to instances of scientific or clinical incompetence, no matter how severe. So long as we operate on the principle that there are no standards of performance in this field, that everybody is equally bright, equally well read, equally skilled, equally logical, and equally experienced, Gresham's Law will, as usual, operate in the clinical case conference. There are too many psychoclinicians who implicitly equate the (valid) Popperian thesis that "Every informed, experienced, and intelligent professional is free to indulge his preferences among competing unrefuted conjectures" with the (preposterous) thesis that "Every professional or student is morally and intellectually entitled to persist in egregious mistakes, and it is wickedly authoritarian or snobbish to point them out." I take it that nobody who values the life of the intellect would subscribe to the latter thesis; and when it is applied in contexts involving psychological misery, physical health, economic dependency, crime, and sometimes death—as it is in the psychiatric case conference—such a maxim is not only foolish, it is downright immoral.

Finally, setting aside the unavoidable residuum of error inherent in the human condition, and the persistence of remediable errors among those professionals whose intellectual competence is simply not adequate to these difficult tasks, I have tried to offer at least the beginnings of a constructive plan for bringing the reinforcement schedule and cognitive feedback of the psychiatric case conference somewhat closer to those which prevail in the clinicopathological conference that has been so successful as a teaching device in the nonpsychiatric fields of medicine.

Addendum

As this volume was going to press, my psychiatric colleague Dr. Leonard L. Heston commented, on reading the manuscript, that an alternative to the somewhat complicated construct-validity approach proposed herein as surrogate for clinicopathological conference criteria would be the use of the follow-up. I am at a loss to understand my omitting this important alternative, except for the fact that my mental set was so strongly oriented toward solving the problem of providing *fairly quick differential reinforcement,* of the kind that the internist receives at the end of each clinicopathological conference when the pathologist presents his quasi-criterial report on what the tissue showed. But, as Dr. Heston reminds me, we ought to be prepared to do some special things in psychiatry and clinical psychology, in trying to make up for the absence of the pathologist's report as a quasi-criterion of diagnosis. Dr. Heston points out that the clinician participating in a psychiatric case conference could be, so to speak, on record (we could even tape-record the conference—which might in itself tend to reduce some of the garbage generated!), and one's differential reinforcements would be forthcoming days, weeks, months (sometimes even years) later. Actually, there would be quite a few patients whose response to therapeutic intervention (e.g., phenothiazines in schizophrenia, electroplexy in psychotic depression, lithium carbonate in hypomania, valium in relatively uncomplicated anxiety states, RET in the "philosophical neurosis") would be ascertainable fairly soon after the case conference. Special provisions, including what might be a considerable financial outlay, would be necessary in order to achieve feedback on longer term forecasts. But I think that Dr. Heston's alternative suggestion is extremely important, and my discussion of the problem would be seriously defective without mention of it.

Of course, he and I agree that these are not really "competing alternatives," since both could be implemented, except insofar as we face the usual problem of opportunity costs. I have little doubt that the impact of some kinds of dramatic follow-up findings, their "convincing power," would be greater than the best souped-up, construct-valid, at-the-time quasi-criterion that could be devised with present methods. Two examples may be given.

Several years ago I had a two-hour diagnostic interview with a theology student from another city who presented with complaints of depression, anxiety, and "loss of interest," but who showed no clinical evidence of textbook schizophrenic thought disorder or markedly inappropriate affect. His flatness was no more severe on Mental Status appraisal than that which we find in many obsessional neurotics or other overintellectualizing, character-armored types. I daresay many of my

American colleagues, and the majority of European clinicians, would say that my interview-based diagnosis, "Schizotype, early stages of decompensation, marginal Hoch-Polatin syndrome," was an example of Meehl indulging his schizotypal hobby again. Nor would most such skeptics have been convinced—although they might have been somewhat influenced—by the (post-interview) scoring of the patient's MMPI profile, which yielded not merely the "gullwing curve" suggestive of pseudoneurotic schizophrenia but had a grossly psychotic (schizophrenic) configuration. As it happened, I subsequently found this patient to have shown up in a Canadian mental hospital with more obvious symptoms of schizophrenia; and then a year or so later, he again showed up (at the Minneapolis Veterans Administration Hospital) with symptoms of schizophrenia so unmistakable that even a very conservative diagnostician, such as Dr. Eliot Slater, would, I am sure, agree with the schizophrenic diagnosis there made.

A quicker but equally dramatic differential reinforcement for the diagnosticians I recall from my graduate school days, at a psychiatric grand rounds conducted by the late J. C. McKinley, M.D., co-author with Dr. Hathaway of the Minnesota Multiphasic Personality Inventory and then head of the Department of Neuropsychiatry. The patient seen in rounds that Saturday morning had presented with complaints of depression and anxiety, plus (as I recall it) rather vague nondelusional feelings that things seemed "not quite solid or real." He had a suspicious Rorschach with some rather bad 0⁻ responses but nothing so gross as confabulation or contamination, and with a marginal over-all form level; his MMPI was also borderline, although somewhat more in the psychotic than the neurotic direction by the then available "eyeballed" profile criteria. On interview a certain flatness, as in the preceding example, was clinically in evidence; but it was not gross and one could not really speak properly of Kraepelinian "inappropriate affect." After the interview was concluded and the patient had left the conference room a spirited debate took place among staff and students about whether the patient was an early schizophrenia or a neurotic with mixed anxiety, depression, and obsessional features. While we were still engaged in this debate (giving arguments pro and con from the history, the resident's Mental Status interview report, the interview that we had just observed, and the MMPI/Rorschach combination) the intern and charge nurse came back to inform us that the patient, after having left the conference

301

to be taken back to his room, had suddenly become mute and immobile, and was now standing in the corridor in a classical catatonic condition! This kind of quick and unmistakable feedback is of course unusual, but I don't think anybody who was present at that conference will ever forget the experience.

Allowing for the fact, as Jevons put it, that "Men mark where they hit and not when they miss," a series of such follow-up findings would either (a) show my colleagues that when I say somebody is a schizotype, I usually know what I am talking about or (b) convince me that I am erring in the direction of schizotypal overdiagnosis. On the other hand, I cannot close this necessarily brief discussion of Dr. Heston's proposed emphasis on follow-up as an alternative criterion without emphasizing that follow-up is unfortunately an asymmetrical affair, in the sense that certain *positive* subsequent developments are capable of strongly supporting some diagnoses as against others; but the theoretical and clinical positions with regard to "open-concept" entities like schizoidia, subclinical manic depression, and the like are such that the *failure* subsequently to develop unmistakable clinical phenomena pointing to diagnosis D_1 and away from diagnosis D_2 cannot, as is recognized by all sophisticated persons, be argued very strongly in the negative. (Cf. the diagnostic situation involving a patient at risk for Huntington's Disease, in a family strain with late onset, who shows irritability but no positive neurology at age 40, and dies of coronary disease two years later. Did he carry the Huntington gene? We will never know.) I regret that the limitations of space (in this already too long chapter) prevent my giving Dr. Heston's suggestion the full consideration that it merits.

I take this opportunity to add that since my scholarly psychiatric colleagues Drs. Leonard Heston and Neil Yorkston are now running a new weekly clinical case conference which is being inched up steadily to clinically and scientifically respectable standards, the title of this essay has become out-of-date for its author, since I am attending their conference regularly, with enjoyment and profit.

REFERENCES

References

Alf, E., and N. M. Abrahams. Mixed group validation: A critique. *Psychological Bulletin*, 1967, 67, 443–444.

Alker, H. A., and H. G. Hermann. Are Bayesian decisions artificially intelligent? *Journal of personality and social psychology*, 1971, 19, 31–41.

American Psychological Association. *Ethical standards of psychologists*. Washington, D.C.: APA, 1953.

American Psychological Association, Committee on Test Standards. Technical recommendations for psychological tests and diagnostic techniques: Preliminary proposal. *American Psychologist*, 1952, 7, 461–475.

American Psychological Association, Committee on Test Standards. Technical recommendations for psychological tests and diagnostic techniques. *Psychological Bulletin*, Supplement, 1954, 51(2, part 2), 1–38.

Anastasi, A. The concept of validity in the interpretation of test scores. *Educational and Psychological Measurement*, 1950, 10, 67–78.

Anastasi, A., and J. P. Foley, Jr. *Differential psychology*. (Rev. ed.) New York: Macmillan, 1949.

Angyal, A., and N. Blackman. Vestibular reactivity in schizophrenia. *Archives of Neurology and Psychiatry*, 1940, 44, 611–620.

Angyal, A., and N. Blackman. Paradoxical reactions in schizophrenia under the influence of alcohol, of hyperpnea, and CO_2 inhalation. *American Journal of Psychiatry*, 1941, 97, 893–903.

Angyal, A., and M. Sherman. Postural reactions to vestibular stimulation in schizophrenic and normal subjects. *American Journal of Psychiatry*, 1942, 98, 857–862.

Arnhoff, F. N., and E. N. Damianopoulos. Self-body recognition and schizophrenia. *Journal of General Psychology*, 1964, 70, 353–361.

Ash, P. The reliability of psychiatric diagnoses. *Journal of Abnormal and Social Psychology*, 1949, 44, 272–276.

Badia, P., A. Haber, and R. P. Runyon. *Research problems in psychology*. Reading, Mass.: Addison-Wesley, 1970.

Barber, B. Resistance by scientists to scientific discovery. *Science*, 1961, 134, 596–602.

Barthell, C. N., and D. S. Holmes. High school yearbooks: A nonreactive measure of social isolation in graduates who later became schizophrenic. *Journal of Abnormal Psychology*, 1968, 73, 313–316.

Bechtoldt, H. P. Selection. In S. S. Stevens, ed. *Handbook of experimental psychology*. New York: Wiley, 1951. Pp. 1237–1267.

Beck, A. T. *Depression: Clinical, experimental and theoretical aspects*. New York: Harper and Row, 1967.

Beck, A. T., B. B. Sethi, and R. W. Tuthill. Childhood bereavement and adult depression. *Archives of General Psychiatry*, 1963, 9, 295–302.

Beck, L. W. Constructions and inferred entities. *Philosophy of Science*, 1950, 17, 74–86. Reprinted in H. Feigl and M. Brodbeck, eds. *Readings in the philosophy of science*. New York: Appleton-Century-Crofts, 1953. Pp. 368–381.

305

Bergin, A., and H. Strupp. *Changing frontiers in the science of psychotherapy.* Chicago: Aldine, 1972.

Betz, B. Studies of the therapist's role in the treatment of the schizophrenic patient. *American Journal of Psychiatry,* 1967, 123, 963–971.

Black, M. Vagueness: An exercise in logical analysis. *Philosophy of Science,* 1937, 4, 427–455.

Black, M. Reasoning with loose concepts. In his *Margins of precision.* Ithaca, N.Y.: Cornell University Press, 1970. Pp. 1–13.

Blair, W. R. N. A comparative study of disciplinary offenders and non-offenders in the Canadian army, 1948. *Canadian Journal of Psychology,* 1950, 4, 49–62.

Bleuler, E. *Dementia praecox; or, the group of schizophrenias* (1911), tr. Joseph Zinkin. New York: International Universities Press, 1950.

Bleuler, E. *The Theory of schizophrenic negativism,* tr. W. A. White. New York: Journal of Nervous and Mental Disease Publishing Co., 1912.

Block, J., and D. Bailey. *Q-sort item analyses of a number of MMPI scales.* Technical Memorandum OERL-TM-55-7. Maxwell Air Force Base, Ala.: Officer Education Research Laboratory, Air Force Personnel and Training Research Center, Air Research and Development Command, 1955.

Blum, M. L., and B. Balinsky. *Counseling and psychology.* New York: Prentice-Hall, 1951.

Braatz, G. A. Preference intransitivity as an indicator of cognitive slippage in schizophrenia. *Journal of Abnormal Psychology,* 1970, 75, 1–6.

Braithwaite, R. B. *Scientific explanation.* Cambridge: Cambridge University Press, 1953.

Broad, C. D. The 'nature' of a continuant. In his *Examination of McTaggart's philosophy,* I. Cambridge: Cambridge University Press, 1933. Pp. 264–278. Reprinted in H. Feigl and W. Sellars, eds. *Readings in philosophical analysis.* New York: Appleton-Century-Crofts, 1949. Pp. 472–481.

Bross, I. D. J. *Design for decision.* New York: Macmillan, 1953.

Bunge, M., ed. *The critical approach to science and philosophy* (essays in honor of Karl R. Popper). New York: Free Press, 1964.

Burks, B. S., D. W. Jensen, and L. M. Terman. *Genetic studies of genius, III: The promise of youth.* Stanford, Calif.: Stanford University Press, 1930.

Campbell, D. P. The vocational interests of American Psychological Association presidents. *American Psychologist,* 1965, 20, 636–644.

Campbell, D. P. *Handbook for the Strong Vocational Interest Blank.* Stanford, Calif.: Stanford University Press, 1971.

Campbell, D. P., and D. W. Fiske. Convergent and discriminant validation by the multitrait-multimethod matrix. *Psychological Bulletin,* 1959, 56, 81–105. Reprinted in E. Megargee, ed. *Research in clinical assessment.* New York: Harper and Row, 1966. Pp. 89–111. Also reprinted in W. Mehrens and R. L. Ebel, eds. *Principles of educational and psychological measurement.* Chicago: Rand McNally, 1967. Pp. 273–302. Also reprinted in D. N. Jackson and S. Messick, eds. *Problems in human assessment.* New York: McGraw-Hill, 1967. Pp. 124–132.

Campbell, D. P., J. H. Stevens, E. H. Uhlenhuth, and C. B. Johansson. An extension of the Whitehorn-Betz A-B Scale. *Journal of Nervous and Mental Disease,* 1968, 146, 417–421.

Carlson, E. A. *The gene: A critical history.* Philadelphia: W. B. Saunders, 1966.

Carnap, R. Testability and meaning. *Philosophy of Science,* 1936, 3, 420–471; 1937, 4, 2–40. Reprinted with corrigenda and additional bibliography, New Haven, Conn.: Yale University Graduate Philosophy Club, 1950.

Carnap, R. Foundations of logic and mathematics. In *International encyclopedia of unified science,* I, no. 3. Chicago: University of Chicago Press, 1939. Pp. 56–69 reprinted as "The interpretation of physics" in H. Feigl and M. Brodbeck,

REFERENCES

eds. *Readings in the philosophy of science.* New York: Appleton-Century-Crofts, 1953. Pp. 309–318.

Carnap, R. Empiricism, semantics, and ontology. *Revue internationale de philosophie,* 1950, 4, 20–40. Reprinted in P. P. Wiener, ed. *Readings in philosophy of science.* New York: Scribner's, 1953. Pp. 509–521.

Carnap, R. The methodological character of theoretical concepts. In H. Feigl and M. Scriven, eds. *Minnesota studies in the philosophy of science,* I. Minneapolis: University of Minnesota Press, 1956. Pp. 38–76.

Castleman, B., and J. Burke. *Surgical clinicopathological conferences of the Massachusetts General Hospital.* Boston: Little, Brown, 1964.

Castleman, B., and H. R. Dudley, Jr. *Clinicopathological conferences of the Massachusetts General Hospital: Selected medical cases.* Boston: Little, Brown, 1960.

Castleman, B., and J. M. McNeill. *Bone and joint clinicopathological conferences of the Massachusetts General Hospital.* Boston: Little, Brown, 1967.

Castleman, B., and E. P. Richardson. *Neurologic clinicopathological conferences of the Massachusetts General Hospital.* Boston: Little, Brown, 1969.

Cattell, R. B. *Description and measurement of personality.* Yonkers, N.Y.: World Book Co., 1946.

Cattell, R. B. *Personality.* New York: McGraw-Hill, 1950.

Cattell, R. B. *Personality and motivation structure and measurement.* Yonkers, N.Y.: World Book Co., 1957.

Cattell, R. B. Taxonomic principles for locating and using types. In B. Kleinmuntz, ed. *Formal representation of human judgment.* New York: Wiley, 1968. Pp. 99–148.

Chapin, F. S. *Experimental designs in sociological research.* (Rev. ed.) New York: Harper, 1955.

Child, I. L. Personality. *Annual Review of Psychology,* 1954, 5, 149–170.

Chyatte, C. Psychological traits of professional actors. *Occupations,* 1949, 27, 245–250.

Clark, K. E. *America's psychologists: A survey of a growing profession.* Washington, D.C.: American Psychological Association, 1957.

Cleave, J. P. The notion of validity in logical systems with inexact predicates. *British Journal of the Philosophy of Science,* 1970, 21, 269–274.

Cleckley, H. *The mask of sanity.* (4th ed.) St. Louis: C. V. Mosby, 1964.

Cleveland, S. E. Judgment of body size in a schizophrenic and a control group. *Psychological Reports,* 1960, 7, 304.

Cleveland, S. E., S. Fisher, E. E. Reitman, and P. Rothaus. Perception of body size in schizophrenia. *Archives of General Psychiatry,* 1962, 7, 277–285.

Colbert, E. G., R. R. Koegler, and C. H. Markham. Vestibular dysfunction in childhood schizophrenia. *Archives of General Psychiatry,* 1959, 1, 600–617.

Collins, W. E., G. H. Crampton, and J. B. Posner. The effect of mental set upon vestibular nystagmus and the EEG. *USA Medical Research Laboratory Report,* 1961, no. 439.

Copilowish, I. M. Border-line cases, vagueness, and ambiguity. *Philosophy of Science,* 1939, 6, 181–195.

Cronbach, L. J. *Essentials of psychological testing.* New York: Harper, 1949.

Cronbach, L. J. Further evidence on response sets and test design. *Educational and Psychological Measurement,* 1950, 10, 3–31.

Cronbach, L. J. Coefficient alpha and the internal structure of tests. *Psychometrika,* 1951, 16, 297–335.

Cronbach, L. J. The counselor's problems from the perspective of communication theory. In V. H. Hewer, ed. *New perspectives in counseling.* Minneapolis: University of Minnesota Press, 1955. Pp. 3–19. (a)

307

Cronbach, L. J. Processes affecting scores on "understanding of others" and "assumed similarity." *Psychological Bulletin,* 1955, 52, 177–193. (b)

Cronbach, L. J., and P. E. Meehl. Construct validity in psychological tests. *Psychological Bulletin,* 1955, 52, 281–302. Reprinted here as Chapter 1. Also available in the Bobbs-Merrill Reprint Series in the Social Sciences, no. P-82.

Cureton, E. E. Validity. In E. F. Lindquist, ed. *Educational measurement.* Washington, D.C.: American Council on Education, 1951. Pp. 621–695.

Dahlstrom, W. G. *Personality systematics and the problem of types.* Morristown, N.J.: General Learning Press, 1972.

Dahlstrom, W. G., G. S. Welsh, and L. E. Dahlstrom. *An MMPI handbook, I: Clinical interpretation.* Minneapolis: University of Minnesota Press, 1972.

Dailey, C. A. The effect of premature conclusion upon the acquisition of understanding a person. *Journal of Psychology,* 1952, 33, 133–152.

Dailey, C. A. The practical utility of the clinical report. *Journal of Consulting Psychology,* 1953, 17, 297–302.

Dalén, P. Causal explanations in psychiatry: A critique of some current concepts. *British Journal of Psychiatry,* 1969, 115, 129–137.

Damrin, D. E. A comparative study of information derived from a diagnostic problem-solving test by logical and factorial methods of scoring. Unpublished doctoral dissertation, University of Illinois, 1952.

Danielson, J. R., and J. H. Clark. A personality inventory for induction screening. *Journal of Clinical Psychology,* 1954, 10, 137–143.

Davenport, B. F. The semantic validity of TAT interpretations. *Journal of Consulting Psychology,* 1952, 16, 171–175.

Dawes, R. M. How clinical probability judgment may be used to validate diagnostic signs. *Journal of Clinical Psychology,* 1967, 23, 403–410.

Dawes, R. M., and P. E. Meehl. Mixed group validation: A method for determining the validity of diagnostic signs without using criterion groups. *Psychological Bulletin,* 1966, 66, 63–67. Reprinted here as Chapter 8.

DeBakey, M. E., chairman. *Report to the president: A national program to conquer heart disease, cancer and stroke.* Washington, D.C.: President's Commission on Heart Disease, Cancer and Stroke, 1964.

Delafresnaye, J. F., ed. *Brain mechanisms and learning.* Springfield, Ill.: Charles C. Thomas, 1961.

Delgado, J. M., W. W. Roberts, and N. E. Miller. Learning motivated by electrical stimulation of the brain. *American Journal of Physiology,* 1954, 179, 587–593.

Dellas, M., and E. L. Gaier. Identification of creativity: The individual. *Psychological Bulletin,* 1970, 73, 55–73.

Dorken, H., and A. Kral. The psychological differentiation of organic brain lesions and their localization by means of the Rorschach test. *American Journal of Psychiatry,* 1952, 108, 764–770.

Dorland's Illustrated Medical Dictionary. (24th ed.) Philadelphia: W. B. Saunders, 1965.

Duncan, O. D., L. E. Ohlin, A. J. Reiss, Jr., and H. R. Stanton. Formal devices for making selection decisions. *American Journal of Sociology,* 1953, 58, 573–584.

Dunnette, M. D. Use of the sugar pill by industrial psychologists. *American Psychologist,* 1957, 12, 223–225.

Edwards, J. H. The simulation of Mendelism. *Acta Genetica et Statistica Mediica,* 1960, 10, 63–70.

Edwards, J. H. The genetic basis of common disease. *American Journal of Medicine,* 1963, 34, 627–638.

Edwards, J. H. Familial predisposition in man. *British Medical Bulletin,* 1969, 25, 58–64.

REFERENCES

Edwards, W. The theory of decision making. *Psychological Bulletin,* 1954, 51, 380–417.

Einhorn, H. J. The use of nonlinear noncompensatory models in decision making. *Psychological Bulletin,* 1970, 73, 221–230.

Einhorn, H. J. Expert measurement and mechanical combination. *Organizational behavior and human performance,* 1972, 7, 86–106.

Erlenmeyer-Kimling, L., ed. Genetics and mental disorders. *International Journal of Mental Health,* 1972, 1, 1–230.

Eron, L. D. Frequencies of themes and identifications in the stories of schizophrenic patients and non-hospitalized college students. *Journal of Consulting Psychology,* 1948, 12, 387–395.

Eysenck, H. J. Criterion analysis—an application of the hypothetico-deductive method in factor analysis. *Psychological Review,* 1950, 57, 38–53.

Faber, K. *Nosography in modern internal medicine.* New York: Hoeber, 1923.

Falconer, D. S. The inheritance of liability to certain diseases, estimated from the incidence among relatives. *Annals of Human Genetics,* 1965, 29, 51–76.

Feigl, H. Existential hypotheses. *Philosophy of Science,* 1950, 17, 35–62.

Feigl, H. Confirmability and confirmation. *Revue internationale de philosophie,* 1951, 5, 268–279. Reprinted in P. P. Wiener, ed. *Readings in philosophy of science.* New York: Scribner's, 1953. Pp. 522–530.

Ferster, C. B., and B. F. Skinner. *Schedules of reinforcement.* New York: Appleton-Century-Crofts, 1957.

Fine, R. *The healing of the mind: The technique of psychoanalytic psychotherapy.* New York: McKay, 1971.

Fish, B. The study of motor development in infancy and its relationship to psychological functioning. *American Journal of Psychiatry,* 1961, 117, 1113–1118.

Fleeson, W., B. C. Glueck, Jr., G. Heistad, J. E. King, D. Lykken, P. Meehl, and A. Mena. The ataraxic effect of two phenothiazine drugs on an outpatient population. *University of Minnesota Medical Bulletin,* 1958, 29, 274–286.

Forer, B. R. The fallacy of personal validation: A classroom demonstration of gullibility. *Journal of Abnormal and Social Psychology,* 1949, 44, 118–123.

Frank, G. H. The role of the family in the development of psychopathology. *Psychological Bulletin,* 1965, 64, 191–205.

Freedman, D. G. Constitutional and environmental interactions in rearing of four breeds of dogs. *Science,* 1958, 127, 585–586.

Freeman, H., and E. H. Rodnick. Effect of rotation on postural steadiness in normal and in schizophrenic subjects. *Archives of Neurology and Psychiatry,* 1942, 48, 47–53.

Freud, S. A reply to criticisms on the anxiety-neurosis (1895). In *Collected papers,* I. London: Hogarth Press, 1950. Pp. 107–127. Also in J. Strachey, ed. *Standard edition of the complete psychological works of Sigmund Freud,* III. London: Hogarth Press, 1962. Pp. 119–139.

Freud, S. Further remarks on the defence neuro-psychoses (1896). In *Collected papers,* I. London: Hogarth Press, 1948. Pp. 155–182. Also in J. Strachey, ed. (under title "Further remarks on the neuro-psychoses of defense"). *Standard edition of the complete psychological works of Sigmund Freud,* III. London: Hogarth Press, 1962.

Freud, S. The dynamics of the transference (1912). In *Collected papers,* II. London: Hogarth Press, 1950. Pp. 312–322. Also in J. Strachey, ed. *Standard edition of the complete psychological works of Sigmund Freud,* XII. London: Hogarth Press, 1958. Pp. 98–108.

Freud, S. *Introductory lectures on psychoanalysis* (1917). In J. Strachey, ed. *Standard edition of the complete psychological works of Sigmund Freud,* XVI. London: Hogarth, 1963.

Fuller, J. L., and W. R. Thompson. *Behavior genetics*. New York: Wiley, 1960. Pp. 272–283.

Garfield, S. *Introductory clinical psychology*. New York: Macmillan, 1957.

Gaylord, R. H. Conceptual consistency and criterion equivalence: A dual approach to criterion analysis. Unpublished PRB Research Note no. 17. Copies obtainable from ASTIA-DSC, AD-21 440.

Gilberstadt, H. *Comprehensive MMPI codebook for males*. IB 11-5. Washington, D.C.: Veterans Administration, 1970.

Gilberstadt, H. *Supplementary MMPI codebook for VA male medical consultation*. IB 11-5, Supplement 1. Washington, D.C.: Veterans Administration, 1972.

Gilberstadt, H., and J. Duker. *A handbook for clinical and actuarial MMPI interpretation*. Philadelphia: W. B. Saunders, 1965.

Glueck, B. C., Jr., P. E. Meehl, W. Schofield, and D. J. Clyde. *Minnesota-Hartford Personality Assay: Doctor's sub-set*. Hartford, Conn.: Institute of Living, n.d.

Glueck, B. C., Jr., P. E. Meehl, W. Schofield, and D. J. Clyde. *Minnesota-Hartford Personality Assay: Forty factors*. Hartford, Conn.: Institute of Living, n.d.

Glueck, B. C., Jr., P. E. Meehl, W. Schofield, and D. J. Clyde. The quantitative assessment of personality. *Comprehensive Psychiatry*, 1964, 5, 15–23.

Glueck, B. C., Jr., and C. F. Stroebel. The computer and the clinical decision process, II. *American Journal of Psychiatry*, Supplement, 1969, 125, 2–7.

Glueck, S., and E. Glueck. *Unraveling juvenile delinquency*. Cambridge, Mass.: Harvard University Press, 1950.

Goguen, J. A. The logic of inexact concepts. *Synthese*, 1969, 19, 325–373.

Goldberg, L. R. Simple models or simple processes? Some research on clinical judgments. *American Psychologist*, 1968, 23, 483–496.

Goldberg, L. R. Man versus model of man: A rationale, plus some evidence, for a method on improving on clinical inferences. *Psychological Bulletin*, 1970, 73, 422–432.

Golden, R., and P. E. Meehl. Detecting latent clinical taxa, IV: Empirical study of the maximum covariance method and the normal minimum chi-square method, using three MMPI keys to identify the sexes. *Reports from the Research Laboratories of the Department of Psychiatry, University of Minnesota*. Report no. PR-73-2. Minneapolis: University of Minnesota, 1973 (in preparation). (a)

Golden, R., and P. E. Meehl. Detecting latent clinical taxa, V: A Monte Carlo study of the maximum covariance method and associated consistency tests. *Reports from the Research Laboratories of the Department of Psychiatry, University of Minnesota*. Report no. PR-73-3. Minneapolis: University of Minnesota, 1973 (in preparation). (b)

Goldsmith, S. R., and A. J. Mandell. The psychodynamic formulation: A critique of a psychiatric ritual. *American Journal of Psychiatry*, 1969, 125, 1738–1743.

Goodenough, F. L. *Mental testing*. New York: Rinehart, 1949.

Goodman, L. A. The use and validity of a prediction instrument, I: A reformulation of the use of a prediction instrument. *American Journal of Sociology*, 1953, 58, 503–510.

Gottesman, I. I., and J. Shields. In pursuit of the schizophrenic genotype. In S. Vandenberg, ed. *Progress in human behavior genetics*. Baltimore: Johns Hopkins Press, 1968. Pp. 67–103.

Gottesman, I. I., and J. Shields. *Schizophrenia and genetics: A twin study vantage point*. New York: Academic Press, 1972.

Gough, H. G., H. McClosky, and P. E. Meehl. A personality scale for social responsibility. *Journal of Abnormal and Social Psychology*, 1952, 47, 73–80.

REFERENCES

Gough, H. G., M. G. McKee, and R. J. Yandell. *Adjective check list analyses of a number of selected psychometric and assessment variables.* Berkeley: Institute of Personality Assessment and Research, University of California, 1953.

Goulett, H. M. *The insanity defense in criminal trials.* St. Paul, Minn.: West Publishing Company, 1965.

Guilford, J. P. New standards for test evaluation. *Educational and Psychological Measurement,* 1946, 6, 427–438.

Guilford, J. P. Factor analysis in a test-development program. *Psychological Review,* 1948, 55, 79–94.

Gulliksen, H. Intrinsic validity. *American Psychologist,* 1950, 5, 511–517.

Hacking, I. *Logic of statistical inference.* Cambridge: Cambridge University Press, 1965.

Halbower, C. C. A comparison of actuarial versus clinical prediction to classes discriminated by MMPI. Unpublished doctoral dissertation, University of Minnesota, 1955.

Hanvik, L. J. Some psychological dimensions of low back pain. Unpublished doctoral dissertation, University of Minnesota, 1949.

Hastings, D. W. Follow-up results in psychiatric illness. *American Journal of Psychiatry,* 1958, 114, 1057–1066.

Hathaway, S. R. A coding system for MMPI profile classification. *Journal of Consulting Psychology,* 1947, 11, 334–337.

Hathaway, S. R. A study of human behavior: The clinical psychologist. *American Psychologist,* 1958, 13, 257–265.

Hathaway, S. R., and E. D. Monachesi. *Analyzing and predicting juvenile delinquency with the MMPI.* Minneapolis: University of Minnesota Press, 1953.

Hedberg, D. L., J. H. Houck, and B. C. Glueck, Jr. Tranylcypromine-trifluoperazine combination in the treatment of schizophrenia. *American Journal of Psychiatry,* 1971, 127, 1141–1146.

Hempel, C. G. Vagueness and logic. *Philosophy of Science,* 1939, 6, 163–180.

Hempel, C. G. Problems and changes in the empiricist criterion of meaning. *Revue internationale de philosophie,* 1950, 4, 41–63. Reprinted in L. Linsky, ed. *Semantics and the philosophy of language.* Urbana: University of Illinois Press, 1952. Pp. 163–185.

Hempel, C. G. Fundamentals of concept formation in empirical science. *International encyclopedia of unified science,* II, no. 7. Chicago: University of Chicago Press, 1952.

Hempel, C. G. A logical appraisal of operationism. *Scientific Monthly,* 1954, 79, 215–220.

Hempel, C. G. *Aspects of scientific explanation.* New York: Free Press, 1965.

Herzberg, A. *Active psychotherapy.* New York: Grune and Stratton, 1945.

Heston, L. Psychiatric disorders in foster home reared children of schizophrenic mothers. *British Journal of Psychiatry,* 1966, 112, 819–825.

Heston, L. The genetics of schizophrenia and schizoid disease. *Science,* 1970, 167, 249–256.

Heston, L. Genes and schizophrenia. In J. Mendels, ed. *Textbook of biological psychiatry.* New York: Wiley-Interscience, 1973 (in press)

Hoch, P., and P. Polatin. Pseudoneurotic forms of schizophrenia. *Psychiatric Quarterly,* 1949, 3, 248–276.

Hoffman, P. J. Criteria of human judgment ability, I: The "clinical" assessment of intelligence and personality. *American Psychologist,* 1958, 13, 388. (Abstract.) (a)

Hoffman, P. J. Human judgment as a decision process. *American Psychologist,* 1958, 13, 368. (Title.) (b)

Hoffman, P. J. The prediction of clinical prediction. *American Psychologist,* 1959, 14, 356.

311

Hoffman, P. J. The paramorphic representation of clinical judgment. *Psychological Bulletin,* 1960, 57, 116–131.

Hollingshead, A. B., and F. C. Redlich. *Social class and mental illness: A community study.* New York: Wiley, 1958.

Hollingworth, L. S. *Gifted children.* New York: Macmillan, 1926.

Holsopple, J. Q., and J. G. Phelan. The skills of clinicians in analysis of projective tests. *Journal of Clinical Psychology,* 1954, 10, 307–320.

Honig, W. K., ed. *Operant behavior: Areas of research and application.* New York: Appleton-Century-Crofts, 1966.

Horst, P., ed. The prediction of personal adjustment. *Social Science Research Council Bulletin,* 1941, no. 48, 286–292.

Horst, P. Pattern analysis and configural scoring. *Journal of Clinical Psychology,* 1954, 10, 3–11.

Hoskins, R. G. *The biology of schizophrenia.* New York: Norton, 1946.

Hovey, H. B. MMPI profiles and personality characteristics. *Journal of Consulting Psychology,* 1953, 17, 142–146.

Humphreys, L. G., C. C. McArthur, P. E. Meehl, N. Sanford, and J. Zubin. Clinical versus actuarial prediction. In *Proceedings of the 1955 Invitational Conference on Testing Problems.* Princeton, N.J.: Educational Testing Service, 1956. Pp. 91–141.

Hunt, W. A. An actuarial approach to clinical judgment. In B. M. Bass and I. R. Berg, eds. *Objective approaches to personality assessment.* Princeton, N.J.: Van Nostrand, 1959. Pp. 169–191.

Jackson, D. D., ed. *The etiology of schizophrenia.* New York: Basic Books, 1960.

Jenkins, J. G. Validity for what? *Journal of Consulting Psychology,* 1946, 10, 93–98.

Jensen, A. R. Counter response. *Journal of Social Issues,* 1969, 25, 219–222.

Kaplan, A. Definition and specification of meaning. *Journal of Philosophy,* 1946, 43, 281–288.

Kaplan, A., and F. Schott. A calculus for empirical classes. *Methodos,* 1951, 3, 165–188.

Kelly, E. L. Theory and techniques of assessment. *Annual Review of Psychology,* 1954, 5, 281–310.

Kelly, E. L., and D. W. Fiske. *The prediction of performance in clinical psychology.* Ann Arbor: University of Michigan Press, 1951.

Kempthorne, O. *An introduction to genetic statistics.* New York: Wiley, 1957.

Kendall, M. G. On the reconciliation of theories of probability. *Biometrika,* 1949, 36, 101–116.

Kety, S., and D. Rosenthal, eds. *The transmission of schizophrenia.* Oxford and New York: Pergamon Press, 1968.

King, H. E. *Psychomotor aspects of mental disease.* Cambridge, Mass.: Harvard University Press, 1954.

Klebanoff, L. B. Parental attitudes of mothers of schizophrenic, brain-injured and retarded, and normal children. *American Journal of Orthopsychiatry,* 1959, 29, 445–454.

Kleinmuntz, B. *Clinical information processing by computer.* New York: Holt, Rinehart, and Winston, 1969.

Kleinmuntz, B., ed. *Formal representation of human judgment.* New York: Wiley, 1968.

Kneale, W. *Probability and induction.* Oxford: Clarendon Press, 1949.

Korman, A. K. The prediction of managerial performance: A review. *Personnel Psychology,* 1968, 21, 295–322.

Kostlan, A. A method for the empirical study of psychodiagnosis. *Journal of Consulting Psychology,* 1954, 18, 83–88.

REFERENCES

Kostlan, A. A reply to Patterson. *Journal of Consulting Psychology,* 1955, 19, 486.
Kraepelin, E. *General paresis,* tr. J. W. Moore. New York: Journal of Nervous and Mental Disease Publishing Co., 1913.
Kuhn, T. S. *The structure of scientific revolutions.* (Rev. ed.) Chicago: Chicago University Press, 1970.
Lakatos, I. Criticism and the methodology of scientific research programmes. *Proceedings of the Aristotelian Society,* 1968, 69, 149–186.
Lakatos, I., and A. Musgrave, eds. *Criticism and the growth of knowledge.* Cambridge: Cambridge University Press, 1970.
Langmuir, I. Science, common sense, and decency. *Science,* 1943, 97, 1–7.
Leach, W. W. Nystagmus: An integrative neural deficit in schizophrenia. *Journal of Abnormal and Social Psychology,* 1960, 60, 305–309.
Levi, I. *Gambling with truth: An essay on induction and the aims of science.* New York: Knopf, 1967.
Lidz, T., A. Cornelison, D. Terry, and S. Fleck. Intrafamilial environment of the schizophrenic patient, VI: The transmission of irrationality. *Archives of Neurology and Psychiatry,* 1958, 79, 305–316.
Lindquist, E. F., ed. *Educational measurement.* Washington, D.C.: American Council on Education, 1951.
Linn, R. L. A note on mixed group validation. *Psychological Bulletin,* 1967, 67, 378.
Little, K. B., and E. S. Shneidman. The validity of MMPI interpretations. *Journal of Consulting Psychology,* 1954, 18, 425–428.
Little, K. B., and E. S. Shneidman. The validity of thematic projective technique interpretations. *Journal of Personality,* 1955, 23, 285–294.
Little, K. B., and E. S. Shneidman. Congruencies among interpretations of psychological tests and anamnestic data. *Psychological Monographs,* 1959, 73(6, whole no. 476).
Littman, R. A., and E. Rosen. Molar and molecular. *Psychological Review,* 1950, 57, 58–65.
Livermore, J. M., C. P. Malmquist, and P. E. Meehl. On the justifications for civil commitment. *University of Pennsylvania Law Review,* 1968, 117, 75–96.
Loevinger, J. Objective tests as instruments of psychological theory. *Psychological Reports,* Monograph Supplement 9, 1957, 3, 635–694. Reprinted in D. N. Jackson and S. Messick, eds. *Problems in human assessment.* New York: McGraw-Hill, 1967.
London, I. D. Some consequences for history and psychology of Langmuir's concept of convergence and divergence of phenomena. *Psychological Review,* 1946, 53, 170–188.
Lorr, M., and E. A. Rubinstein. Factors descriptive of psychiatric outpatients. *Journal of Abnormal and Social Psychology,* 1955, 51, 514–522.
Lucas, C. M. Analysis of the relative movement test by a method of individual interviews. *Bureau of Naval Personnel Research Reports,* Contract Nonr-694 (00), NR 151-13. Princeton, N.J.: Educational Testing Service, March 1953.
Lundberg, G. A. Case-studies vs. statistical methods—an issue based on misunderstanding. *Sociometry,* 1941, 4, 379–383.
Lykken, D. T. A study of anxiety in the sociopathic personality. *Journal of Abnormal and Social Psychology,* 1957, 55, 6–10.
Lykken, D. T. Statistical significance in psychological research. *Psychological Bulletin,* 1968, 70, 151–159. Reprinted in P. Badia, A. Haber, and R. Runyon. *Research problems in psychology.* Reading, Mass.: Addison-Wesley, 1970. Pp. 263–277. Also reprinted in D. E. Morrison and R. E. Henkel, eds. *The significance test controversy.* Chicago: Aldine, 1970. Pp. 267–279.

313

McArthur, C. C. Analyzing the clinical process. *Journal of Counseling Psychology*, 1954, 1, 203–207.

McArthur, C. C., P. E. Meehl, and D. V. Tiedeman. Symposium on clinical and statistical prediction. *Journal of Counseling Psychology*, 1956, 3, 163–173.

McConaghy, N. The use of an object sorting test in elucidating the hereditary factor in schizophrenia. *Journal of Neurology, Neurosurgery, and Psychiatry*, 1959, 22, 243–246.

MacCorquodale, K., and P. E. Meehl. On a distinction between hypothetical constructs and intervening variables. *Psychological Review*, 1948, 55, 95–107.

Macfarlane, J. W. Problems of validation inherent in projective methods. *American Journal of Orthopsychiatry*, 1942, 12, 405–410.

McKinley, J. C., and S. R. Hathaway. The Minnesota Multiphasic Personality Inventory, V: Hysteria, hypomania and psychopathic deviate. *Journal of Applied Psychology*, 1944, 28, 153–174.

McKinley, J. C., S. R. Hathaway, and P. E. Meehl. The Minnesota Multiphasic Personality Inventory, VI: The K scale. *Journal of Consulting Psychology*, 1948, 12, 20–31.

McNair, D. M., D. M. Callahan, and M. Lorr. Therapist "type" and patient response to psychotherapy. *Journal of Consulting Psychology*, 1962, 26, 425–429.

McNemar, Q. Lost: Our intelligence? why? *American Psychologist*, 1964, 19, 871–882.

Major, R. H. *Classic descriptions of disease*. Springfield, Ill.: Charles C. Thomas, 1932.

Malmquist, C. P. Depression and object loss in acute psychiatric admissions. *American Journal of Psychiatry*, 1970, 126, 1782–1787.

Manning, H. M. Programmed interpretation of the MMPI. *Journal of Personality Assessment*, 1971, 35, 162–176.

Manosevitz, M., G. Lindzey, and D. D. Thiessen. *Behavioral genetics: Method and research*. New York: Appleton-Century-Crofts, 1969.

Marks, P. A., and W. Seeman. *The actuarial description of abnormal personality*. Baltimore: Williams and Wilkins, 1963.

Marks, P. A., and J. O. Sines. Methodological problems of cookbook construction. In J. Butcher, ed. *MMPI: Research developments and clinical applications*. New York: McGraw-Hill, 1969. Pp. 71–96.

Masserman, J. H., and H. T. Carmichael. Diagnosis and prognosis in psychiatry with a follow-up study of the results of short-term general hospital therapy of psychiatric cases. *Journal of Mental Science*, 1939, 84, 893–946.

Meehl, P. E. An examination of the treatment of stimulus patterning in Professor Hull's *Principles of behavior*. *Psychological Review*, 1945, 52, 324–332. (a)

Meehl, P. E. An investigation of a general normality or control factor in personality testing. *Psychological Monographs*, 1945, 59(4, whole no. 274). (b)

Meehl, P. E. A simple algebraic development of Horst's suppressor variables. *American Journal of Psychology*, 1945, 58, 550–554. (c)

Meehl, P. E. *Clinical versus statistical prediction: A theoretical analysis and a review of the evidence*. Minneapolis: University of Minnesota Press, 1954. (a).

Meehl, P. E. Comment on "Analyzing the clinical process." *Journal of Counseling Psychology*, 1954, 1, 203–208. (b)

Meehl, P. E. Clinical versus actuarial prediction. *Proceedings of the 1955 Invitational Conference on Testing Problems*. Princeton, N.J.: Educational Testing Service, 1956. Pp. 136–141. (a)

Meehl, P. E. Symposium on clinical and statistical prediction. *Journal of Counseling Psychology*, 1956, 3, 163–173. (b)

Meehl, P. E. Wanted—a good cookbook. *American Psychologist*, 1956, 11, 263–272. Reprinted here as Chapter 3. (c)

REFERENCES

Meehl, P. E. When shall we use our heads instead of the formula? *Journal of Counseling Psychology*, 1957, 4, 268–273. Reprinted here as chapter 4. Available also in the Bobbs-Merrill Reprint Series in the Social Sciences, no. P-519.

Meehl, P. E. A comparison of clinicians with five statistical methods of identifying psychotic MMPI profiles. *Journal of Counseling Psychology*, 1959, 6, 102–109. (a)

Meehl, P. E. Some ruminations on the validation of clinical procedures. *Canadian Journal of Psychology*, 1959, 13, 102–128. Reprinted here as Chapter 5. Also available in the Bobbs-Merrill Reprint Series in the Social Sciences, no. 517. (b)

Meehl, P. E. The cognitive activity of the clinician. *American Psychologist*, 1960, 15, 19–27. Reprinted here as Chapter 6. Also available in the Bobbs-Merrill Reprint Series in the Social Sciences, no. P-518.

Meehl, P. E. Schizotaxia, schizotypy, schizophrenia. *American Psychologist*, 1962, 17, 827–838. Reprinted here as Chapter 7. Also available in the Bobbs-Merrill Reprint Series in the Social Sciences, no. P-516.

Meehl, P. E. *Manual for use with checklist of schizotypic signs.* Minneapolis: Psychiatric Research Unit, University of Minnesota Medical School, 1964.

Meehl, P. E. Detecting latent clinical taxa by fallible quantitative indicators lacking an accepted criterion. *Reports from the Research Laboratories of the Department of Psychiatry, University of Minnesota.* Report no. PR-65-2. Minneapolis: University of Minnesota, May 25, 1965. (a)

Meehl, P. E. Discussion of Eysenck's "The effects of psychotherapy." *International Journal of Psychiatry*, 1965, 1, 156–157. (b)

Meehl, P. E. Seer over sign: The first good example. *Journal of Experimental Research in Personality*, 1965, 1, 27–32. (c)

Meehl, P. E. Problems of strategy in research on schizotaxia. Unpublished memorandum to D. T. Lykken, February 15, 1966.

Meehl, P. E. Theory-testing in psychology and physics: A methodological paradox. *Philosophy of Science*, 1967, 34, 103–115. Reprinted in P. Badia, A. Haber, and R. P. Runyon. *Research problems in psychology.* Reading, Mass.: Addison-Wesley, 1970. (a)

Meehl, P. E. What can the clinician do well? In D. N. Jackson and S. Messick, eds. *Problems in human assessment.* New York: McGraw-Hill, 1967. Pp. 594–599. Reprinted here as Chapter 9. (b)

Meehl, P. E. Detecting latent clinical taxa, II: A simplified procedure, some additional hitmax cut locators, a single-indicator method, and miscellaneous theorems. *Reports from the Research Laboratories of the Department of Psychiatry, University of Minnesota.* Report no. PR-68-4. Minneapolis: University of Minnesota, August 15, 1968.

Meehl, P. E. Comment in 'Input.' *Psychology Today*, 1969, 3, 4. (a)

Meehl, P. E. Nuisance variables and the ex post facto design. *Reports from the Research Laboratories of the Department of Psychiatry, University of Minnesota.* Report no. PR-69-4. Minneapolis: University of Minnesota, April 15, 1969. (b)

Meehl, P. E. Nuisance variables and the ex post facto design. In M. Radner and S. Winokur, eds. *Minnesota studies in the philosophy of science*, IV. Minneapolis: University of Minnesota Press, 1970. (Expanded version of Meehl, 1969b.) Pp. 373–402. (a)

Meehl, P. E. Psychology and the criminal law. *University of Richmond Law Review*, 1970, 5, 1–30. (b)

Meehl, P. E. Some methodological reflections on the difficulties of psychoanalytic research. In M. Radner and S. Winokur, eds. *Minnesota studies in the philosophy of science*, IV. Minneapolis: University of Minnesota Press, 1970. Pp. 403–416. (c)

315

Meehl, P. E. A taxonomic statistic for loose genetic syndromes. Paper read at the First Meeting of the Classification Society, Columbus, Ohio, April 9, 1970. (d)

Meehl, P. E. High school yearbooks: A reply to Schwarz. *Journal of Abnormal Psychology,* 1971, 77, 143–148. (a)

Meehl, P. E. Law and the fireside inductions: Some reflections of a clinical psychologist. *Journal of Social Issues,* 1971, 27, 65–100. (b)

Meehl, P. E. A critical afterword. In I. I. Gottesman and J. Shields. *Schizophrenia and genetics: A twin study vantage point.* New York: Academic Press, 1972. Pp. 367–416. (a)

Meehl, P. E. Reactions, reflections, projections. In J. Butcher, ed. *Objective personality assessment: Changing perspectives.* New York: Academic Press, 1972. Pp. 131–189. (b)

Meehl, P. E. Specific genetic etiology, psychodynamics and therapeutic nihilism. *International Journal of Mental Health,* 1972, 1, 10–27. Reprinted here as Chapter 11. (c)

Meehl, P. E. MAXCOV-HITMAX: A taxonomic search method for loose genetic syndromes. 1973. Printed here as Chapter 12.

Meehl, P. E. The concept 'specific etiology': Some quantitative meanings. To appear.

Meehl, P. E., and W. G. Dahlstrom. Objective configural rules for discriminating psychotic from neurotic MMPI profiles. *Journal of Consulting Psychology,* 1960, 24, 375–387.

Meehl, P. E., D. T. Lykken, M. R. Burdick, and G. R. Schoener. Identifying latent clinical taxa, III: An empirical trial of the normal single-indicator method, using MMPI scale 5 to identify the sexes. *Reports from the Research Laboratories of the Department of Psychiatry, University of Minnesota.* Report no. PR-69-1. Minneapolis: University of Minnesota, January 15, 1969.

Meehl, P. E., D. T. Lykken, W. Schofield, and A. Tellegen. Recaptured-item technique (RIT): A method for reducing somewhat the subjective element in factor-naming. *Journal of Experimental Research in Personality,* 1971, 5, 171–190.

Meehl, P. E., and A. Rosen. Antecedent probability and the efficiency of psychometric signs, patterns, or cutting scores. *Psychological Bulletin,* 1955, 52, 194–216. Reprinted here as Chapter 2. Also available in the Bobbs-Merrill Reprint Series in the Social Sciences, no. P-514.

Meehl, P. E., W. Schofield, B. C. Glueck, Jr., W. B. Studdiford, D. W. Hastings, S. R. Hathaway, and D. J. Clyde. *Minnesota-Ford pool of phenotypic personality items.* (August 1962 ed.) Minneapolis: University of Minnesota, 1962.

Mehlman, B. The reliability of psychiatric diagnoses. *Journal of Abnormal and Social Psychology,* 1952, 47, 577–578.

Melrose, J. P., C. F. Stroebel, and B. C. Glueck, Jr. Diagnosis of psychopathology using stepwise multiple discriminant analysis, I. *Comprehensive Psychiatry,* 1970, 11, 43–50.

Meltzoff, J., and M. Kornreich. *Research in psychotherapy.* New York: Atherton Press, 1970.

Meyers, D., and W. Goldfarb. Psychiatric appraisals of parents and siblings of schizophrenic children. *American Journal of Psychiatry,* 1962, 118, 902–908.

Minnesota Hunter Casualty Study. St. Paul, Minn.: Jacob Schmidt Brewing Company, 1954.

Mirabile, C. S., J. H. Houck, and B. C. Glueck, Jr. Computer prediction of treatment success. *Comprehensive Psychiatry,* 1971, 12, 48–53.

Morrison, D. E., and R. E. Henkel, eds. *The significance test controversy.* Chicago: Aldine, 1970.

Mosier, C. I. A critical examination of the concepts of face validity. *Educational and Psychological Measurement,* 1947, 7, 191–205.

Mosier, C. I. Problems and designs of cross-validation. *Educational and Psychological Measurement,* 1951, 11, 5–11.

Murphy, E. A. One cause? Many causes? The argument from a bimodal distribution. *Journal of Chronic Diseases,* 1964, 17, 301–324.

Myers, J. K., and L. Schaffer. Social stratification and psychiatric practice. *American Sociological Review,* 1954, 19, 307–310.

Nash, L. K. *The atomic-molecular theory.* Cambridge, Mass.: Harvard University Press, 1950.

Nash, L. K. *The nature of the natural sciences.* Boston: Little, Brown, 1963.

Newell, R. R., W. E. Chamberlain, and L. Rigler. Descriptive classification of pulmonary shadows: A revelation of unreliability in the Roentgenographic diagnosis of tuberculosis. *American Review of Tuberculosis,* 1954, 69, 566–584.

Olds, J., and P. Milner. Positive reinforcement produced by electrical stimulation of septal area and other regions of rat brain. *Journal of Comparative and Physiological Psychology,* 1954, 47, 419–427.

Pankoff, L. D., and H. B. Roberts. Bayesian synthesis of clinical and statistical prediction. *Psychological Bulletin,* 1968, 70, 762–773.

Pap, A. Reduction-sentences and open concepts. *Methodos,* 1953, 5, 3–30.

Pap, A. Disposition concepts and extensional logic. In H. Feigl, M. Scriven, and G. Maxwell, eds. *Minnesota studies in the philosophy of science,* II. Minneapolis: University of Minnesota Press, 1958. Pp. 196–224. (a)

Pap, A. *Semantics and necessary truth.* New Haven, Conn.: Yale University Press, 1958. (b)

Pap, A. *An introduction to the philosophy of science.* New York: Free Press, 1962.

Paterson, D. G. Character reading at sight of Mr. X according to the system of Mr. P. T. Barnum. Unpublished, mimeographed. First printed in M. L. Blum and B. Balinsky. *Counseling and psychology.* New York: Prentice-Hall, 1951. P. 47. Reprinted in M. D. Dunnette. Use of the sugar pill by industrial psychologists. *American Psychologist,* 1957, 12, 223.

Patterson, C. H. Diagnostic accuracy or diagnostic stereotypy? *Journal of Consulting Psychology,* 1955, 19, 483–485.

Payne, R. S., and J. H. G. Hewlett. Thought disorder in psychotic patients. In H. J. Eysenck, ed. *Experiments in personality,* II. London: Routledge and Paul, 1960. Pp. 3–106.

Payne, R. W. Cognitive abnormalities. In H. J. Eysenck, ed. *Handbook of abnormal psychology.* New York: Basic Books, 1961. Pp. 248–250.

Peak, H. Problems of objective observation. In L. Festinger and D. Katz, eds. *Research methods in the behavioral sciences.* New York: Dryden Press, 1953. Pp. 243–300.

Penrose, L. S. The distal triradius *t* on the hands of parents and sibs of mongol imbeciles. *Annals of Human Genetics,* 1954, 19, 10–38.

Peppard, T. A. Mistakes in diagnosis. *Minnesota Medicine,* 1949, 32, 510–511.

Peterson, C. R., and L. R. Beach. Man as an intuitive statistician. *Psychological Bulletin,* 1967, 68, 29–46.

Peterson, D. R. The diagnosis of subclinical schizophrenia. *Journal of Consulting Psychology,* 1954, 18, 198–200. Reprinted in G. S. Welsh and W. G. Dahlstrom, eds. *Basic readings on the MMPI in psychology and medicine.* Minneapolis: University of Minnesota Press, 1956. Pp. 415–418.

Piotrowski, Z. The Rorschach inkblot method in organic disturbances of the central nervous system. *Journal of Nervous and Mental Disease,* 1937, 86, 525–537.

Platt, J. R. Strong inference. *Science,* 1964, 146, 347–353.

Pollack, M., and H. P. Krieger. Oculomotor and postural patterns in schizophrenic children. *Archives of Neurology and Psychiatry,* 1958, 79, 720–726.

317

Popper, K. R. *The logic of scientific discovery.* New York: Basic Books, 1959.

Popper, K. R. *Conjectures and refutations.* New York: Basic Books, 1962.

Porteus, S. D. *The Porteus maze test and intelligence.* Palo Alto, Calif.: Pacific Books, 1950.

Rado, S. *Psychoanalysis of behavior.* New York: Grune and Stratton, 1956.

Rado, S. Theory and therapy: The theory of schizotypal organization and its application to the treatment of decompensated schizotypal behavior. In S. C. Scher and H. R. Davis, eds. *The out-patient treatment of schizophrenia.* New York: Grune and Stratton, 1960. Pp. 87–101.

Rado, S., and G. Daniels. *Changing concepts of psychoanalytic medicine.* New York: Grune and Stratton, 1956.

Raiffa, H. *Decision analysis: Introductory lectures on choices under uncertainty.* Reading, Mass.: Addison-Wesley, 1968.

Ramey, E. R., and D. S. O'Doherty, eds. *Electrical studies on the unanesthetized brain.* New York: Hoeber, 1960.

Reik, T. *Listening with the third ear: The inner experience of a psychoanalyst.* New York: Farrar, Straus, 1948.

Reiss, A. J., Jr. Unraveling juvenile delinquency, II: An appraisal of the research methods. *American Journal of Sociology,* 1951, 57, 115–120.

Robinson, R. *Definition.* Oxford: Clarendon Press, 1950.

Roessel, F. P. MMPI results for high school drop-outs and graduates. Unpublished doctoral dissertation, University of Minnesota, 1954.

Rogers, C. R., and R. F. Dymond. *Psychotherapy and personality change.* Chicago: University of Chicago Press, 1954.

Roller, D. E. *The early development of the concepts of temperature and heat.* Cambridge, Mass.: Harvard University Press, 1950.

Roller, D. E. *The development of the concept of electric charge.* Cambridge, Mass.: Harvard University Press, 1954.

Rosen, A. Detection of suicidal patients: An example of some limitations in the prediction of infrequent events. *Journal of Consulting Psychology,* 1954, 18, 397–403.

Rosen, E., R. E. Fox, and I. Gregory. *Abnormal psychology.* (2nd ed.) Philadelphia: W. B. Saunders, 1972.

Rosenberg, M., B. C. Glueck, Jr., and C. F. Stroebel. The computer and the clinical decision process. *American Journal of Psychiatry,* 1967, 124, 595–599.

Rosenthal, D. Problems of sampling and diagnosis in the major twin studies of schizophrenia. *Journal of Psychiatric Research,* 1962, 1, 116–134.

Rosenthal, D. *Genetic theory and abnormal behavior.* New York: McGraw-Hill, 1970.

Rotter, J. B., J. E. Rafferty, and A. B. Lotsof. The validity of the Rotter Incomplete Sentences Blank: High school form. *Journal of Consulting Psychology,* 1954, 18, 105–111.

Rozeboom, W. W. Mediation variables in scientific theory. *Psychological Review,* 1956, 63, 249–264.

Salter, A. *Conditioned reflex therapy.* New York: Creative Age Press, 1949.

Sarbin, T. R. A contribution to the study of actuarial and individual methods of prediction. *American Journal of Sociology,* 1942, 48, 593–602.

Sarbin, T. R. The logic of prediction in psychology. *Psychological Review,* 1944, 51, 210–228.

Savage, L. J. *The foundations of statistics.* New York: Wiley, 1954.

Sawyer, J. Measurement *and* prediction, clinical *and* statistical. *Psychological Bulletin,* 1966, 66, 178–200.

Schilpp, P., ed. *The philosophy of Karl Popper.* Library of Living Philosophers. LaSalle, Ill.: Open Court, in press.

318

Schmidt, H. O., and C. P. Fonda. The reliability of psychiatric diagnosis: A new look. *Journal of Abnormal and Social Psychology,* 1956, 52, 262–267.

Schofield, W. *Psychotherapy: The purchase of friendship.* Englewood Cliffs, N.J.: Prentice-Hall, 1964.

Schofield, W., and L. Balian. A comparative study of the personal histories of schizophrenic and nonpsychiatric patients. *Journal of Abnormal and Social Psychology,* 1959, 59, 216–225.

Schwarz, J. C. Comment on "High school yearbooks: A nonreactive measure of social isolation in graduates who later became schizophrenic." *Journal of Abnormal Psychology,* 1970, 75, 317–318.

Scriven, M. Definitions, explanations, and theories. In H. Feigl, M. Scriven, and G. Maxwell, eds. *Minnesota studies in the philosophy of science,* II. Minneapolis: University of Minnesota Press, 1958. Pp. 99–195.

Sellars, W. S. Concepts as involving laws and inconceivable without them. *Philosophy of Science,* 1948, 15, 287–315.

Sellars, W. S. Some reflections on language games. *Philosophy of Science,* 1954, 21, 204–228.

Sellars, W. S. Counterfactuals, dispositions, and the casual modalities. In H. Feigl, M. Scriven, and G. Maxwell, eds. *Minnesota Studies in the philosophy of science,* II. Minneapolis: University of Minnesota Press, 1958. Pp. 225–308.

Shaffer, L. F. Of whose reality I cannot doubt. *American Psychologist,* 1953, 8, 608–623.

Simon, H. A., and N. Rescher. Cause and counterfactual. *Philosophy of Science,* 1966, 33, 323–340.

Simons, D. J., and O. Diethelm. Electroencephalographic studies of psychopathic personalities. *Archives of Neurology and Psychiatry,* 1946, 55, 619–626.

Sines, J. O. Actuarial versus clinical prediction in psychopathology. *British Journal of Psychiatry,* 1970, 116, 129–144.

Sines, L. K. An experimental investigation of the relative contribution to clinical diagnosis and personality description of various kinds of pertinent data. Unpublished doctoral dissertation, University of Minnesota, 1957. Published in reduced form: The relative contribution of four kinds of data to accuracy in personality assessment. *Journal of Consulting Psychology,* 1959, 23, 483–492.

Skinner, B. F. *The behavior of organisms.* New York: Appleton-Century-Crofts, 1938.

Sokal, R. R., and P. H. A. Sneath. *Principles of numerical taxonomy.* San Francisco: W. H. Freeman, 1963.

Soskin, W. F. Bias in postdiction from projective tests. *Journal of Abnormal and Social Psychology,* 1954, 49, 69–74.

Spiker, C. C., and B. R. McCandless. The concept of intelligence and the philosophy of science. *Psychological Review,* 1954, 61, 255–266.

Stephenson, W. The significance of Q-technique for the study of personality. In M. L. Reymert, ed. *Feelings and emotions.* New York: McGraw-Hill, 1950. Pp. 552–570.

Stern, C. *Principles of human genetics.* (2nd ed.) San Francisco: W. H. Freeman, 1960.

Strong, E. K., Jr. *Vocational interests of men and women.* Stanford, Calif.: Stanford University Press, 1943.

Sundberg, N. D. The acceptability of "fake" versus "bona fide" personality test interpretations. *Journal of Abnormal and Social Psychology,* 1955, 50, 145–147.

Tallent, N. On individualizing the psychologist's clinical evaluation. *Journal of Clinical Psychology,* 1958, 14, 243–244.

Taulbee, E. S., and B. D. Sisson. Rorschach pattern analysis in schizophrenia: A cross-validation study. *Journal of Clinical Psychology,* 1954, 10, 80–82.

319

Taylor, L. W. *Physics, the pioneer science.* New York: Houghton Mifflin, 1941.

Terman, L. M. *Genetic studies of genius, I: Mental and physical traits of a thousand gifted children.* Stanford, Calif.: Stanford University Press, 1925.

Terman, L. M., and M. H. Oden. *Genetic studies of genius, IV: The gifted child grows up.* Stanford, Calif.: Stanford University Press, 1947.

Terman, L. M., and M. H. Oden. *Genetic studies of genius, V: The gifted group at mid-life.* Stanford, Calif.: Stanford University Press, 1959.

Thiesen, J. W. A pattern analysis of structural characteristics of the Rorschach test in schizophrenia. *Journal of Consulting Psychology,* 1952, 16, 365–370.

Thorndike, R. L. The psychological value systems of psychologists. *American Psychologist,* 1954, 9, 787–789.

Thorndike, R. L. The structure of preferences for psychological activities among psychologists. *American Psychologist,* 1955, 10, 205–207.

Thurstone, L. L. The criterion problem in personality research. *Psychometric Laboratory Reports.* Report no. 78. Chicago: University of Chicago, 1952.

Tolman, E. C. *Purposive behavior in animals and men.* New York: Century, 1932.

Ulrich, R. E., T. J. Stachnik, and N. R. Stainton. Student acceptance of generalized personality interpretations. *Psychological Reports,* 1963, 13, 831–834.

Waismann, F. Verifiability. *Proceedings of the Aristotelian Society,* Supplement, 1945, 19, 119–150.

Wender, P. H. On necessary and sufficient conditions in psychiatric explanation. *Archives of General Psychiatry,* 1967, 16, 41–47.

Werts, C. E., and R. L. Linn. Path analysis: Psychological examples. *Psychological Bulletin,* 1970, 74, 193–212.

Whitehorn, J. C., and B. J. Betz. A study of psychotherapeutic relationships between physicians and schizophrenic patients. *American Journal of Psychiatry,* 1954, 111, 321–331.

Whitehorn, J. C., and B. J. Betz. Further studies of the doctor as a crucial variable in the outcome of treatment with schizophrenic patients. *American Journal of Psychiatry,* 1960, 117, 215–223.

Winch, R. F., and D. M. More. Does TAT add information to interviews? Statistical analysis of the increment. *Journal of Clinical Psychology,* 1956, 12, 316–321.

Wittenborn, J. R. *Wittenborn Psychiatric Rating Scales.* New York: Psychological Corporation, 1955.

Wittgenstein, L. *Philosophical investigations,* tr. G. E. M. Anscombe. Oxford: Blackwell, 1953.

Wolpe, J. Objective psychotherapy of the neuroses. *South African Medical Journal,* 1952, 26, 825–829.

Zubin, J., and C. Windle. Psychological prognosis of outcome in the mental disorders. *Journal of Abnormal and Social Psychology,* 1954, 49, 272–281.

Complete List of P. E. Meehl's Publications on Psychodiagnosis

The dynamics of "structured" personality tests. *Journal of Clinical Psychology,* 1945, 1, 296–303.

An investigation of a general normality or control factor in personality testing. *Psychological Monographs,* 1945, 59 (4, whole no. 274).

A simple algebraic development of Horst's suppressor variable. *American Journal of Psychology,* 1945, 58, 550–554.

The Hunt-Minnesota Test for organic brain damage in cases of functional depression (with M. Jeffery). *Journal of Applied Psychology,* 1946, 30, 276–287.

The K factor as a suppressor variable in the Minnesota Multiphasic Personality

REFERENCES

Inventory (with S. R. Hathaway). *Journal of Applied Psychology*, 1946, 30, 525–564.

Profile analysis of the Minnesota Multiphasic Personality Inventory in differential diagnosis. *Journal of Applied Psychology*, 1946, 30, 517–524.

Minnesota Multiphasic Inventory. *Fifth Annual Industrial Relations Conference Report*. Minneapolis: Center for Continuation Study, University of Minnesota, 1947.

Schizophrenia, catatonic form. In A. H. Burton and R. E. Harris, eds. *Case histories in clinical and abnormal psychology*. New York: Harper, 1947. Pp. 71–83.

The Minnesota Multiphasic Personality Inventory, VI: The K scale (with J. C. McKinley and S. R. Hathaway). *Journal of Consulting Psychology*, 1948, 12, 20–31.

Configural scoring. *Journal of Consulting Psychology*, 1950, 14, 165–171.

Using the Minnesota Multiphasic Personality Inventory in counseling. St. Paul: Advisement and Guidance Section, Vocational Rehabilitation and Education Division, Veterans Administration, 1950.

An atlas for the clinical use of the MMPI (with S. R. Hathaway). Minneapolis: University of Minnesota Press, 1951.

The Minnesota Multiphasic Personality Inventory (with S. R. Hathaway). In *Military Clinical Psychology*. Technical Manual 8-242. Washington, D.C.: Department of the Army, July 1951. Pp. 71–111.

A personality scale for dominance (with H. G. Gough and H. McClosky). *Journal of Abnormal and Social Psychology*, 1951, 46, 360–366.

A personality scale for social responsibility (with H. G. Gough and H. McClosky). *Journal of Abnormal and Social Psychology*, 1952, 47, 73–80.

Technical recommendations for psychological tests and diagnostic techniques: Preliminary proposal (with L. J. Cronbach, E. S. Bordin, R. C. Challman, H. S. Conrad, L. G. Humphreys, and D. E. Super—APA Committee on Test Standards). *American Psychologist*, 1952, 7, 461–475.

Clinical versus statistical prediction: A theoretical analysis and a review of the evidence. Minneapolis: University of Minnesota Press, 1954.

Comment on "Analyzing the clinical process." *Journal of Counseling Psychology*, 1954, 1, 207–208.

Relationships between objective and oral examinations in psychology (with C. Bird and K. E. Clark). In R. E. Eckert and R. J. Keller, eds. *A university looks at its program*. Minneapolis: University of Minnesota Press, 1954. Pp. 153–156.

Antecedent probability and the efficiency of psychometric signs, patterns, or cutting scores (with A. Rosen). *Psychological Bulletin*, 1955, 52, 194–216. Reprinted here as Chapter 2.

Construct validity in psychological tests (with L. J. Cronbach). *Psychological Bulletin*, 1955, 52, 281–302. Reprinted here as Chapter 1.

Clinical versus actuarial prediction. *Proceedings of the 1955 Invitational Conference on Testing Problems*. Princeton, N.J.: Educational Testing Service, 1956. Pp. 136–141.

Symposium on clinical and statistical prediction (with C. C. McArthur and D. V. Tiedeman). *Journal of Counseling Psychology*, 1956, 3, 163–173.

Wanted—a good cookbook. *American Psychologist*, 1956, 11, 263–272. Reprinted here as Chapter 3.

When shall we use our heads instead of the formula? *Journal of Counseling Psychology*, 1957, 4, 268–273. Reprinted here as Chapter 4.

The ataraxic effect of two phenothiazine drugs on an outpatient population (with W. Fleeson, B. C. Glueck, Jr., G. Heistad, J. E. King, D. Lykken, and A. Mena). *University of Minnesota Medical Bulletin*, 1958, 29, 274–286.

A comparison of clinicians with five statistical methods of identifying psychotic MMPI profiles. *Journal of Counseling Psychology,* 1959, 6, 102–109.

Q-technique, pros and cons. In B. C. Glueck, Jr., ed. *Report of Conference on Social Adjustment Rating Scales.* Minneapolis: University of Minnesota Center for Continuation Study, 1959. Pp. 11–18.

Some ruminations on the validation of clinical procedures. *Canadian Journal of Psychology,* 1959, 13, 102–128. Reprinted here as Chapter 5.

Structured and projective tests: Some common problems in validation. *Journal of Projective Techniques,* 1959, 23, 268–272.

Approaches to the quantitative analysis of clinical assessment (with B. C. Glueck, Jr., and G. T. Heistad). *American Psychiatric Association District Branches Publication No. 1.* Washington, D.C.: American Psychiatric Association, 1960. Pp. 202–212.

The cognitive activity of the clinician. *American Psychologist,* 1960, 15, 19–27. Reprinted here as Chapter 6.

Objective configural rules for discriminating psychotic from neurotic MMPI profiles (with W. G. Dahlstrom). *Journal of Consulting Psychology,* 1960, 24, 375–387.

Logic for the clinician. Review of T. R. Sarbin, R. Taft, and D. E. Bailey, *Clinical inference and cognitive theory. Contemporary Psychology,* 1961, 6, 389–391.

Minnesota-Ford pool of phenotypic personality items (with W. Schofield, B. C. Glueck, Jr., W. B. Studdiford, D. W. Hastings, S. R. Hathaway, and D. J. Clyde). (August 1962 edition.) Minneapolis: University of Minnesota, 1962.

Schizotaxia, schizotypy, schizophrenia. *American Psychologist,* 1962, 17, 827–838. Reprinted here as Chapter 7.

Manual for use with checklist of schizotypic signs. Minneapolis: Psychiatric Research Unit, University of Minnesota Medical School, 1964.

The quantitative assessment of personality (with B. C. Glueck, Jr., W. Schofield, and D. J. Clyde). *Comprehensive Psychiatry,* 1964, 5, 15–23.

The creative individual: Why it is hard to identify him. In G. A. Steiner, ed. *The creative organization.* Chicago: University of Chicago Press, 1965, Pp. 25–32.

Detecting latent clinical taxa by fallible quantitative indicators lacking an accepted criterion. *Reports from the Research Laboratories of the Department of Psychiatry, University of Minnesota.* Report no. PR-65-2. Minneapolis: University of Minnesota, May 25, 1965.

Seer over sign: The first good example. *Journal of Experimental Research in Personality,* 1965, 1, 27–32.

Contributions to the problem of evaluating autonomic response data: 1 (with D. T. Lykken). *Reports from the Research Laboratories of the Department of Psychiatry, University of Minnesota.* Report no. PR-66-2. Minneapolis: University of Minnesota, January 15, 1966.

Mixed group validation: A method for determining the validity of diagnostic signs without using criterion groups (with R. M. Dawes). *Psychological Bulletin,* 1966, 66, 63–67. Reprinted here as Chapter 8.

The virtues of M'Naghten (with J. M. Livermore). *Minnesota Law Review,* 1967, 51, 789–856.

What can the clinician do well? In D. N. Jackson and S. Messick, eds. *Problems in human assessment.* New York: McGraw-Hill, 1967. Pp. 594–599. Reprinted here as Chapter 9.

Detecting latent clinical taxa, II: A simplified procedure, some additional hitmax cut locators, a single-indicator method, and miscellaneous theorems. *Reports from the Research Laboratories of the Department of Psychiatry, University of Minnesota.* Report no. PR-68-4. Minneapolis: University of Minnesota, August 15, 1968.

On the justifications for civil commitment (with J. M. Livermore and C. P. Malmquist). *University of Pennsylvania Law Review,* 1968, 117, 75–96.

Comments on the invasion of privacy issue. In J. N. Butcher, ed. *MMPI: Research developments and clinical applications.* New York: McGraw-Hill, 1969. Pp. 273–278.

Identifying latent clinical taxa, III: An empirical trial of the normal single-indicator method, using MMPI scale 5 to identify the sexes (with D. T. Lykken, M. R. Burdick, and G. R. Schoener). *Reports from the Research Laboratories of the Department of Psychiatry, University of Minnesota.* Report no. PR-69-1. Minneapolis: University of Minnesota, January 15, 1969.

Nuisance variables and the ex post facto design. In M. Radner and S. Winokur, eds. *Minnesota studies in the philosophy of science,* IV. Minneapolis: University of Minnesota Press, 1970. Pp. 373–402.

Psychology and the criminal law. *University of Richmond Law Review,* 1970, 5, 1–30.

High school yearbooks: A reply to Schwarz. *Journal of Abnormal Psychology,* 1971, 77, 143–148. Reprinted here as Chapter 10.

Recaptured-item technique (RIT): A method for reducing somewhat the subjective element in factor-naming (with D. T. Lykken, W. Schofield, and A. Tellegen). *Journal of Experimental Research in Personality,* 1971, 5, 171–190.

Clinical issues. In S. S. Kety and S. Matthysse, eds. *Prospects for research on schizophrenia. M.I.T. Neurosciences Research Program Bulletin,* 1972, 10 (4).

A critical afterword. In I. I. Gottesman and J. Shields. *Schizophrenia and genetics: A twin study vantage point.* New York: Academic Press, 1972. Pp. 367–416.

Detecting latent clinical taxa, IV: Empirical study of the maximum covariance method and the normal minimum chi-square method, using three MMPI keys to identify the sexes (with R. Golden). *Reports from the Research Laboratories of the Department of Psychiatry, University of Minnesota.* Report no. PR-73-. Minneapolis: University of Minnesota, 1973.

Detecting latent clinical taxa, V: A Monte Carlo study of the maximum covariance method and associated consistency tests. *Reports from the Research Laboratories of the Department of Psychiatry, University of Minnesota* (with R. Golden). Report no. PR-73-. Minneapolis: University of Minnesota, 1973.

Reactions, reflections, projections. In J. Butcher, ed. *Objective personality assessment: Changing perspectives.* New York: Academic Press, 1972. Pp. 131–189.

Specific genetic etiology, psychodynamics and therapeutic nihilism. *International Journal of Mental Health,* 1972, 1, 10–27. Reprinted here as Chapter 11.

MAXCOV-HITMAX: A taxonomic search method for loose genetic syndromes. In P. E. Meehl. *Psychodiagnosis: Selected papers.* Minneapolis: University of Minnesota Press, 1973. Chapter 12 above.

Why I do not attend case conferences. In P. E. Meehl. *Psychodiagnosis: Selected papers.* Minneapolis: University of Minnesota Press, 1973. Chapter 13 above.

INDEX

Index

Ability, second-order disposition to develop achievements, 188
Abstract ideas, boring to some students, 283
Academic achievement, as nuisance variable to be "controlled," 175
Academicians, lack of intellectual excitement among, 283
Acceptance: essential in content validation, 5; of set of operations as definitive, 5; involved in construct validity, 18
Accessory symptoms in schizophrenia, absence of not exclusion test, 231
Achievement: academic, as nuisance variable to be "controlled," 175; disposition of first order, 188
Acting-out neurotic, distinguished from sociopath and cultural delinquent, 93
Activity preferences of psychologists, "social" versus "scientific" (R. Thorndike), 283
Actualizing condition, probability of, 192
Actuarial, see Statistical
Ad hoc fallacy, in case conferences, 261–262
Additivity, departures from in clinical judgments, 126
"Adjustment" concept, in assessing psychopathology, 245
Administrative dimensions, 65
"Advance knowledge," utility of to therapist, 132
Affective disorder, not excluded by delusions or hallucinations, 230
Aggressive parameter, as potentiator of schizophrenia (diagram), 190
Alcohol, paradoxical effect of: in schizophrenia, 204; as schizotypal indicator, 206
Allergies, example of rare disposition, 249
Allport-Vernon-Lindzey values: characteristic profiles of clinical psy-

chologist, 130; author's score on "theoretical," 281
Ambivalence, in schizophrenia, 140
American culture, and polygenic causal contributors to schizophrenia, 177
American Psychological Association Committee on Test Standards, 3, 33: four kinds of validity, 91
Analyses, interminable: and unrecognized schizotypy, 194; based on unrealistic therapeutic goals, 194
Anhedonia: in schizophrenia, 140; as subjective aspect of deficit in positive reinforcement parameter, 146; improvable by psychotherapy, 147; mainly interpersonal in defective inhibition theory of schizophrenia, 150–152; less characteristic of schizotypy than kinesthetic integrative defect, 154; as provisional indicator for schizotypy, 206
Antecedent, commonly or rarely realized, 248
Antecedent conditions, 40
Antecedent probabilities, 40
Anti-biology bias of social scientist, 263
Antidiagnostic argument: formal diagnoses extremely unreliable, 273–274; understand rather than label patient, 274; formal diagnoses prognostically worthless, 276–280; diagnosis does not help treatment, 280–281
Antinosological bias of American psychiatry and clinical psychology, 272–281
Anxiety, potentiating cognitive slippage and etiology, 139
Anxiety parameter, as potentiator of schizophrenia (diagram), 190
Anxiety-proneness, as polygenic causal contributor to schizophrenia, 177
Anxiety-readiness, higher in decompensated than compensated schizotypes, 142
Applied psychology emphasis, as self-

manded by clinician, 166. *See also* Clinical versus statistical issue

Clerical procedure for combining information, studies comparing with human judges, 71

Clinical case conference, *see* Case conference, clinical

Clinical decision making: general philosophy of, 40; probabilistic character of inference, 119, 255; departures from linearity and additivity in judgments, 126; pragmatic utility of theoretical constructs in, 131; countermands clerical, 166; six factors or circumstances theoretically favoring prediction, 168–169; departures from established empirical frequency, 234; increase in errors by choosing clinical inference over actuarial data, 256; on inadequate evidence, 265. *See also* Clinical versus statistical issue

Clinical inference: ideally based on objective probability statement, 119; probabilistic transition from episodes to dispositions, 119; probabilistic character of, 255

Clinical periodicals, need for inclusion of standard overlap measures in manuscripts, 261

Clinical population: and cookbook method, 79; marked departure from base rates of, 132

Clinical practice: in disparity with research evidence, 115; data available in, comparable to data in clinical-actuarial studies, 171

Clinical prediction, six factors or circumstances theoretically favoring, 168–169

Clinical psychologists: disillusionment with profession (E. L. Kelly), 117; justification of existence of, 133

Clinical psychology: emphasis shifting from diagnosis to therapy, 90; in state of ferment, 90; vocational dissatisfaction in, 90; psychodiagnosis as original role, 90–91; curse of, 113–114

Clinical psychology students: betting odds on schizophrenia, 135–136; value orientation of, and quality of clinical case conferences, 282–283

Clinical psychology training, goals of, and quality of clinical case conferences, 282

Clinical versus statistical (actuarial) issue: pragmatically unavoidable, 82, 166–167; Meehl-Dahlstrom Rules created by combination, 126; author's book on, 165; formulation as opposition, 166; studies of use data comparable to those in routine practice, 171; unusual uniformity of study outcomes, 172; ethical aspects of in treatment selection or withholding, 251–252; identifying softhearted and softheaded, 255. *See also* Clinical decision making; Clinician; Statistical experience; Statistical method

Clinician: straight prediction not greatest strength, 64; as inefficient computer, 77, 78; costly middleman, 79; inventor of new theoretical relations or variables, 79; wastes time concocting personality descriptions, 80; as hypothesis maker, 81; as discerner of gestalted stimulus equivalences, 83; can exemplify laws that he can't formulate, 83; cannot escape monitoring by actuary, 88; calibration of, not best approach, 89; confidence of predictions defines subset, 89; cognitive functions, 118; elimination of not proposed, 165; not attacked in author's book on prediction, 165; performs unique and important functions, 165; wastes time on functions he does inefficiently, 165; countermanded by actuarial prediction, 166; hypothesizing behavior by, 166; nonformalized judging by, 166; as constructor of hypotheses, 167; functions only he can perform, 167; "doesn't merely predict" argument answered, 168; can respond to patterns without mathematical formulation of them, 170; seasoned, and personality research, 226; must not fear to act rationally on evidence, 258; as decision maker willy-nilly, 265; motives of, 268

Clinicopathological conference: useful analogue for improving format of clinical case conference, 284; epistemological structure of, 288; withholds high-validity information until end, 288–289

Cluster, loose, in schizotypy, 202

337

338

Linearity, departures from in clinical judgments, 126

Locus minoris resistentiae, in complete etiological equation, 286

Logical validity, 4

Logicians: terminology, 195; less stringently "positivistic" or "operational" than formerly, 196

Loose syndromes, study of demands nonarbitrary choice of cutting scores, 210–211

Magnetic, as first-order disposition, 188

Magnetizable, as second-order disposition, 188

Manic-depressive diagnosis, not excluded by delusions or hallucinations, 230

Marks-Seeman atlas, 293

Massachusetts General Hospital Conferences, advent of clinicopathological conferences, 284

Matched pairs, tend to yield atypical samples from both populations, 179

Matching cases, as method of "controlling" nuisance variables in nonexperimental studies, Chapter 10 *passim*

Matching method, very high success required to support network, 29

Matching on variables, crucialness of, 175

Matching studies, in "global" interpretation, 29

Mathematical models, other than factor analytic needed, 116

MAXDIFF-HITMAX, alternative method of hitmax cut location, 223

"Me too" fallacy, in clinical case conferences, 237

Meaning stipulations, not sharply distinguished from empirical assertions, 196

Medical complaints, as one indicator of behavior pathology, 245

Medical diagnosis: unreliable, 114; study of, differentiating types of jaundice, 172

Medical model: as unclear concept, 194; used as catchphrase to dissolve problems by incantation, 194; incompetent discussions of, 198–199; usually considered incompetently, 275

Meehl-Dahlstrom Rules: concurrent validity of, 125; sorting of MMPI

profiles, 125; created by combination of statistical checking and clinical experience, 126; as example of objective configural method of profile analysis, 133

Mellaril, study of, 129

Mental hygiene movement, spun-glass theory of mind an undesirable side effect of, 252–253

Mental illness, pathogenic background factors statistically related to, 246

Mental status: actuarial use of variables, 168; probably superior to existing tests, 168; usually done before psychometrics available, 294

Mesomorphic toughness, and etiology of schizophrenia (diagram), 190

Meteorology, actuarial method in, 173

Methodology: shifting standards of rigor, 136; commitment of clinical psychologists, 133–134; conflicts in internal medicine, 197

Mice, as example of genome-environment interaction, 184–187

Military induction: personality inventory for use in, 34; appropriate situation for "successive hurdles" approach, 52

Mind, spun-glass theory of, 252–255

Mixed group: as basis for estimating sign validity, Chapter 8 *passim*; proportions of types known without individual diagnoses, 157

Mixed-group validation: includes criterion-group validation as special case, 159; advantages of, 160–162; and future time, 160–161; and open concepts, 161; sampling error of, 162–164; conditions for overestimating and underestimating sign validity, 163; sample size in relation to base rates, 164

"Mixture," population, as generator of covariance within intervals, 211–212

MMPI: psychopathic deviate scale example of construct validation by multiple evidence, 20–21; cookbook interpretation versus rule-of-thumb, 70–76; finite set of scores, 71; coarseness of grouping similar profiles, 72; construction of modal Q sort for curve type, 72–73; cookbook interpretation versus "average patient" stereotype, 76–77; interpretation, Chapter 4 *passim*; low congruency

Operational approach: defended, 9; using many specific criteria, 9; in formal diagnosis, 94

Operational definition: sometimes appropriate, 8; of inner states, 120; and mixed-group validation, 161

Operational methodology: claimed when not used, 31; forcing research into mold, 31

Operationism, and schizophrenia research, 196

Operations, experimental, efficacy of in detecting genome-environment interaction, 187

Optimistic illusions, and treatment efficacy, 194

Orders of dispositions, 187–189

Ordinary language movement, 195

Organic causal factors, and taxonomy, 275

Outcome research, adequate for studying practical value of psychometrics, 110

Outpatient psychotherapy, test to select those who continue, 44

Overlap: of normal with abnormal, not refutation of disease entity concept, 196; numerical example of, 260–261; measures of should be required by journal editors, 261

Painful thoughts, pseudoneurotic schizophrenic's inability to turn off, 149

Pancakes in attic, example of "me-too" fallacy in case conferences, 239

Parameter and parameters: of behavioral acquisition function, as phenotypic expression of gene, 137; of nervous system, in theory of schizophrenia, 183; differences in strains and learning theory of behavior content, 186; of CNS function, as example of disposition, 189

Paresis, as example of diagnostic problem, 95

Parole violation, index of prediction of (Goodman), 36

Past-pointing, in schizophrenia, 204

Path analysis, and antecedent knowledge about some causal arrows, 181

Pathogenic background factors, statistical relation to mental illness, 246

Pathognomonic sign and signs: rare in organic medicine, 99; not required for behavior genetics research, 196;

unlikely in schizotypy, 202; detectable by using fallible indicators, 216

Pathological findings, as quasi-criteria, 285

Pathological set ("sick-sick" fallacy), in case conferences, 237

Pathologist: and clinicopathological conference, 285; psychopathological equivalent of report of, 291

Pathology: minimizing sign or symptom of, 239; behavior defined by multiple criteria, 245; with etiology defines disease entity in organic medicine, 285–286; distinguished from etiology in functional psychiatry, 286–288

Patients: time for contacts with exceeded by interstaff contacts, 167; underprivileged, treatment by paramedical professionals and physicians, 251; sources of data on, 291; "best estimate" of characteristics for case conference purposes, 293

Penetrance: inappropriate concept for formal diagnosis, 137; derivative concept, 210; nonarbitrary quantity when expressivity curves have no overlap, 210; analogous to sensitivity in epidemiology, 210; arbitrary function of cut on expressivity distributions, 210; as doubtful concept in schizophrenia, 218; complex analogy to in schizophrenia theory, 220–221

Perceptual-cognitive parameters, as potentiators of schizophrenia (diagram), 190

Performance, evidence for construct but distinct from it, 10–11

Persistence, low, as polygenic causal contributor to schizophrenia, 177

Personality assessment: one function of tests, 91, 102–114, 118; as function of psychodiagnostician, 118; genotypic, 118; phenotypic, 118. See also Personality tests

Personality descriptions, 65: time wasted in concocting, 80

Personality research, theoretical, 226

Personality tests: use in military induction, 34; upper limit of predictive validity of, 58–59; skepticism about predictive power of, 168; genetic factors as co-determiners of, 183

Phenocopy, stipulated as lacking specific genetic etiology, 196

Phenotype, description of, 65

Phenotypic attributes, as domain dispositions, 102–103

Phenotypic characterization: one function of tests, 91; involves concurrent validity, 103; pragmatic function obscure, 103; qualitative and quantitative deficiencies in clinical staff's domain sample, 103; criteria of validation studies, 103; four levels of validity question, 104–108; early and incremental, 107–108; therapist stabilizes early, 108–109

Phenotypic criterion, 58

Phenotypic indicators, highly fallible, of dominant gene, 203

Phenotypic pool, patient described in terms of, 131

Phenotypic trait, family of atomic dispositions, 103

Phenylalanine intake, 188

Philosophers: and metatheory of loose concepts, 195; mistaken arguments on schizophrenia, 196

Philosophy, toughness in, contrasted with psychiatry and clinical psychology, 228

Philosophy of science: in construct validation, 16; two attitudes toward theoretical mistakes, 181; and speculative formulations, 184; less stringently "operational" than formerly, 196; instrumentalist, as dogmatically imposed, 268

Pigeonhole: formal diagnosis as, 95; taxonomic rubric, 274

Pitch, absolute, as example of non-pathological deviance, 245

PKU: genotype, examples of orders of dispositions, 188; genome, as producing higher order dispositions, 188–189; analogy to schizophrenia and therapeutic nihilism, 191; as disposition, labeled "cause" on grounds of rarity, 247–250; as example of statistical criterion of disposition versus actualizing event as specific "cause" of disease, 247–250; syndrome, as example of hereditary disease with rare disposition, 248; syndrome, "cause," genetic mutation, 248

Plague serum, shortage of, analogized to psychotherapy situation, 252

Plasma, shortage of, analogized to psychotherapy situation, 252

Pleasure: capacity for, defective in schizophrenia, 140; and reinforcement in schizophrenia theory, 145–146; deficit, as explanation of cognitive slippage, 146–147; capacity for improvable by psychotherapy, 147; in cognitive and aesthetic domains, among schizotypes, 147

Point-predictions: generated by "strong" theories, 201; not generated by environmentalist, 201

Politicization tendency among students, psychiatric diagnosis as example of, 273

Polygenic contributors to schizophrenia, 177–178

Polygenic theory, may be hard to test against monogenic, 201

Polymorph-perverse eroticism, as potentiator of schizophrenia (diagram), 190

Poor adjustment cases, efficiency in detecting, 34–35

Popper, Sir Karl: philosophy of science of, 184; on "weak" versus "strong" theories, 201

Population and populations: rarely defined, 33; to which psychometric devices are applied, 35–40; all patients versus all referred for testing, 39; importance in test interpretation, 39; parameter values for, 41; restricted, 43; cookbook generalizability over, tied to construct validity, 111; may permit using same predictive function with shifted cutting scores, 111–112; invariance of sign probability over, assumed, 160; mixture of, as generator of covariance within intervals, 211–212; mixture of, as greatest when split is even, in MAXCOV-HITMAX method, 212

Positive sign, follow-up as, 302

Positives, false, 34

Positives, valid, 34

Positivism, and empirical meaning, in schizophrenia research, 196

Postulate system, constitutes implicit definition of theoretical primitives, 21

"Potentiator": term preferred over "modifier" in behavior genetics, 217;

tient is mentally ill, 96, 115, 139, 244; emphasis on in American psychiatry, 235; inferred in case conference on superficial basis, 235; as implied by nosological labels, 274–276

Psychological test data, low congruency in interpretation of, 118

Psychologists, activity preferences of (R. L. Thorndike), 283

Psychology department, reputation of, as factor in clinical students' value orientation, 283

Psychometric devices: as means of increasing accuracy of classifications and predictions, 32; difficulty of evaluating efficiency of, 32–33

Psychometric differentiators, majority almost worthless, 261

Psychometric signs, efficiency of, Chapter 2 *passim*

Psychometric validity, naive view of, 240

Psychometrics: time wasted on noncontributory, 61; value to therapist of "advance knowledge" from, 107–108; "advance knowledge" from investgable by therapy-outcome research, 110; combined actuarially with life-history data, 112; clinical practice and research evidence, 115; "advance knowledge from" not highly valued by therapists, 118; and rapid stabilizing of therapist's patient image, 122; disparity between clinical reliance on and research evidence, 133; data of not to be confused with actuarial data confirmation, 168; conflict of with clinician's opinion, 240–244; to be explained rather than explained away, 241; aim of in case conference, 242; disagreement of with other data, 244; used pointlessly to infer easily obtainable facts, 262–263; not usually available at initial interview, 294; "blind" diagnosis from, 294–295

Psychoneurotic patients, less socially participant in high school than controls, 174

Psychopathic personality: as wastebasket category, 93; clinical skill in diagnosing, 93; diagnosis "at sight," 93; not mainly matter of legal delinquency, 93

Psychopathology, attributing causal role to factor not connected with, 247

Psychoses, affective, nosological distinction from other disorders with regard to efficacy of EST, 280

Psychosis, probability of: impressionistic profile placement by clinicians, 126; as function of pooled MMPI sortings, 127; as function of sorter consensus, 128

Psychotherapists: unique powers of, 64; rapid stabilizing of view of patient, 122–123; time pressures on for decision making, 170; shortage of, 251

Psychotherapy: process research inadequate for investigating usefulness of test-based "advance knowledge," 110; "art of applying a science which does not yet exist," 117; and specific genetic etiology of schizophrenia, Chapter 11 *passim,* especially 183, 189; selection of patients for, 251

Psychotic depression: suicide risk in, 277–280; mutism in differential diagnosis of, 279

Psychoticism: clinician's judging behavior of, 126; judged from MMPI profile, 128

Pulmonary shadows, unreliability in classifying, 114

Q sort, 61: MMPI interpretation, 71; advantage in presenting standard set of dispositions and constructs, 121; advantages and disadvantages as standard set of items, 121; description from MMPI actuarial atlas, 293

Quadratic equation in $p =$ proportion of schizotypes, 213

Rage-depression: contrasted with object-loss depression, 269–270; construct validity for, 271

Random sample, adequacy as control group, 175–181

Rare event, actuarial table fails to include, 84

Rare patterns, probabilities too unstable for clinical use, 86

Rarity, as one basis of labeling factor specifically "causative" of disease, 247–250

93; academic underachievement in differential diagnosis of, 231

Sociotropes, 183

"Soft" neurology: signs reported in schizophrenia, 152–154; in schizophrenia, clinician's alertness to, 153; in schizotypy, why put into provisional indicator set, 204

Special cases: countermanding formula, 82; importance of, 84–85

Specific criteria: multiple, in operational approach, 9; inadequacy of validation, 9–11; used temporarily, 11

Specific etiology: life history as example of, 97; as interaction effect, 137; as sine qua non, 137; in analysis of variance terms, 137; misconceptions about, 137; necessary but not sufficient condition, 137; causing two different disease entities, 285; Freud and, 286

Specific genetic etiology: and psychodynamics, 96; and psychodynamics, in case conference, 264

Specificity, in epidemiology, 210

Speculation: and philosophy of science, 184; interplay with fact in history of genetics, 200; freewheeling, not objectionable, 265; not same as errors, 299

Spun-glass theory of mind: fallacy, 252–255; countertherapeutic effect of, 253; extreme example of, 254–255

"Spurious" correlation, not optimal terminology, 179

Stability: bearing on construct validation, 14; statistical versus idiographic detail, 113–114

Staff conferences, time taken may exceed staff-patient contact time, 167

Standards of performance, needed in case conference, 299

States: one of four kinds of entities in world, 188; altered synaptic condition as example of, 189

Statistical "assumption," versus "hypothesis," 205

Statistical-clinical issue, see Clinical versus statistical issue

Statistical control: of nuisance variables in nonexperimental research, Chapter 10 passim, 175–176; as "playing it safe," 181

Statistical deviation, in assessing psychopathology, 245

Statistical (actuarial) experience: may do better than composite of tests and interviews, 106; Meehl-Dahlstrom Rules created by combination with clinical experience, 126; techniques aimed at unscrambling causal questions, 176; search techniques for taxonomic entities, 197–198; departures from, save some cases at expense of missing others, 234; applied to single case, in Russian roulette situation, 257

Statistical (actuarial) formula: reasons why lacking, 83; broken leg case, 84

Statistical inference, pre-Fisherian fallacies in, 40

Statistical logic, ignorance or repression of in case conferences, 232–235

Statistical (actuarial) method: development could proceed more rapidly, 89; applicable to interview and life-history data as well as tests, 115; formal arguments for, 167; studies showing difference in favor of, 172; opposed because medicine practiced without, 172; in meteorology and forecasting security prices, 173; formal proof that it cannot determine causal arrows, 181; single case objection to, Russian roulette example, 257. See also Clinical versus statistical issue

Statistical power, for detecting genome-environment interaction, 187

Statistical (actuarial) prediction: and quality of data used, 171; rejection of, 255. See also Clinical versus statistical issue

Statistical rarity, not sufficient condition for psychopathology, 245

Statistical significance, pragmatic application of, 259–260

Statistical (actuarial) tables (base rates), 32

"Statistical twin," restraints imposed in finding, 179

Statisticians: fussy about wrong things, 207; unrealistic assumptions made by, 207

Stereotype: of "average patient" versus cookbook, 76–77; description as baseline for evaluating test's incremental validity, 103; of patients as